Eurographics

Wolfgang Herzner, Frank Kappe (eds.)

Multimedia/Hypermedia in Open Distributed Environments

Proceedings of the
Eurographics Symposium
in Graz, Austria, June 6–9, 1994

Springer-Verlag Wien New York

Dr. Dipl.-Ing. Wolfgang Herzner
Forschungszentrum Seibersdorf, Seibersdorf, Austria

Dr. Dipl.-Ing. Frank Kappe
Institut für Informationsverarbeitung und Computergestützte Neue Medien,
TU Graz, Graz, Austria

Typesetting: Camera ready by editors and authors

Printed on acid-free and chlorine-free bleached paper

With 105 Figures

ISSN 0946-2767

ISBN-13: 978-3-211-82587-7   e-ISBN-13: 978-3-7091-9361-7
DOI: 10.1007/ 978-3-7091-9361-7

Preface

Over the last few years, multimedia hardware and applications have become widely available in the personal computer and workstation environments, and multimedia is rapidly becoming an integral part of stand-alone, single-user systems. In contrast, the problems encountered when moving to open, distributed environments are only just beginning to be identified. Examples are the transmission of dynamic data (video, sound) over large distances and cooperative work.

Following on from two successful workshops on multimedia, EG-MM '94 concentrates on topics related to multimedia/hypermedia in open, distributed environments. The goal of this symposium was not only to give a comprehensive overview of the current state of research, development, and standardisation in the field, but also to provide an opportunity for live demonstrations to experience directly the presented results.

The symposium program consists of two invited keynote speeches, eight technical sessions, one tutorial, and one demonstration session. A workshop following immediately after the symposium provides an opportunity for in-depth discussions of open problems among experts. It is intended to fill a gap often experienced at larger meetings and conferences: the lack of time to discuss in detail issues raised during the event, such as the characteristics of different approaches to a certain problem. It is intended that the results of the workshop be published as a Eurographics Technical Report.

The program committee consisted of M. Gervautz, Austria, M. Gomes, Portugal, R. Guedj, France, W. Herzner, Austria (chairman), Ch. Hornung, Germany, W. Hübner, Germany, K. Kansy, Germany, F. Kappe, Austria, L. Kjelldahl, Sweden, K. Meyer-Wegener, Germany, S. Owen, Georgia, P. Purcell, UK, M. Rhiner, Switzerland, P.Stucki, Switzerland, J. Teixeira, Portugal, R. Took, UK, H. Vin, Texas, P. Willis, UK. We thank them all, especially Michael Gervautz, Klaus Kansy, Klaus Meyer-Wegener, and Patrick Purcell, who supported the preparation of the technical program to a degree going beyond the normal reading and refereeing of contributions.

To conclude, we would also like to thank all of the authors and speakers for their effort as well as the referees for their kind support and cooperation.

Special thanks also go to Eurographics for their support and Springer-Verlag for publishing these proceedings.

A special expression of gratitude goes to Dr. Doris Florian from Joanneum Research as well as the many local helpers without whom the event could not have been successful, and to all those who financially supported the symposium and workshop.

Wolfgang Herzner, Frank Kappe
Editors
March 1994

Contents

Architectures

CSCW and Information Services

Standards
and
Standards Exploitation

The MHEG standard
principles and examples of applications

Françoise COLAITIS, Convenor of ISO/IEC JTC1/SC29/WG12, MHEG
colaitis@ccett.fr
Florence BERTRAND, Co-Editor of the MHEG Standard
bertrand@ccett.fr

France Telecom CCETT, 4 rue du Clos Courtel, BP 59,
35512 Cesson Sévigné Cedex, FRANCE.

Abstract. This paper presents the main concepts of the ISO International Standard/ITU-T Recommendation for Multimedia/Hypermedia objects, prepared by the ISO/IEC JTC1/SC29/WG12 known as MHEG, as well as examples of the use of MHEG in different communicating environments. It presents the different approaches in the multimedia/hypermedia domain, leading to different possible levels of standardization. Each level corresponds to a different balance between Genericity and Specificity or adequation to a given application domain. The level of MHEG is a compromise between genericity across various application types, and support for a minimum set of basic, essential functionalities. The requirements are introduced and expressed in terms of synchronization/linking between elementary units of information, real time interchange and presentation. The MHEG standard is then introduced, and the way the MHEG specifications meet the application requirements is discussed. The specification process is accompanied by experiments and prototype developments.

1. Introduction

This paper introduces the main concepts and field of applications of the emerging MHEG standard prepared by the Working Group 12 of ISO/IEC JTC 1/SC 29, known as MHEG (Multimedia and Hypermedia information coding Expert Group).
This presentation provides the reader with clear insights into the technical context of the MHEG standard (development of open multimedia applications and underlying requirements), and into the consequences of the application requirements on the design of a generic interchange format for multimedia/hypermedia information. In this perspective, several issues are discussed in this paper:
Is there a need for a standard defining the representation and encoding of data structures (objects) suited to multimedia applications or services ? and if yes, what are the required features for such objects ?
How the design of multimedia/hypermedia objects can meet the requirements of their different types of using applications ?
How multimedia/hypermedia objects may be used in real applications ?

4

2. Why a standard for multimedia/hypermedia Objects

2.1.   General context of multimedia/hypermedia applications development

In recent years, an explosion of multimedia applications has been seen in many domains such as: education, training systems, office and business systems, information and point of sales systems, digital television, etc...
In all these three fields, multimedia interactive programs have been developed, providing their users with pictures, video sequences and audio sequences, presented in interactive situations.

This major trend can be explained as follows:
a• The availability of multimedia resources on many computers. Compression standards, such as JPEG or MPEG have allowed the development of dedicated chips, installed on computer motherboards as basic system resources.
b• The increasing availability of optical disks and digital transmission media such as ISDN, digital broadcasting networks and broadband telecommunication networks, which allow the exchange of very large amounts of data.

Many multimedia applications will be designed to run on heterogeneous workstations, or to be interconnected to offer a multimedia service: computer supported multimedia cooperative work, multimedia messaging systems, electronic publishing and electronic books, audiovisual telematic systems for training and education, simulation and games, sales and advertizing, TV guides and entirely new classes of multimedia applications.

The production of the large quantities of multimedia/hypermedia information necessary for the expansion of such services represents a significant investment, and it is vital that this information remains available in a world of rapidly evolving systems and technologies, and is not lost because of incompatibilities in the data structures supported by the applications. This is why a "common language" is required for all those multimedia/hypermedia communicating systems which will appear in the forthcoming years is required. An important issue remains: what "level" of interchanged information should be standardized ? How to define the appropriate "unit of information" to be interchanged between heterogeneous multimedia/hypermedia systems ?

2.2.   Multimedia/hypermedia application model

An OSE (Open System Environment) reference model is proposed for heteregeneous multimedia/hypermedia technologies presently being developed. This model is composed of:
a• application software (specific programs and data);
b• application platform (the actual hardware and software);
c• platform external environment (system elements such as communication services, peripheral devices, ...);
and interfaces between these entities:
1• API (Application Programming Interface) between the application software and the application platform (man/machine interaction services, information interchange services, communication services, internal system services);

2• and EEI (External Environment Interface) between the platform and the external environment (protocols and data formats).

This type of model, which basically consists in a clear separation between platform-dependent and platform-independent modules, is very commonly used in many delivery systems architectures (e.g CDI players, MHEG terminals as described in section 6, etc ...).

In this OSE model, a number of basic multimedia/hypermedia services are described as the sets of functionalities necessary for the support of multimedia/hypermedia applications. These services are summarized in figure 1.

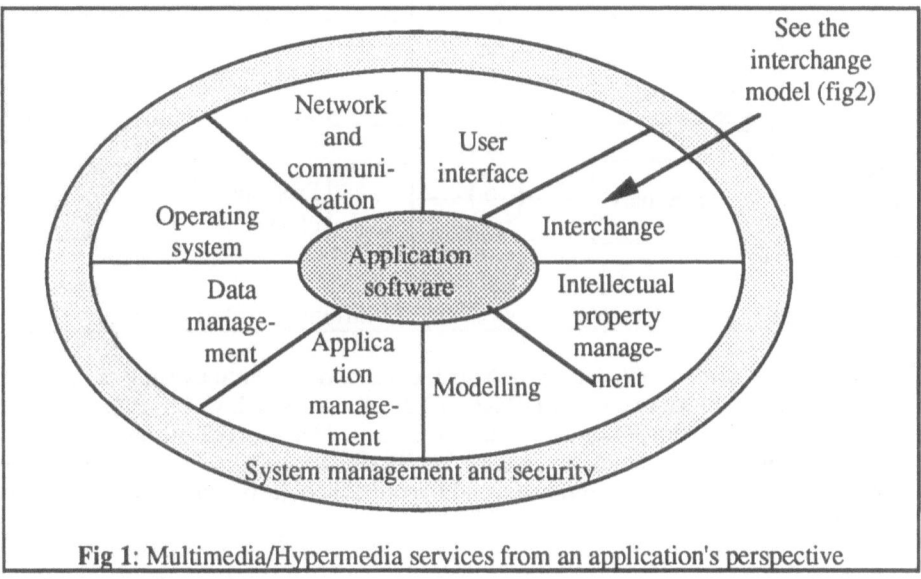

Fig 1: Multimedia/Hypermedia services from an application's perspective

The figure 2 shows the position of MHEG with respect to other hypermedia data interchanges:

6

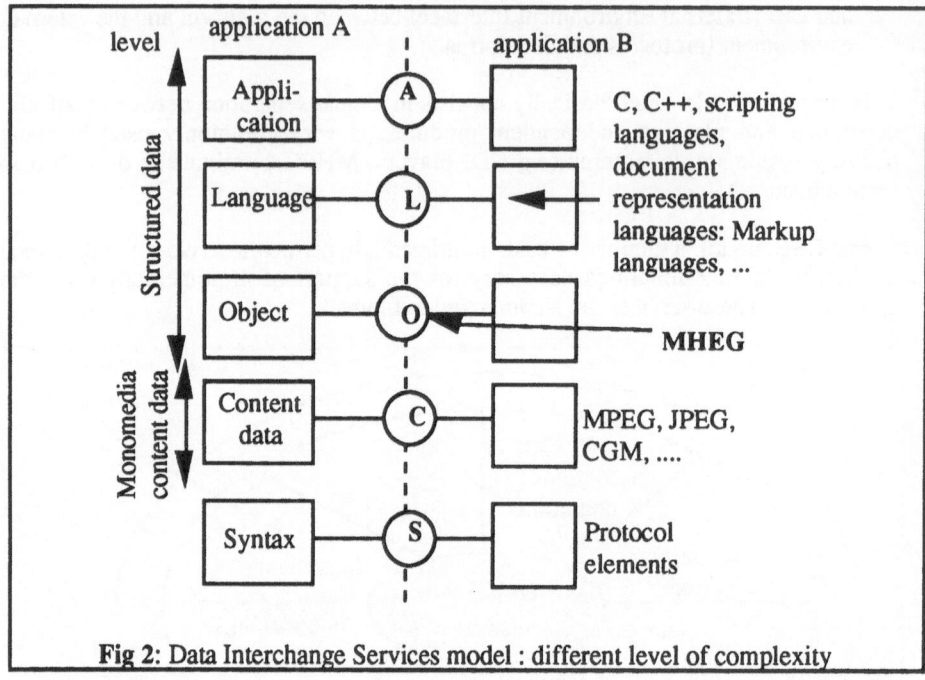

Fig 2: Data Interchange Services model : different level of complexity

In this figure, some of the data interchange levels correspond to existing or emerging standards: monomedia contents (JPEG, JBIG, MPEG, MIDI, CGM, ...), languages and scripts (international standards such as C, C++, SGML, HyTime and proprietary scripting languages such as Hypertalk, ToolBook, ScriptX, ...). The Object level defines representation for multimedia and hypermedia objects and is addressed by the MHEG standard.

From the above model, we see that there are various levels of data interchange between applications, according to the level of genericity which is targeted:
Genericity: If communicating applications interchange low level unstructured data, they do not need to share any high level representation of the information that they are handling. In this way, standards such as JPEG or MPEG define algorithms suited to data compression independently of the application domain.
No genericity: The interchange of high level structured data (e.g hypertext documents) assumes that communicating applications share the same representations and semantics of a hypertext document. The interchanged information is specific to a given context.

Future hypermedia applications will go far beyond the old limits between categories and will use cross-domain concepts and facilities, e.g multimedia document retrieval and consultation associated to hypertext navigation, groupware associated with multimedia messaging, training program plus direct interpersonal communication. It is essential to find the adequate unit of information communication to reconcile the required genericity with a correct level of structuration.

The MHEG committee has adopted the following methodology:
1• Start from the hypermedia application requirements and define the level of genericity required to meet the needs of a broad range of communicating applications;
2• Deduce the features of the generic structures from the application requirements.

2.3.   Hypermedia application requirements

From the list of typical applications enumerated in paragraph 2.1, a number of underlying requirements can be identified:
- Portability in a multi-vendor environment, i.e the possible use of a wide range of terminals and workstations;
- Multimedia information, i.e to be able to group several monomedia entities into a single "container";
- Information structured in such a way that real-time interactivity, including acquisition of multimedia data, as well as real-time interchange can be ensured;
- Composition and Synchronization in space and time;
- Definition of links between data elements;
- Definition of interaction with the user;
- Reusability of data in other documents;
- Ability to update the data, and manipulate sets of data elements.

These requirements call for the design of structured entities called multimedia/hypermedia objects or MHEG objects in the standard, able to encapsulate a limited set of functionalities while remaining sufficiently generic to be usable by a range of applications:
- Standardization only at the level of monomedia information is not enough to garantee applications portability, because applications do not use the monomedia data individually
- Monomedia information is not well suited to the design and interchange of hypermedia information
- The design of distributed hypermedia applications will be eased if the internal details of the information presentation are masked from the application.

The MHEG abstractions are communication oriented and are suited to:
- Real-time presentation
- Final form representation: the objects do not require additional processing of their structure.

3. The main concepts of the MHEG standard

3.1.   Methodology

The object-oriented approach was chosen for the design of the standard because it fits the requirements of active, autonomous and reusable objects. The standard focuses on the generic structuring aspects of the objects.

The base representation (Part I of the standard) uses ASN.1, and the Part II of the standard will provide an isomorphic representation in SGML.

These alternate structure representations are equivalent, as shown in Figure 3.

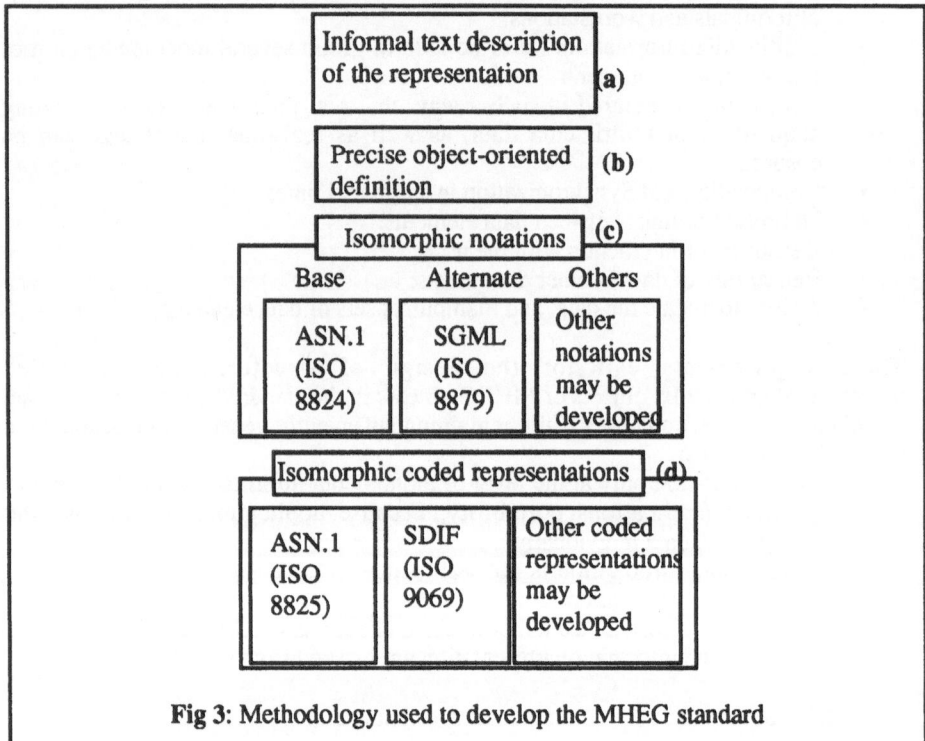

Fig 3: Methodology used to develop the MHEG standard

For each class, the standard provides (a) an informal textual description (for intuitive understanding), (b) an object-oriented definition expressed in a formal context free grammar, (c) a set of equivalent notations of the formal definition, and the corresponding encodings (d).

3.2.   MHEG object classes

The MHEG standard defines classes of objects, instances of these classes will be interchanged between using applications. Figure 4, shows the MHEg inheritance tree:

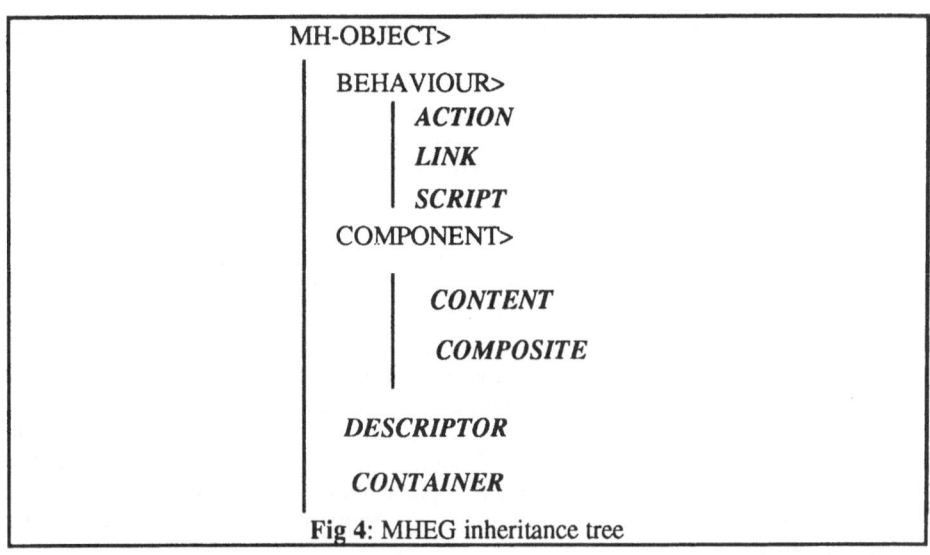

Fig 4: MHEG inheritance tree

MH-Object class. The standard provides the required information for the identification and addressing of MHEG Objects.

Action Class. The action class defines a set of actions to be applied to a specified target. Different types of actions can affect the following behaviours of an MHEG object, presentation and script instances:
• *Preparation*: controls the availability of the object in the system. For example, "Prepare" and "Destroy" actions may be applied to add and remove an object from the system.
• *Creation*: creation of presentation instances from a component object or script instances from a script object.
• *Presentation*: controls the progress of the presentation instances in the system. For example, "Run" and "Stop" actions may be applied to control the progression of a time-based presentation instance.
• *Rendition*: controls the rendition of the presentation instance on the system. These actions vary according to the media type, for example, "Set Speed" for time-based media and "Set Size" for visible media.
• *Interaction*: controls the results of interaction with a presentation instance in the system. For example, "Set Selectable" specifies the selectability of a presentation instance and "Set Modifiability" speficies the modifiability of a presentable.
• *Activation*: controls the activation of the script instances in the system. For example, "Run" and "Stop" actions may be applied to control the progression of a time-based presentation instance.
• *Getting value*: get the attribute, status or behaviour value of MHEG object, presentation instance and script instance. These actions are used to express the link condition in a link object.

Link Class. The link class specifies sets of relationships between a "source" and a list of "targets". The relationship is composed of conditions associated with the source and actions to be applied to the targets when the conditions are satisfied.

Script Class. The script class defines a container for *complex* relationships between objects, defined by a non-MHEG language.

Content Class. The content class contains or refers to the coded representation of monomedia information together with a parameter set which identifies the coding method, and application-oriented parameters such as fonts, colour table.

Composite Class. The composite class provides the support for associating multimedia and hypermedia objects. This mechanism provides a consistent approach to the synchronisation in time and space and linking of a set of objects. This class provides also the logical structure to describe the list of possible interactions offered to the user but does not define the interaction facilities provided by the user interface. Such interaction may be achieved in a variety of ways, for example, Graphical User Interfaces, keyboards, etc. This standard does not define the "look and feel" of multimedia interactive presentations, neither does it propose to change or add concepts to those that exist in typical Graphical User Interfaces. As this standard is generic and independent of platform and implementation, it describes interaction at a virtual level. It is for a using application to apply these mechanisms using its specific "look and feel".

Descriptor Class. The descriptor class defines the interchange of resource information about sets of interchanged objects and is used to facilitate installation and resources negotiation.

Container Class. The container class provides a container for regrouping multimedia and hypermedia data interchange.

3.4.   Presentation and script instances

For the purpose of reusing component objects or script objects in different presentations or activations, a clear separation has been made between the MHEG *content* interchanged object which contains the original reusable media data and the *presentable* corresponding to a specific presentation of the original media data. The same distinction has been made between the MHEG *composite* object which contains the original arrangements of information and the *tree* corresponding to a specific presentation of the original arrangements. The same distinction has been also made between the MHEG *script* object which contains the original script data and the *script instance* corresponding to a specific activation of the original script data.

The presentation of a presentable or a tree does not affect the original component object, this allows the reuse of the same original component object in different presentation instances. The activation of a script instance does not affect the original script object, this allows the reuse of the same original script object in different script instances.

A component object is considered as an 'original' or 'model' object, any number of presentation instances may be created based on instructions given by the author. An instance of presentation made from a content object is called a presentable. An instance of presentation made from a composite object is called a tree. A script object is considered as an 'original' or 'model' object, any number of script instances may be created based on instructions given by the author.

This standard defines an explicit action 'make' to create an instance of presentation from a component object or 'make_script' to create a script instance from a script object

This standard defines also an initial expected behaviour of the presentables, trees, and presentation instances it defines also actions that will modify this behaviour.

The internal representations of the presentable, tree and script instance are not defined by the standard, each MHEG engine will have its own internal representation technique. However, this standard defines the overall structure and the identification techniques to reference a presentation instance in order to modify its behaviour.

3.5. Schedule

Part I: "Information Technology - Coding of Multimedia and Hypermedia Information - MHEG object representation - Base notation (ASN.1)"
CD approved: November 93, Start of DIS ballot: Mid 94, Planned IS: 1994

Part II : "Information Technology - Coding of Multimedia and Hypermedia Information - MHEG object representation - Alternate notation (SGML)
Planned CD ballot: End 94, Planned DIS ballot: 1995, Planned IS: 1995

Part III : "Information Technology - Coding of Multimedia and Hypermedia Information - MHEG-S : MHEG extensions for scripting language support"
Planned CD ballot: End 94, Planned DIS ballot: 1995, Planned IS: 1995

4. Uses of MHEG Objects in communicating environments

The standard defines an encoded format for the interchange between applications. Once interchanged, the MHEG objects are handled by the MHEG engine in an internal representation. There is only one representation defined in the MHEG standard for the interchange of objects, but there will be many possible MHEG engines, each with their own internal format.

The purpose of the MHEG standard is not the specification of the MHEG engine, however, the standard makes some assumptions on different processes that may exist in an MHEG engine.

4.1. The interchange process

The protocol used for the interchange is not described in the MHEG standard.
The interchange process may have two sub processes: the formatter and the parser.

- When an MHEG engine in a using application sends MHEG objects to another using application, a formatter may be used to convert the internal format used in this mheg engine to the encoded format defined by the MHEG standard.

- When an MHEG engine in a using application receives an MHEG object, the object is decoded by a parser. The values within the object are passed to the MHEG engine which may convert them to an internal format.

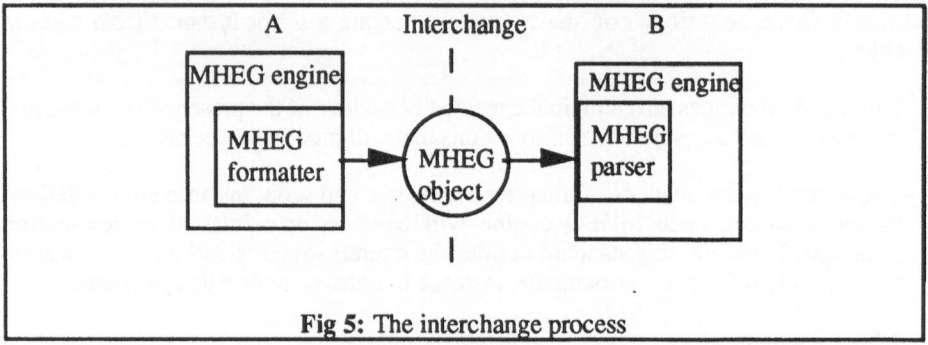

Fig 5: The interchange process

If the exchange between two using applications is bidirectional, the two interchange processes may have both a formatter and a parser.

4.3. The preparation process

This process prepares MHEG objects for processing by the MHEG engine. For example, retrieval of an audiovisual sequence content data from a disk may require so much time that it may be efficient to start loading it before it is needed.

Specific MHEG actions invoke the preparation process: *prepare* and *destroy* . The *prepare* action makes the object available to the MHEG engine, the *destroy* action removes the MHEG object from the MHEG engine.

4.4. The make process

This process make presentation instances or script instances from MHEG original model object and render them available for presentation or activation by the MHEG engine.

Specific MHEG actions invoke the make process: *make* and *kill*. The *make* action makes the presentation or script instance from the object model, and render it available to the MHEG engine, the *kill* action removes the presentation or script instance from the MHEG engine.

4.5. The presentation process

This process presents the presentation instances to the user.

The *run* action places the presentation instance under control of the presentation process, the *stop* action removes this control. The presentation status of a presentation instance in an MHEG engine shows whether the presentation instance is running or not running.

The *rendition* actions may change the rendering of the presentation instance to the user dynamically. Parameters may modify the volume of an audible media data, the size of a visible media data or the presentation of a selection item as a menu item or as a button .

An application may extend the actions with its specific renditions, e.g. colour, character fonts.

4.6. The interaction process

This process enables interactions with the user. The MHEG standard does not aim at defining the look and feel of multimedia presentation, it interworks with graphical user interface tools existing on the system. The interaction process is composed of two sub-processes: selection and modification of presentation instances.

4.7. The synchronization and linking process

This process enables the dynamic variation of presentation of a presentation instance, the spatial and temporal synchronization of a set of objects and the presentation of objects after an interaction. The information interchanged in action, link and script objects are handled in this process.

4.8. The activation process

This process activate a script instance. This may have user effect or not, depending of the content of the script data.

The *activate* action places the script instance under control of the activation process, the *deactivate* action removes this control. The activation status of a script instance in an MHEG engine shows whether the script instance is activated or not activated.

4.9. Interface between MHEG objects and using applications

The MHEG standard has been designed to allow simple relationships between an MHEG object and a user application. The interface between an application and an MHEG engine is not defined by the standard, it is defined by each MHEG engine. In the case of an object oriented MHEG engine, the interface is based on sending messages and receiving results.

Multimedia applications may manipulate MHEG objects at different levels of details, the object (as a whole or attribute per attribute). The standard does not define the structure of data passing across the interface.

However, the following facilities are suggested features which may be provided by an MHEG engine interface :

- Start, stop the MHEG engine
- Supply objects (or references) to the engine, accept objects (or references) from the engine
- Start, stop the processing of an object
- Facilities equivalent to those provided by the action class
- Facilities to access to data within the MHEG engine (attributes, statuses, ...)
- System management information (error indications, ..)

5. Examples of models of user applications

5.1.   Model of an interactive telematic training service

The figure shows an example of an interactive telematic service in the educational environment described in CCITT Recommendation F.740.

It shows the possible actions of a student terminal which is in session with a central server, for example the school system, and is receiving MHEG objects.
The student is studying a hypermedia document in an interactive manner, and as the MHEG engine analyses the responses of the student, it may request either further MHEG objects or the content data required by the objects it has already received from the server.

The formal responses of the student are returned to the server as MHEG objects which may in turn be received by the more sophisticated system used by the tutor. Note in that case the requirement to code these "answers" using the MHEG standard, since the tutoring and student equipments may be the subject of separate procurement policies.

The student system has the "look and feel" defined by the interaction process in conjunction with the graphical user interface.

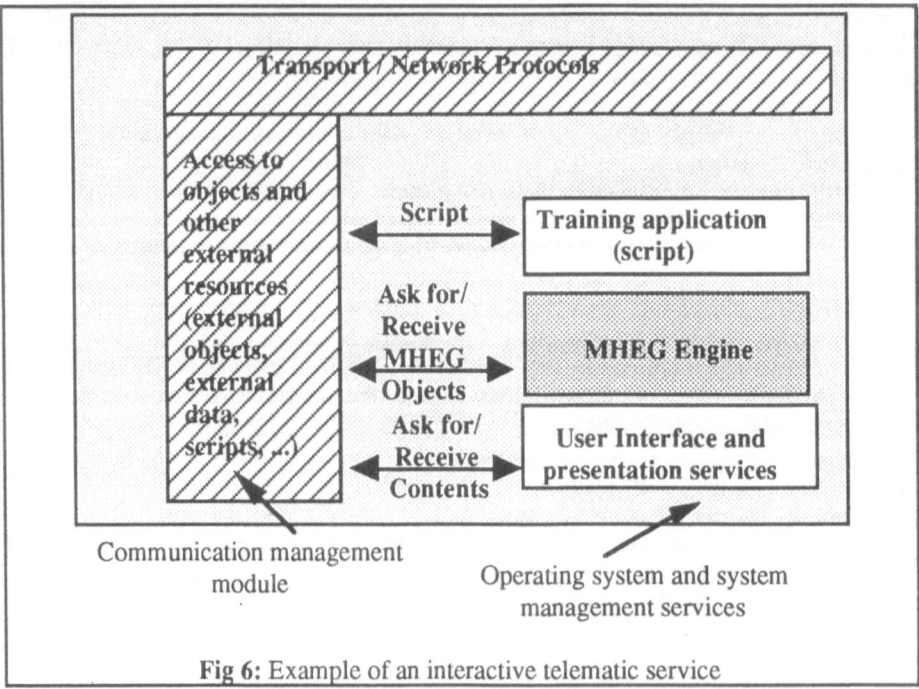

Fig 6: Example of an interactive telematic service

5.3.   Example of an authoring application

The authoring application creates MHEG objects and relies on the services of the

MHEG engine for the dialog with the author, the allocation of identifiers to the objects and the exchange of MHEG objects.

In this generic functional model, the MHEG engine as well as the application can access a specific module to allocate unique identifiers to each MHEG object at creation time.

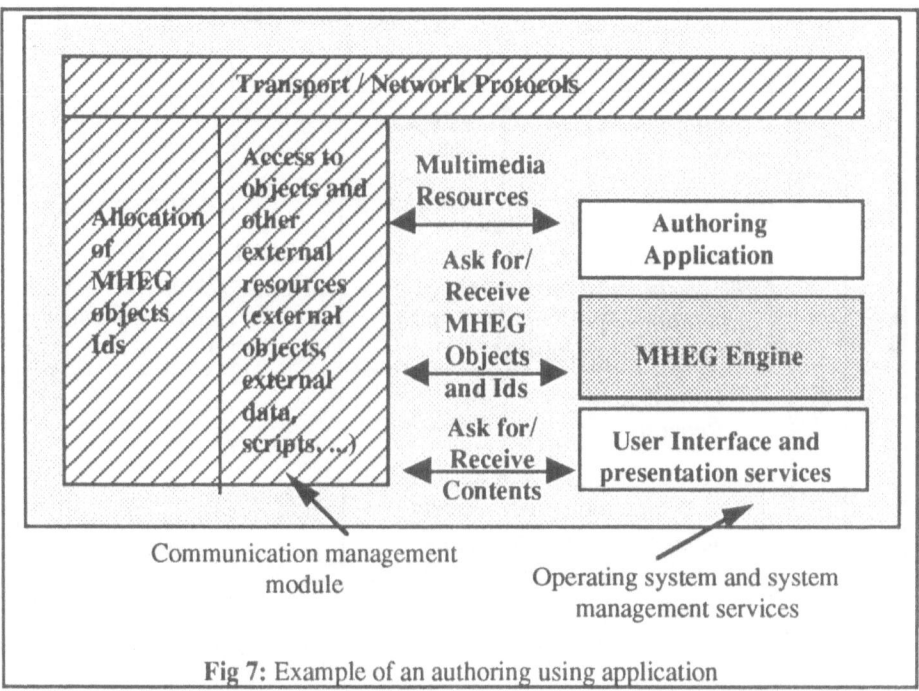

Fig 7: Example of an authoring using application

6. COMIS : An implemented example of the use of MHEG objects and MPEG video sequences

In 1992, CCETT participated in a CEC (Commission of the European Communities) ESPRIT project "COMIS" (COding of Moving Images on digital Storage media) which developed an application showing the interworking of MHEG, JPEG and MPEG standards. This is an interactive game consisting of a tour of different capitals in Europe.

For this project, CCETT has developped an initial version of MHEG engine, integrated into a multimedia platform according to the software architecture outlined below:

The platform consists of three software components, each of which corresponds to a logical layer and implemented as a separate Windows application, which communicates by messages with its neighbouring layers:
- The windowing presentation server: manages windowing resources, deals with user-generated events, displays visual and auditive information.

- The MHEG object manager: accesses, decodes and analyses MHEG objects, interprets the associated methods as series of presentation requests or feedback answers.
- The game scriptware: executes the algorithmic structure of the scenario.

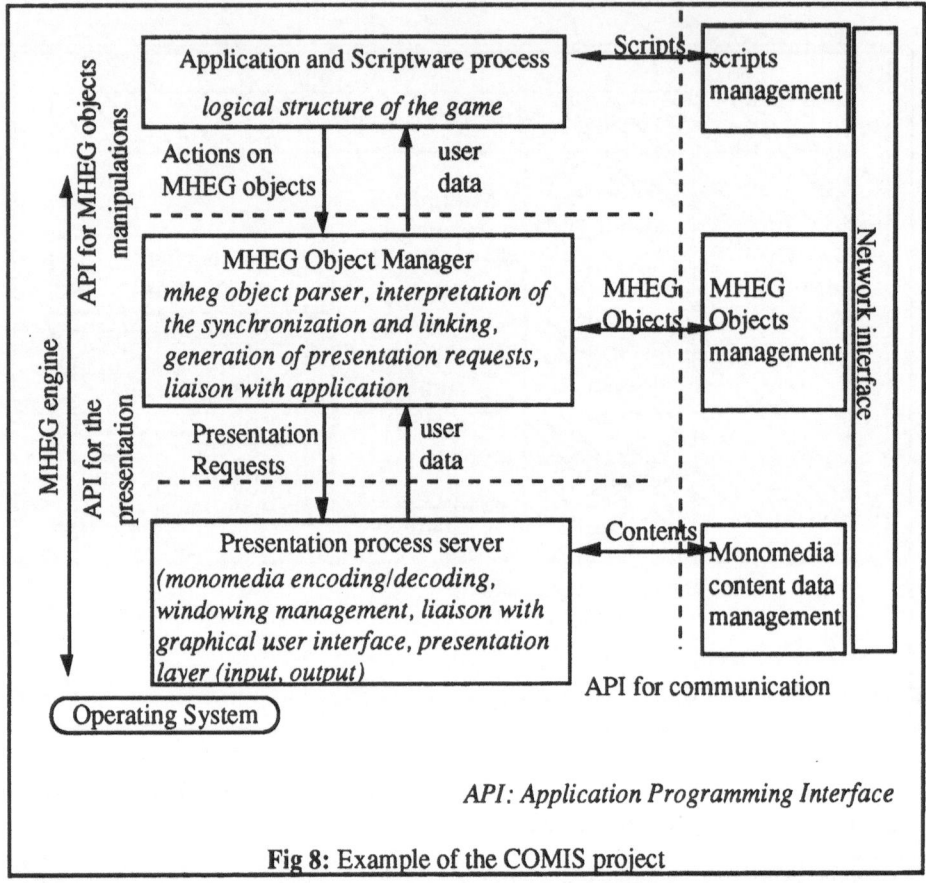

Fig 8: Example of the COMIS project

In a communicating version, the voluminous MPEG video sequences are located in a remote server. After a user selection, the interchange process of the MHEG engine accesses the corresponding video sequences via a broadband network for real-time presentation.

Following the achievement of the COMIS project, the MHEG engine has been continuously improved to stick to the progress of the MHEG standard specifications. A complete toolkit, composed of an Object Editor, a MHEG Class Library, an ASN.1 Codec, and an Interpretor, is now available in CD version.

7. Other ongoing projects

Since the beginning of the MHEG standard development, the MHEG partners have been collaborating in experimental programs based on interchange and validation of test objects and pilot implementations.

By the end of 1993, the MHEG specifications have stabilized, allowing for more significant developments and full size experiments. Early products and licensing announcements are expected as the MHEG standard progresses to the DIS and IS stages.

A European initiative funded by the EEC, European Economic Commission, known as "OMHEGA" (Open MHEG Applications) has been launched at the beginning of 1994, with the following objectives:

- Elaboration of a generic architecture and API specifications by a set of industry partners and telecommunication operators, to be available and widely published as the reference architecture of a MHEG system;
- Design and realisation of MHEG prototypes;
- Promotion of the MHEG standard through regular information exchange, conferences.

Other european projects, using MHEG objects in Video-On-Demand applications, and in multimedia TV guides for digital television broadcasting, have also begun in January 1994.

8. Conclusion

The MHEG standard is a key to the development of communicating multimedia applications and services. The standard supports the interchange of multimedia information, and it specifically meets the needs of applications which run under the following constraints:

Need for multimedia synchronisation between the components of a single and easily addressable "composite" object;

Need for specific structures to support interactivity with the end-user;

Need for real time interchange, through simple and efficient mechanisms to optimize interchange of composite objects;

Final form representation of information, without additional processing needed to restructure the information.

Acknowledgments

The authors wish to thank all the MHEG members for their contribution to this international effort.

References

1. Information Technology - Coded Representation of Multimedia and Hypermedia Information Objects (MHEG), Part I : Base Notation (ASN.1), ISO/IEC CD 13522-1.
2. Colaïtis Françoise, Kretz Francis: "Standardizing Hypermedia Information Objects", IEEE Communications Magazine, May 1992.
3. Colaïtis Françoise: "MHEG, an emerging standard for interchange of multimedia and hypermedia objects", ICC'93 Conference and Proceedings, Geneva, May 23-26, 1993.
4. Price Roger: "An introduction to the future MHEG international standard for Hypermedia Object interchange", ACM 93 Conference and Multimedia Proceedings, Anaheim, August 93.

Distributed Hypermedia Link Service on WAN:

An Experiment with MHEG on the ATM network

Antoine RIZK, Francis MALEZIEUX

EUROCLID, Promopole, 12, avenue des près, 78180 Montigny-le-bretonneux, France.
email : rizk@nuri.inria.fr, Tel: ++.33.1.30.44.14.56, Fax: ++33.1.30.57.18.63

Alain LEGER

CCETT, 4, rue du clos courtel, 35512 Cesson Sévigné, France.
email : leger@ccett.fr, Tel: ++.33.99.12.42.23, Fax: ++33.99.12.40.98

Abstract. The concept of separating hypertext facilities from data storage and from presentation applications is now well established. The idea of hypertext facilities, known as link service, has been proposed and implemented on local area network by many [4,19,20,21,22,23].

In this paper we describe an architecture and implementation that extend the link service concept to the wide area network. The proposed architecture defines a hypermedia protocol and uses the MHEG standard as a common information representation and exchange format.

We address the majors issues such as data exchange of node contents and open access to hypermedia facilities. In the implementation, all MHEG compatible stations will have access to hypermedia link servers to manage hyper objects, and to content servers to retrieve content objects with the requested quality of service.

1. Introduction

First and second generations of hypertext systems were conceived as autonomous applications, having a proprietary data representation format and a specific form of management of the hypertext facilities they offer. It has now become clear that the moderate success that these systems have gained is largely due to their closed architecture and the absence of any form of open exchange mechanism or protocol that would allow them to cooperate interactively with other applications.

There have been a few research achievements around the open hypermedia approach in the recent past, namely [1,3,4]. More recently, the need for open and distributed hypermedia seems to be more pressing judging by the success of systems such as WWW, the DNE proposal [13], the attention the hypermedia standards such as MHEG and Hytime receive, and the emergence of workshops that have been newly organised specifically on this topic[17,18].

Open cooperation in hypermedia systems could be developed along two major aspects : data exchange of node contents and open access to hypermedia facilities such as link management and hypermedia objects organisation. In this paper we develop both aspects by introducing a hypermedia architecture that consists of WAN based link servers and content servers and uses the MHEG standard representation for the exchange of data. Applications access hypermedia facilities through a hypermedia protocol.

We have made the choice of MHEG since it could be used for the exchange of multimedia content data as well a means of coding more complex hyper objects. This was shown in a previous study in the context of the hypermedia system Multicard[5][6].

In this way, our architecture allows the real distribution of data "objects" as well as hypermedia "documents" and third party applications[12]. By using hypermedia facilities such as following links, applications may have access both to remotely stored data objects and to other applications or service elements registered in specialised servers.

The concept of separating hypertext facilities [2](delivered by the link server) from the data storage (the contents server) and from applications (presentation servers) is now well established, but has never been implemented on a Wide Area Network. Quality of service is of paramount importance in the context of hypermedia navigation on WAN. The implementation of the architecture we describe here makes use of the most recent high speed communication services proposed by ATM.

2. Using MHEG standard in multimedia communication

The future international standard known as MHEG [7](ISO Multimedia and Hypermedia information object Expert Group) defines the representation and encoding of multimedia and hypermedia objects to be interchanged within or across applications or services, by any means of interchange including storage devices, telecommunications or broadcast networks.

These objects, encoded using ASN.1 or SGML will provide a common base for other ITU-TS Recommendations and ISO standards and for the many multimedia and hypermedia applications which will be developed in the forthcoming years in a wide range of domains.

The MHEG standard is designed to meet the requirements of communicating multimedia applications and services running on heterogeneous workstations and interchanging information in real time to perform a specific set of services to their users : computer supported multimedia cooperative work, multimedia messaging systems, audiovisual telematic systems for training and education, simulation and games, video on demand services, interactive TV guides, etc.

Users requirements, regarding the interchange of multimedia information, include : real-time interactivity through specific interaction structures, real-time interchange of multimedia data, composition and synchronisation of multimedia data in space and time, linking between elements of composite multimedia objects, reuse of multimedia data by integration in different contexts, portability in a multi-vendor environment, frequent updates of multimedia data, manipulation of a set of data elements.

The scope of the MHEG standard is to fulfil the above requirements by defining the representation and encoding of final form multimedia and hypermedia information objects.

Additionally, the MHEG Objects provide multimedia abstractions particularly suited to real-time presentation (through the synchronisation functionalities), and real-time interchange through telecommunication or broadcast networks.

The standard defines classes of objects, the design of which relies on the analysis of their common behaviour and the commonalities of properties between object categories. The standard provides an ASN.1 representation of the objects (Part I), and an alternate SGML representation (Part II).

Among the main MHEG object classes we find : the Content class, the Link Class, the Script class, the Composite class, the Selection class and Modification class, the Descriptor class (general information about a set of interchanged objects, for presentation resources negotiation).

3. An Hypermedia architecture based on a link server

3.1. General architecture

We describe here the different architecture elements (see Fig. 1.):

Kiosk. From the end-user workstation point of view, the front-end of our architecture, the *service entry point*, is what a telecommunication operator calls a "kiosk" service. The kiosk service, which itself could be a hypermedia application, is the only address known by the user station. The main function of the service entry point is to connect the user requesting a service to the application server that offers the service. In any case, the architecture is totally masked to the user station. The kiosk may deliver sophisticated services based on the use of the link server and, for instance, periodically makes a search of the newest applications registered in the link server.

The kiosk ensures the quality of service by adapting the proposed contents formats to the user station resources and by choosing the network session profile.

User station. A user station typically consists of presentation/editing resources, like graphical interface and monomedia decoders, storage and network resources. The hypermedia protocol will be implemented to support the link server dialogue and the content server dialogue. A MHEG engine is responsible for the interpretation and execution of the MHEG objects. The MHEG engine resolves the object internal links and relies on the link server to resolve external links.

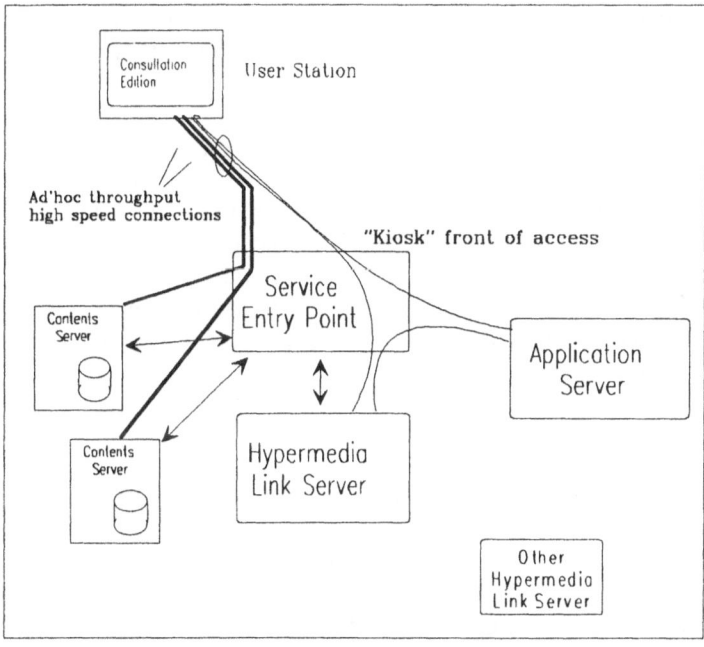

Fig. 1. General Architecture

Application Server. An application server defines application service elements and must register its own services in the link server (service nodes). Each service element interface is coded in a MHEG representation (e.g. a MHEG composite) by the application server. The resulting MHEG object will be proposed to the user stations invoking the service.

Like a user station does, the application server uses the link server facilities to store and access distributed data or to call services from other applications servers. By using the hypermedia facilities of the link server, each application service element develops its own view of data and delivers an added value on these data [8].

Content Server. The contents servers are responsible for the multimedia data management in close cooperation with the link server. Each server could be dedicated to a data type like video, sound... to give the optimal quality of service.

Two types of dialogues have to be implemented in a content server. On one hand lies the dialogue which allows the kiosk to request storage, retrieval, update or any other management functions to be applied to a content object. This dialogue only requires the exchange of light objects, that is to say, objects description without the content data.

On the other hand, the dialogue with the user station must permit the exchange of the content data between content servers and user stations. The implied protocol must support high speed transfer from/to the user station with adapted mechanisms to ensure a good quality of service.

Link Server. Heart of the system, the link server provides a set of hypermedia primitives independently of the applications[8,9,10,13]. The server stores the hyper objects such as nodes and their definition attributes, links and groups of nodes in a hypergraph. Following the MHEG standard, the node attributes will be the "Hook", "descriptor" and "comments" facilities. The set of node attributes is useful to define the resources needed for transfer (transfer rate, asynchronous or synchronous transport service...) and for content data presentation (type of monomedia decoders...)[11].

3.2. Kiosk types of dialogues

The kiosk implements three types of dialogue with the three entities :

Firstly, the kiosk delivers access to hypermedia facilities (provided by the link server) for the user applications and applications servers. This dialogue enables management of nodes of information, the creation of links between nodes and anchors, the invocation of links and so on. The link server could deliver any extra facilities for the computation of views following user requirements or to select data formats in accordance with the user station profile.

Secondly, the kiosk must dialogue with contents servers to perform the content data storage and retrieval. The protocol between these two entities must support all the management and consistency functions like moving, duplicating, deleting... the contents data. This protocol provides the means to set up the data transfer dedicated connection between content server and client user station.

Finally, the kiosk could dialogue with other link servers. This dialogue allows to spread over many network nodes the hypermedia information according to exploitation considerations (multiple access to the server) or semantic organisation.

4. Access and exchange of hypermedia information

A powerful aspect of this architecture is to support heterogeneous applications environments. On the application servers, application service elements don't need to have the same internal environment but are expected to conform to the MHEG exchange representation. Figure 2 shows the distribution of MHEG objects and their exploitation by the kiosk.

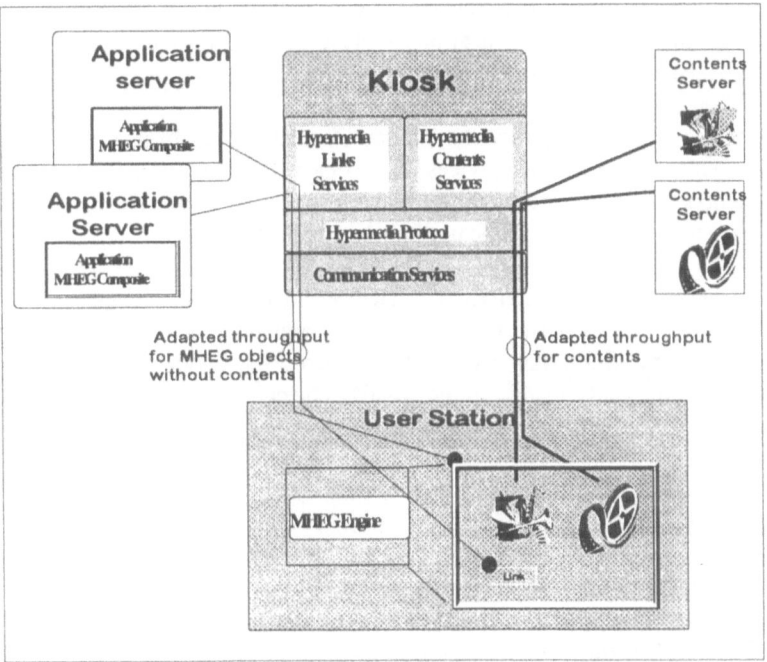

Fig. 2. Exchange of distributed MHEG objects

4.1. Exploiting the MHEG coded hypermedia information

Manipulation of multimedia data. Figure 2 illustrates both the manipulation of light MHEG objects and the transfer of content objects when necessary. Each MHEG light object includes a content data reference which is requested by the kiosk content service to deliver access to content server.

Moreover, MHEG representation provides a full description of the content data with the "hook" attribute and the needed resources for the good rendition of data with the "descriptor" object. These hook attributes and descriptor object are employed in the MHEG "prepare action". When preparing a MHEG object for the presentation, a user station calls the kiosk content to obtain the content data (in case of discrete data) or to set a session (in case of continuous data).

Using MHEG standard to call services. By using MHEG representation, we allow the user station to access application services in two ways (e.g. the application elements coded in application MHEG composites).

The exchange of simple application service elements coded in a composite MHEG object is a solution for simple services. In this case, the user station will take charge of the composite object interpretation and execution. We suppose the user station able to execute the script language used in the composite object.

For complex services we prefer the second way. In this case the application server will only deliver an interface composite object and perform the real execution of service. Following links, the user station invokes the services elements and the application server reply using simple MHEG objects or link references to MHEG objects.

In any case, the user station will always obtain the content data of MHEG objects from the kiosk.

4.2. A hypermedia protocol

All requests sent to the kiosk service and link server are based on the exchange of MHEG objects in a hypermedia protocol. We define a set of hypermedia primitives coded with MHEG action and composite objects. Replies to primitives are also coded with MHEG results objects.

The following scenario illustrates the use of a subset hypermedia primitives :

We suppose that a user station is using the "public" mode to access the kiosk services. The public mode defines a subset of hypermedia primitives with basic access rights.

Firstly, the kiosk uses the link server facilities to search the registered services, their description and access means. So, the kiosk defines a MHEG object which embeds link objects to the different services. The MHEG object will be delivered to a user station requesting an overview of available services.

The following schema illustrates the scheduled steps of dialogue between user station and kiosk :

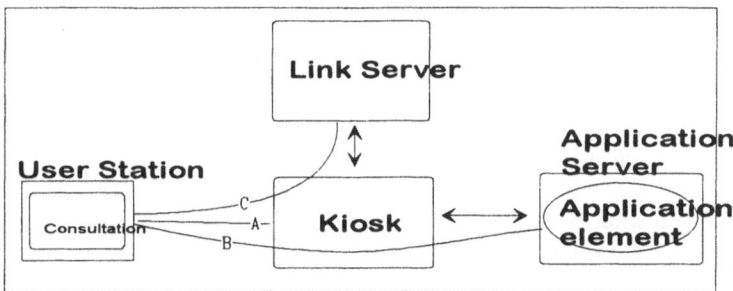

Fig. 3. Access scenario

Step A. User station asks for the available services with the request Navigate[Service_Id]. The kiosk sends it the MHEG composite object he prepared before (the composite embeds links to node services) with ReplyNavigate[Object].

Step B. User station asks for a particular service with Navigate[link_Id]. The kiosk interrogates the link server to obtain the application server address corresponding to the requested service (link_Id) and download the MHEG object from the application server. It replies with ReplyNavigate[Service_Object].

Step C. Traversing an external link (in the service object) to a content object (may be a video), the user station requests more information. User station uses Navigate[link_to_content_object]. The kiosk interrogates the link server and sends the node description with ReplyNavigate[Node, Descriptor_Object].

Finally the user station can obtain the content data by using its reference embedded in the Node object (with the primitive GetContent[Node_Id]). In this example, we have not described the session initialization with the kiosk which allows the user station to give a descriptor object of its own resources. The station descriptor is used by the kiosk to choose the content data type when the user station sends a GetContent primitive.

5. Communication features of the architecture

In this architecture, the separation of the hypermedia information from the multimedia data means that different transport services will be called upon at different times according to the specific need [15]. The ATM transport technology was considered an adequate support because of its flexibility in this sense [14,16].

Briefly, from a communication point of view, we can identify many kinds of flow and interaction while using the hypermedia protocol to access link servers or contents facilities.

Communication between link servers is based on signalling. The transmission unit is the message and interactivity is not a heavy constraint. At the transport level we will choose the datagram based communication but enhanced with the appropriate mechanisms for ensuring data integrity.

The communication between link servers and user stations or application servers must be very interactive with a low connection latency to ensure a good response time. The connection could be message based because in this case only light MHEG objects are exchanged.

Finally the connection between user stations and content servers requires high throughput with many types of service and quality constraints. In the case of resources negotiation, the profile information, encoded in a MHEG object, will determine the choice of the right connection setting in accordance with the user station capacities (nature of data and encoding format).

6. Conclusions

In this paper we have described an architecture and implementation that extend the link service concept to the wide area network. The proposed architecture defines a hypermedia protocol and uses the MHEG standard as a common information representation and exchange format.

The described Architecture is the result of two serious studies realised by Euroclid and the CCETT (a French research centre of France Telecom) that focused on architectures for the distributed hypermedia systems and implementation of MHEG in the open hypermedia system MultiCard.

7. Acknowledgements

The authors wish to thank the ISO-JTC1 SC29/WG12 (MHEG) members and CCITT SGVIII (terminals and protocols) for their invaluable work that allowed the present effort. The constructive and sometimes provocative comments of Françoise

Colaïtis (MHEG convenor), Florence Bertrand and Roger Price (MHEG standard editors) are also gratefully acknowledged.

References

1. Kacmar, C., Leggett, J.: PROXHY : a process oriented extensible hypertext architecture. ACM Trans. on Information Sys., Vol. 9, n°. 4, pp. 399-419, Oct. 1991.

2. Halasz, F.G., Schwartz, M.: The Dexter hypertext reference model. Proceedings of NIST Hypertext Standardization Workshop, Gaithersburg, MD. (January 16-17), 1990.

3. Haan, B., Kahn, P., and all.: "IRIS hypermedia services", Communication of the ACM, vol.35, n°1, pp. 36-51, Jan 92.

4. Rizk, A., Sauter, L.: MULTICARD ; An open Hypermedia System. Proceedings of the ACM Conference ECHT'92.

5. Rizk, A., Malézieux, F., Léger, A.: Using the MHEG standard in the Hypermedia System Multicard, EPodd, special issue on hypermedia, 1994.

6. Leggett, J., Killough, R.L.: Issues in Hypertext exchange. Hypermedia Vol. 3, N° 3, pp. 159-186, 1991.

7. MHEG Part I (ISO-13522-1): "Coded Representation of Multimedia and Hypermedia Information objects. Base notation". This is a complete description of all the classes, and representation and encoding of Objects following the ASN.1 notation and encoding rules.

8. Hatzimanikratis, A., Gaviotis, I., Christodoulakis, D.: An architecture for distributed hypermedia systems. Computer Technology Institute, Greece. ISA Project, 1992.

9. Macartney, A.J., Blair, G.S.: Flexible trading in distributed multimédia systems. Computer Networks and ISDN Systems 25(1992) 145-157.

10. Pearl, A.: "Sun's link service : a protocol for open linking", Proceedings of Hypertext'89, pp. 137-146.

11. Cordes, R., Wybranietz, D., Vautz, R.: An object-oriented transaction-oriented approach including signalling aspects. Telenorma GmbH Bosch Telecom.

12. ESPRIT Project Multiworks. Specifications of the Multicard distributed release on the Multiworks distributed plateform . BNR Europe Limited.

13. Acksyn B.: The Dynamic Node Exchange, personal communication and demonstration at HT'93, Seattle.

14. Tawbi, W., Horlait, E., Dupuy, S.: High Speed Protocol, State of the Art in Multimedia Applications. Laboratoire Masi, Université de Jussieu. Second International Workshop on Network and Operating System for support digital audio and video. Heidelberg 91.

15. Hehmann, D.B., Salmony, M.G., Stüttgen, H.J.: Transport Services for Multimedia Applications on Broadband Networks. Computer Communications Vol. 13 No 4, May 1990.

16. Salmony, M.G., Shepherd, W.D.: Support of Future Multimedia Applications Beyond OSI. IBM European Networking Center, Heidelberg. IFIP March 91.

17. Kuhlen, R.: Workshop on open hypermedia systems. Konstanz, March 1994.

18. Leggett, J.: Workshop on open and large data hypermedia systems, Seattle, Nov. 1993.

19. Campbell, B, Goodman, J.: "HAM: A general purpose hypertext abstract machine", Communications of the ACM, Vol.13, N°. 7, 1988, pp.856-861.

20. Schütt, H.A, Streitz, N.: "Hyperbase: A hypermedia engine based on a relational database management system", in: A.Rizk, N.Streitz and J.Andrè, (Eds.), Hypertext: Concepts, systems and applications, Cambridge University Press, 1990, pp. 95-108.

21. Wang, B, Hitchcock, P.: "InterSect: A general purpose hypertext system based on an object oriented framework", in: D.Karagiannis, (Ed.), Database and Expert Systems Applications, Springer-Verlag, 1991, pp. 459-464.

22. Haan, B.J, Kahn, P, Riley, V.A, Coombs. J.H, Meyrowitz, N.K.: "IRIS hypermedia services", Communications of the ACM, Vol. 35, N°. 1, 1992, pp. 36-51.

23. Wiil, U.K, Leggett, J.J.: "Hyperform: Using extensibility to develop dynamic, open and distributed hypertext systems", in: D.Lucarella, J.Nanard, M.Nanard and P.Paolini, (Eds.), Proceedings ACM Conference on Hypertext, Milano, Italy, December 2-4, 1992, pp. 251-261.

MHEG, Scripts, and Standardisation Issues

Thomas Casey, CIHE, UK[*]
Joseph Fromont, CCETT, France[**]

Abstract. Complex issues involve the relationship between MHEG objects and scripts, and the problems encountered in developing standards within this domain. MHEG, ISO 13522 -1, is a DIS (Draft International Standard)*[MHEG 93]* that specifies the encoding for Multimedia Hypermedia information for interchange. This same ISO working group is responsible for the standardisation of encoding for Audio Visual Interactive Scriptware (AVIs) and providing extensions to MHEG encodings for support of scripting languages, MHEG part 3. Within ITU, Study Groups are developing recommendations for services and protocols that will support AVI services*[ITU-T 93]*. Much of the activity in ISO JTC 1/SC 29/WG 12, and ITU SG 11/Q.8 is aligned; in some cases joint text may be published.

The purpose of this paper is to explore the nature of the problems involving multimedia hypermedia object interchange, presentation and interaction supported by scripts in a distributed environment, and the current status of the work of ISO and ITU-T standards groups with respect to their views of the problems.

1. The Framework

Significant improvements in network and computer technologies in recent years provide new opportunities for the different actors of information technology and telecommunications.

Telecommunication operators want to provide new interactive services that allow users to access and interchange various types of information in a convenient and efficient way. IT industries are developing a new generation of equipment to exploit the multimedia and hypermedia technologies.

A common feature of these new interactive services is the interactive multimedia and hypermedia nature of the information being accessed and interchanged by users.

---

[*] Thomas Casey is a Snr Lecturer CIHE, Cardiff, Wales, UK and a member of SC29/WG 12 "MHEG" E-mail: tcasey@uk.ac.cihe.

[**] Joseph Fromont is a Research scientist at CCETT Rennes, France, Rapporteur of ITU-T Study Group 8 Question 11 on protocols and representation for the interchange of Multimedia and Hypermedia information on AVIs Services. Co-editor of the MHEG standard (part III): " Extension to MHEG for scripting languages support" E-mail: fromont@ccett.fr.

Hence a consistent concept of an AVI (AudioVisual Interactive) service must be identified as a prerequisite to determining the standardisation requirements for such services. These requirements comprise several levels and fields of activity in the communications domain. Consequently, standardisation effort is shared among and within different organisations, their committees, or working groups.

General model aspects, especially those concerning definition of services are treated by ITU-T (Recommendations F.740 and T.170 draft). Functional aspects concerning multimedia and hypermedia applications are addressed through a collaborative framework between ISO/IEC JTC 1/SC 18, and ITU-T. Representation and coding aspects of the various components, objects and aggregates involved in these applications are the responsibility of SC 29/ WG 12(MHEG); SC 29/ WG 09(JBIG), 10(JPEG), & 11(MPEG) provide codings for compression of Mono and Multimedia data content. Protocols definition work has been assigned to ITU-T SG 8.

An Illustration of the general framework for providing AVI Telematic services is shown in the AVI model diagram below.

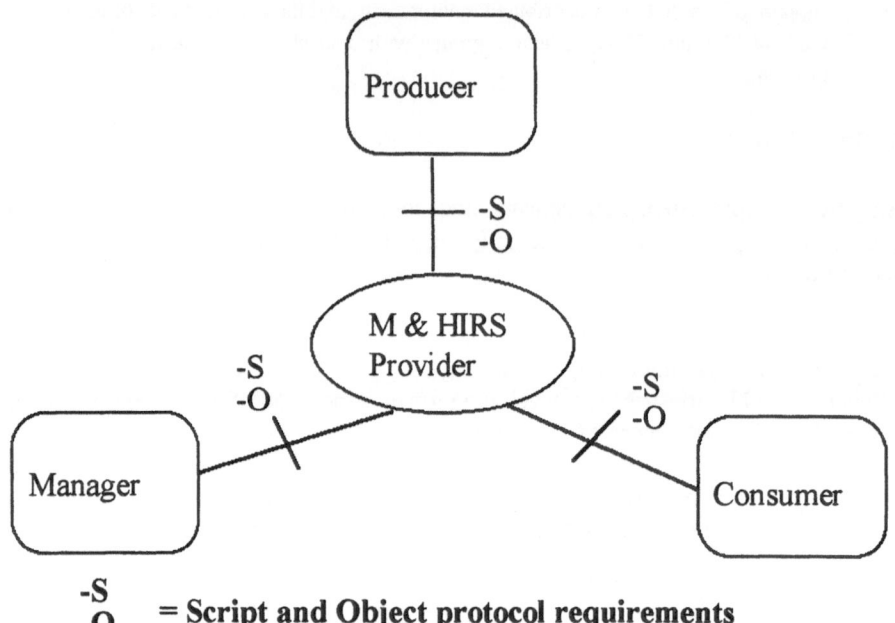

$-S$
$-O$ = Script and Object protocol requirements

M & HIRS = Multimedia & Hypermedia Information
Retrieval Service

Figure 1: Model of AVI Service System

As this illustration indicates several protocols, each with specific requirements need to be developed with respect to the objects and scripts that will be interchanged among the actors in such a system.

This presents interesting protocol problems in the relationship among MHEG, objects, scripts, and requirements for Audio Visual Interactive (AVI) Telemetric services.

2. MHEG

MHEG refers to ISO 13522-1, currently at DIS stage (Draft International Standard, the last stage before publication as an International Standard (IS)), which specifies the standards for MH (Multimedia Hypermedia) information objects. MHEG defines the coded representation of object classes required for the interchange of MH information. It defines the structure and as much of the semantics as is necessary for providing standardised encoding of the objects. MHEG is object-oriented but implementation does not require the use of object-oriented techniques or languages. MHEG objects are defined at four levels, A - D. Level A provides an informal English definition of the object. Level B provides a rigorous definition. At level C of Part I, the standard provides an ASN.1 notation for each of the object classes; and level D provides an ASN.1 encoding according to the BER (Basic Encoding Rules)[1] specification.

It is intended that Part II of the standard will provide for an isomorphic encoding of the MHEG object classes using SGML notation. Isomorphism between Part I and II will be supported at level B, the formal Object Class definition level.

MHEG defines object classes for component, composite and content objects. It also defines behaviour, link, script, descriptor, and macro objects. Within the composite object class the container or encapsulation concept is explicitly defined and the concept of presentable is supported via a graphic or tree structured addressing mechanism. A presentable or view allows for the reuse of objects in various presentations.

Taken together the MHEG composition, link and behaviour objects provide for a rich, expressive set of multimedia-media hyper-media facilities for interchange. The use of script and descriptor objects further enhance the capability to interchange complex interactive multimedia hypermedia applications.

---

[1] BER, refers to ISO 8825:1987 Specification of Basic Encoding Rules of Abstract Syntax Notation One (ASN.1), is one of many and probably the most widely used encoding rules of the ISO 8824: 1987 Specification of Abstract Syntax Notation One (ASN.1).

MHEG is not a scripting language nor is it considered a complete scriptware package. MHEG provides a standard definition of Multimedia Hypermedia (MH) objects for interchange among a heterogeneous set of platforms; it supports reuse of objects, and different views of presentables. Using the forthcoming extensions for script language support and the presently specified script object, MHEG can be a standard mechanism which will support a wide range of AVI service applications.

3. Scriptware

Scriptware is comprised of MH objects and algorithms which express relationships among the objects, and the processing applied to objects and their scripts; these form a complete and consistent production and/or exploitation unit, that is:

- presentation of multimedia and hypermedia objects referring to specific content data;
- use of a script representation allowing the handling of objects;
- production and handling of traces which consist of data produced during information exploitation and made available by services.

The first aspect to consider is the nature of scriptware, and more particularly, whether it is necessary to define a representation for encompassing the set of objects that comprises scriptware.

It appears that scriptware does not imply the use of a specific standardised representation. Scriptware may be considered as a view on a set of objects (scripts) assembled for a particular usage.

3.1 Scripts

Scripts can be defined as software implementations expressing the handling of multimedia and hypermedia information objects, spatiotemporal and conditional sequencing, and additional processing required during exploitation by the information consumer (retriever).

A script can be seen as an instance of a Scripting Representation. The concept of script is quite general and applies to many fields: not only to multimedia or hypermedia domains. However, in the present document the word "script" and its derivatives refer to an "AVI script" (AudioVisual Interactive script).

3.1.1 Scripting Representation

A scripting representation is a result of the processing (typically compilation, or at least, coding optimisation) of a Scripting Language module (script source) or of the use of a Scripting Tool. The scripting representation is generally designed to achieve compactness and to allow execution. Such a representation is not human-readable, and frequently non-reversible for copyright protection.

3.1.2 Script Interchange Format (or Script Interchange Representation)

Script Interchange Representation is designed to allow script interchange and delivery over networks, as well as exploitation on heterogeneous configurations. Usually, the creation of scripts and scriptware is associated with the use or execution of a scripting language.

3.2 Scripting Language

In the field of interactive multimedia/hypermedia applications, an author uses a scripting language to bring together a set of multimedia/hypermedia information in an organised way so that further users will be able to consult it interactively. Indeed, a scripting language can be easily compared to a programming language and the attributes which differentiate scripting from programming languages are subtle and often have more to do with marketing than with clear technical distinctions *[MARK 93]*.

However, several characteristics of scripting languages can be recognised.

- *A scripting language is composed of a simple-to-use syntax offering enhanced functionalities.* Thus, an author is able to create applications very easily which handle a complete multimedia environment including user's interactivity.

- In a multimedia environment, applications editing requires the use of dedicated software. These software are aimed to users (authors) whose objectives are more to conceive and display than program. Indeed, *scripting languages are usable by people who are not professional programmers.* Most industrial products currently available offer *scripting languages looking like natural ones in user-friendly environments.*

- *A same scripting language is usable on a various range of operational systems* either entirely local such as personal computers equipped with CDs, or remote or distributed such as in networking systems.

Various scripting languages are available on multimedia platforms enabling authors to produce their applications:

Amongst them, Hypertalk® can be considered as a first reference in this domain. It provides a way to include procedural processings in Hypercard® stacks.

Lingo® is used by the Macromind Director authoring system. Here, the user is provided with a story board onto which certain events are placed. The position of the events on the storyboard suggests their sequencing and synchronisation relationships. Behind the scenes, Director creates a Lingo® script which is interpreted during the playback of the presentation.

Kaleida, a joint venture between IBM and Apple, is launching a new product called Script/X® which is based on object oriented concepts.

Toolbook's "Openscript" is a popular scripting language which works "under" a graphical user friendly Toolbook authoring system. It builds Windows compatible applications for PC's.

4. Implementation Specificity

In scriptware scenarios, it is important to realise that scriptware development cannot be analysed independent of the presentation environment; this is a typical API (Application Programming Interface) problem. For the most part implementers will always assume that their applications are supported by some type of graphic user or windows environment: Windows 3.1, Window NT, X Windows, Motif, Apple Mac graphic interface, are some of the more popular environments. It is unlikely that scriptware will be written such as to provide the presentation process as well as the scripts. This could however be the case for certain videotex applications; but these will have to be dealt with elsewhere.

5. The Interchange Model

In both the ISO IEC/JTC1/SC18/WG1 Technical Report *[TR SC18 93]* and the MHEG CD standard *[MHEG 93]* , an interchange model is described comprising several layers showing the relative positions of the various kinds of data used in multimedia/hypermedia environments. This model is illustrated below in *Figure 2*.

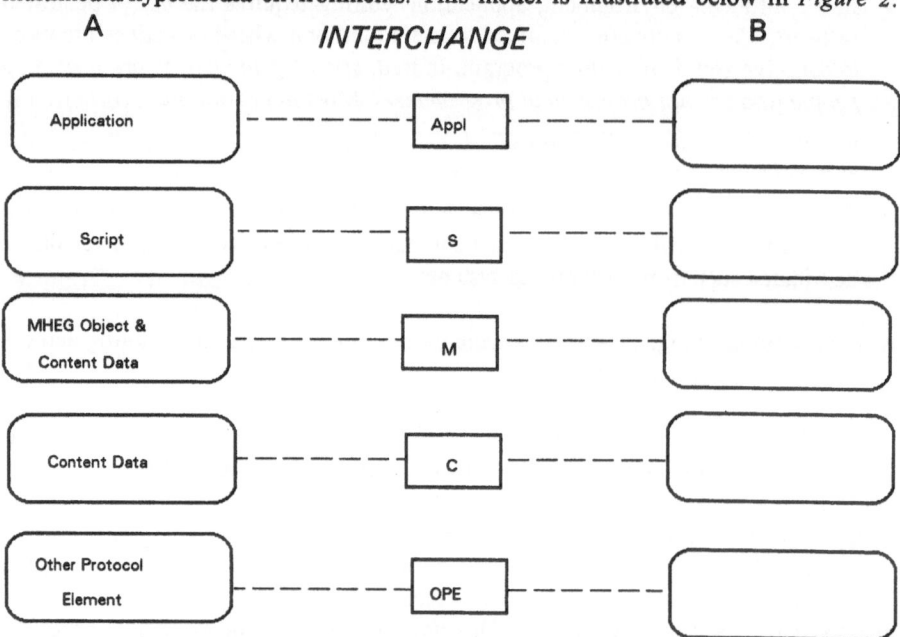

FIGURE 2: DIFFERENT LEVELS OF INTERCHANGE BETWEEN COMMUNICATING APPLICATIONS

In this figure, the level of content data corresponds to generic unstructured data (audio, graphics, video, etc.), whereas the upper levels correspond to structured data (applications, hyperdocuments, scripts, etc.).

The script level belongs to the language layer together with document representations, mark-up and programming languages. It relies on a set of other layers referring to existing or emerging standards: standards for monomedia contents (JPEG, JBIG, MPEG, MIDI, CGM, etc.), standards for multimedia and hypermedia objects (MHEG etc.).

- **It goes beyond the presentation by aiming at standardising the application level, especially in the design of a syntax describing a set of functions (inputs, outputs, processings, decisions etc.) [Fro&al. 89]**

- It supports the creation of pre-edited structures and their consultation in a hypermedia way.

- It provides abstractions independent of the execution configuration's heterogeneity.

- Lastly, its operation in communication environments takes place on the basis of several functional models characterising a general multimedia operational system including editing, management and execution [ITU-T 93].

As a conclusion, these four assignments point out the need for two kinds of standardisation requirements, that is:

- the representation of script elements;

- their interchange between varied platforms (editing, management, execution).

5.1 Real-Time and Non-Real-Time Interchange Over Networks

Protocols need to be defined for the setting up of services in a distributed networking environment. Work on protocols must take as a starting point a very precise definition of service architecture. Its precise definition is the subject of work undertaken within ITU-T Recommendations F.740 & T.170 [ITU-T 93].

Providing protocols for Telemetric services is complex within the milieu of ITU-T. Service definitions are provided by Study Group 1 and protocols for the service tasks are within the domain of Study Group 8.

Many ideas are forthcoming with respect to:

- terminal architectures;

- multimedia-media hypermedia applications.

An important question is how can these applications be made to run on ATM, ISDN, and PSDN networks. If we analyse the protocol requirements in terms of service tasks such as, conferencing, conversational, retrieval, sending, collection, and distribution, it become evident that protocol complexity is an important consideration.

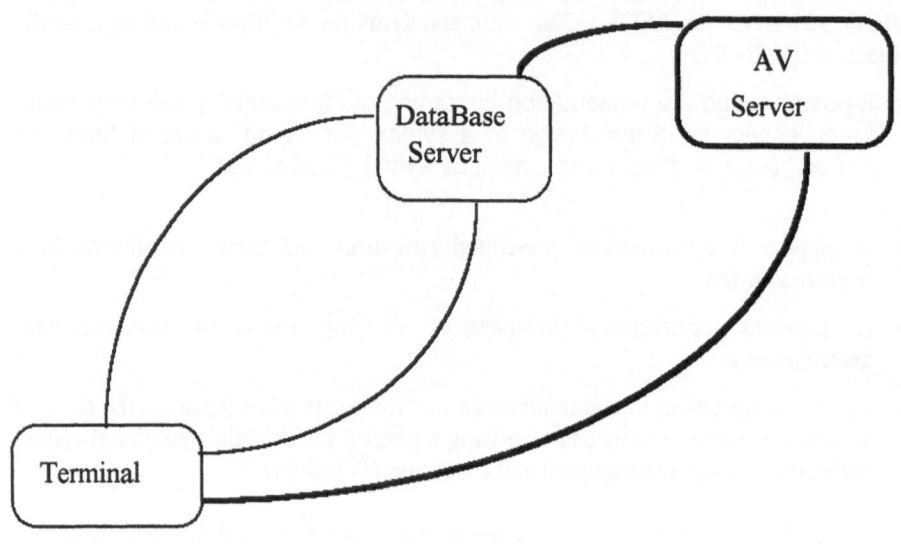

Figure 3: AVI Services & Protocol Complexity
Lines = protocols; Rectangles = services
Thick lines and rectangle outlines indicate additional requirements

The illustration of Figure 3 shows an AV server added to a database and indicates the added protocol complexity that this entails. The heavy lines indicate complex multi-channel protocol requirements associated with the addition of the AV server.

Adding an AV server to a database requires multichannel & link protocols for Multimedia Hypermedia control and presentation between the servers and the using terminal.

Different protocols are to be specified according to the network they rely on and to the transfer mode they implement: real-time interchange or non real-time interchange. Real-time means that information is interchanged for immediate use within time constraints given by the service. Protocols do not depend on the representation of the information they are carrying but it should be noticed that all the information representations are not adapted to real-time interchange.

Protocols for non real-time interchange will be based upon existing file transfer protocols enhanced with using rules. The four levels of information (content data, multimedia and hypermedia information, script information, scriptware-specific information) must be supported by these protocols.

Real-time (timing relationship) protocols allow the interchange of data, multimedia and hypermedia information and application-specific information. The real-time interchange of multimedia and hypermedia information is a critical issue because of the need of linearisation of a basically non-linear, "hyper" information. ITU-T objects may be composed of various kinds of components which may require different Quality of services (e.g. time constraints). It must be noticed that these constraints may be applied to procedural information.

6. Some General Aspects of AVI Applications

6.1. Technical Typology of Multimedia Applications

In the numerous fields where multimedia and hypermedia technologies apply, a simple analysis of their related applications allow their sorting according to the following technical typology decomposed in three families:

6.1.1 "Intrinsically Multimedia" Applications.

Those applications are composed of fully constitutive multimedia components, namely the application semantics is brought by the multimedia components themselves. In such applications, the multimedia components development process is closely linked, even associated with the application development process itself.

Typical representatives of this category are Computer Aided Learning applications, museographic applications, games, multimedia booths etc.

6.1.2 Applications with Multimedia External Interface.

In those applications, multimedia components are mainly used to improve the interface user-friendliness. This interface subset may be voluminous and structured and aims to hide an application's main body which requires no multimedia or hypermedia technology.

Representatives are simulations, process control applications etc.

In this last case of process control, multimedia-hypermedia features must comply with real-time constraints.

6.1.3 Applications Managing Multimedia Components.

These components are not intrinsic constituent parts of the application. In fact, they result from or are the basis for the applications exploitation which are rather tools or information management systems.

Typical examples correspond to medical records systems, estate agencies applications, multimedia banks of documents, electronic publishing, video on demand systems etc.

In such applications, the multimedia components development process is usually dissociated from the application development process itself, except for validation purposes.

Obviously the above typology is simply indicative. Some applications may correspond to several of these categories. For example, "multimedia catalogues" may be interpreted as a combination of types 1 and 3 (use of a multimedia dialogue for navigation and selection inside the catalogue, which lies itself upon a multimedia database). Computer Assisted Maintenance also often presents mixed characteristics.

6.2. Characterisation of Script-Based Applications

In the above typology, script-based applications mainly correspond to type a) , but they can also be seen to correspond to the multimedia sub-parts of type b) applications.

In general terms, these applications have the functional characteristics of being "execution control oriented". The multimedia components are attached to execution control structure elements. They are managed through a "scenario" that provides the spatiotemporal-temporal sequencing and the conditional relationships between the objects.

On the other hand, type c) applications are "data-oriented". The number of multimedia objects can be very large compared to the control structure size and these objects may be indistinguishable from the control structure features.

It is possible to position script-based applications within a global layered presentation of multimedia applications; these are described below with several examples identified within the table.

Info Type	Category of Applications	CD	MH	S	A
T1 Resident Algorithms	Video on Demand Multimedia Journals	X X			X X
T2 Down-Loaded Hypermedia	Tele-Karaoke Tele-Shopping	X X	X X		X X
T3 Complex Procedures	Video Games Maintenance Tele-Shopping	X X X	X X X	X X X	X X X

Table 1: Classification of MH Application Types
CD: Content Data
MH: Multimedia Hypermedia Object
S: Script
A: Application Specific

T1 corresponds to (control-)unstructured or poorly-structured applications. The structuration, when it exists, is mainly the result of a preparation by the system manager.

T2 corresponds to the intermediate case of a minimal structuration of multimedia objects and their related links at the information producer's initiative.

T3 corresponds to highly-structured applications comprising complex procedures.

Considering this global classification, some general characteristics of script-based applications can be enunciated. These applications can be seen as :

- *autonomous*

- It does not mean that the applications are "independent" (it is quite the opposite for type b)) but they can be considered as individual entities during their specific execution;

- It does not mean that these applications do not exchange information with outside processes, such as at the beginning by receiving parameters, at the end by sending results or even during all their execution (case of the front-end of a process control), but these eventual exchanges can be clearly isolated.

- *pre-edited*

The contents and the structure are created and edited in a separate phase before the execution.

- It does not exclude updating (in real time or not)

- *indivisible*

Only a whole application is meaningful for the purpose of execution.

- It does not exclude capability to be inserted in more global sets and contexts (macro-applications), or to co-operate with external processes (see above).

7. Standardisation

Standards for the interchange of Data, Objects, Documents, Architectural Forms, and Multimedia Hypermedia Information is an ongoing process that takes place in a variety of forums. The most important of these for our concerns are the international committees, study groups, and working groups of ISO and ITU-T that are currently working in the scripting and Telematics services areas.

7.1 State-of-the-Art of Work in Standards Organisations

Many standards' working and study groups have recently taken on the tasks of extending their activity into field of Multimedia and Hypermedia, as extensions to work they were doing in document, graphics, architectures and other areas of standardisation. ODA, Open Document Architecture, SC 18/WG 3, has a collaborative project with MHEG to produce a TR Technical Report on the use of MHEG Objects in ODA documents and Vice-versa. ISO working groups SC 18/WG 8, SGML, and SC 29 have special relationships with ITU-T, because of their current responsibilities to produce standards dealing with scripts, scripting languages, and script language interfaces.

7.1.1 ISO IEC JTC 1/SC 18/WG 8/SGML

Members of ISO SC 18/WG 8 Hypermedia Languages SWG have proposed that the SMSL project proceed by first defining a data model, based on the HyTime and SGML standards [MARK 93]. This data model could then be used to define a set of services which would map, at least roughly, to a set of operators for typical objects classes. The framework of services (which should be defined in as generic a manner as possible, with arguments consisting of data headers encoded using SGML) could then be implemented as an API in various system implementations. The API would provide a consistent programming interface for applications.

This approach will allow the current scripting language vendors to provide language tools specific to classes of applications, while maintaining portability. Better still, this approach will allow other companies to enter the scripting arena with languages designed specifically for their applications while still providing a high degree of portability and interchange ability.

A first objective of SC 18/WG 8-SGML has been to collect contributions from interested parties and to prepare a dossier in this area that will constitute the basis of their work. They expect to launch an ISO CD in Mid-94.

7.1.2 ISO IEC JTC1/SC29/WG12-MHEG

Being responsible for the coding aspects, the ISO SC 29/WG 12, MHEG, group is studying the appropriate coding methods for scripts as a possible extension of multimedia and hypermedia objects encoding [MHEG 93]. They are keen to issue a standard that supports ASN.1, SGML, as well as other notations and syntax.

As the script world is already populated by many industrial products, MHEG is studying how these products could join, or be aligned with future *International* standards. Indeed, three levels of standardisation are worth being taken into account:

- A first level will enable the interchange of non-standardised scripts within scriptware and the access to a set of standardised objects.

- A second level is currently under consideration as part 3 of the MHEG standard. The scope of this part is being defined with respect to providing mappings between a standardised core of scripting functionalities and other run-time script interpretation environments.

During the SC 29 plenary, November 1993 a decision was made to support an MHEG Part 3 that would provide the required AVI Scripting extensions for MHEG object.

7.1.3 ITU-T Q11/8

ITU-T Q11/8 is defining architecture and protocols for AVI services. It is preparing a number of recommendations on the technical facilities required for the provision of AVI services, i.e. for the interchange of AVI scriptware, among which the following are scheduled:

- T.170: "General introduction";

- T.171: "Coded representation of MH objects"; referenced text to ISO CD 13522 Part 1 MHEG.

- T.172: "Functional description of AVI scriptware";

- T.173: "Coded representation of scripts";

- T.174: "Protocols for non real-time interchange of scriptware";

- T.175: "Protocols for real-time interchange of scriptware".

In order to avoid duplication of efforts and willing to arrive at a common standard for scripts, this group has already established a collaborative working group with ISO SC29/WG12/MHEG for T.173 and has proposed during its April 93 plenary meeting the same mechanism to ISO SC18-WG8-SGML.

7.2 Industry Associations

Interesting references are the Interactive Multimedia Association (IMA), the Association for Binary Compatibility (ABC):

- The mission of IMA is to promote the development, application and use of interactive multimedia, to expand markets for interactive products and services, to encourage greater public awareness of the industry, and to demonstrate the uses and values of the new technologies. Membership in the IMA is open to organisations, institutions, and individuals who are actively involved in the production and use of interactive technology and optical media systems, who provide services to the industry, and those who wish to track the forward motion of this emerging technology. The IMA has recently launched a Request For Technology (RFT) on scripting languages. It means that an industry standard should be supported by the IMA in the next future.

- The Association for Binary Compatibility may offer a container architecture and application programming interface known as Bento.

Bento is a specification for object containers. These containers can be used by applications to store document objects. Bento is intended to be platform and content neutral, so that it provides a convenient container for transporting any type of content between multiple platforms. The current Bento specification describes a label format, a data model, and a few (primitive) standard objects. Work is underway to define a set of standard objects.

Currently, Bento is implemented for Macintosh (by Apple) and Windows 3.x (by Lotus). The intent is to distribute Bento as a public domain offering from the Association for Binary Compatibility (ABC).

8. Conclusion

The standardisation of a scripting language in ISO and ITU-T has only recently begun despite the fact that the corresponding work items was approved two years ago by JTC1. It is certainly due to the fact that the focus in ISO has been firstly put on standardising multimedia/hypermedia objects; for example, SC 29/WG 12 has just produced it's IS ISO 13255 -1 on the coding of multimedia and hypermedia objects and SC18/WG 8 has recently published the SGML\ HyTime IS providing among other things a way to express links between heterogeneous distributed documents *[NEWC 91]*.

Once the standards work on scripts is complete at the structured data level it will be possible to create and use multimedia and hypermedia applications by referring exclusively to internationally agreed standards for any level of information, content, structure, and link relationships.

What the impact of these standards will have on industry generally and the hardware and software OEMs is still a speculative and difficult to answer question. Unlike other standardisation efforts which usually evolved from the de facto standards of industry, in the MH domain standards may at last be driving industry to conformance in order to protect their markets. This will probably be true as long as no single de facto standard comes to dominate the MH markets.

9. References

[AFN 92] Norme experimentale AFNOR Z62040-1-2-3-4 "Représentation Des Applications Audiovisuelles Interactives"

[A.0 92] Coded representation of AVI scripts, PART I : Base notation, Working document *A.O* DRAFT, SOURCE SC29/WG12(MHEG)

[AVI 93] The AVI initiative: Functional requirements and proposed framework for standardisation, ITU-T Q8/11 & ISO SC29/WG12-MHEG reference working document.

[ITU-T 93] ITU-T Rec. F.740 "Audiovisual Interactive Services: General Description" (1993)

[FRO&al. 89] La RAVI: Objectifs, Aperçu des spécifications, Produits industriels, évolution, Technical Report CCETT/RT/1989/N°5, J. FROMONT, F. KRETZ, PL MAZOYER, F. OGUET

[MARK 93] ISO IEC JTC1/SC18/WG8 SMSL Working Document, B. MARKEY

[MHEG 93] Committee Draft ISO/IEC CD 13522-1 (1993): "Coded Representation Of Multimedia And Hypermedia Objects (MHEG)".

[NEWC 91] HyTime: Hypermedia/Time-based Document Structuring Language, Communication of the ACM, Nov. 1991, Vol. 34 N°11, Steven R. NEWCOMB, Neill A. KIPP, Victorai T. NEWCOMB

[TR SC18 93] Technical Report on Hypermedia and Hypermedia: Model and Framework, Source: SC18/WG1 (1992)

[Z60R 89] Report Of The AFNOR Z60R Adhoc Group on Audiovisual Interactive Applications, AFNOR Document (1989)

The BERKOM Multimedia Teleservices

Joachim Schaper

Digital Equipment GmbH,
CEC Karlsruhe Vincenz-Priessnitz-Str.1,
D-76131 Karlsruhe,
E-MAIL: schaper@kampus.enet.dec.com

Abstract. This paper reports the BERKOM Multimedia Teleservice project, which is a joint effort between the German PTT and various companies and research organizations to build prototypes for future broadband public services. The goal of this paper is to give an introduction to the overall design of the services, their architecture and to describe the current implementation state. After a problem description of multimedia applications according to open heterogenous network environements, the specific project context of BERKOM is introduced. The services Multimedia Collaboration (MMC), Multimedia Mail (MMM), and the Multimedia Transport system (MMT) will be described. A summary on our current experience in providing an implementation on top of Alpha AXP and OSF/1 of the 3 subsystems provides the Digital expierence within the consortium. An outline of the future work gives directions for the focus for the next few years.

1.0   Introduction

1.1 Background

The motivation to start the BERKOM programme was the fact that larger organizations such as corporations or administrations are becoming more and more geographically distributed. The increasing communication need between the different parts within the organizations make the use of high bandwidth communication facilities (e.g. high speed network links) necessary and useful. The advent of powerful systems expands currently the scope of traditional datatypes, such as text and graphics, to multi-media including images, video, and audio. The advent of high performance networks and current evolution of multimedia workstations with a resonable price/performance relation build the technical foundation to introduce new public teleservices as a standard telecommunication infrastructure. BERKOM [5] (the BERliner KOMmunikationssysteme) is one of the most prominent Broadband ISDN trial projects world wide.The first phase of the project ended in 1991 after 5 years. Unlike the first phase, which explorred numerous independent broadband network solutions, the second phase which is planned until end of 1994 concentrades on providing a single uniform communication infrastructure. This infrastructure should be the base for future broadband multimedia applications. The goal is to provide three prototypes of teleservices which are implemented in a standards based open, and heterogenous environment of networked multimedia workstations and PCs. The 3 subprojects comprise the areas of network transport, realtime conferencing, and multimedia extensions to mail grouped as:

1. The Multimedia Transport Service (MMT) provides the communication platform for audiovisual communication. MMT is based on the Internet Stream Protocol ST-2. It allows the creation of multi-endpoint connections with guaranteed throughput and delay. The current transport medias the consortium is focusing on are Ethernet, FDDI and ATM.

2. The Multimedia Mail Service (MMM) allows the exchange of multimedia messages consisting of text, image, video, audio and structured documents (ODA). It provides extensions to the X.400 functionalities and also prepares gateways to other multimedia mail systems such as e.g. Internet MIME.

3. The Multimedia Collaboration Service (MMC) supports concurrent work of persons in a distributed network environment. The services enables the user to share applications among the participants and to use an audiovisual conference from their desktop computer.

1.2 Partners

The consortium lead by the DeTeBerkom consists of

Partner	Location	Platform
DeTeBerkom	Berlin	
Danet	Darmstadt	HP 7000
Digital/CEC and TU Karlsruhe	Karlsruhe	Alpha OSF/1
FhG	Darmstadt	SUN
GMD Fokus	Berlin	SUN, NeXT
HP	(TU) Berlin	HP 7000
IBM/ENC	Heidelberg	RS/6000
Liebing & Ullfors	Berlin	PC
MacConsult	Berlin	Apple
Siemens	München	SGI, UNIX-PC's
SIEtec	Berlin	SUN, SGI

Table 1. Project Partners

The consortium has agreed to design and implement the teleservices under contract with the consulting group of the German Telecom (Deutsche Bundespost Telekom), DeTeBerkom which supervises the overall project. The objective of the group is to provide the teleservices targeted to the working environments of large, geographically distributed organizations (e.g. office administration, medicine , or manufacturing). Within these scenarios, the use of broadband WAN's and the interconnection of heterogenous LAN's becomes obvious as the communication takes place from the desktop of the individual user and not within a special video conferencing room by using specialized expensive equipment.

The final goal is to create an open, homogenous framework for collaborative computing running on a variety of hardware platforms. So already during the design phase the team had a strong focus on using international standards (ISO/CCITT) where ever feasible.

The following chapte's will describe the services to a first level of detail. Current publications have been completed for MMC [6], MMM [7] and MMT [8]. For more details please refer to the specification documents [1], [2], and [3].

2.0   Multi-media Mail

2.1 Overview

The Berkom MMM Teleservice uses the X.400 e-mail standard to define an open multi-media mail system which supports text, structured office documents (ODA) [10], image, audio (G.711 [11], G.721 [12]) and video (SMP [9], MPEG [13].

Beyond the X.400 extensions, the teleservice has two distinguishing features which will be described at length in later sections.

1. support for the creation and resolution of external references, including real-time viewing of the external data.

2. support for structuring single mail messages; this structure can range from the relatively simple, e.g. cross referencing or annotating a text, to the more complex, e.g. hyper-media networks.

X.400 and New Body-Part Types

For those interested, this section gives more information about X.400 and how it is used by the Berkom Teleservice. For those less interested, all but the next paragraph can safely be skipped.

X.400 structures a message into a header and a sequence of typed body parts. It also specifies how to encode some types such as text and ODA. In addition, it specifies how to define new types by using a type called externally-defined. The Berkom Teleservice uses this mechanism to define the types image, audio, video, link and external reference. The last two are used to implement message structuring and external references, respectively.

Supporting a new type requires the addition of viewers/editors or converters for the new type to the User Agent (UA), the program which enables the user to send and receive mail. But, it requires no changes to the X.400 MTS (Message Transport System) which transports the mail from UA to UA. See Figure 1 for a diagram of the X.400 mail system components.

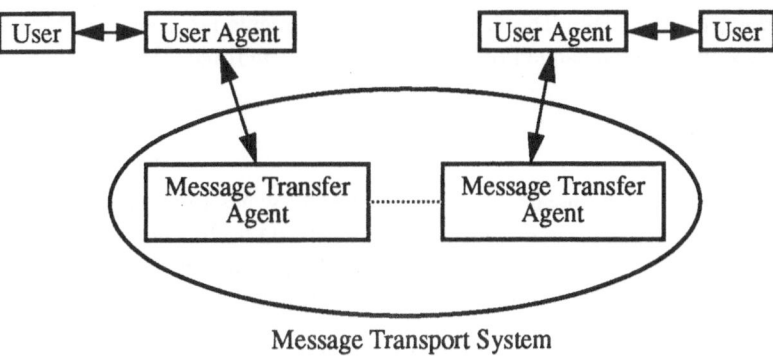

Message Transport System

Fig. 1. X.400 Mail System, is a Store and Forward System, where each message is copied to each MTA before forwarding starts

Figure Note: X.400 '88 is needed because '84 does not have the body type 'externally defined' which is used to define new types.

Information about the encoding of body parts is given in the following table:

Component	Representation
text	IA5 (8 bit)
document	ODA/FOD26 + Corrigenda

Table 2. Supported Types of Body Parts (include encoding, etc.)

Component	Representation
audio	Industries Implementation of G.711, G.721
image	Image Interchange Format
audio/video	Phase 1: SMP[a]
	Phase 2: MPEG, MPEG, or M-JPEG
external reference	Distinguished Object Reference
link	textual

Table 2. Supported Types of Body Parts (include encoding, etc.)

a. The SMP [9] Software Motion Picture software codec is a privat format from DEC which has been ported to all partner platforms.

Table Note: (about ODA) The ODA-encoded documents are converted from/to the Digital Document Interchange Format (DDIF) by the DIGITAL UA.

2.2 External References

The etiquette of e-mail dictates that when someone wants to share a large file with others, she sends a pointer to the file rather than the data itself. This etiquette increases in importance with audio and video because of the potentially large quantity of data involved, e.g. 1 minute of compressed SMP video is about 9 megabytes[1] long.

Turning from the social to the practical side, another reason for sending external references is that either the receiver or some of the MTAs in the store-and-forward chain might not have enough disk space to handle such large messages.

The Berkom MMM teleservice provides a solution to this problem. It defines services which enable a mail sender to move data to a server, create an external reference to it and mail the external reference encoded in an X.400 body part.

The receiving user can resolve the external reference and copy the data from the server to a local file. Alternatively, the receiver can take advantage of a real-time viewing service to view the data as it arrives from the server. This is an extremely useful feature for receiving systems with limited disk space. (Note: The transport service defined by MMT can be used to implement a real-time viewing service with guaranteed quality, e.g. throughput and delay.)

Myriad uses for external references can be envisaged, e.g. an e-mail video-of-the-week club whose subscribers receive a weekly mailing of video previews (trailers) and

---

1. This figure is based in an assumed data rate of 150 KBytes/second, a typical CD-ROM data rate.

external references to the previewed videos. The next figure shows the sequence of actions required to provide and use such a service using external references.

(Note: one interesting problem is how to prevent users from stealing the videos and passing them on for free)

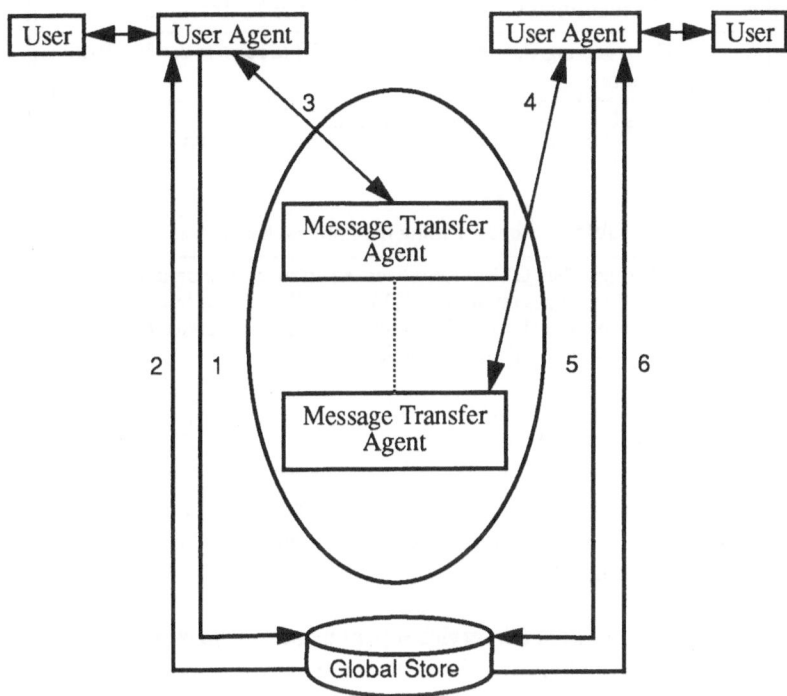

Fig. 2. USING EXTERNAL REFERENCES: If a mail contains an external reference body part, the following steps occur to pass the external data to the user:

Step	Action
1.	The User Agent gives data to the Global Store which stores it.
2.	The Global store returns a DOR[a] containing a reference to the stored data.
3.	The User Agent mails the DOR as a bodypart in an X.400 message.
4.	The receiving User Agent receives the X.400 message.
5.	The receiving User Agent uses the DOR to request the data from the store.
6.	The store returns the requested data.

Table 3. Steps for using the External References

a. DOR - Distinguished Object Reference is part of the standard on Distributed Office Application Model [14]. A DOR contains information on the datatype of the referenced data object, qualitiy of service parameters and transport mechanism information.

2.3 Structured Messages

The rising popularity of methods and systems, such as SGML and WWW, for structuring and linking related information are evidence that users prize this capability and would welcome it in a mail system.

With this in mind, the Berkom teleservice superimposes on the basic X.400 structure (a sequence of body parts) a hyper-media structure. It enables a user to superimpose networks of links on the bodies, thus allowing a reader to jump between related pieces of information. This can be used, e.g., to annotate text with audio or video comments by defining links between the text and other (e.g. audio or video) body parts.

As shown in the example below the linkends -- the information the user can jump to or from -- can be sections within a body as well as the entire body. In this case the link ancors are parts of an image, where the target body parts are audio clips.

All the information about where the linkends are and how they are related is put into the link body-part. This decision has at least two desirable consequences.

1. Multiple ways of relating the same information can be sent in one mail message by sending a link body-part for each.

2. Mail programs which do not support linking can ignore the link body-part, but still process all the other parts since they are sent exactly as they would be if the message had no links.

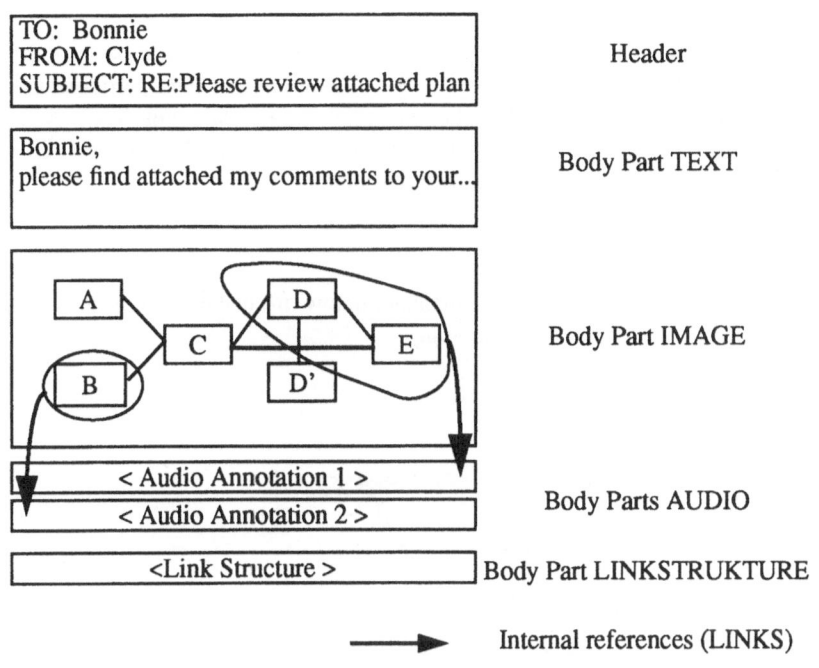

Fig. 3. enumerates the different body parts of an example mail.

Additionally to the internal link structure an external reference mechanism will allow to store parts of a mail on a global server (e.g. hugh image or video data) and give the user the option to decide if he wants to view the data or not. If he decides to view it, the data would be transmitted at presentation time. This concept allows to extend the current store and forward mail systems to a more flexible system which is designed to easily cope with large amounts of data (giga up to tera byte).

3.0   Multi-Media Collaboration

The teleservice multimedia collaboration extends the current usage of distance communication such as audio or video conferencing by adding a third channel of information called application sharing. Application sharing allows to simultaneous display of information that is manipulated using a computer application e.g. a document processor. The control over the application can be passed between the participants of the conference just as a boardmarker is passed between people discussing in front of a whiteboard.

The MMC teleservices also envisions various levels of service depending on the systems available for the conference participants and the network performance such as various audio and video qualities.

The conferencing system is partitioned into various servers e.g.a conference directory service which provides information of conference setups and their participants similar to the yellow pages keeping the telephone numbers of a certain area. These servers are defined within a standard protocol using an ISO standard (ASN.1) and are implemented using the ISODE programming environment.

3.1 Architectural overview

For each conference session the components below are needed. On each workstation the components are arranged as following

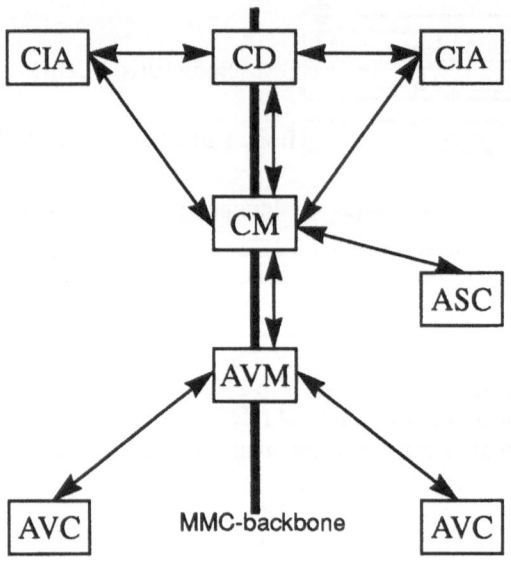

Fig. 4. MMC Architecture

The major components for the MMC-backbone service are the Conference Directory (CD), the Conference Manager (CM) and the Audiovisual Manager. Every workstation has to have a Conference Interface Agent (CIA) and an Audiovisual Component (AVC). Also one of the participant workstations need to have the Application Sharing Component running. The backbone services (CD, CM, and AVM) might either run on a remote server host or on one of the participants workstations. The application sharing component (ASC) allows to transparently distribute the output of Windows and X applications between the conference participants.

3.2 Application sharing

A major difference of the MMC service to existing video conferencing systems is the capability to include standard applications into the conference context. This allows to reuse ordinary end-user applications as collaborative applications such as e.g. DIGI-TALs DECwrite word processor as a joint-editing tool without modifying the application code. A restriction to this approach is that only one member of the conference is able to edit a document a the same time. The control on the application can be easily passed between the conference participants. A more enhanced version of the ASC will also allow to integrate existing group-aware applications such as e.g. shared-whiteboards which allow a simultaneous editing.

The application sharing component for X windows has been tested with various complex applications such as image manipulation, desktop publishing packages, and CAD applications. The ASC for MS-Windows also works for standard PC applications such as word processors or spreadsheets. Current development involves a gateway function between X windows and MS-windows inorder to share PC applications to the workstation (the other direction form X to MS-windows was already solved by using a X server on the PC).

4.0   Multi-Media Transport

4.1 High Speed Networks

As one of the goals of the BERKOM II project is to explore the use of high speed network infrastructure for the common use in companies and organizations, the bandwidth that is needed in order to use the teleservices defined above ranges from S-ISDN (small band ISDN starting at 2 x 64kbit channels) up to B-ISDN providing 155 Mbit channel or even more using ATM technology. The current focus of BERKOM II is to use 155 Mbit fiber optic links between the major development and test sites, but the migration to ATM is part of the BERKOM strategy.

4.2 MMT Overview

The Multi-Media Transport (MMT [3]) subproject will provide the layers 1 to 4 that are necessary to efficiently support the fast transport of huge amounts of multi-media data. Referring to the ISO/OSI reference model layer 3 is provided by the ST/2 proto-

54

col, where as layer 4 are provided by an modification of XTP called XTP-Lite. The data link layer for the LAN will be based on FDDI.

Note:
In Phase 1 of the project Ethernet has been used as infrastructure based on TCP/IP will be used to implement the MMM and MMC prototypes. This phase was completed in mid 1993.

The following picture shows the network topology provided for the BERKOM II project.

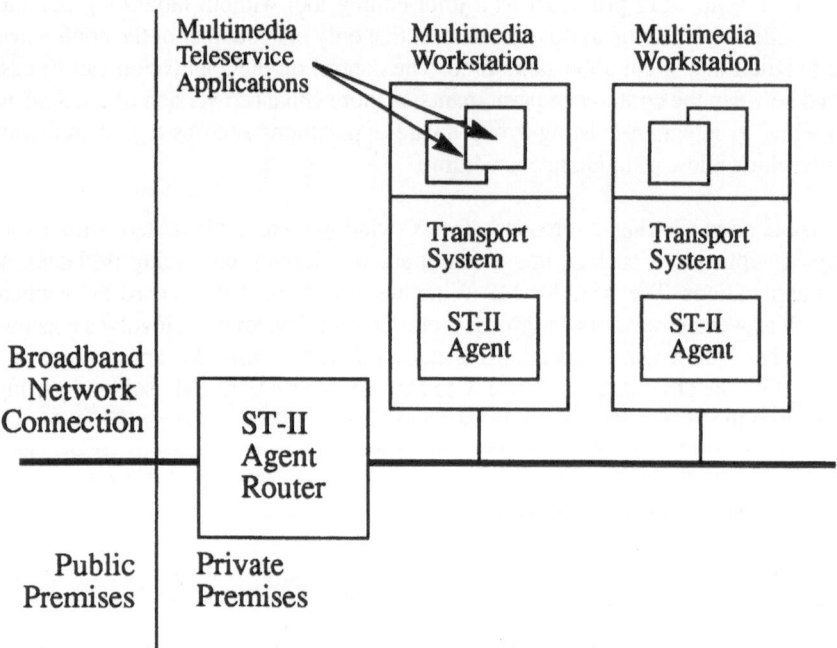

Fig. 5. Network Topology

4.3 Requirements for MMT

The major requirements identified for MMT are to

• allow the user to specify the desired **quality of services** for the communication and provide guarantees on it, to

- support **isochronous traffic**, which reflects the behavior of audio and video devices, as well as
- **high-speed data communications** as well as audio and video communication, and
- support for **real-time communication** where the reaction time to given events in the system is critical.

5.0   Status

The current implementation of all partners will be presented at the spring computer exhibition CeBIT'94 in Hanover/Germany. All major UNIX platforms and the PC will demonstrate the MMC and MMM services over TCP/IP, as the MMT will be added during 1994. The network infrastructure will be Ethernet, FDDI and ATM. The current Digital implementation is based on OSF/1 on Digital's Alpha based workstation series. In order to have a potential migration path from prototypes to supported products a series of existing Digital software components is used. Currently the MMM services relies on DECmailbus and a derivation of Mailworks. A realtime multimedia server prototopye has been adopoted to the special needs of the Global Store. The MMC service is built on top ISODE and uses G.711 as the audio format, SMP and M-JPEG as the video format. Digital has one of the reference backbones for MMC, so all components have been implemented and are stable. The MMT implementation is partioned in a kernel implemtation of ST-2 into OSF/1 and a user level implemetation of XTP-lite. Currently the interoperability tests are an ongoing effort inorder to enable the network connectivity.

5.1 Future Work

The future work of the Multimedia Teleservices is targeting to perform first user trial by mid of 1994, so various end-user applications have been selected to test the usability in day-to-day work. A phase of stabilization and documentation will deliver a first version to a broader user community within a one year time frame. The network specific focus will be achieved by adopting the MMT part towards ATM environment to also enable a heterogenous test environement for inhouse switches from various vendors (DEC, IBM, HP, Siemens). The goal is to use the MMTS as well within the German B-ISDN pilot that also starts during spring 1994. The next exhibition is planned for the International Switching Symposium in Berlin 1995.

References

1. DeTeBerkom[1], The BERKOM-II MultiMedia Mail System (MMM) Version 2.4

2. DeTeBerkom, The BERKOM-II MultiMedia Collaboration System (MMC) Version 3.1

3. DeTeBerkom, The BERKOM-II MultiMedia Transport System (MMT) Version 3.0

4. DeTeBerkom, The BERKOM Multimedia -Mail teleservice API description of External Reference Manager, Distinguished Object Reference and Referenced Data Transfer Guide, Release 1.0

5. H. Ricke, J. Kanzow: BERKOM - Breitbandkommunikation im Glasfasernetz, R. v. Deckers Verlag, Heidelberg, 1991

6. Michael Altenhofen e.al.:, The BERKOM Multimedia Collaboration Service, Proc. ACM Multimedia, 1993 Anaheim CA

7. Eckard Moeller, Angela Scheller, Gerd Schuermann: Der BERKOM-Teledienst 'Multimedia Mail', PIK, Praxis der Informationsverarbeitung und Kommunikation 3/93

8. S. Böcking, a. al.: The BERKOM Multimedia Transport System, IS&T/SPIE 94

9. Burkhard Neidecker-Lutz, Software Motion Pictures, Digital Technical Journal Volume 5 No. 2 1993, ISSN 0898-901X

10. ISO/IEC 8613: 1989, Inforamtion processing - Text and office systems - Office Document Architecture (ODA) and Interchange Format

11. CCITT Recommendation G.711: 1988, Pulse Code Modulation (PCM) of Voice Frequencies

12. CCITT Recommendation G.721: 1988, 32kbit/s Adaptive Differential Pulse Code Modulation (ADPCM)

13. ISO/IEC DIS 11172: 1992, Information technology - Coding of moving pictures and associated audio for digital storage media up to about 1.5 Mbit/s - MPEG

14. ISO/IEC 10031-2; 1991 Information technology - Text and office systems - Distributed-office-application-model - Part 2 Distinguished-object-reference and associated procedures

---

1. For all references to the consortium documents please contact:
DeTeBerkom, Peter Egloff
Voltastr.5
D-13355 Berlin

Toward Automatic Generation of HyTime Applications

John F. Buford, Lloyd Rutledge, John L. Rutledge

Interactive Media Group
Department of Computer Science
University of Massachusetts--Lowell
Lowell, MA 01854
(508) 934-3618
{buford,lrutledg,jrutledg}@cs.uml.edu

Abstract. Hypermedia/Time-based Structuring Language (HyTime) provides a comprehensive set of primitives for composing hypermedia documents. HyTime engines have been developed that process the HyTime-encoded information in arbitrary conforming documents. Applications of HyTime can use engines in initial document processing, but the non-HyTime functionalities of applications must be explicitly coded. In this paper we discuss a model for generating HyTime applications. We also present a paradigm for the automatic generation of application code within the content of this model.

1 Introduction

Hypermedia/Time-based Structuring Language (HyTime) is an international standard for defining the structure of multimedia and hypermedia documents [10]. It is encoded using Standard Generalized Markup Language (SGML), which defines the structure of text documents. SGML specifies the syntax of a document textual representation and attaches descriptive labels to document objects. HyTime establishes certain SGML-encoded constructs as having hypermedia structuring semantics. Although there are a few other research models for multimedia document architectures [7, 8], HyTime has generated attention for its perspective on fundamental hypermedia modeling concepts and status as an international standard, particularly with respect to its relationship with SGML [12].

SGML and HyTime define the functionalities of the tools which process them: the SGML parser and the HyTime engine. Applications of HyTime use these two tools for the initial processing of documents. This processing generates information about the application-independent and presentation-independent structure of a document. This information is further processed by an application to determine how the document is to be presented. Applications define their own SGML-encoded constructs and apply presentation semantics to them. Applications also specify the interpretation of HyTime concepts into presentation concepts. While SGML parsers and HyTime engines are developed for use by any application, the applications themselves must be individually crafted by developers.

A HyTime application uses one or more document models as defined by SGML document type definitions (DTDs). The DTD is used in both authoring and delivery of the hypermedia document. The presentation of the document is based on the presentation semantics that the DTD designer associates with the document elements. Some of the elements will have HyTime semantics, such as scheduling and links. Elements which refer to non-HyTime content such as video and audio will be interpreted according to the appropriate content model. Additional constructs may be present in the DTD that have application-specific semantics. The interpretation of these elements must be handled by the application. In this paper we are concerned with generating the application software from the corresponding DTD. The model that we present is based on our experience of developing both DTDs and HyTime application software.

Presentation software for a HyTime application requires application-specific interaction semantics, since HyTime does not model input or behavior aspects of hypermedia documents. Hypermedia applications will typically rely upon a user interface toolkit to implement input and behavior aspects of interactive HyTime documents. In our approach we assume that the toolkit services can be represented using a class hierarchy, and that there are presentation services for the media and interaction objects used in the DTD. We describe a procedure for generating the presentation code using the DTD as input. The DTD is parsed and elements within the DTD are associated with generated application layer classes which are subclasses from the existing HyTime engine and toolkit classes. This requires that the DTD follows certain conventions if the default toolkit behavior is desired. The DTD designer can also create custom behavior not defined by the toolkit, but then custom code must be written to extend the toolkit. We present our approach using a sample toolkit class hierarchy, but the approach described here does not depend upon the use of a specific toolkit.

In the next section we present the HyTime engine class hierarchy and API that we have defined for our prototype HyTime engine called HyOctane. Section 3 presents the application generation model. This is followed by a detailed example in section 4. Section 5 discusses a number of issues involved in the generation process. We conclude with a discussion of implementation status, related work and a summary of the paper.

2 HyTime Engine, Classes, and API

In previous work we have outlined a three-layered database model for HyTime-conforming documents [1]. These three layers are the SGML layer, the HyTime layer, and the application layer. The SGML layer is generated by parsing SGML code. It contains objects representing instances of SGML constructs. It also contains the descriptive markup, which associates document objects with descriptions that have significance to HyTime engines and applications. SGML layer information reflects only the syntax of the document as encoded by SGML. The HyTime layer is derived from the SGML layer and contains objects representing instances of HyTime constructs defined by the SGML code. The information here reflects the semantics of HyTime. These semantics regard mainly the structuring of the hypermedia aspects of a document, including hyperlinks, schedules, and document object location definitions. The application layer is derived from the SGML and HyTime layers and contains objects representing the application's semantic interpretations that fall outside of the scope of HyTime. The information on this layer is application-specific and presentation format-specific. It reflects all of the SGML code that does not represent HyTime constructs and it reflects application-specific interpretations of HyTime construct patterns.

Within the corresponding HyTime processing model, each of these three layers corresponds to a component which generates its contents [1]. The SGML layer is generated by an SGML parser. The parser processes SGML code and calls appropriate database operations to generate the objects of the SGML layer. The HyTime layer is generated by a HyTime engine which queries the SGML layer for instances of SGML-encoded HyTime constructs and then builds representations of them on the HyTime layer. The application loader queries the SGML and HyTime layers to determine the contents of the application layer. Once the contents of the three layers are loaded, the application presentation procedure queries the contents of the application layer (see figure 1).

Our HyOctane engine provides a programming interface based directly on the HyTime constructs, called architectural forms (see figure 2). These classes are instantiated in the HyTime database layer when the document is created or loaded. Each class has private attributes given by the associated SGML attlist construct for the HyTime architectural form. Each class has a reference to the corresponding object in the SGML database.

The HyOctane engine is built on an object-oriented database which provides persistent object storage, object-life cycle functions, and object access functions. In particular, the ability to manipulate collections of objects and search for objects by name or attribute is provided by the database. The need for a hyperbase system to provide additional functionality beyond that of an object-oriented or semantic database has been discussed by several researchers [5, 13]. We provide similar services related to the HyTime model through the HyTime class hierarchy. We discuss the services for links, scheduling, and location addressing modules next.

2.1 Link Module

A HyTime hyperdocument is the root of a collection of documents that are interconnected using HyTime link architectural forms. The definition of link types, anchor types, link attributes, and browsing semantics are key aspects of the definition of a hypermedia model. HyOctane link services include the following functions:

```
Link FindLinkByType()
Link FindLinkByLevel()
```

60

```
Link FindLinkByDistance()
Object TraverseLink()
void PushLink()
Link PopLink()
```

Fig. 1. HyOctane HyTime Engine Design (adapted from [2])

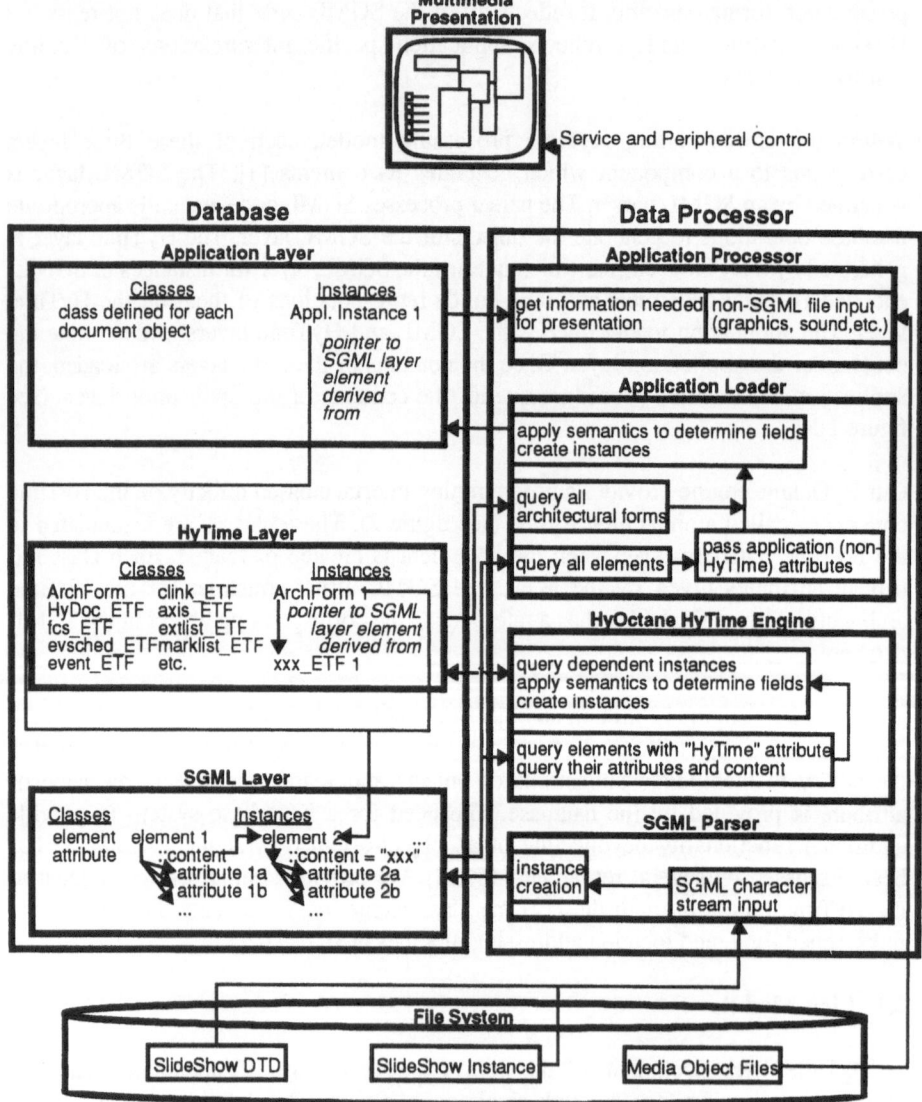

The first three functions are examples of specialized link search functions that depend on application links having attributes of type, level, and distance respectively. The traverse link operation returns the object which is the target of the link. Push and pop can be used to maintain a history of link access.

Fig. 2. Partial HyOctane class hierarchy; only classes needed in the paper are shown

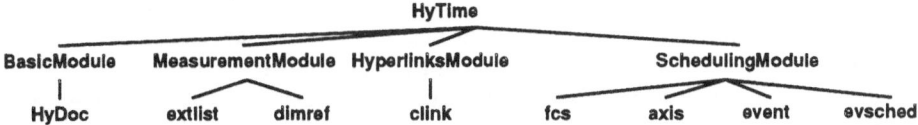

2.2 Schedule Module

HyTime's scheduling facilities can be applied equivalently to time, space, and any other measurable dimension. Here we concentrate on time and describe the HyOctane functional interface for timeline processing. In HyOctane, time is distinguished from other dimensions not because of the way HyTime is defined but because of the functional needs of typical applications. An application's scheduling along timelines provides different computational challenges than, for example, placement within space.

Document elements are positioned in time as events in an event schedule. Event position can be either absolute or relative to other events, and events can be grouped. In order for an event schedule to be used for presentation, the schedule has to be interpreted in the context of a presentation timer. We provide the following functions for this purpose. The application receives time events through pre-registered event handlers.

```
SetVirtualTimeUnitMapping()
CreateClock()
StartClock()
SetClockPosition()
StopClock()
RegisterEventHandler()
```

2.3 Location Address Module

The location address module of HyTime provides a range of object content identification models, including semantic and lexical. The actual pattern matching facilities available depend upon the engine. The location address services include functions for traversing the document tree and searching by pattern or path.

```
Object FindElementByName()
Object FindElementParent()
Object FindElementSibling()

Object FindElementByLexPattern()
Object FindElementBySemanticPattern()
```

```
Object FindElementByPath()
```

2.4 Engine Services and the Application Layer

Typically, an SGML parser and a HyTime engine will work for multiple applications of HyTime. With an existing parser and engine providing the determination of a multimedia document's structure and descriptive markup, what is left for a developer to encode is the application which translates this structure and these descriptions into a hypermedia presentation. Removing the encoding of the functionality of SGML and HyTime from the developer's responsibilities makes code creation easier. In the next section we describe ways in which the functionalities of SGML and HyTime can be used to further simplify the application developer's job by having the some of application code automatically generated.

3 Application Generation Model

Our model for the generation of HyTime application code has three stages: the writing of the application DTD, the defining of the application classes residing on the application database layer, and the coding of the application that processes these classes and creates the presentation. In our experience we have found it most useful to generate an application's DTD first and then generate the code which processes it. We have also found that application code tends to follow certain patterns; particular constructs within the application's DTD tend to correspond to particular sections of application code. This is because a DTD for HyTime-conforming documents contains much information that is useful for the creation of application code. This information includes definitions of document object types, how these objects use HyTime constructs, and how instances of these types can be placed within a document. Constructs that represent this information can be detected and processed by an SGML parser and HyTime engine. Given this, we find that application code can be partially generated by processing the application's DTD. This generation is partial because there is likely to be information needed for code determination that is not available in a DTD, such as information provided by the developer's intuition. Despite the incompleteness of the generated code, we feel that enough useful code would be generated to expedite the total creation of code.

We have developed a HyTime environment that includes an SGML parser, our prototype HyTime engine HyOctane, and an application [1, 2]. The database management system shared by the SGML parser, HyOctane, and application is object-oriented (see figure 1). C++ code is used to define the classes that exist on the three layers. The primary classes on the SGML layer correspond to the element and attribute SGML constructs. The primary classes on the HyTime layer consist of a class definition for each architectural form specified by the standard. Roughly speaking, each architectural form's class has a field for each of that form's attributes. On the application layer of a HyOctane environment database, there is a class defined for each element type in the application's DTD and each class has a field for each of that element type's non-HyTime attributes. This pattern of application layer class definitions is the basis for how we design the processes that determine a partial encoding for an application given a DTD.

The application development facility takes into account the existence of HyTime architectural form instances. As such, HyTime attributes are not represented as fields in element type class definitions of the generated code, as are non-HyTime attributes. Furthermore, references to corresponding HyTime layer form class instances are made in the appropriate element type class definitions and instances.

3.1 Application Class Definition Code Generation

Each element type defined in the DTD corresponds to a class definition in the application code. If an element type is an instance of a HyTime architectural form, then that type's class has a field referencing the HyTime layer object for that form instance. For each attribute of that element type that is not an attribute of that type's HyTime architectural form a field is defined for that class to represent that attribute's value. The variable type of this field is determined by the SGML type of its attribute. For example, if an attribute's type is "SGML unique identifier reference" (IDREF), that attribute is a reference to another element, and its field's type is defined as a reference to an element type class instance.

Fields for a type class are also generated by processing that type's content model. Individual references to element types as content model units each correspond to a field whose value is a reference to an instant of that element type's class. Portions of content models that are non-SGML data each correspond to a field whose value is a direct representation of that data. Each grouping in a content model corresponds to a composite field that in turn has a field for each of the groupings components.

SGML content models also have occurrence modification symbols. The symbol "?" means a content model's component's appearance is optional. A Kleene star, indicated by a "*", means the component can appear zero, one, or multiple times in sequence. These modification symbols affect the definition of element type classes. Fields corresponding to model components which are optional have a possible null value which indicates that the component did not appear in the element instance content. A Kleene star affects a model field by making it a list whose entries are instances of that component.

3.2 Generation of Application Code for Presentation and Access

An application is typically divisible into two components: the loader and the presenter. The application loader creates instances of objects on the application database layer when the document is initially processed. This object creation relies on the contents of the HyTime and SGML layers. The application presenter accesses these created objects to determine the presentation of the document to the user. In our model for code generation these two components are created separately. C++ class constructors are generated for use by the loader to construct class instances. C++ class methods are generated for use by the presenter to access these instances.

Constructor Code Generation. A constructor is made for each element type class. Such a constructor is given an SGML element reference as an input parameter. This element is of the type the constructor makes class instances for, and the constructor generates such an instance for the input SGML element. Field values are designed for the non-HyTime attributes. The constructor is coded so that a reference value for the element's HyTime architectural form instance, if there is one, is assigned to the form reference field. The resulting constructor also performs the appropriate SGML layer queries to determine the element's contents and places the appropriate values and references in the content model fields.

The assignment of fields containing references to other application class instances is dependent on the creation of those class instances. For this reason, the assignment of content model reference fields is made more efficient because the code is generated so that constructors for elements are called in bottom-up order along the document's hierarchical structure. This way, an element's content elements have class instances already created and available for referencing when that element's constructor is called. However, there is no guarantee that instances for elements referenced by IDREFs will have been constructed when the referencing element's instance is being constructed. Because of this, IDREF attribute fields are not assigned until all element instances have been created.

Method Code Generation. For each field of each class a method is created that when given a reference to an instance of that class returns the value of that field within that instance.

4 Detailed Example

We have developed a HyTime application called SlideShow [1, 2]. SlideShow is an interactive presentation program. It presents slides where each slide is a backdrop image and a series of media object presentations. These media objects can be images, animations, audio playbacks, and script playbacks. They can be positioned on the screen and presented at particular times. Also displayed with a slide are buttons, each of which when pressed by the user's mouse triggers the presentation of another slide or terminates the program.

Appendix 1 contains the DTD used by SlideShow. Figure 3 diagrams this DTD. Table 1 describes the document objects used in the DTD. Elements of type slidesho act as root objects for their documents. Elements of type slides contain multiple elements of type slide and define a presentation space for them. This presentation space consists of a workstations screen, with an x and y axis, and a timeline. Elements of type slide represent the presentation of a slide, including its background, its component presentation units, and its buttons. An element of type button associates the display of button pressing feedback with the selection of a particular screen area. These button screen areas are specified by button event (butnevnt) elements. An element of type butnpres (button press) schedules the feedback of a button selection and schedules the occurrence of a butndone (button done) event which triggers the linking to a new slide. A background (backgrnd) element is a screen-sized background image display. A slidevnt element can contain one of four media object element types, and it assigns a time and place for that object's display. The media object elements are SGML external entities. As such, they specify an external file and its format. The timing and positioning of background, slide event, and button event elements are specified by placment elements which are reference by the exspec attribute. Each coordinate in the three-dimensional space is specified either directly by a number or indirectly as a dimension reference (dimref) element. Dimension reference elements specify a coordinate number as some function of a particular coordinate of a slide event.

Fig. 3. Multimedia document structure corresponding to the SlideShow DTD in Appendix 1 (adapted from [1, 2]).

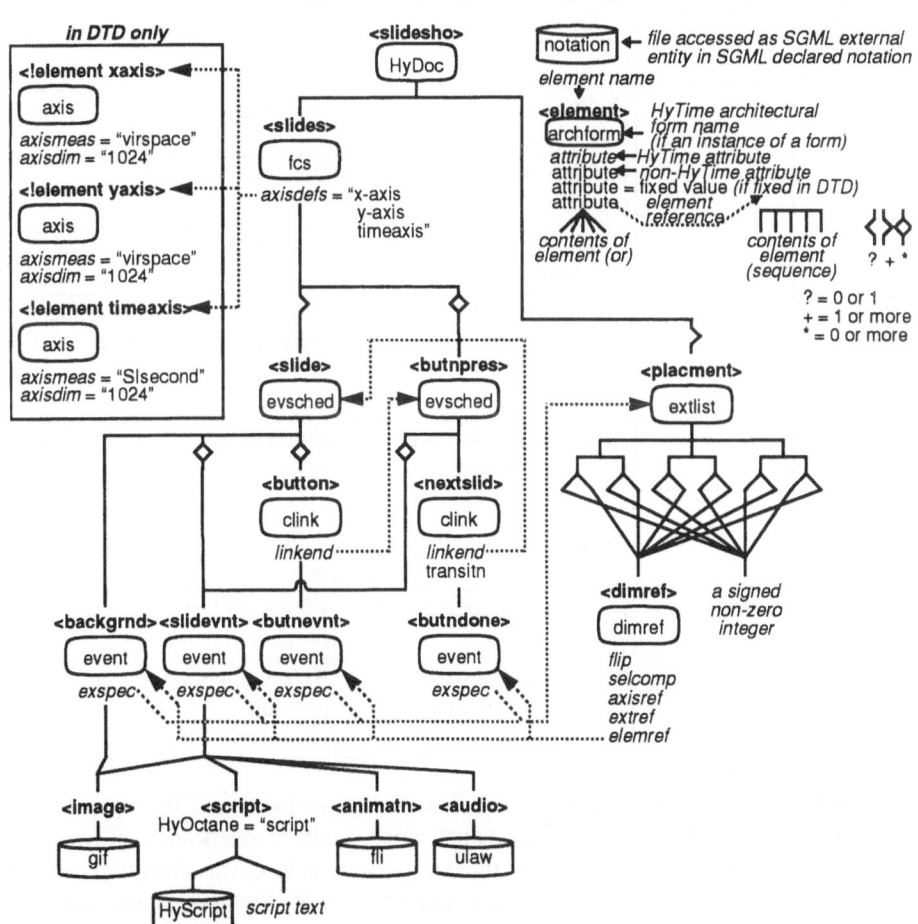

This DTD and application demonstrate HyTime's ability to establish hyperlinks and to place document objects in relation to one another in a shared space.

Figure 4 shows a partial class hierarchy for the toolkit and HyTime engine when processing this application. The objects with the "SS" prefix are application objects and reside on the application database layer. The highest level object is the collection object, which specifies different types of collections that can exist. One of these types is space, which defines the context in which documents objects are positioned, and of which the HyTime finite coordinate space (fcs) architectural form is a subclass. Another of these types is document, of which the HyTime document (HyDoc) architectural form is a subclass. The figure defines HyTime architectural form objects for each form used by the application. These exist in the layer below the objects for the four HyTime modules used. Each form object has as subobjects the elements from the SlideShow DTD that are instances of that form.

Table 1. Document objects used in SlideShow DTD (adapted from [1]).

SGML Element Type	HyTime Architectural Form	HyTime Semantics	SlideShow Semantics
slideshow	HyDoc	Contents are whole hyperdocument	Root object of document
slides	fcs	Definition of a finite coordinate space	Defines context of slide presentations
slide	evsched	Group of events in same fcs instance	One slide
backgnrd, slidevnt, butnevnt, butndone	event	Existence of an object in an fcs	Existence of a media object presentation in a slide
button, nextslid	clink	Link from contained object to another object	When contained area is select present slide linked to
xaxis, yaxis, timeaxis	axis	Reference for object position and dimension	The workstation screen dimensions and seconds after start of slide
placment	extlist	Position of an object along several axes	Where and when an object is presented in a slide
dimref	dimref	Reference to another object's position for relational placement	Reference to another object's position for relational placement

The toolkit has as components the types of media that are presented, the input that can be supplied by the user, the behavior an application can have independent of responses to user interaction, the composition of the document, and the events that are positioned in the document. The media type objects that are used by the application each have

SlideShow element types as subclasses. The link object represents a hyperlink between two object components and can be an instance of a database link, which specifies object location independent of user interaction, a toolkit button, which indicates a user activated link traversals, or a transition, which represents a change in the presentation's behavior that is defined as a hyperlink traversal.

Fig. 4. Partial HyOctane engine and toolkit class hierarchies for SlideShow application

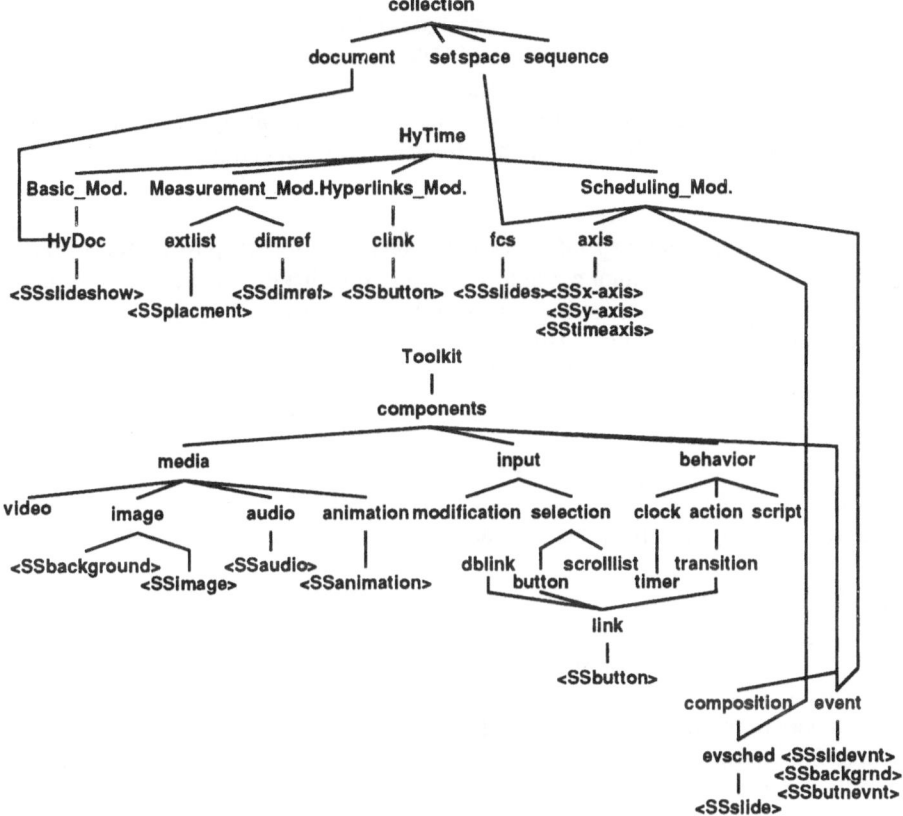

5 Discussion

5.1 HyTime Support for Code Generation

The automatic generation of application code is derived from information contained in an application's DTD. Often this information is embodied in SGML syntactical definitions such as content model and attribute type declaration. These definitions place restrictions. They provide limited forms in which data are contained. When these restrictions and limitations are taken into account, generated code has data structure definitions which more efficiently represent the data. HyTime has facilities that extend

SGML's ability to limit the format in which data can appear. These facilities include reference type declaration and lexical modeling.

HyTime reference type declarations further specify SGML element unique identifier references. In SGML, a document element can be given a unique identifier, and the attributes of other elements can refer to that element with a reference to that unique identifier. When such an attribute is defined in SGML code, it is stated to be of type "IDREF" and can be a reference to any element. A HyTime reference type can specify that a certain IDREF attribute can only reference elements of a certain type or one of a list of types. Attributes which are lists of IDREFs can have each entry of the list be confined to referencing one of a certain set of element types. In the application presented in this paper, reference types are used (see appendix 1). They are contained in the attributes named *reftype* in the element types *backgrnd*, *slidevnt*, *butnevnt*, *button*, and *dimref*.

HyTime lexical modeling specifies regular expressions for the possibilities of string contents. SGML places minor possible restrictions on what the character string content of elements or the character string values of attributes can be. With lexical modeling, element content and attribute values that are strings can be specified as following certain patterns. Lexical models can be processed in automatic code generation to tailor data structures for those patterns rather than defining those structures as simple strings.

A DTD author can maximize an application generator's ability to create code by properly including such reference type and lexical model definitions in DTDs.

5.2 Media Objects

The representation of media objects falls outside the scope of SGML and HyTime. However, certain SGML constructs state how documents objects are stored in the file system. Use of these constructs in a DTD can guide a code generator in developing the proper file system calls for retrieving a stored media object. These constructs include SGML external entities and SGML data content notation declarations.

SGML external entities state that at their point in the document exists the contents of an external file. External entities are used in the application presented in this paper to specify that the media objects exist in external files. Application code generators can associate with DTD external entities the appropriate file processing code. Applications can be coded to access these files directly or they can allow the SGML parser to process the files and pass their contents to the application indirectly.

SGML data content notations specify that certain streams of text follow a certain named notation. When an element's contents are defined in this manner to follow a notation, then the application code generator can specify that the element's contents are to be processed by the subsection of code designed for that notation.

5.3 Interaction Classes

There are presentation-specific document objects that are common to many applications. Examples of these include graphical user interface objects. The defining of such objects falls outside the scope of SGML and HyTime and cannot be recognized by a code generator for an arbitrary DTD. However, a set of common presentation-specific objects can be designed and encoded using SGML constructs, and application code generators can be made to recognize these constructs. For example, a scrollbar element type or architectural form could be defined whose contents are to be displayed along with a scroll bar for what portion of those contents are to be displayed. Then a scrollbar-aware code generator could associate with the contents of each scrollbar element the code for presenting those contents in conjunction with a scrollbar.

5.4 Updating the Database Layers

If during the course of a document's presentation an editing tool is invoked, any changes by the application are performed only on objects in the application layer. These objects propagate changes to the corresponding HyTime and SGML objects. If a HyTime document instance is to be generated for interchange with another application, this file is created directly from objects in the SGML layer.

In modifying an object on the application layer, that object's interdependence with other objects will often need to be accounted for. For example, if a class instance that is referenced by another instance's IDREF field is deleted, then that field now references a non-existent instance. Inconsistencies such as these must be prevented. Application code generated for performing such updating must account for object interdependencies.

Information about object interdependencies is available from an application's DTD. IDREF attributes are one example of the DTD encoding of this information. When one element references another, it is dependent on that other element's existent to prevent an inconsistency. Code could be generated for the application that checks for or automatically performs the modification or removal of all references to an application instance before the instance itself is deleted. Furthermore, this code should prevent an IDREF from being made unless the referenced instance exists. A similar dependency exists between an element and its content elements. Generated application code may handle this dependency by requiring or automatically performing the removal of an element's descendents in the document hierarchical structure before the element itself is removed. This dependency can also be handled by requiring that new elements be placed in the document structure only in ways that are consistent with the definition of the structure in the DTD.

Interdependencies with HyTime layer objects can also be determined from DTD processing and accounted for in generated application code. All of these dependencies derive from the association of architectural form instances on the HyTime layer with element instances on the application layer. Generated application code should remove a form instance when its element instance is removed. When an element instance is created, its corresponding form instance should also be created, and the appropriate form field values should be supplied by the creating method. Access should be provided through the application layer for modifying the values of HyTime attributes. Finally, the generated code should cooperate with the HyTime engine's consistency-maintaining facilities (if it has them) to ensure the validity of the HyTime components of the modifications.

5.5 Semantic Assumptions

HyTime constructs are intended to be independent of presentation format. However, code generators can apply default assumptions to how certain HyTime constructs map to certain presentation schemes. The measure of usefulness of a code generation tool is how much effort it spares the human developer. If default assumptions create code that is appropriate most of the time and is easily adaptable to more appropriate presentation schemes then it is likely that the developer's work will be facilitated.

For example, the HyTime architectural form *clink* specifies that a hyperlink exists between the content of the current object and another referenced object. The content of a clink can be a selectable area of a presentation. This is the case with the application presented in this paper. Elements of type *button* are clinks and contain elements of type *butnevnt* (button event). Button events are instances of HyTime *event* architectural forms and as such specify some part of a schedule orchestrating events along several dimensions which can include space and time. In this case, the dimensions are the amount of time since a slide was first presented and the x and y coordinates of a screen display. Button events specify a certain screen area and a certain period of time. A mouse click which occurs in that screen area during that time act as one end of a hyperlink. The other end of such a hyperlink is the display of a new slide, represented as an element of type slide, which is an event schedule (evsched) architectural form instance.

An application generator can look for occurrences of clinks which contain events, are contained in event schedules, and whose linkend attributes reference other event schedules. When such an occurrence is found, code can be generated for the application which triggers the presentation of the other event schedule when the user selects the event's area.

6 Related Work

A number of research groups have built hypermedia systems, for example [6, 11]. Many of these systems have been concerned with user interface issues and specific hypertext models, and have not addressed the management of hypermedia document structuring information and its associated services. HAM [3] is an abstract hypertext machine which does not provide hypermedia facilities. Some hypermedia systems have used databases for storing link information such as [5, 13]; these systems have similar goals to the HyOctane research, but do not use HyTime modeling concepts. Since HyTime is not a hypermedia model per se, a HyTime engine needs to support a broader range of models than a system which is designed for a specific hypermedia model. Little work has been reported on the design of HyTime services and applications. A number of other hypermedia models have been described [7, 8]. The implications of these models on hyperbase services has not received much attention.

7 Summary

A model for HyTime application code generation and an accompanying paradigm for automating this code generation was presented. The SGML Document Type Definition (DTD) is the code which describes the format of an application's documents and is the first code generated in this model. The DTD contains certain types of information that either specify or suggest particular processing. This information includes hierarchical structure modeling and object type definition. Using a DTD as input, this information can be automatically processed into partial application code. Such a generator is a valuable tool for HyTime application development.

8 References

1. Koegel (Buford), J.F., Rutledge, L., Rutledge, J.L., and Keskin, C.: HyOctane: A HyTime Engine for an MMIS. Proceedings of ACM Multimedia 93. (August 1993).

2. Buford, J.F., Rutledge, L. and Rutledge, J.L.: Integrating Object-Oriented Scripting Languages with HyTime. Proceedings of IEEE International Conference on Multimedia Computing and Systems (May 1994).

3. Campbell, B., and Goodman, J. M.: HAM: A General Purpose Hypertext Abstract Machine. Communications of the ACM, vol. 31, no. 7, pp. 871-879 (July 1988).

4. Goldfarb, C.F.: The SGML Handbook. Oxford University Press (1991).

5. Haan, B.J., Kahn, P., Riley, V.A., Coombs, J.H., and Meyrowitz, N.K.: IRIS Hypermedia Services. Communications of the ACM, vol. 35, no. 1, pp. 36-51 (January 1992).

6. Halasz, F.G.: Reflections on Notecards: Seven Issues for the Next Generation of Hypermedia Systems. Communications of the ACM, vol. 31, no. 7, pp. 836-855 (July 1988).

7. Hardman, L, Bulterman, D.C.A., and Rossum, G.V.: The Amsterdam Hypermedia Model: Extending Hypertext to Support Real Multimedia. Hypermedia, vol. 5, no. 1, p. 47-69 (1993).

8. Herzner, W., and Kummer, M.: MMV--Synchronizing Multimedia Documents: An Extension of CDA for Synchronization and Presentation of Multimedia Documents. Computation and Graphics, vol. 17, no. 3, pp. 229-241 (1993).

9. Horak, W.: Office Document Architecture and Office Document Interchange Formats: Current Status of International Standardization. Computer, vol. 18, no. 10, pp. 50-60 (October 1985).

10. ISO: ISO/IEC IS 10744, Hypermedia/Time-based Document Structuring Language (HyTime) (April 1992).

11. McCracken, D.L., and Yoder, E.A.: KMS: A Distributed Hypermedia System for Managing Knowledge in Organizations. Communications of the ACM, vol. 31, no. 7, pp. 820-835 (July 1988).

12. Newcomb, S.R.: The "HyTime" Hypermedia / Time-based Document Structuring Language. Communications of the ACM, (December 1991).

13. Schnase, J.L., Leggett, J.J., Hicks, D.L., and Szabo, R.L.: Semantic Data Modeling of Hypermedia Associations. ACM Trans. on Information Systems. vol. 11, no. 1, pp. 27-50 (January 1993).

Appendix 1: SlideShow DTD

```
<!-- Copyright 1994 Interactive Media Group University of
     Massachusetts Lowell -->

<!-- SLIDESHO (slideshow) is the element with contains the
     entire document. It is of the HyTime architectural
     form "doc". It contains a list of slides followed by
     supporting constructs. The first slide on this list
     is the first slide displayed. -->

<!element slidesho - o (slides, placment+)>
<!attlist slidesho HyTime name #fixed HyDoc>

<!-- SLIDES (slides) is the finite coordinate system in
     which all of this document's slides and their objects
     are mapped according to. It is of the HyTime AF
     "fcs". -->

<!element slides - o (slide+,butnpres*)>
<!attlist slides
 HyTime name #fixed fcs
 -- x, y, and time axes (defined below) are used --
 axisdefs cdata #fixed "xaxis yaxis timeaxis">

<!-- SLIDE (slide schedule) contains all of the
     information for a particular slide. It is of the
     HyTime AF "evsched", and as such it is the schedule
     for placing the background and all of the individual
     images and button placements for the slide. -->

<!element slide - o (backgrnd, slidevnt*, button*)>
<!attlist slide
 HyTime name #fixed evsched
```

```
     -- enables nextslid links --
     id id #required>
```

```
<!-- BACKGRND (background) contains to a slide file to be
     used as a backdrop for this slide. It is of the AF
     "event", and as such specifies the placement of the
     background image, which is always the entire screen
     for the entire display time of the slide. -->
```

```
<!element backgrnd - o (image)>
<!attlist backgrnd
 HyTime name #fixed event
 -- referenced extlist must specify placement as whole
 screen, all time --
 exspec idref #fixed wholscrn
 reftype cdata #fixed "exspec placment">
```

```
<!-- SLIDEVNT (slide event) is the mapping of the
     contained slide object within the schedule. It is of
     the AF "event", and as such it specifies the
     placement and time in which the object is presented.
     If the object is an audio then the placement is
     irrelevant. -->
```

```
<!element slidevnt - o (image|script|animatn|audio)>
<!attlist slidevnt
 HyTime name #fixed event
 -- an extlist spec'n a placement and time period --
 exspec idref #required
 reftype cdata #fixed "exspec placment">
```

```
<!-- IMAGE (image) specifies a file containing an image as
     an external entity. -->
```

```
<!element image - o empty>
<!attlist image file entity #required>
```

```
<!-- SCRIPT (script) specifies a file containing a script.
     The cdata content can be directly contained or can be
     en external entity reference. -->
```

```
<!element script - - cdata>
<!attlist script
 -- specifies to HyOctane this is a script --
 HyOctane name #fixed script>
```

```
<!-- ANIMATN (animation) specifies a file containing an
     animation -->
```

```
<!element animatn - o empty>
<!attlist animatn file entity #required>
```

```
<!-- AUDIO (audio) specifies a file containing an audio
     clip or sample -->
```

```
<!element audio - o empty>
```

```
<!attlist audio file entity #required>

<!-- BUTTON (button) references the feedback presented
     when a button is pressed. It is of the HyTime AF
     "clink", which indicates that this element's content
     is an object which triggers a link. In this case, the
     triggering object is the area occupied by a
     particular area on the workstation screen. -->

<!element button - o (butnevnt)>
<!attlist button
 HyTime name #fixed clink
 -- link to an action --
 linkend idref #required
 reftype cdata #fixed "linkend butnpres">

<!-- BUTNEVNT (button event) contains information for a
     screen's button area. It is of AF "event", and as
     such it specifies the area on the screen which, when
     clicked by the mouse cursor, activates the button
     containing it. -->

<!element butnevnt - o empty>
<!attlist butnevnt
 HyTime name #fixed event
 -- an extlist spec'n a placement and time period --
 exspec idref #required
 reftype cdata #fixed "exspec placment">

<!-- BUTNPRES (button press) contains the information for
     presenting to the user feedback for pressing a
     button. As a HyTime AF "evsched", it is the schedule
     for placing the image and other media feedbacks for
     the button's pressing. -->

<!element butnpres - o (slidevnt*,nextslid)>
<!attlist butnpres
 HyTime name #fixed evsched
 -- enables button links --
 id id #required>

<!-- NEXTSLID (next slide) references the slide presented
     after a button is pressed. It is of the HyTime AF
     "clink", which indicates that this element's content
     is an object which triggers a link. In this case, the
     triggering object is the passing of a period of time,
     typically the time it takes for the feedback media
     objects to be presented. -->

<!element nextslid - o (butndone)>
<!attlist nextslid
 HyTime name #fixed clink
 -- link to an action --
 linkend idref #required
 reftype cdata #fixed "linkend slide"
```

```
-- non-HyTime attributes --
-- visual transition between slides --
transitn (dissolve|cut|wipeup|wipedown|
wipeleft|wiperite|fade|chckbrd) cut>
```

```
<!-- BUTNDONE (time out), as an "event" AF, specifies the
        period of time after which the next slide is
        displayed. -->
```

```
<!element butndone - o empty>
<!attlist butndone
 HyTime name #fixed event
 -- an extlist spec'n a placement and time period --
 exspec idref #required
 reftype cdata #fixed "exspec placment">
```

```
<!-- PLACMENT (placement) specifies a particular screen
        area and time period. It is of AF "extlist" and as
        such its contents resolve to a pair of coordinates
        for each axis. -->
```

```
<!element placmnt - o
  ((dimref|#pcdata),(dimref|#pcdata),(dimref|#pcdata),(dim
  ref|#pcdata),(dimref|#pcdata),(dimref|#pcdata))>
<!attlist placmnt
 HyTime name #fixed extlist
 -- referred to by events --
 id id #required>
```

```
<!-- DIMREF (dimension reference) specifies a coordinate
        as relative to a particular coordinate of some event.
        It is of AF "dimref". -->
```

```
<!element dimref - o empty>
<!attlist dimref
 HyTime name #fixed dimref
 -- the id of the reference event --
 elemref cdata #required
 -- the axis with the coordinate --
 axisref name #required
 -- which coordinate the axis: first, last, or length --
 selcomp (first|last|qcnt) qcnt
 -- invert the coordinate or not --
 flip (flip|noflip) noflip
 reftype cdata #fixed "elemref slidvnts">
```

```
<!-- SLIDEVNTS (slide events reference model) exists
        solely as en element type to provide dimref with an
        or group reference type. -->
```

```
<!element slidvnts o o (backgrnd|slidevnt|butnevnt) >
```

```
<!-- XAXIS, YAXIS, and TIMEAXIS are the axes in the finite
        coordinate system. They are of AF "axis". They are
```

```
                used to define a coordinate system with a 1024 by
                1024 screen and a large expanse of time. -->

<!element xaxis - o empty>
<!attlist xaxis
 -- HyTime attributes for this architectural form --
 HyTime name #fixed axis
 -- measurement domain, the system of measure used --
 axismeas cdata #fixed "virspace"
 -- default: equal to fcsmdu,virspace --
 axismdu cdata #fixed ""
 -- this axis has 1024 units, the length of a workstation
  screen in pixels --
 axisdim cdata #fixed "1024">

<!element yaxis - o empty>
<!attlist yaxis
 -- HyTime attributes for this architectural form --
 HyTime name #fixed axis
 axismeas cdata #fixed "virspace"
 axismdu cdata #fixed ""
 axisdim cdata #fixed "1024">

<!element timeaxis - o empty>
<!attlist timeaxis
 -- HyTime attributes for this architectural form --
 HyTime name #fixed axis
 -- one second --
 axismeas cdata #fixed "SIsecond"
 axismdu cdata #fixed ""
 -- default highest number in HyTime --
 axisdim cdata #fixed "4294967295">

<!-- This document uses the non-HyTime measurement unit
        virspace -->

<!notation virspace public -- Virtual Space Unit -- "+//
  ISO/IEC 10744//NOTATION Virtual Measurement Unit//EN">

<!-- This document uses the non-HyTime measurement unit
        second -->

<!notation SIsecond public -- Time -- "+//ISO/IEC 10744//
  NOTATION Systeme International second//EN">

<!-- This document requires that the HyTime modules BASE,
        MEASURE, LINKS, and FCS be supported with certain
        options. -->

<?HyTime support base refctl>
<?HyTime support measure dimref>
<?HyTime support links>
<?HyTime support sched manyaxes=2 splitfcs>
```

PREMO
An Architecture for Presentation of Multimedia Objects in an Open Environment

Horst Stenzel, FH Köln Abt. Gummersbach
George S. Carson, GSC Associates, Redondo Beach
Ivan Herman, CWI Amsterdam
Klaus Kansy, GMD Sankt Augustin

Abstract. The PREMO (Presentation Environment for Multimedia Objects) project is a multimedia project within the International Organisation for Standardization which will define a programming environment for the presentation of, construction of, and interaction with a variety of media. Based on experiences with previous computer graphics standards, PREMO will focus on an open environment which allows for an easy configuration, customization, and extension of standardized components which deal with single aspects of presentation, construction and interaction using many different media. PREMO is based on the object model of the Object Management Group (OMG) that facilitates portability of applications and interoperability of software and hardware components in a distributed heterogeneous environment.

Keywords: Multimedia, standards, object oriented, computer graphics, PREMO

1 Introduction

There is an urgent need for standards in the important area of multiple media, not only for interchange or storage, but also for services in the area of presentation of and interaction with multimedia information, as well as the development, modification, and support of multimedia documents.

The PREMO work falls within the scope of ISO/IEC JTC1/SC24 (International Organization for Standardization/International Electrotechnical Commission - Joint Technical Committee 1/Subcommittee 24). The scope of work of SC24 was recently expanded from computer graphics and image processing to include presentation of and interaction with other media as well. SC24 expects to base much of the functionality of PREMO on existing technology from ISO standards for single-media and intends to cooperate closely with other organizations that are developing standards and specifications in other areas of multimedia.

One of the primary goals of PREMO is to support presentation using a variety of media, that is to support output to physical devices as well as accepting operator input from physical devices. Presentation is the aspect which distinguishes PREMO from other related multimedia activities in ISO/IEC (ODA and HyperODA [7], MHEG [8], HyTime [6], etc.) where the focus is on structuring and coding of documents. It is the express intention of SC24 to develop a standard which is designed to interoperate with existing and emerging standards. Close liaisons to other relevant projects will be maintained to identify areas for possible co-operation and exchange.

PREMO is the first of a second generation of computer graphics standards. The transition from first to second generation begun in 1992 is characterized by two things: reliance in object technology and seamless integration of computer graphics with other media (such as audio and video) in the context of windowing and non-windowing environments.

PREMO is being designed as an open standard, in contrast to the "kernel" approach followed in previous computer graphics standards. Some of the problems recognized in these earlier functional standards were:

- they were outdated when finished due to the lengthy international standardization process (which typically took at least five to seven years);

- by their prescriptive nature they are difficult to adapt to specific needs or changed environments;

- through the desire of the standards bodies to cover a broad area, many diverse requirements resulted in standards that were complex to use, even for restricted tasks; and

- new technology typically could not be included.

For multiple media as well as for computer graphics, PREMO aims at open environments which are easily extensible, configurable, and customizable to cover the needs of the rapidly changing computer graphics community. PREMO covers all presentation media such as still computer graphics, sound, animated sequences, and video. This task cannot be achieved by a monolithic standard, but rather requires a common framework which also allows for the integration of existing de-facto standards as well as of emerging new standards.

The PREMO standard is currently an ISO Working Draft [10] (an early stage of standards processing.) This paper is based on this Working Draft and emphasizes concepts that appear to be stable.

2 Requirements and Basic Concepts of PREMO

2.1 Scope and Purpose of PREMO

According to the "New Work Item Proposal" [9] the scope and purpose of PREMO is described as follows: PREMO "specifies a programming environment for the presentation of, construction of, and interaction with simple as well as complex multidimensional entities. It will support modelling and interaction at different levels of abstraction. The interaction can be dynamic, adaptive, and responsive. PREMO will allow related and integrated presentation using a variety of appropriate media. ... A unified object model is adopted to define the fundamental behaviour of PREMO objects. PREMO objects can be combined in a standardized way to construct more complex functionality."

By multimedia, the PREMO work means any media type or combination of media types, including:

- still computer graphics,

- animated computer graphics,

- all types of synthesized graphics,

- audio, synthesized as well as replayed captured sound,

- text,

- still images,

- moving images, video,

- results of imaging operations.

PREMO is intended to satisfy the presentation requirements of a wide range applications, including medical imaging, CAD/CAM, and virtual reality.

One of the major insights of the past years is, however, that isolated standards for synthetic graphics cannot cope with the requirements of these (and new) applications any more. Technology made it possible to create systems which use, within the same application, different presentation techniques not necessarily related to synthetic graphics, eg, video, still images, or sound. Examples of applications where video output, sound, etc, and synthetic graphics (eg, animation) coexist are numerous and well-known. It is therefore a natural demand to have development environments which can include the techniques to display different media in a consistent way, and which allow for the various, media-specific presentation techniques to coexist within the same system.

"Coexistence" is not enough though; *integration* is also necessary. For example, an audio display is not necessarily independent from the (synthetically generated) image being displayed: the viewer's position in the model, or indeed the model itself being displayed, may influence the attributes of audio display. This influence may be very simple (eg, the volume may depend on the virtual distance from the viewer), but it may also require very complicated sound processing techniques (eg, to take the room's model into account for sound reflection, absorption). In other words, it should be possible to describe media objects integrated with geometry and with one another, with possibilities to describe their mutual influence. The complete integration of various media and their presentation techniques within the same consistent framework is one of major goals (and challenges) of PREMO, and one of the features which will make it very different from earlier computer graphics standards.

Introduction of new media brings new problems into PREMO, hitherto unknown for earlier computer graphics standards. One of the most intricate requirements is the issue of synchronisation, eg, synchronisation of video and sound display. This problem is well-known in the multimedia community; its integration with the general demands of a presentation system will obviously be a challenge.

Computer graphics is no longer an isolated component of an information processing system. Thus, not only must computer graphics standards coexist with other media standards, but there must be a common underlying functional basis to enable interaction among all media. This functionality must be available in such a way that it can be built upon and bound into many as yet unforeseen environments. By defining PREMO as an open architecture and a set of rules that offer frames for interoperable components it is capable of adressing these needs.

2.2 Requirements

With PREMO, experiences with previous computer graphics standards are considered. The graphics standards of the first generation, like GKS, PHIGS, and CGM, did what they were supposed to do: they solved the predominant problems in computer graphics of the seventies and early eighties. However, when they were completed in 1985-1992, it was obvious that they did not solve all problems of the eighties and nineties. This especially applies for application programmer's interface standards which had to cope with the rapidly changing functionality of graphics workstations and requirements of new applications.

Customizability. Having finished a computer graphics standard with specific user communities and application areas in mind, it was surprising to notice that these communities were not as happy as expected. Many application areas have unique requirements which are not used outside the area. Examples are specific hatchings, markers, text handling in cartography and special types of line caps and joins as well as shielding of annotations in technical drawings. Such functionality could not be included into a kernel standard which should contain only commonly used features. But these specific features are very important for the respective groups. To achieve the required functionality, the applications had to re-program major parts of the standard which significantly reduced the benefits of using a standard interface.

The conflict between the minimality of a kernel system and the unlimited list of possible requirements by applications can only be solved by providing a standardized means for customizing existing functionality.

Extensibility. Graphics technologyis evolving at the rapid pace that is typical for computer technology. New computer graphics techniques have become available which offered new capabilities. The advent of raster display technology generated a demand for standardized raster-oriented primitives and attributes which had been less important for vector-oriented graphics in the seventies. The cost of graphics hardware has dropped and computing power has increased significantly making computer graphics possible for new application areas and new user communities. Powerful primitives and rendering attributes allowing for realistic lighting and shading of three-dimensional (3D) scenes have become affordable.

The rapid progress of technology is expected to continue; thus any computer graphics standard is likely to be partly obsolete when it is published. This problem can only be mitigated by defining extensible standards which can develop further with the evolving technology.

When the GKS standard was defined, this problem was recognized and provisions were made for a later addition of graphics primitives via a so-called "generalized drawing primitive," for new attributes via open ended lists, and for other unforeseen functionality via an "escape function." Specific user groups could define the functionality needed in their context and could register these items with an registration authority to avoid conflicting definitions and to achieve a standardized set of optional functions.

However, the registration procedure for additional functionality has not been very successful. The compatibility problem is not really solved but moved to a different place. The problem can only be solved by providing a standardized extension mechanism by which new functionality can be added without compromising the compatibility.

Configurability. It is unpractical to fulfill all wishes with a single monolithic standard. Such a standard would be huge and unmanageable. Everybody would have to pay for all the functionality. It would be very expensive for implementors to implement numerous special functions. Users not interested in exotic functionality would have to pay in price and performance for unneeded features.

The inclusion of different media into a new standard makes this kind of problems only more accute. The techniques to achieve integration of media are extremely disparate, and they use the results of various fields of computing technology like, for example, high quality synthetic graphics, image processing, speech synthesis, etc. Some of the techniques are also highly application dependent. It is almost impossible to define a closed programming environment which would encompass all needs.

A configurable system can provide rich functionality without putting too much a burden on smaller applications.

2.3   Object-Orientation

The limitations of the data-oriented view employed in previous computer graphics standards can be overcome by combining static and dynamic behaviour of graphical entities into the concept of objects containing both data and methods.

Object-orientation has proven to be a useful concept for increasing the productivity and the quality of software production. Today, the designer of a multi media system has more or less to start from scratch by designing the class hierarchies and interfaces necessary for his specific task. Experience has shown that this is a demanding process which is hard to be done right on the first try.

It is well recognized that each new application area has its own "optimal" class design which cannot be predicted or even prescribed by a standard. What PREMO will supply are components containing services for dynamic presentation, control, and interaction of multi media objects.

PREMO aids the application designer by supplying basic functionality for constructing interactive multimedia applications in a well structured manner. PREMO provides a "middleware" toolkit upon which application-specific functionality can be built.

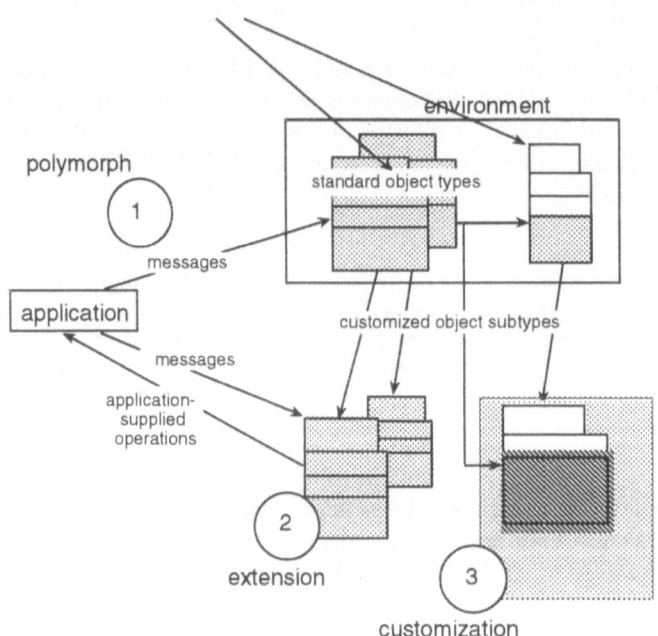

Fig. 1. Customizing a component (from [17])

Object-oriented technology can give appropriate tools for configurability and extensibility, features which are asked for in current systems. Fig. 1 [17] shows different possibilities object-oriented systems have. One characteristic feature of object-oriented systems is polymorphism (1). This means that the sender of a message has no knowledge of the recipient except that it is ready to accept a message of a given kind. Therefore, new objects can freely be added and used by the existing components as long as they obey a certain message pattern. Subclassing can be used for re-using existing code and extending (2) or modifying (3) the predefined behaviour of existing objects.

In a distributed environment, object-oriented technology has the advantage of offering an appropriate framework for the description of distribution in a consistent manner.

Objects in such an environments are closed entities which provide "services" via their methods; from the point of view of the object specification it is absolutely immaterial whether an object method has been invoked from the same "program", so to say, or via a network to encompass the need of distributed services. In other words, object-orientedness will have a dual role in PREMO: it will provide the technique for user extensibility, configurability, etc, and, also, it will offer a consistent framework for distribution.

Defining complex object-oriented systems to be used in a distributed environment leads to complicated software engineering issues, whose complete solution would go far beyond the activities and the experiences of the relevant working group within SC24 WG6. Instead, the PREMO specification will make use of techniques developed elsewhere, both within and outside ISO. These are: OMG [15] and SC21 WG7's "Open Distributed Computing initiative" (ODP) [2]. Active liaison agreements are set up with these groups to ensure mutual compatibility between the design of PREMO and the systems defined by these groups.

3 Fundamentals and Architecture of PREMO

The intended functionality of PREMO is much broader than that of previous computer graphics standards. How can one manage that complexity? One answer is the "divide and conquer" approach of the layered model of the "Computer Graphics Reference Model" (CGRM) [5] where different aspects of the graphics pipeline are considered separately. Due to the lessons learned from the past, PREMO does not attempt to establish a monolithic architecture for a monolithic kernel supporting one API for all applications.

Instead, the new standard will be based on the concept of an architectural framework and sets of components. The architecture specifies guidelines for the construction of each component as well as for the interfaces between components. A component contains a set of related functionality which is implemented following the guidelines of the framework. Components could be implemented as class libraries with predefined classes and methods which can be used by the applications.

According to this component/framework approach, different components can be developed which are tailored to the needs of specific user groups and application areas. Components replacing or complementing existing ones can be developed at any time thus providing for extensibility and an incremental, separable development of the overall system.

A user may configure a system to meet particular needs by selecting one or more appropriate components of each type. Existing standards and systems can be integrated by encapsulating their functionality into objects which conform to the framework rules.

3.1 PREMO Object Model

Similar to other functional standards, PREMO has to establish a suitable foundation in software technology. It would be preferable if the object model employed by PREMO could be based on other already standardized work, but none was available. PREMO intends to use the capabilities defined in the Common Object Request Broker [15] provided by the Object Management Group (OMG) as a firm basis of the starting work. OMG comprises major commercial companies interested in the development of an object-oriented tool kit. It is hoped that CORBA work will evolve into a formal standard.

The Common Object Request Broker provides a mechanism by which objects transparently make requests and receive responses. Its purpose is to provide interoperability between applications on different machines in distributed environments.

Basic PREMO Object Characteristics. PREMO objects are instances of types. They can be referenced and operated upon. PREMO object types can be specialized and refined by subtyping, allowing for multiple inheritance.

PREMO objects are considered to have a lifecycle from creation to destruction during which its reference (and probably its type) can be altered.

It is important to note that PREMO objects are dynamic and come to life by programming. They can represent and "model any kind of entity, e.g., a person, a ship, a document, a graphic segment, a colour value", an outcome of a user's input action [10].

A PREMO object may be active and have its own thread of control due to the need for synchronization. This is not contradicting the OMG model; however, some details on object requests had to be specified in in more precise terms for PREMO as it is the case in OMG. In order to pass synchronization information amonst objects, *events* are provided as a special elementary category of PREMO types (not objects). Synchronization and events are discussed below more detailed.

So called *non-opbjects* are basic types within PREMO that are necessary for any kind of processing but that cannot be the object of an operation defined by PREMO. Typical non-object for PREMO are integers or events.

It appears desirable but is still under debate whether PREMO objects can change their type or their signature by explicit action. This is considered a useful capability for interactive and animated scenes where it is impossible to have apriori knowledge of all the operation that might be performed on an object during its life time.

Requests and Services. The behaviour of a PREMO object that is externally visible is determined by the services the object provides upon a request or the operations that can be performed on the object. A request for a service is the only means how information can be transfered with and among PREMO objects.

The requestor of a service can only ask for the service in an atomic way, and the request is passed to the servicing object at most once.

The servicing object can decide to handle an incoming request either

- synchronously, the requestor is suspended until servicing is completed and possible results are returned, or

- asynchronously, control returns directly to the requestor who has no control over the time or order of service given to his request, or

- sampled, control returns directly to the requestor, too, and it is even possible that a later request for the same service will overwrite the request so that it will never receive service.

3.2 Components

Whereas the object model together with the concepts related to it give a clear conceptual framework for all basic notions in PREMO, components provide for a structuring of the PREMO standard in terms of the provided services.

A component in PREMO is a collection of object types and non-object data types, from which objects can be instantiated. Objects within one component are designed for a close cooperation to offer a well-defined set of functionalities for other objects external to the component. A component can be the source of a set of services as in OMG, ie, services usable in a distributed environment, or may be used as a set of objects directly linked to an application.

Components may be defined to be dependent upon other components. This can be done by organising them in component inheritance hierarchies. If component B inherits from component A, this means that all object types in B are subtypes of types defined in A which also means that all objects in B inherit from objects in A. All PREMO objects are subtypes of a common PREMO supertype, so this rule allows for the definition of essentially new types of objects, too. As far as subtyping and/or inheritance are concerned, objects within components which are related by inheritance are all distinct types: no type in one may be a subtype of a type in the other and vice versa.

Components may also depend on other components by requiring the availability of services offered by instances of objects defined in other components. They may also specify how they exploit functionality from other components, with the option of hiding this from the client. Hence components may become clients of other components services.

Underlying all PREMO components is a Foundation Component providing functionalities which are fundamental for all other PREMO components. It is mandatory that all PREMO component would inherit from this Foundation Component; see also below for a more detailed presentation of this component.

The rules for components are part of the standard. These rules form the basis for the properties of configurability, customisability, extendibility and interoperability.

4 Foundation Component and its Objects

The foundation component contains the definitions and services every other PREMO component can build upon since it must be available in every PREMO implementation. These include elementary data types, data oriented objects, active objects that control other objects (porters, producers, life cycle), events, and syncronization objects.

All PREMO objects are derived from a common super type supplying life cycle control and basic interrogation and inquiry methods. This basic behaviour is automatically inherited by all PREMO objects.

In their simplest form PREMO objects are called data objects. Data objects are carriers of information together with related operations and additional attributes. e.g., 2D or 3D points, matrices, frequency spectra.

Existence, references, and perhaps types of objects are controlled by a conceptual "life cycle manager" object. It brings PREMO objects existence through a creation service; their existence is ended by a destroy operation. During the life span of an object it is possible to alter the scope of its reference. An object's type is also determined by the life cycle manager.

4.1 Networks of Producers and Porters

Important PREMO foundation objects can be categorized as Porter objects or Producer objects by the way they act upon data objects. The basic behaviour of these object types is specified in the foundation component. It is the task of the specific components to define specific objects with behaviour particular to their needs.

Producer Objects. Producer objects are intended for processing data objects. Data objects can be presented to a producer object from one or several other objects, other producer objects or porter objects. They act on it, possibly altering their internal state, and in turn present data objects to other producers or porters. The behaviour of producer objects that is inherent in the foundation component covers elementary methods such as controlling connections, inquiring internal states, and transmitting data. An example of a producer object is a clipping stage in an output pipeline.

Porter Objects. Porter objects connect the PREMO system to the outside. Porter objects are able to import into or to export out of PREMO. Examples of porter objects are objects that give access to and provide abstract models of the behaviour of hardware such as a mouse or a speaker, etc., but also external services like database systems. Porter objects are not intended to do much processing with the data except for formatting it. They have, like all othe PREMO objects, the possibility to be asynchronously active.

4.2   Events and Synchronization

Central for reacting to changing environmental states and for synchronization is the notion of events, which is rooted in PREMO's object model as a basic, non-object type.

Events differ from other PREMO types because, while a request is sent to a specific servicing instance, events are delivered to all recipients that requested to be informed of events of a specific kind. The message receptor for a specific kind of event can be asynchronous or sampled.

Events contain the information associated with the occurence that brought them into existence. Events are created by events sources and consumed by event clients.

Event clients register their interest in specific events or categories of events with a special event handler. PREMO components will specify the event handlers they need and that will know about the occurence of events, filter them, and pass them to the interested objects.

Common of event sources are timer ticks, user input operations, results of other asynchronous activities, or results from constraints supervision.

Synchronization mechanisms are supplied by the components that need them. For example, several output streams can be synchronized by an object that defines and processes a suitable set of requests. That is, an event source generates messages at specific synchronization points, and the output services halt at the respective reference positions in their streams. In order to synchonize with the other streams, the output services may wait for the event to occur, or, if late, send a delay message to the message handler, thus delaying all other streams, or just skip some data.

The emphasis on the possible presence of active objects in PREMO stems from the need of synchronisation. Conceptually, different media (ie, a video sequence and a corresponding sound track) may be considered as parallel activities that have to reach specific milestones at distinct and possibly user definable synchronisation points. In many cases, specific media types may be directly supported in hardware. In some cases, using strictly specified synchronisation schemes, the underlying hardware can take care of synchronisation. However, a general object model should offer the possibility to describe synchronisation in general terms as well (see also [1, 11, 12] for similar approaches taken in multimedia programming systems). This means that a PREMO object may have its own thread of control, or may implement its interface by using, internally, several threads of control.

Using active objects, synchronisation appears to be no more and no less than synchronisation of concurrent processes, ie, concurrent active objects in PREMO. This does not mean that synchronisation becomes easy. What it does mean is that the terminology, the results, the machinery, etc, of the theory and the practice of concurrent programming can be reused in PREMO.

5   Multimedia System Services Component

The Multimedia System Services (MSS) component of PREMO will be based on the Multimedia System Services Recommended Practice defined by the Interactive Multimedia Association (IMA) [4]. The IMA is an international trade association with over 250 members worldwide. Its projects are aimed at accelerating the acceptance of multimedia in information technology applications by providing timely solutions to important problems.

The IMA's Multimedia System Services specification defines a standard set of services that can be used by multimedia application developers in a variety of computing environments. Enabling multimedia applications in a heterogeneous, distributed computing environment was chosen as the design center for the Multimedia System Services. This is an increasingly prevalent computing model, and a solution that meets the needs of this environment can more easily be scaled to stand-alone systems than vice versa.

Active cooperation has been set up between the ISO PREMO group and IMA, and it has been decided to merge MSS with PREMO. MSS functionality will form a separate component within PREMO, relying on the objects defined in the Foundation Component. The design of these objects already reflect the requirements of MSS, too. A first implementations of MSS will be available independently of PREMO in the course of 1994. The integration with PREMO will be made in a later stage, which may also lead to a slight restructuring of MSS to accomodate with the PREMO rules on component inheritance.

5.1   Goals of Multimedia System Services

The primary goal of PREMO Multimedia System Services is to provide an infrastructure for building multimedia computing platforms that support interactive multimedia applications dealing with synchronized, time-based media in a heterogeneous distributed environment. While there are several commercially-available products today that provide multimedia services to support interactive applications which deal with synchronized, time-based media, these operate only in a stand-alone environment. Thus, the major distinction of PREMO Multimedia System Services is the ability to support such applications in a heterogeneous, distributed environment.

Multimedia operation in a distributed environment is important for two reasons:

1. to allow users and applications to leverage shared remote "multimedia" resources (e.g., storage of titles and source material for the creation of titles, special processing elements such as video compressors or converters, special devices such as professional VCRs, etc.), and

2. to enhance collaborative working environments (e.g., adding video conferencing to shared application technology).

Why is operation in a heterogeneous, but interoperable, distributed environment important? In a large distributed multimedia environment, one which may span hundreds of computers and associated multimedia devices, there is little chance that all the equipment will be provided by a single vendor. In order for an environment to exist in which application platforms, multimedia sources, and multimedia destinations interoperate despite being built by different vendors, the Multimedia System Services must be built upon interoperable protocols, for both controlling devices and for passing data among them. The Multimedia System Services supports abstractions that make it possible for applications to deal with media devices without regard to specific characteristics of a platform or attached devices, or the network(s) connecting the platforms and devices.

While the emphasis of the Multimedia System Services is on a distributed multimedia environment, the Multimedia System Services does not preclude stand-alone systems. In fact, the converse is true. The support required for stand-alone systems is a proper subset of that required for distributed systems. Therefore, there is no reason why the Multimedia System Services cannot be used for a stand-alone environment. In fact, stand-alone systems will likely benefit from Multimedia System Services features such as object orientation, extensibility, and reliance on standards.

The Multimedia System Services is intended to address a broad range of application needs. It extends the multimedia capabilities of today's stand-alone computers to capabilities that are usable both locally and remotely. The Multimedia System Services gives applications the ability to:

− handle live data remotely;

− handle stored data remotely;

− handle both live and stored data simultaneously;

− handle multiple kinds of data simultaneously; and

− handle new kinds of devices and media types.

5.2 Summary of Multimedia System Services Functions

Multimedia System Services constitutes a framework of "middleware" - system software components lying in the region between the generic operating system and specific applications. As middleware, the Multimedia System Services marshals lower-level system resources to the task of supporting multimedia processing, providing a set of common services which can be used by multimedia application developers on an industry-wide basis.

The Multimedia System Services encompasses the following characteristics beyond those provided by the PREMO foundation component:

- provision of an abstract interface for a media processing node, extensible through subclassing to support abstractions of real media processing hardware or software;
- provision of an abstract interface for the data flow path or the connection between media processing nodes, encapsulating low-level connection and transport semantics;
- grouping of multiple processing nodes and connections into a single unit for purposes of resource reservation and stream control;
- provision of a media dataflow abstraction, with support for a variety of position, time and/or synchronization capabilities;
- separation of the media format abstractions from the dataflow abstraction;
- application visible characterization of object capabilities;
- registration of objects in a distributed environment by location and capabilities;
- retrieval of objects in a distributed environment by location and constraints;
- adoption of a Media Stream Protocol to support media independent transport and synchronization;
- provision of a local library to simplify the task of writing Multimedia System Services based applications.

6 Modelling and Presentation Components

One interesting area are components covering the functionality of an advanced computer graphics system with important geometrical aspects, and extending them to other media. An example is an animation system including sound and video. The animated scene is defined in application-specific modelling coordinates which are transformed by the graphics system to device coordinates. Within such a system, sound (loud speaker) and video screen also have geometrical positions which are subject to the same transfomations and have to be considered for sound and video rendering.

For the currently envisioned modelling and presentation components, environments and the scene are central concepts.

6.1 Environments

The Computer Graphics Reference Model (CGRM) [5] defines five environments which describe different levels of abstraction between application and operator and are traversed by graphics output primitives and geometrical input (see fig. 2):

1. The construction environment allows for modelling at the application level.

2. In the virtual environment, a device-independent representation of the graphics, the scene, is created.

3. In the viewing environment, a specific view of the scene is defined (e.g., projection from 3D into 2D).

4. In the logical environment, device-dependent attributes are bound.

5. In the realization environment, the picture is finished, e.g., by consulting a colour lookup table to generate a frame.

The environments are useful for describing the successive transformation of geometrical coordinates from application-oriented coordinates to device coordinates and the evaluation of abstract attributes into the display capabilities of a workstation. Modern high performance graphics systems emphasize the modelling and the presentation (rendering) aspects of computer graphics and other media where the scene can be regarded as the interface between both. These aspects can be easily mapped onto the levels of the CGRM with the lower three levels combined into one. The lower three environments are normally combined in one component, e.g., for sound rendering and ray tracing, such that PREMO-at this level of abstraction-is only concerned with the interface to such components.

Multimedia data associated with a geometrically specified scene has to traverse the same layers although the actual combination of the different media may be postponed until the media are physically combined in the display.

Input traverses the environments in the opposite direction. For geometrical input, the inverse transformations take place. Besides the classical graphical input devices like LOCATOR (inputs positions) and PICK (selects picture parts), other input sources like video cameras and microphones will be included which can be controlled by a PREMO application and their input be integrated into a graphics scene.

6.2 Presentation and Modelling Objects

From existing computer graphics systems we can identify a number of objects which provide modelling or presentation aspects. Modeller include sets of functionality needed for a specific application to transform application-specific objects into output objects which can be inserted into the scene. Sets of related objects form modelling components. Examples are:

- solid modellers with set operations (union, intersection) of bodies,

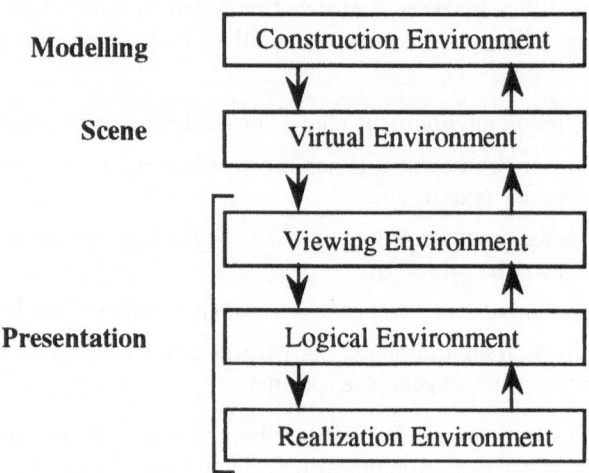

Fig. 2. Environments of the CGRM as seen in PREMO [10, Part 1 Annex C]

- time-dependent primitives and attributes of animation systems,
- objects for physically based modelling,
- primitives and attributes for virtual reality,
- objects needed for building up a HyperODA or MHEG document.
  Presentation components include:
- ray-shading (following single light rays passing through a single pixel or emanating at a light source considering possible reflections)
- radiosity (calculating an energy balance for all surfaces within a scene)
- video rendering with projective distortions,
- stereo sound renderering considering speaker positions.

Modelling and presentation components are combined via the scene interface (see fig. 3). For these purpose, scene objects have a double nature defined by two interfaces: the creation and modification interface used by the modeller and an interface which allows the interrogation of attributes like geometry and surface characteristics as needed by presentation components.

A scene comprises objects to be rendered as a whole, e.g., by one camera. The objects may originate from different modellers. A scene may be presented by one or more renderers allowing for different views, e.g., from different view points or by different rendering mechanisms.

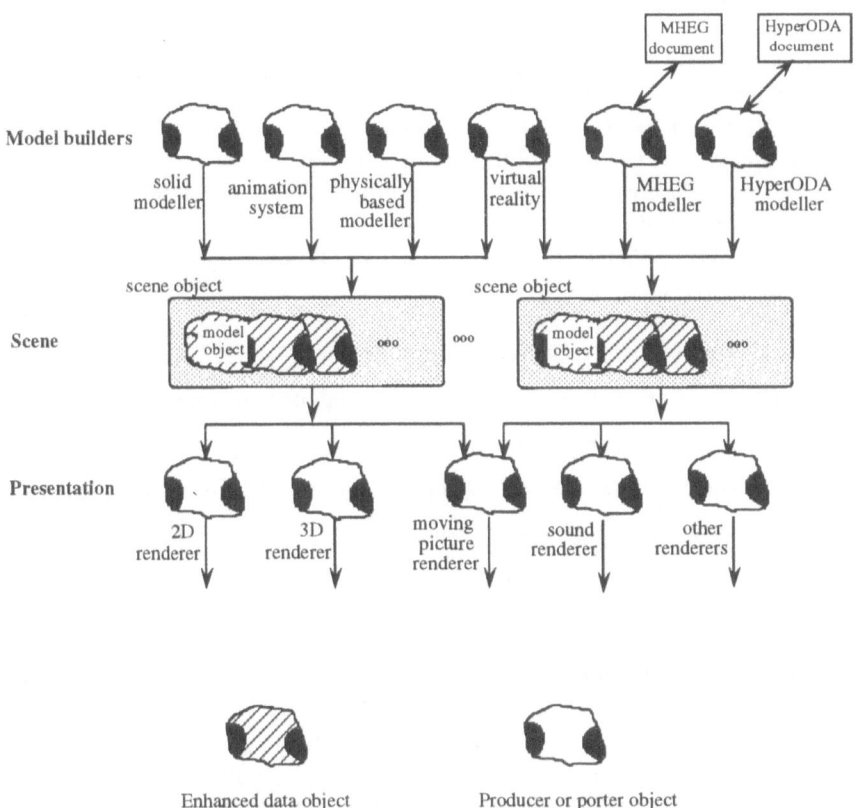

Fig. 3. The scene as mediator between different modelling and presentation components [10, Part 3]

The designer of a computer graphics system can choose the most suitable components for his applications. This tailoring of a system may considerably improve the efficiency and usability of the system.

Additional components to replace or extend existing components may be developed later. This facility also enables the inclusion of future techniques and new functionality appearing on the market during the development of the standard.

7 Outlook

7.1 Intended Progression of PREMO

Relevant projects concerned with multimedia are well underway within other committees, e.g., HyTime [6] and HyperODA [7] in SC18, MHEG [8] in SC29, as well as outside ISO, e.g., within the Interactive Multimedia Association (IMA). It is intended to progress PREMO in coordination with with such projects.

The PREMO standard will be developed incrementally. The first parts, containing the architecture, the object model, the foundation component, and an MSS component, are expected to reach international standard (IS) status in 1997, their technical contents becoming stable by 1995.

Further parts of PREMO are intended in the near future for components like:

- simple Audio/Video capture/replay,

- interface to standards for storage/interchange of multi media information,

- interaction, interfacing to users,

- functionality comparable to existing standards (GKS/R, PHIGS PLUS)

- high quality rendering/presentation,

- advanced modelling of geometric and other physics based systems.

7.2 Expected Impact

Through its layered object-oriented design PREMO supports compartmentalizing of software development, thus increasing the productivity of application development and increasing the quality of the software produced. In general, it benefits from the proven advantages of object oriented software design, merging them with the benefits gained from standardizing software interfaces.

Through the designed-in user extensibility PREMO is able to address emerging markets as well as existing application areas.

The market intended for PREMO is notoriously fast moving. PREMO is supposed to be usable in this market not only by facilitating maintenance of applications but also by making them adaptable to new requirements staying within the scope of PREMO. The cost of adapting an existing application to new resentation media or techniques will be considerably reduced.

It will also be possible to develop taylored applications that address small niche markets in a timely and cost effective manner.

It is also expected that other future standards, de facto or official, will emerge that will be interoperable with one another by adhering to PREMO.

8 Acknowledgements

The authors want to acknowledge the contributions from various collegues in the international PREMO RG and their national counterparts.

References

1. Arbab, F., Herman, I., and Reynolds, G., An object model for multimedia programming.Computer Graphics Forum (Eurographics'93 Conference Issue) 12, 3 (September 1993), C101-C114.

2. CCITT — ISO/IEC, Basic Reference Model of Open Distributed Processing, CCITT Recs.X.901 to 904 — ISO/IEC 10746:1992.

3. R. Erstling, K. Kansy, M. Müller, H. Stenzel, P. Wißkirchen, Prego Framework - Initial Draft Version 0.7, DIN NI 24/37-92 (1992).

4. International Multimedia Association, Multimedia System Services Version 1.0, Submission by Hewlett-Packard Company, International Business Machines Company, SunSoft Inc. in Response to MSS Request for Technology by IMA (1993).

5. ISO/IEC, Information technology - Computer graphics - Reference model, International Standard ISO/IEC 11072:1992.

6. ISO/IEC, Information technology - Hypermedia/Time-based Structuring Language (HyTime), International Standard ISO/IEC 10744:1992.

7. ISO/IEC, Information technology - Open Document Architecture (ODA) and Interchange Format - Temporal relationships and non-linear structures, Draft International Standard ISO/IEC DIS 8613-14:1993.

8. ISO/IEC, Information technology - Coded Representation of Multimedia and Hypermedia Information Objects (MHEG) - Part 1: Base Notation (ASN.1), Committee Draft, ISO/IEC CD 13522-1:1993.

9. ISO/IEC JTC1/SC24, Proposal for a New Work Item for PREMO (Presentation Environment for Multimedia Objects), Document ISO/IEC JTC1/SC24 N846rev. (1993).

10. ISO/IEC JTC1/SC24/WG6/OME, PREMO Working draft 1, ISO/IEC JTC1/SC24/WG6/N32 (1994).

11. de May, V., Breiteneder, C., Dami, L., Gibbs, S., and Tsichritzis, D., Visual composition and Multimedia. Computer Graphics Forum (Eurographics'92) 11, 3 (1992), C-C21.

12. de May, V., and Gibbs, S., A multimedia component kit., In Proceedings of ACM Multimedia'93 (Anaheim, CA, August 1993), P. Rangan, Ed., ACM Press, pp. 2-300.

13. M.Müller, R.Erstling, M.Bräckelmann, Architektur zur Normung von objektorientierten Graphiksystemen. In K.Kansy, P.Wißkirchen (eds), Neue Architekturkonzepte zur Gestaltung graphischer Systeme, GMD-Studien Nr. 223 (1993).

14. J.R.Nicol, C.T.Wilkes, F.A.Manola, Object Orientation in Heterogenous Distributed Computing Systems, IEEE Computer, June 1993, Vol.26, No.6.

15. Object Management Group, The Common Object Request Broker: Architecture and Specification, OMG Doc. 91.12.1 (1992).

16. P. Wißkirchen, Object-Oriented Graphics - From GKS and PHIGS to Object-Oriented Systems, Springer-Verlag Berlin (1990) 236 p.

17. P. Wißkirchen, K. Kansy, The New Graphics Standard - Object-Oriented! In: E. Blake, P. Wißkirchen (Eds), Advances in Object-Oriented Graphics I, Springer-Verlag Berlin (1991) pp. 199-215.

Demonstrations

The Department Information System of the Information Systems Department at the Technical University of Vienna

E. Valsky, M. Herzog, R. Peratello, W. Slany

Department of Information Systems, Division for Database and Expert Systems,
Technical University of Vienna, A-1040 Wien, Austria.

Abstract. This paper describes our approach towards constructing an electronic information system. The purpose of this information system is to provide information about activities and research work done at our department. Firstly we investigate relevant design targets and requirements and their influence on the implementation process. Secondly we review different approaches towards hypermedia developments in respect to our previous analysis. The authoring process is a crucial point in the generation of hypermedia documents. In the last part we emphasize our experience with the authoring process and describe details of the implementation process.

1 Introduction

During the last years our faculty at the department has been facing a growing burden through organizational overhead. The increasing number of students as well as a growing information demand led us to reconsider our conventional methods of information providing. Our hitherto used blackboard method seemed not to be suitable anymore. Information is too often outdated, unorganized, and there is no common knowledge of how to present information. Students rely on members of our staff to satisfy their information needs which causes a growing load as stated above.

Besides this proposing a new way to present our department to people was another challenging idea. This service will not only be useful to students, but in general to any person who is interested in organizational, personal, or administrative details of the department. Potential users will be visitors, new members of the department, foreign colleagues, etc. Additionally, providing information in a uniform way will also foster communication within the department, thus making collaborative work much easier.

While we are concentrating on organizational information in a first stage, a seamless integration of education will be the aim of upcoming work. The system can not only be used to provide accompanying information like important deadlines, latest news, results, etc. but also lecture notes in addition to traditional means of education. The advantage of this system will be its universal availability, extendibility, and accuracy.

In the remaining part of this paper we will concentrate on the following topics: Firstly we will define desired targets which should be accomplished within this project. These include aims of the design as well as the implementation cycle of the project. Secondly we will investigate different existing approaches towards the generation of such systems. Thirdly we will discuss details of our system design and lessons learned during the implementation process.

2 Project Targets and Requirements

The main target of this project is to gain the highest achievable effect within the least amount of time. This is due to the fact that we are working under a tight time-table. Moreover we do not want to spend too much time during the specification phase. Thus we are looking for a system that highly supports a prototype approach to the system design, thus reducing the redesign phase.

Besides this we are attaching high importance to an easy user-handling. The system interface should be self explanatory and the user should be able to handle the system without being forced to study complicated instructions. Hypermedia is a promising technique in this field and we choose it as general information delivery model.

The support for collaboration of all members of the department is another important point in the design considerations. The ease of handling should not only be important in regard to information consumers (e.g. students) but also to information providers (e.g. staff). The possibility for including already existing material into the information system will result in a better acceptance of the overall approach.

Clearly a high availability to all users is of crucial significance to this kind of service. As we are working in a heterogeneous network environment we have to assert the usefulness from different types of hardware platforms. This shall not result in a penalty for users of certain platforms but ensure the same functionality on any kind of platform.

Taking these design targets into account we can compile the following list of design requirements:

- Powerful development tools to build a satisfying system in a short amount of time.
- Hypermedia as the underlying information modeling and presentation methodology.
- Distributed information organized by an universal access interface.
- Heterogeneous network support

3 System Design

3.1 Choosing the Development Platform

Taking our development time into account it is clear that we cannot build all needed parts from scratch. Thus we have to rely on already existing work. We can identify two different approaches within the hypermedia research towards development of new systems.

On the one hand new systems have been build which address the development of a certain Hypermedia model (e.g. DHM [1]) As a consequence, most of them necessitate distinguished software settings (e.g. underlying database systems) and require a high system knowledge of all participating users. We can think of these as "system centered" approaches, as they all introduce a certain kind of hypermedia engine.

On the other hand some research initiatives concentrate on the definition of hypermedia document languages. Among these "document centered" approaches are HyTime [2], MHEG [3], Adobe Acrobat, and HTML(+) [4]. Concentrating on documents relieves authors from dealing with complicated systems and we can compare the implementation process to the authoring process within text systems.

This helps novice users to get familiar with the new environment as they can draw on already well known principles.

We think, that HTML(+) as part of the WWW-project is best suited for our requirements. This is due to the fact, that it is available free of charge, embedded in a growing research community, usable on different platforms across heterogeneous networks (via HTTP [5]), and easy to use.

3.2 Authoring the System

HTML(+) supports the common Hypermedia link-node paradigm. This means the single author can create documents incorporating links to other documents. These links rely on so-called URLs, which specify a unique document within the universe of documents.

Documents can be accessed on a client-server basis. WWW-servers (currently there are around 1500 servers on the Internet) send these documents on request to clients which can be located all over the Internet.

Our first step in the authoring process is the construction of several documents, which serve as starting points for the information providing process. This is usually done in the form of directories, indices, and other collections of pointers to more information. This information is discovered by employing the well known browsing strategy.

A basic set of documents is used to render information about members of the department, projects, courses of classes, descriptions to the local library, software manuals, etc. This documents are highly interlinked and have been authored by the project team.

The advantage of our approach during this phase of the construction process is that we can include already existing material (files, documents in other formats) through gateways. This helps gathering a "critical" amount of information that makes the system worth to use. Moreover this prevents repeating already done work.

Up to now most of our documents have been authored by the same persons. In the future we want to encourage all members of the department to write their own documents. This will shorten the "publishing" process, thus making information more accurate. Supporting distributed documents is one of the core ideas of the WWW-project. The only problem one has to consider is the organizational part how "publishers" can make their information available. A strategy has to be formulated which is reliable for all participants.

Additional to this basic information service we want to include a seamless integration of our already existing anonymous-ftp server. This will add a new quality to this service, as technical reports and other publications can be viewed on-line in a hypermedia-like style. Reports can be viewed without changing the viewing tool, thus freeing the user from permanent switching between different tools.

Another important point is the compilation of a collection of links to other relevant information on the internet. This will be similar to constructing a virtual library, which can be used by every interested person to locate up-to-date information on various topics. We are exploring different possibilities how this process could be - at least partial - automated.

We are also investigating the possibility to incorporate feedback from the user. This would be of great interest for automating simple procedures as register to an examination, inquire test results, or looking for a particular book in our library. HTML+ supports this by providing so-called forms, which are used to generate query masks.

4 Conclusion

Starting from design requirements and targets we have shown how we came up with our final design. Major influences have been the limited development time, the support for distributed information in a heterogeneous network, and the simplicity to interact with the system.

If we evaluate our approach so far, we must also admit some drawbacks. Due to the lack of a powerful hypermedia engine, we have to work without features like automatic version control of documents, extended CSCW capabilities, automatic link management, and other services available in sophisticated systems. Nevertheless we think that considering our purposes we got the right pay-off between development time and effect.

The ratio between effort and effect is a crucial rate for the usefulness of any system. We tried to minimize that by using existing software and the well established authoring paradigm. Moreover we can rely on results of joint-efforts of the WWW project and other corresponding initiatives. Thus our system is embedded in a community of similar projects and is able to interfere with documents from all over the world.

References

1. Gronbaek, Kaj, Trigg, Randall H., Design Issues for a Dexter-Based Hypermedia System, in: Communications of the ACM, Volume 37, Number 2, pp. 40-50, February 1994

2. Information technology - Hypermedia/Time-based Structuring Language (HyTime), ISO/IEC DIS 10744, ISO, 1991

3. Price, Roger, MHEG: An Introduction to the Future International Standard for Hypermedia Object Interchange, in: Proc. 1st ACM Multimedia 93, pp. 121-182, August 1993

4. Berners-Lee, Tim; Connolly, Daniel: Hypertext Markup Language; A Representation of Textual Information and Metainformation for Retrieval and Interchange; Internet Draft, 13.; Juli 1993; ftp://info.cern.ch/pub/www/doc/html-spec.ps HTTP:.

5. Berners-Lee, Tim: Hypertext Transfer Protocol; A Stateless Search, Retrieve and Manipulation Protocol; Internet Draft, 5.; November 1993; ftp://info.cern.ch/pub/www/doc/http-spec.ps.

Teaching Computer Simulation with Multimedia/Hypermedia Application

Gabor Balogh and Dr. Istvan Molnar

Department of Computer Science, Budapest University of
Economics,
Budapest, Hungary

Abstract. The paper starts with discussion of the present way of teaching computer simulation and contrasts it with teaching of the same subject with the help of multimedia instruments. The practical implementations of the main principles are demonstrated with the help of a multimedia teaching material, which is a PC stand alone application for teaching mathematical ecology and computer simulation.

1 Introduction

The traditional university teaching of computer simulation today in no way differs from teaching other subjects of computer science. That statement no doubt holds true not only in Hungary. Theoretical knowledge fundamentally is obtained in the form of lectures, seminars and written technical literature, while practical knowledge can be acquired within the framework of seminars and exercises developed by using computers. As regards media employed, the dominance of written and vocal instruments can be observed, supplemented by diagrams and pictures, occasionally by animation.

Although individual learning has special significance, neither the teaching material, nor the technical instruments are suitable for taking into account the differences stemming from the individual training of the˘students.

During learning in addition to computer usage interactivity is made possible in a limited way by seminars and exercises.

Reporting is done on oral or written examinations, or perhaps by using the results of computer programs done by the students.

Computer simulation is employed first of all in the technically most developed areas. In a controversial way the technical level of teaching simulation applications at university level is not at all advanced. In our opinion the difference between the technical level of application and education can be reduced with the help of multimedia education systems.

2 Possibilities of media applications

On the basis of [1] the process of simulation can be divided into the following steps: problem formulation, model building, data acquisition, model translation, verification, validation, strategic and tactical planning, experimentation, analysis of results, implementation and documentation. Teaching simulation is connected to the activities to be done during simulation steps.

The characteristic of the education of the various steps is that it needs the employment of more than one medium and naturally individual steps require and put into the fore different media. As can be seen from table no. 1, it is preferable to use all the media.

Besides the previous characteristics, teaching simulation also requires the carrying out of a great number of numerical calculations, consequently the computer not only directs the storage and display of voice, pictures, etc. , but as a universal computer, it performs calculations, as well.

We find that during teaching, especially in model translation and result analysis phase increased interactivity is required even when giving the information or when learning. Naturally, recollection and reaching of the aim can also be done interactively.

Table No. 1 : Phases of the simulation process and the preferred media and interactivity to be used

Phases of simulation process	Type of media to be used	Interactivity
System definition, problem formulation	Text, pictures, voice, movie	
Model building	Text, pictures, voice	
Data acquisition and preparation	Text, pictures	
Model translation	Text, pictures, voice	X
Verification and validation	Text, pictures, voice	
Strategic and tactical planning, experimentation	Text, pictures	X
Analysis of results	Text, pictures, voice, movie	X
Implementation and documentation	Text, pictures, voice	

3. Lotka-Volterra systems: a multimedia demonstration program

In order to make education complete we wanted to create as an accompanying material a multimedia-application which presents the technical solutions needed for fulfilling the above requirements. The characteristics of the demonstration program are the following:

Subject: interactive teaching of mathematical ecology and ecological application of simulation modelling

Hardware requirement: Intel486 CPU, 8MB RAM, 120MB HD

Software requirement: MS-WINDOWS 3.1

Duration of execution: about 35-45 minutes

Main characteristics: Students can make experiments with parameters of the model without knowing anything about the programming environment or the simulation software, and can look at the effects of the changes almost immediately. They are able to gain elementary knowledge about the process of simulation, especially about
- examination of real systems,
- building of simulation models,
- building a corresponding mathematical model,
- making experiments for parameter calibration,
- examination and evaluation of the results.

The demonstration program has been developed with international cooperation, in which Open University Hagen supplied hardware, the authoring tool (Multimedia Toolbook from Asymetrix Co.) and some of the featured pictures and video clips (including their digitalisation), while the Hungarian participants concieved the idea itself, developed and programmed the whole scenario, building together the simulation program written in GPSS-FORTRAN Version 3. [4] and the presentation application, evaluated the missing pictures and videos and finally put the system together.

Our training program is not complete. It has some shortcomings that are the consequence of the short time we had to develop it and our small budget. We have ideas how to finish it and we are working on these modifications.

References

1. Pritsker, A.A.B, Pegden, C. D.: Introduction to simulation and˝SLAM. New York, John Wiley and Sons, Inc. 1979

2. Bossel, H: Simulation dynamischer Systeme. Vieweg Verlag, 1989

3. Metzler, W.: Dynamische Systeme in der Oecologie, Stuttgart,˝Teubner Verlag , 1987

4. Schmidt, B.: Modellbildung mit GPSS-FORTRAN Version 3.,˝Berlin Heidelberg New York Tokio: Springer Verlag, 1984

Tools

A Distributed Audio System

Ning LI

Computing Laboratory, University of Kent at Canterbury
Kent CT2 7NF, UK

Abstract. This paper introduces the design and implementation of a distributed audio system that is used to build multimedia applications. The system is based on the ANSAware distributed system which can be run on different platforms. The system is implemented in the client-server model. It provides a set of programming interfaces for audio data storage, data management and audio communication connections. Various applications can be built using these interfaces. The audio editor is such an application which can manipulate the sounds in a myriad of ways – playing, recording, labelling, trimming and so on.

1 Introduction

Sound is an important medium. Nowadays, more and more widely used hardware is equipped with multimedia facilities, that allow computers to process audio and visual signals digitally in a distributed environment [2, 10, 14].

The audio system introduced in this paper is a part of the Palantir project, a multimedia project carried out at the University of Kent during 1989-1992. This system provides the basic programming interfaces for audio data storage, data management, and audio communication connections. It enables users to develop their own applications, for instance the audio editor and speaking clock, using these interfaces. It is different from most of the conventional audio tools, such as SUN Microsystems' AudioTool [1], MicroMedia's SoundEdit, Microsoft's WaveEdit or Macintosh's SoundEdit [13], in that the Palantir audio system is built in a distributed environment.

There are a number of similar systems which were built in the distributed collaborative environment. Etherphone system has provided facilities to manage and to share audio data among multiple workstations and multiple networks [12]. Some other projects have extended the principle of Etherphone to incorporate video applications [8]. SuitSound[9] has provided a conventional tool for building object based applications that include audio. Almost all these systems use primary remote procedure calls under the TCP/IP protocol. The hardware environment usually influences the design decisions. Researchers have begun to investigate the communication protocols to support audio[3]. For example, Terek and Pasquale describe an extension to the X Window System to support audio applications. The modified X server accepts audio requests from across the network and executes them on workstations[11]. This kind of system meets the difficulty of unexpected time delay and slow response, since the X server, which is a single process, does not support multi-threads, as X is a protocol designed for graphical user interface.

The Palantir audio system is different from the above systems because it is built on a mature distributed system, i.e., the ANSAware 4.0[6]. This creates several advantages:

- The audio processing is separated from the network communication. It makes the system 'neat' and efficient.

- Little effort is needed to incorporate audio into a general multimedia environment with unified programming interfaces. Palantir project uses ANSAware as the communication platform to support various video and audio applications. Audio is treated in the same way as other multimedia objects.

- ANSAware can run on a wide range of hardware including SUN, DEC or HP workstations, and personal computers running UNIX, VMS or MS-DOS operating systems. ANSAware allows the system to be heterogeneous. By setting up the bridge between traders, the audio system can be used in wide area networks.

- ANSAware provides the programmer with a number of programming tools and libraries that enable the construction of distributed systems. The multi-thread ability, the synchronisation support and dynamic interface binding are extremely useful in the implementation of a distributed audio system.

This system has been used successfully in the applications apart from the Palantir project. It has been applied to construct a phonetic system which can synthesis modern Chinese pronunciations [4].

2   System overview

The audio system was developed on Sun Sparc stations, HP stations and PCs running conventional UNIX operating system and MS-DOS. All the platforms have ANSAware installed. The system includes the following parts: the audio server, the voice storage and management server and user applications like the audio editor and speaking clock. Fig 1 shows the relationship between these parts.

The audio server has two functions, one of which is to set up the link of different audio streams, the other is to transfer the audio data from the clients to the audio device. It is supported by the audio facilities standardly available on the Sun Sparc workstations. It provides 64 kbps PCM speech input and output in either μ-low or A-low form. The audio data is sent by spurt packages, each of which has the length of 512 bytes (16 packages per second). All the communication is via the ANSAware 4.0 mechanisms.

The concept of voice rope comes from D.B.Terry and D.C.Swinehart's paper [12]. A rope is a sequence of stored voice with logical meaning. The voice storage management in the audio system is designed with the intention of sharing the audio data among different users and using the minimum space to store the data. For this purpose,

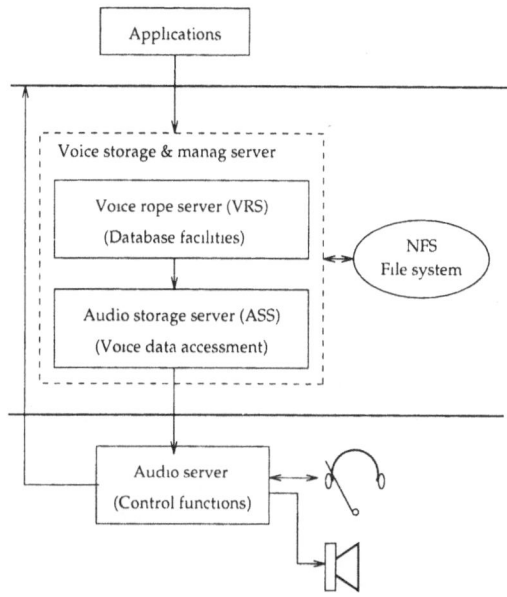

Figure 1: The construction of the audio system

a two-level storage hierarchy is employed: a voice rope represents a sequence of stored voice segments by referring to the intervals of these voice segments. A given voice rope may consist of intervals recorded in several audio files, and a given audio file can be referred by several voice ropes; a database stores the $n : n$ relations between the voice rope and audio file. Editing operations simply create new ropes from the old ones and add them into the database.

The voice ropes rely on a simple database management system for implementation. The database facilities need only store the immutable objects, provide basic query and update mechanisms, and support sharing among many client users.

In reality, the voice storage management is divided into two parts:

1. Voice Rope Server (VRS): provides the database management facilities to manage the logical relationship between voice segments (voice ropes)

2. Audio Storage Server (ASS): provides the file management functions, such as reading and writing audio files through the network

The audio editor is a real application of the audio system. It is designed for trimming or editing the sound segments via a graphical user interface (GUI). It has the functions for recording or playing sound, generating or deleting ropes, labelling ropes, changing speed and various control operations. The speaking clock is another application that provides the audio time inquiry service using the voice ropes generated dynamically.

3 Implementation details

This section introduces the implementation details including the user interface and programming interface used in the audio server, audio storage server, voice rope server and audio editor respectively. The programming interfaces are specified in the Interface Definition Language (IDL) of ANSAware 4.0, see [5].

3.1 Audio server

The user interface of the audio server is shown in Fig 2. It provides the manual control facilities to set up audio communication links and to adjust the volume.

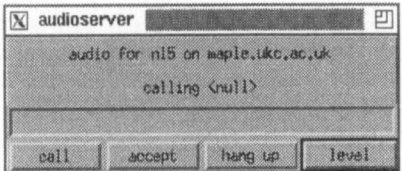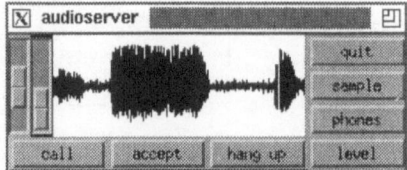

Figure 2: The user interface of the audio server

In the view of object interaction, Fig 3 shows the interfacing between two audio servers when a communication link is set.

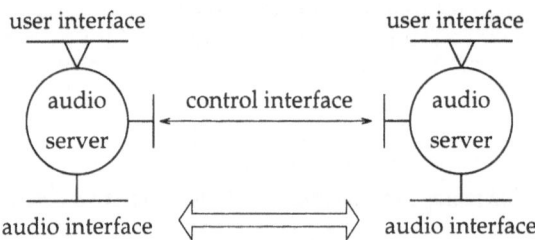

Figure 3: The communication interface of the audio server

A communication link can be set up between two audio servers by the user from the user interface in one of the three modes: create, request port and request user, see [7]. The audio interface reference (channel for transferring the audio data) is obtained when the link has been set. The audio data then can be transferred into or out from the audio server. The audio transfer is handled by the ANSAware remote procedure call with buffer mechanism for stabilising the audio input and output.

The audio interface is as below:

```
Spurt:          OPERATION    [ in_status:      Boolean;
                               in_delay:       CARDINAL;
                               in_samples:     SEQUENCE OF OCTET]
```

```
RETURNS        [ out_status:      Boolean;
                 out_delay:       CARDINAL;
                 out_samples:     SEQUENCE OF OCTET]
```

where delay is the time difference between the sample being sent and received. It is measured in units of 1/8192 of a second, which currently matches the PCM sampling rate.

3.2   Voice storage management

The voice storage management which is further specified as the audio storage server and the voice rope server provides the programming interface only.

3.2.1   Audio storage server

The audio storage server is user-transparent. It is only used by the voice rope server. Its major operations are: **AssRead()** – reads an audio file from the specified position untill the indicated length; **AssWrite()** – picks up the data from the audio interface and writes them into an audio file. Apart from these two operations it provides the operations for canceling the sound playing and recording which may be useful in some of the audio applications.

3.2.2   Voice rope server

```
VrsBuildRope:   OPERATION   [ rope_segments:   RopeSegments;
                              ropename:        STRING ]
                RETURNS     [ VrsStatus ];
```

VrsBuildRope() builds a new rope ropename from the existing old ropes which are indicated by rope_segments, with or without inheriting the labels.

The voice rope server has a function to "label" a sound. A label is a mark in the audio sequence with the attributes of name and position (offset from the beginning). An audio sequence may have many labels. Each label may trigger an action specified by the user. For example, the user may want to flash the screen when the sound "flashing the screen" is playing.

```
VrsFileToRope:  OPERATION   [ ropename:        STRING;
                              filename:        STRING ]
                RETURNS     [ VrsStatus ];
```

VrsFileToRope() registers a file in the database, i.e., generates a new rope from this file. Since a rope is the basic unit in the audio system, all the plain audio files have to be registered before being processed.

```
VrsDeleteRope:  OPERATION   [ ropename:        STRING ]
                RETURNS     [ VrsStatus ];
```

VrsDeleteRope() deletes a specified rope.

```
VrsPlayRope:     OPERATION    [
                    audio_interface_ref:        ansa_InterfaceRef;
                    display_interface_ref:      ansa_InterfaceRef;
                    display_scan_rate:          INTEGER;
                    ropename:                   STRING;
                    play_range:                 Interval;
                    label_events:               LabelEvents;
                    callback_interface_ref:     ansa_InterfaceRef;
                    filename:                   STRING;
                    preload:                    INTEGER;
                    speed:                      INTEGER  ]
                 RETURNS      [ VrsStatus ];
```

VrsPlayRope() plays a rope in one of the following circumstances:

- Producing the sound as well as the graphical data (signal waveform)

- Producing the sound but no graphical data

- Producing the graphical data but no sound

These three modes are for different applications having different requirements. Which mode is applied, when the operation is called, depends on the value of audio_interface_ref and display_interface_ref – nothing will happen if the interface reference is an empty one.

The parameter display_scan_rate is the sampling rate for the graphic lines. For instance, eight graphic lines per sample will be generated if display_scan_rate is set to 64 when the sample size is 512 bytes ($512 / 64 = 8$).

VrsPlayRope() first assembles the rope to be played by building up a chain which contains all the rope segments. The AssRead() is called to locate the physical audio data and to send them to the audio interface. All the related audio files are opened in advance to avoid the time delay during the play operation. While each sample is read, the graphic data that represent the waveform are sent to the display interface. Crossed labels are reported through the callback interface. The synchronisation of sound, waveform graphics and label callbacks are implemented by ANSAware event sequencer and event counter.

The callback facility is provided in the rope server, which notifies the user application to take an action when a particular label is being crossed while the sound is playing. That is why callback_interface_ref is needed in VrsPlayRope().

Sound is a continuous medium that no interruption is desired. However, since the graphical data generated from the rope server needs to be transferred rapidly into the user application through network, it puts a heavy burden on network. Also it takes time to generate the graphics in the user application, the client may not response to the server in time. Sounds might be interrupted under the heavy loading of network and machine, thus the quality of sound is poor. To solve this problem, the parameter preload is used which lets the server produce the sound and the graphical data asynchronously, i.e., the graphical data is generated and sent to a local temporary file beforehand. While the sound is playing, the user application receives only the time-stamps (one for every eight samples) and reads the graphical data from the local file. This method significantly improves the sound quality since the audio data and graphical data are sent in the different phases. The sacrifice is that, in this way, extra time is needed to send the graphical data and the synchronisation of the sound and waveform is not so perfect. This is because it is impossible to correct the delay produced in the sample transferring when preload is applied.

The start position and length of the rope for playing is indicated by play_range. All the labels requiring callback are specified in label_events. The parameter filename is used when the user wants to save the sound into an audio file while playing.

```
VrsRecord:        OPERATION    [
                        audio_interface_ref:        ansa_InterfaceRef;
                        filename:                   STRING;
                        interval:                   Interval;
                        callback_interface_ref:     ansa_InterfaceRef ]
                  RETURNS      [ VrsStatus ];
```

VrsRecord() records a piece of sound in a file.

The voice rope server maintains a set of data structures:

- Voice rope head pool (VRH)
  Each voice rope has this head. Every rope name recorded in VRH has a rope-ID corresponding to the VRH entry. This structure also contains the pointer to the entry of its first segment in the voice rope table (VRT), and the pointer to its label chain in the voice label table (VLT).

- Voice rope table (VRT)
  This is a table consisting of one direction chains. Each entry points to a voice segment in the voice segment table (VST). It also contains a pointer to its next segment in VRT.

- Voice segment table (VST)
  This table contains the locations of all the voice segments in the distributed audio files. Actual audio data can be indexed through this table.

- Voice label table (VLT)
  All the logical labels, each of which is expressed by a label name and the offset, are recorded in this table. Each rope has two default labels, i.e., StartLabel and EndLabel which represent the beginning and end of the rope respectively.

The relationship between the data structures described above is shown in Fig 4.

There are a set of disk files (database) used as the storage of the in-memory data structures. Any in-memory data changes will update the related disk files. A unique timestamp is stored in the beginning of these files for the safety reason. The server checks the timestamp in each file before the disk files are loaded into memory to make sure that all the files are of the same version. An old version of the files is available to make the server able to recover from failure. A Locking mechanism is applied to prevent the reading and writing conflict of the database data.

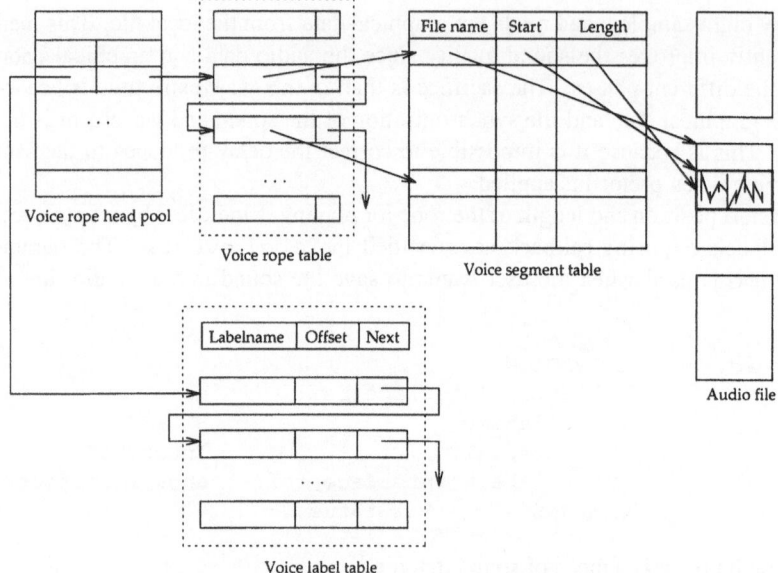

Figure 4: The relationship between the data structures used in the voice rope server

3.3   Audio editor

The audio editor, as an application, is built on top of the interfaces provided by the voice rope server. The audio editor, on one hand, is the client of the voice rope server, which in turn is the client of the audio storage server; on the other hand, the audio editor itself is a callback server for event callback and a display server for displaying the signal waveform. Fig 5 shows the relationship between all the interfaces used by the audio editor.

The audio editor user interface is shown in Fig 6. It provides a window composed of the following seven areas:

Command section – the area contains all the buttons to activate the operations, such as to build a rope, play a sound, record a sound, stop and continue operating, reset the system; change, delete or list ropes; request labels, choose sample size and so on.

Input area – the input data is edited and accepted through this area.

Speed panel The playing speed can be changed by sliding the speed marker in this area. This can achieve the fast play and slow play in a forward or backward direction.

Rope display area – the area displays all the mother-ropes which are drawn to scale according to their length. The mother-ropes are shown by rectangles which also are buttons. By pressing one of the rope patterns, the current rope name will be displayed in the system message window.

Segment display area – the area displays all the segments which are picked up from the mother-ropes. The segments are represented by the dark bars which also are buttons. By pressing one of the segment patterns, the current position (the offset from

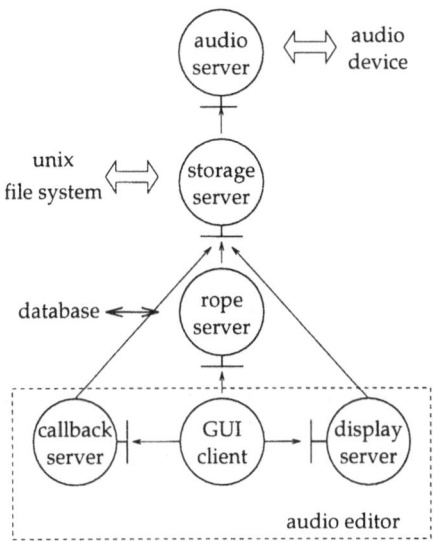

Figure 5: The relationship between the interfaces used by the audio editor

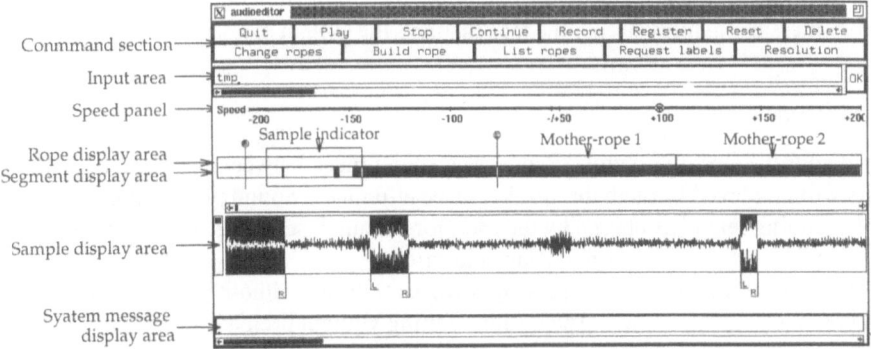

Figure 6: The audio editor user interface

the beginning of the rope) will be displayed.

Overlaid on both the rope and segment display area, there is a sample indicator which indicates the location within the new rope of the sample currently being displayed in the sample display area (described below). It runs from left to right or right to left depending on the speed value while the sound is playing, and can be located manually at other times. The width of the indicator, which is determined by the sample size and the length of ropes to be played, can be selected by the button "Resolution" in the command section (described below). Two other indicators, which are set by the user, mark the start and stop positions of the sound for playing.

Sample display area – a graphic window which displays the audio signal waveforms. The amplitude of the level being displayed can be controlled by the slider next to the trace. The resolution is of either 32, 16, 8, 4, 2 or 1 lines per sample, which means that a sample (currently 502 bytes of audio data) will be drawn in 32, 16, 8, 4, 2 or 1 line(s) in this graphic window. The resolution is selected by the button "Resolution" which is a popup menu in the command section. A scroll bar can scroll the sample displaying window in both directions. This scroll bar together with the sample indicator can locate the samples in both rough and fine modes. There might be some label indicators under the window which signify the labels in the corresponding positions. Selecting a place under the sample window will popup a window which shows the details of a label including its name and offset. The label can be modified by changing the contents in the window. The possible operations include adding and deleting labels, or changing label positions.

In the sample window, the foreground and background of the sounding segments (where the sound will be produced) are swapped to differentiate from the dump segments (silent part) which are displayed in the normal foreground and background colour. Under each segment boundary, there is a boundary marker which can be moved by the mouse. It allows the user to change the segment boundary easily. Pressing a button in the sample display window will popup a menu which has four marker types for dividing or adding a segment and extending the left or right boundaries.

System message display area – the area displays the system messages fed back to the user.

The main operations:

Play a sound Select the button "Play". The sound piece between the start/stop indicators will be played through the speaker or head-phones. Sound playing only covers those sounding segments chosen by the user; for the dumb segments, no sound is given but an equivalent amount of time delay is inserted.

There are three methods of playing a rope: "editing without preload", "editing with preload" and "preview". The option "editing without preload" gives fairly good synchronisation of sound and waveform graphics, and is also fast. However the quality of sound is poor when the network or machine is heavily loaded. The option "editing with preload" improves the sound quality but the synchronisation of sound and waveform is not as good as in the first option (reference to 3.2.2). By using the third option "preview", the user can have a "preview" listening of the sound from all the sounding segments, without any dumb intervals. There is no waveform displayed in this option and looks like the sound comming from a new rope which was built by the sounding segments being chosen.

Record a sound After pressing the button "Record" and inputing the audio file name, the record session will start. It can be cancelled by pressing the button "Stop". When the recording is finished, a registering operation automatically follows. It asks the user to input the new rope name so as to get the audio file registered.

Register a file After pressing the button "Register" and inputing the audio file name and the new rope name, the whole audio file becomes a new voice rope which can be managed in various ways by the audio system.

Delete ropes After pressing the button "Delete" and inputing the rope names, the ropes will be deleted from the internal database irreversibly.

Change ropes After pressing the button "Change ropes", the sequence of the previous mother-rope names will be displayed in the input window, if there was a rope being built before; otherwise the mother-rope names have to be input by the user one by one. The user can do any modification to the sequence of mother-rope names by text editing. When finished, a new rope composed of the mother-ropes in the selected sequence will be shown.

Build a rope or change a rope to file There are three options for building a rope: "build with inheriting labels", "build without inheriting labels" and "a new audio file". The first two options determine whether a new rope will inherit the labels of their mother-ropes or not. The last option will generate a new audio file with the audio data from the current rope. The user has to input a new rope name or file name at this stage.

Change resolutions A menu will popup after pressing the button "Sample size". There are six options on the menu – 32, 16, 8, 4, 2 and 1. This means there will be the same number of line(s), which represent the waveform, to be drawn in the graphic window for each sample. The sample indicator will be updated after a new value has been selected.

Change the playing speed By pressing and sliding the speed marker, the playing speed can be changed widely. If the speed changes to negative, the playing will be changed from forwards to backwards.

3.4 Speak Clock

Speak clock is another application built on the audio system. It continuously or interactively reports the current time in hours, minutes or seconds by sound. A typical sentence is:

Now the time – fifteen hours twenty three minutes thirty seconds

It is played as a generated rope, which contains the segments of: 1) a bell ring; 2) "now the time"; 2) "fifteen"; 3) "hours"; 4) "twenty three"; 5) "minutes"; 6) "thirty"; 7) "seconds". These come from the existing ropes being recorded, which include the bell ring, words of "now the time", "hours", "minutes" and "seconds", and the digital numbers from one to fifty nine. In the above sentence, 2), 4) and 7) are figured out dynamically by the time functions provided by the operating system. The speaking clock builds the new rope which is the sentence listed above by concatenating all the pre-stored ropes in the right order. The user does not need to manage the server (rope

server and storage server) as the ANSAware factory and node manager can start up and
terminate the service automatically.

4 Summary

The audio system was designed with the intent of sharing the audio data by many
users and using disk space as little as possible. To make full use of the facilities in
distributed systems, the audio system was built in a distributed environment supported
by ANSAware. The networking communication has been well separated from the
audio processing.

The client-server model was adopted in the implementation of distributed processing. The audio server is used to set up the audio communication link. It also returns
the audio interface to the user to transfer the audio data over the link. The two-level
voice storage and management facility was built, on top of which is the voice rope
server which maintains the logical relations of audio segments in ropes and provides
the basic programming interface for user applications, for example, building, deleting,
playing or recording operations for ropes. Under the voice rope server, there is an
audio storage server which is used to manage the physical audio files. It provides the
operations which are called only by the rope server for reading and writing distributed
audio files.

The audio editor is an application instance using the programming interface provided by the audio system. It supports the basic editing operations as well as various
control functions through GUI. Special effort has been made to reduce the network and
CPU loading to preserve the sound quality. Another application, the speaking clock,
provides the audio time inquiry service using the voice ropes generated dynamically.

Some further work might carry on to make the system lighter-weight.

5 Acknowledgement

I would like to acknowledge my gratitude to Prof. Peter F. Linington for his valuable
supervision to this research, and his remarkable programming of the audio server. I
am grateful to Mr Chris Scott who has given me great help in the development of this
audio system. I am also thankful to Mr Jonathan C.Roberts for having proofread this
paper.

References

[1] *OpenWindows Version 3 DeskSet Reference Guide*. Sun Microsystems, Inc, 1991.

[2] *European multimedia yearbook*. Interactive Media Publications, 1993.

[3] B. Arons, C. Binding, et al. The VOX audio server. *Multimedia '89: 2nd IEEE
    COMSOC Inter. Multimedia Comm. Workshop*, pages 20–23, 1989.

[4] Ning Li. *Computer Method in the Study of Han4-Zi4 – An Intelligent Approach to the Computing of Chinese Writing History.* PhD thesis, Univ. of Kent at Canterbury, 1993.

[5] Architecture Projects Management Limited. *ANSAware 4.0 Application Programmer's Manual.* On-line manual, 1992.

[6] Architecture Projects Management Limited. *An Overview of ANSAware 4.0.* On-line manual, 1992.

[7] P.F.Linington. *Audio facilities for use in Palantir.* internal report of University of Kent (palantir/ukc/050), 1990.

[8] P. Venkat Rangan, Walter A. Burkhard, et al. A testbed for managing digital video and audio storage. *Proceedings of the Summer 1991 USENIX Conference,* pages 199–208, 1991.

[9] John Riedl, Vahid Mashayekhi, et al. SuitSound: A system for distributed collaborative multimedia. *IEEE Transactions on Knowledge and Data Engineering,* 5(4):600–609, 1993.

[10] D Simpson. Multimedia premieres on Unix workstations. *System Integration,* 25(1):32–36, 1992.

[11] Robert Terek and Joseph Pasquale. Experiences with audio conferencing using the X Window System, UNIX, and TCP/IP. *Proceedings of the Summer 1991 USENIX Conference,* pages 405–417, 1991.

[12] Douglas B. Terry and Daniel C. Swinehart. Managing stored voice in the Etherphone system. *ACM Transactions on Computer Systems,* 6(1):3–27, 1988.

[13] Tay Vaughan. *Multimedia Making it Work.* Osbone McGraw-Hill, 1993.

[14] Tom Yager. The multimedia PC: High-powered sight and sound on your desk. *BYTE,* 17(2):217–226, 1992.

Uniform Access to Images within Open Distributed Environments[1]

Rüdiger Strack and Christof Blum
Fraunhofer Institute for Computer Graphics,
Wilhelminenstraße 7, D–64283 Darmstadt, Germany

David Duce and Dale Sutcliffe
Rutherford Appleton Laboratory,
Chilton Didcot, Oxon OX11 0QX, United Kingdom

Narciso García
Universidad Politècnica de Madrid,
E–28040 Madrid, Spain

Abstract. A huge variety of (de facto) standards for image interchange, compression, and communication is employed today in different systems, applications, and environments. Within the AMICS project a framework, called *Image Communication Open Architecture* (ICOA) was elaborated that enables the various standards and standardization activities both in the imaging area and in the wider area of image communication to be related and the necessary support tools to be identified. Although the framework sets a clear emphasis on the handling of images, the ICOA fulfills the image communication requirements from a wide range of application areas including multimedia.

Based on the ICOA framework, software tools that support that framework were developed that focus on different requirements for image communication. Within AMICS, one image communication requirement was perceived to underlie all the others, that of providing uniform access to images whether they are stored locally or remotely. Such uniform access is provided through the *ICOA Image Handling Interface* (IHI). The IHI is realized by means of the *ICOA Image Handler* that is modelled as an *Open Distributed Processing* (ODP) object. The Image Handler encompasses the support of various compression schemes and (image) data formats, as well as different conversion facilities.

1 Introduction

The communication, storage, and manipulation of the information type "digital image" is one of the most challenging tasks within the development of multimedia systems and telecommunication services. If the technological issues on image storage, image communication, and image manipulation (including image compression, image conversion and the synchronization of images with other information types) are solved then the most serious obstacles towards the usage of multimedia technology in open, distributed environments will be removed.

---

[1]The work has been performed within the RACE II project *Advanced Multimedia and Image Communication Services* (AMICS) (R2056) partially supported by the Commission of the European Community (CEC).

A huge variety of image interchange and communication (de facto) standards is employed today in different systems, applications and environments. Most often, these standards have been developed separately and in isolation from each other, each addressing particular needs. Nevertheless, for the development of systems for open image communication, the standardization of compression schemata, data formats and communication protocols turns out to be a key issue.

Within the RACE II project *Advanced Multimedia and Image Communication Services* (AMICS) a framework, called *Image Communication Open Architecture* (ICOA) [16] [17], was elaborated that illuminates the broad area of imaging and image communication. Although the framework sets a clear emphasis on the handling of images, the ICOA fulfills the image communication requirements from a wide range of application areas including multimedia.

Based on the ICOA, software tools that support that framework were developed. The software tools focus on different requirements for image communication.

Within AMICS, one requirement was perceived to underlie all the others, that of providing uniform access to images whether they are stored locally or remotely. By providing such uniform access, communication services can be invoked as necessary, without the knowledge of the application, and other related services such as compression and conversion can be integrated. Such uniform access is provided through the *ICOA Image Handling Interface* (IHI). The IHI is realized by means of the ICOA Image Handler. This paper focuses on the concepts and aspects of the Image Handler.

The remainder of this paper is organized as follows: First, an overview about the ICOA framework is given. The ICOA Image Data Model (IDM) and the relation of the ICOA to open distributed systems are described in more detail. Then, the concepts, functional requirements, and the architecture of the Image Handler are outlined. Finally, a conclusion is given.

2 Image Communication Open Architecture

Standards for imaging and communication have been developed separately and in isolation from each other. Moreover, even the standards for imaging have been developed in an uncoordinated manner, each addressing the needs of a particular application area. Terminology has been developed in different areas such that the same terms are used to mean different things.

Image data is used in widely differing application areas and many diverse requirements are placed upon it. The image data may represent many differing properties and/or data may be organized in various ways. Thus, there are many different uses of image data. Knowledge of the precise properties of a particular use enables the most appropriate encoding scheme to be employed for storage or transfer of the image data. Many of these encodings have been designed with a particular use in mind and without regard to a more general framework. It is believed that, by looking at the whole field of images and image communication, a framework encompassing the various requirements can be derived.

AMICS gives the opportunity, through its work to develop an *Image Communication Open Architecture* (ICOA) to characterize images, leading to the production of a framework, which identifies the operations on images, and to relate these operations to the required standards. The ICOA enables the various standards and standardization activities both in the imaging area and in the area of image communication to be related and the necessary support tools to be identified.

The ICOA embraces the widest range of digital images fulfilling the image communication requirements from different application areas including multimedia. Several standards were inspected with respect to images according to information and data structures, communication and other aspects, such as storage, processing, and management. Services were inspected in order to identify specific requirements for image communication. The concepts of open, distributed systems were inspected in regard to image handling. A mathematical model of an image and the operations that might be carried out on that image was developed. A comprehensive, generic image data model was defined to provide broad and flexible data structures which can be used to describe any kind of digital image. A reference model for image formats which comprises a set of distinct criteria (image format characteristics) was derived, which can be used to characterize existing image interchange formats. The project decided to restrict the ICOA at this stage to end–to–end communication. As advanced communication services become available (e.g. video on demand) there will be a greater use of end–to–end communication in the TV–world.

The functional building blocks of the ICOA are described in detail in [16] [17].

3 ICOA Image Data Model

The ICOA Image Data Model (IDM) provides broad and flexible data structures and attributes which can be used to describe any kind of digital image used in the area of imaging and image communication. The IDM allows the description of images according to the derived mathematical model for digital images. Also, it defines all relevant attributes (e.g. identifiers, metric descriptions, channel descriptions, colour model, etc.). Furthermore, the model is independent of data encodings.

A broad and flexible image data model is defined within the *Image Processing and Interchange Standard* (IPI) which has reached the status of a "Draft International Standard" (DIS) by November 1992 [10]. The IPI will reach the status of an "International Standard" (IS) by April 1994. The IDM is in part based on this generic data model, since the latter has most of the characteristics considered important for the IDM. However, the scope of the ICOA is much wider than the scope of the IPI. For this reason, extensions to the IPI data model have been elaborated and integrated into the IDM. These extensions address the support of interlaced/time–variant data, non–linear relationships for external spatial references, and undefined values for the image domain. The concepts and data types of the IDM are introduced below.

3.1 Image data types

The IDM uses a mechanism to constructively define image data types in order not to be limited to particular applications. Comparable constructive descriptions can be found in well–known areas, e.g., the CSG method (*constructive solid geometry*) for computer graphics and CAD applications.
Three categories of data types are defined within the IDM:

- basic data types: basic data types are either elementary or compound. The definitions of the basic data types directly comply with the *Common Language–Independent Data Types* (CLIDT) [9] that are currently being standardized within ISO/IEC JTC1/SC22. The elementary data types defined within the ICOA Image Data Model are bit, boolean, character, real, complex, enumerated, null, integer, real, state). Data types constructed by one of the mechanisms $N_1 \times \ldots \times N_n$ array, choice, list, range, record, table are called compound data types.

- image data types and associated attributes: image data types are either fundamental or compound.

  A fundamental image data type consists of arrays and records whereby the dimensions of all arrays refer to the same coordinate space and record components refer to the bands (of a multi–band image). The arrays of the bands may differ in size and element structure but not in dimensionality. The leaves of a fundamental image data type are elementary data types. A fundamental image data type includes a region of definition (ROD) which indicates for each pixel in the image whether that pixel is defined or not.

  A compound image data type describes an image, in which the following construction mechanisms are used to combine images, which may themselves be either fundamental or compound: $N_1 \times \ldots \times N_n$ array, list, and record. The images to be grouped to not refer to the same coordinate space. The leaves of a compound image data type are fundamental images. The definitions comply with the definitions of the forthcoming IS document of the third part of the IPI standard, IIF.

  Image attributes are attached to the image data types. They carry information on how to correctly interpret the associated image data. The IDM defines the following image attributes:

  - metric attribute: the metric attribute provides all information regarding the spatial nature of an image.

  - channel attribute: an image may be composed of several channels of data. The channel attribute provides the information about the capture–related attributes (sensor models) underlying the channels of an image.

  - colour attribute: the colour attribute provides the information necessary to reproduce a colour image accurately.

- fidelity attribute: different kinds of techniques may be used to represent the image data. The fidelity attribute provides the information necessary to describe the image data representation.

- image–related data types: Image–related data types cover data which may be used in conjunction with a digital image as input or output parameters for any operation performed on images. The IDM defines the following image–related non–image data types:

  - look–up table: a look–up table is defined as a structure that contains pairs of entries. The first entry of the pair is an input value to be matched, while the second contains a corresponding output value.

  - region of interest: a region of interest (ROI) is a general mechanism for selecting specific pixels, comprising a boolean value for each each pixel location of the image which indicates whether or not that pixel is in the ROI.
  A ROI may or may not be anchored to a particular point in the image.

  - feature list: a feature list is defined as a collection of pairs of elements. The first element of the pair is a coordinate of a pixel, while the second refers to a basic data type storing the associated feature.

3.2 Operations on images

Since images are used within many types of applications it is helpful to consider the types of operations that are applied to images. The *Computer Graphics Reference Model* (CGRM) [12] identifies six classes of operations. The ICOA is restricted to supporting the transfer of images between those classes of operations which use or produce images.

It is helpful to understand the operations that are applied to images as a precursor to discussing communication services. Image communication is the ability to perform image operations across a communications channel.

The motivation for thinking about operations on images is the concept of *abstract data types* (ADT). The idea behind ADTs is that data are characterized by both the values they can take and the operations that can be applied to the data values. In this approach, data values are constructed and retrieved through operations, thus enabling a separation between the precise details of the representation of data values and the operations through which data are accessed, constructed and manipulated.

The most important general groups of image handling operations are

- image operations (*createImage, deleteImage*)

- image attribute operations (*inquireAttributes, setAttributes*)

- image structure operations (*groupImage*)

- image data manipulation operations (*retrieveImage, storeImage*)

The *createImage* operation creates an "empty" image with specified characteristics. The characteristics are essentially the image structure and the image attributes in the ICOA Data Model. The purpose of the image characterization is to define the semantics of the image and includes entities such as the dimensionality of the image, identification of the coordinate axes, the base vectors (and hence lattice structure), the range of the base vector coefficients generating the region of the lattice over which the image extends, spatial reference, and data type of the pixel values. The result of the operation is an image consisting of image data (null values at all the lattice points within the extent of the image) and values of image attributes corresponding to the specified characteristics.

The *deleteImage* operation deletes the image. All data related to the image, i.e. pixel data and attributes will be removed.

The *inquireAttributes* operation returns the characteristics of a specified image. The values returned are the values of the attributes of the image. The information returned by this operation might well be used in a communications environment to negotiate the best way in which to carry out a particular operation.

The *groupImage* operation is used to compose already existing images — either fundamental or compound images — using a constructor mechanism as described in Section 3.1 to build compound images respectively image families and image sets.

The image data returned by *retrieveImage* and specified with *storeImage* are an n-dimensional array of tuples whose type corresponds to the type of the pixels of the image each operates upon. The *retrieveImage* operation returns the pixel values of particular lattice points defined by a ROI. The *storeImage* operation sets the pixel values at the lattice points in the image corresponding to the specified ROI. The new pixel values overwrite the previously defined (or undefined) value at that point.

The purpose of the IDM is to model in a programming language independent manner, the types of data that are specified as parameters to these basic operations.

4 ICOA and Open Distributed Systems

Information processing within an open environment has to deal with the two general aspects distribution and heterogeneity. Hereby, distribution encompasses e.g. the distribution of resources, processing, archiving, usage (or users), management, and administration; heterogeneity includes e.g. heterogeneous computers, operation systems, networks, end systems, user interfaces, APIs, and software tools.

The reasons to support both aspects are manifold. There may be, for example, the necessity to share resources, the need to improve the system reliability by replicating resources, the necessity to optimize access to specialized resources, the requirement to multiply the performance for information processing and archiving, and/or specific resources may be only available from distinct manufacturers or enterprises.

4.1 Concepts of open, distributed processing

The area of building heterogeneous distributed systems from unlike components in a standardized way has been addressed by the *Advanced Network Systems Architecture* (ANSA) [5] [1] that started in 1985. ANSA focuses on the development of software which sits between the application and the collection of hardware and networks which support it. Many of the concepts of ANSA have influenced and guided the development of international — i.e. the forthcoming ISO/IEC and ITU–T standard *Basic Reference Model of Open Distributed Processing* [13] [6] [7] [8]) and de–facto standards (e.g. OMG CORBA [14], OSF DCE [15]). Adopting an open standards–based approach for distributed systems has significant benefits for the user, e.g. vendor independence, technology independence, user support, availability of new applications, and ease of application development.

The objective of the work on *Open Distributed Processing* (ODP) is to provide a framework for the standardization of distributed systems. The ISO/IEC and ITU–T standard *Basic Reference Model of ODP* (RM–ODP) provides such a framework.

In order to fulfill the requirements and characteristics of distributed systems, an architectural approach to standardization is used. This involves a framework or model, supported by suitable concepts and terminology, within which interfaces for further standardization effort and the relationships between them are identified.

Viewpoints The RM–ODP defines distributed processing as follows ([6]):

> *Distributed processing comprises that class of information processing activities in which discrete components may be located at more than one location, or where there is any reason which necessitates explicit communication among the components.*

To describe the full complexity of a system that supports distributed processing may be rather intricate. Therefore, the RM–ODP defines the concept of *viewpoints* that reflect a specific set of design concerns. A viewpoint (on a system) is defined within RM–ODP ([6], Page 2) as *a form of abstraction achieved using a selected set of architectural concepts and structuring rules, in order to focus on particular concerns within a system*. The following viewpoints are defined ([13], Page 19):

- Enterprise viewpoint: focuses on the expression of purpose, policy, and boundary for an open distributed system.

- Information viewpoint: focuses on the expression of information and information processing functions in a distributed system.

- Computational viewpoint: focuses on the expression of the functional decomposition of an ODP System, and of the interworking and portability of ODP functions.

- Engineering viewpoint: focuses on the expression of the infrastructure required to support distributed processing.

- Technology viewpoint: focuses on the expression of technologies to support aspects of open distributed processing.

The most significant viewpoints from the ICOA perspective are the information viewpoint, the computational viewpoint, and the engineering viewpoint. While the information viewpoint of the ICOA describes the information flow in the context of images, the computational viewpoint identifies the functions and data types of applications independently of the computer system on which the applications run. The IDM as a generic data model for images encompassing a set of functions that are used for image handling, can be seen from the computational viewpoint. The engineering viewpoint identifies the system components that enable the distribution of operations and data. Here, transparency and communication mechanisms that play a major role for digital images have been discussed.

Transparency   A transparency is defined within RM–ODP as *the property of hiding from a particular user the potential behaviour of some parts of the system* ([6], Page 12). The concept is limited for the various forms of distribution transparency, namely access transparency, failure transparency, federation transparency, group transparency, migration transparency, replication transparency, resource transparency, and transaction transparency.
Within the context of the ICOA, access and location transparency are further discussed. These are defined within the RM–ODP ([13], Page 3) as follows:

- access transparency: a transparency which masks differences in data representation and invocation mechanisms to enable interworking between heterogeneous computer system.

- location transparency: a transparency which masks interface location (including the distinction between local and remote invocations), to enable location–independent interface identification and continued use of interfaces after their relocation.

Modelling concepts and the client–server model   Within the RM–ODP, an object defines a set of services that can be offered to clients of the object in the form of interfaces. Each interface comprises the set of operations that may be invoked by other objects. Each object encapsulates its data and the operations to act on that data. The information contained by an object is only accessible via invocation of the services provided by the interface of the object. Thus, the way the service is provided is internal to the object.
All objects interact in the same way. Two different roles have to be distinguished in the context of object interaction. When objects interact, one object acts as a client, the other as the server. Objects can act as a client in one interaction and as a server in the other direction. In addition to interacting to each other,

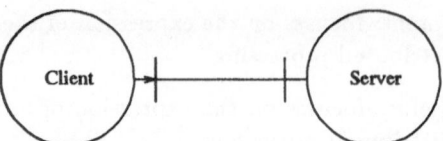

Fig. 1.: Simple client–server model.

objects interact with their environment. These interactions are rules by means
of a contract. One type of contract encompasses particular QoS properties of
invocations such as jitter, resolution, timing constraints, etc.
Fig. 1 illustrates a simple–client server model. Objects (i.e. client and server)
are denoted by circles, object interfaces by ⊢, and interrogation modes (request
directions) by arrows.
The trading concept within the RM–ODP is used to link objects. The trader
keeps a listing of what services are available. This is used to find suitable servers
to meet requests from clients.

4.2   The ICOA Image Handler within open distributed systems

In general, the purpose of the Image Handler is the storage and retrieval of digital
images whether they are stored locally or remotely. Thus, the Image Handler
can be regarded as a communication service or component able to handle the
broad range of images defined in the IDM, thus providing a sophisticated, general
handling facility which can be used as a kernel for any application dealing with
the handling of digital images. Also, the Image Handler provides the basic set
of operations necessary for the storage, retrieval and control of images (similar
to those described in Section 3.2).

The Image Handler as an ODP object   As described in Section 4.1 an
object defines a set of services that can be offered to clients in form of interfaces.
Thus, the Image Handler can be regarded as as object whose interface, called
Image Handling Interface (IHI), provides the basic set of operations for the
handling of digital images. Thus, the Image Handler acts as a server offering
an image handling interface to clients, i.e. various applications. This aspect is
illustrated in Fig. 2.

Selective transparencies   From a certain point of view, using selective transparencies (see Section 4.1) the communication aspect of the Image Handler may
not be of interest. As a result of location transparency, the computational model of the two interacting objects client (i.e. any application) and server (i.e.
Image Handler) with the IHI, as illustrated in Fig. 3, can be mapped into an
engineering specification where distribution is explicit (see Fig. 4).
This may be, however, not feasible in the context of the handling of the broad
range of images provided by the Image Handler. Thus, from the service specification point of view, a further refinement of the interfaces regarding explicit

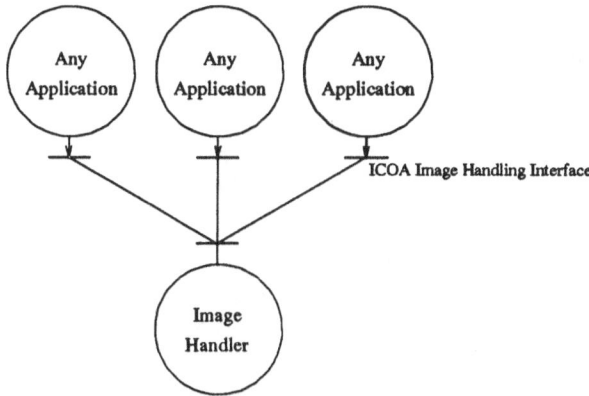

Fig. 2.: The Image Handler used by various applications.

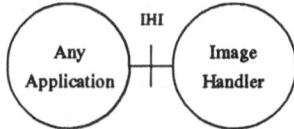

Fig. 3.: Computational model providing location transparency.

reference to communication, i.e. supporting the *visibility* of the separation of components, together with selecting mechanisms to bridge the separation, may be necessary. Then, communication comes into play explicitly in the computational viewpoint. Hereby, especially the requirements for image communication that were identified within the ICOA framework — transmission bit–rates, timing constraints (e.g. delay, jitter, throughput), synchronization requirements (e.g. type, quality), — have to be taken into account for the specification of an IHI. The computational objects (see Fig. 4) — i.e. the communication objects — should be specified in such a way that they are able to negotiate specific QoS parameters that result from an analysis of the image communication requirements. The communication objects itself may interact with the environment in form of a contract (see Section 4.1) that encompasses particular properties.

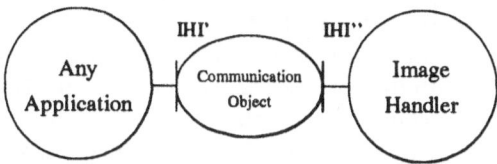

Fig. 4.: Engineering model resulting from a computational model providing location transparency.

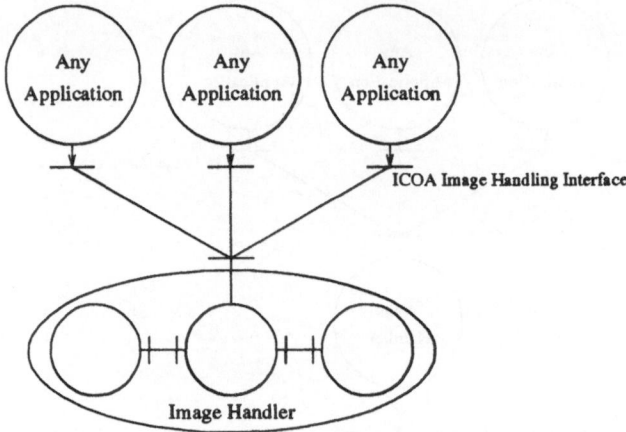

Fig. 5.: Decomposition of the ODP object Image Handler.

Decomposition criteria Various different image formats are in use today. The Image Handler provides a means to describe the images stored in the different image formats by the IDM. Thus, it provides a common view on different image formats.

To support the different image formats, the Image Handler may be regarded as a configuration of objects, i.e. a *composite* ODP object. In other words, the Image Handler as an ODP object may be internally decomposed into objects that support the specific features of an image file format in an optimized manner. The internal interfaces are hidden. The external view to the Image Handler object is still provided by the IIH. This aspect is illustrated in Fig. 5.

5   The Architecture of the Image Handler

The ICOA Image Handling Interface (IHI) provides for the storage, retrieval, and control of images whether they are stored locally or remotely. This includes the storage and retrieval of image data, the creation and deletion of images, the setting and inquiry of image attributes, and the creation of compound images by grouping of existing images. The IHI is realized by means of the ICOA Image Handler. This section focuses on the architecture of the Image Handler.

First, the different representation layers in regard to the architecture are described. Then, the architecture of the Image Handler is described from the viewpoint of open distributed processing. Moreover, since the ICOA fulfills the image communication requirements from a wide range of application areas including multimedia, the Image Handler is inspected in regard to its use within a multimedia environment.

5.1   Representation layers

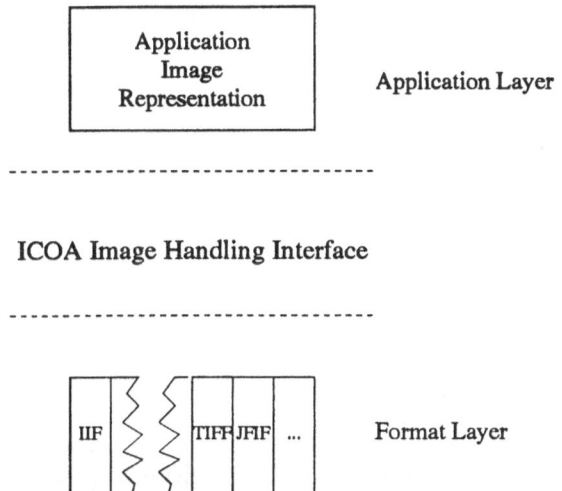

Fig. 6.: Representation layers in regard to the Image Handler.

Within the ICOA the relationship between image, data format, compression, and conversion was depicted. According to these definitions the following representation layers in regard to the Image Handler have to be distinguished:

- Application layer: Each application may have its own application specific data types for the representation of images. Thus, not all images dealt with by an application will be ICOA images and hence handled through the IHI. ICOA images are characterized by the property of 'open communicability'. They can be passed through the IHI between applications and between different parts of the same application.

- ICOA Image Handling Interface: The IHI provides the user — the application programmer — with a uniform interface for the handling of images, that is based on the IDM. Thus, it supplies broad and flexible data structures which can be used to describe any kind of digital image and the basic set of operations necessary for the storage, retrieval and control of images. Since the Image Handler provides a means to describe images stored in different data formats by the IDM, it establishes a common view on different data formats.

- Format layer: The data format layer focuses on the representation of images within a distinct (image) data file/interchange format. The Image Handler provides access to different data formats. Thus, it is not tied to a specific format. This is necessary in order to provide access to already existing image archives, databases, etc.

The different representation layers in regard to the Image Handler are illustrated in Fig. 6.

5.2 Image data handling and conversion within the Image Handler

The design of the Image Handler in regard to the handling of image data has to consider the current status of data handling by applications. Thus, not all images dealt with by an application will be ICOA images and hence handled through the IHI. Specific image devices (sinks, sources) dealt with by those applications may be restricted to support only raw or compressed data. Thus, the Image Handler allows raw and compressed data to be passed through the IHI, in a form and representation which is understandable to the application.

Different compression schemes might be applied in parallel to compress an image. In fact, this holds for ICOA images since the IDM allows different data units of an image to be compressed differently. Conversion comes into play, if the compression scheme[2] used by the application does not match the compression schemes supported by the data format. In this case, either the application or the Image Handler has to provide the necessary conversion functionality.

The Image Handler was established with the ultimate goal to provide uniform access for the wide range of digital images. As a consequence, the Image Handler has to accommodate the flexibility needed to access the variety of data formats supporting different compression schemes. Also, the application should be freed from complex conversion tasks. Therefore, conversion is provided by the Image Handler underneath the IHI. The application may have control of conversion processes, by appropriately setting up the environment in which conversion takes place, but the details of conversion are hidden from the application. It should be possible for applications to function totally unaware of any conversions taking place, if they so desire, by providing appropriate default settings for conversion processes.

Dealing with various data formats supporting different compression schemes, an open concept concerning conversion within the Image Handler was elaborated. Compressed data is passed through the IHI together with the specific set of parameters used by the respective compression scheme to control the (de)compression. This provides for the inclusion of additional, forthcoming compression schemes.

The use of a particular compression scheme for image data does not rely on the use of a particular data format. All compression schemes that are supported by the Image Handler can be used by the application. If a particular compression scheme for image data is requested by the application that is not used or supported by the data format used to store the image the conversion mechanism is invoked.

5.3 Communication mechanisms of the Image Handler

The Image Handler provides for the storage, retrieval, and control of images whether they are stored locally or remotely. For this reason, the Image Handler provides sophisticated communication mechanisms underneath the IHI.

---

[2] This includes the representation of raw data defined as a specific compression scheme.

Within Section 4.2 the Image Handler was discussed as an ODP object offering the basic set of operations for the handling of digital images by its interface, i.e. the IHI, to various applications. In an ideal world, image communication would be simple. Every site a user wishing to transfer images from would offer an ODP object Image Handler, that would process requests and return results accessed by the Image Handler through the IHI. Unfortunately, this is not the case.

For this reason, an alternative approach to the problem of image communication has been developed. The aim of this approach is to provide the appearance of the ODP object Image Handler, although the underlying services, called *Image Handling Services*, may not all be in place. This allows applications to be written independently of services available at any one time. As a service becomes available, it is used transparently by the Image Handler, without any changes needing to be made to an application. Provision of such a concept could make use of the trading facilities for locating suitable service providers.

The following scenario may illustrate this concept: An application requests a subset of an image located at a particular site. The Image Handler requests the trader to find what services for transferring images are available at the given site. If an Image Handling Service is available, it can be used to transfer only the subset of image by reducing the volume of data transferred. If a Image Handling Service is unavailable, the Image Handler may have to fall back to an available, common, lower level of service, such as FTP[4] or FTAM[11]. A bulk transfer of the entire image would be performed and the subset would be extracted from the image using local services.

The outlined concept results in the decomposition of the Image Handler as described in the following Section.

Decomposition of the Image Handler   The Image Handler supports various data formats (see Section 5.1). The requirements of the data formats in regard to image structure, image attributes, compression schemes, QoS parameters, etc. differ. Thus, data formats represent one adequate criteria in regard to the decomposition of the Image Handler.

Conversion between various compression schemata can be regarded as another functional building block of the Image Handler (see Section 5.2). Conversion can be performed either in software or with the support of specific hardware (i.e. the AMICS DIP chip [3]). For this reason, various conversion facilities may coexist. Considering these aspects, the Image Handler is decomposed as follows:

- For each data format a distinct ODP object is established, that provides the functionality of the Image Handling Service in regard to the respective data format.

- An ODP object in regard to conversion is established.

The resulting Image Handler is depicted in Fig. 7.

In regard to the interaction between the different objects of the Image Handler the following clients/servers can be distinguished:

- The application as a client of the Image Handler

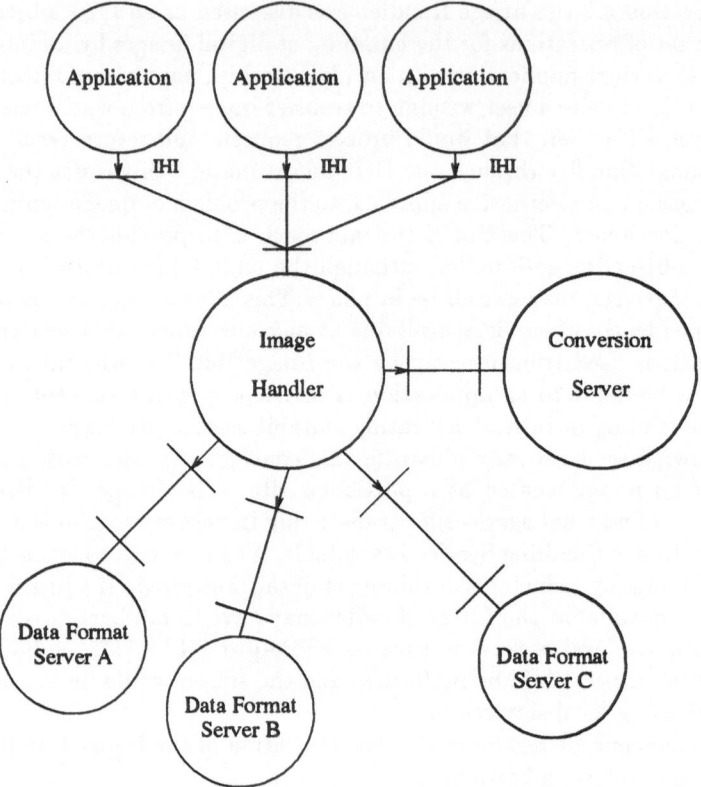

Fig. 7.: Decomposition of the Image Handler into specialized ODP objects.

- The Image Handler as a client of the conversion server

- The Image Handler as a client of the data format server

The trading concept is used to establish the links between the different Image Handler objects.

Trading Within RM–ODP, the trading concept is used to link objects within a distributed system. Objects interact on the basis of a client requesting a service from another, which is acting as a server (see Section 4.1). A very important service provider within RM–ODP is the trader object. The role of the trader is to locate other service providers when requested. The trader keeps a listing of what services are available. The list is used to find suitable service providers to meet requests from clients. It is kept up to date by periodic updates from the service providers advertising that they are available for use.

The Image Handler makes usage of the trading concept since it is of great advantage for its communication concept. The trader is called upon by the Image Handler to find a suitable service provider. The trader keeps a list of all available Image Handler service providers. This includes other Image Handlers, data format services, and conversion services. If more than one service provider for a distinct Image Handler request exists, the trader evaluates some other relevant criterion. A choice may be made dependent on several (QoS) factors:

- basic QoS factors in regard to temporal requirements like delay, delay jitter, throughput (bandwidth), etc.

- error handling requirements like treatment of corruption, loss, and alteration of transmitted data sequences and the provision of respective recovery mechanisms

- costs (network, provision, etc.)

The concept established enables different Image Handler to use the same data format and conversion service providers. Applications are not allowed to trade an Image Handler. Thus, there is only one Image Handler per application. Nevertheless, several Image Handler may be realized. Thus, Image Handlers can coexist. Fig. 8 illustrates the coexistence of different Image Handler that share data format and conversion service providers.

5.4 The Image Handler within multimedia environments

The usage of the Image Handler within a multimedia environment is illustrated in Fig. 9. The Image Handler acts as one media handler that is responsible for the entire range of digital images.

The necessary functionality for the interlinking of multimedia objects is provided by an object called *Multimedia Handler*. The Multimedia Handler provides the necessary multi/hypermedia functionality for the handling of different media objects. This encompasses aspects like

- time synchronization,

- spatial synchronization,

- navigation, and

- content location.

The different media handlers have to provide hooks necessary for the realization of these aspects. For the Image Handler, these hooks are provided e.g. by the path object, providing for the addressing of any part of an image.

5.5 Implementation aspects

The aim of the communication concept established for the Image Handler is to provide the appearance of the ODP object Image Handler, although the underlying Image Handling Services may not all be in place (see Section 5.3). Trading facilities are of great advantage for the realization of this concept (see Section

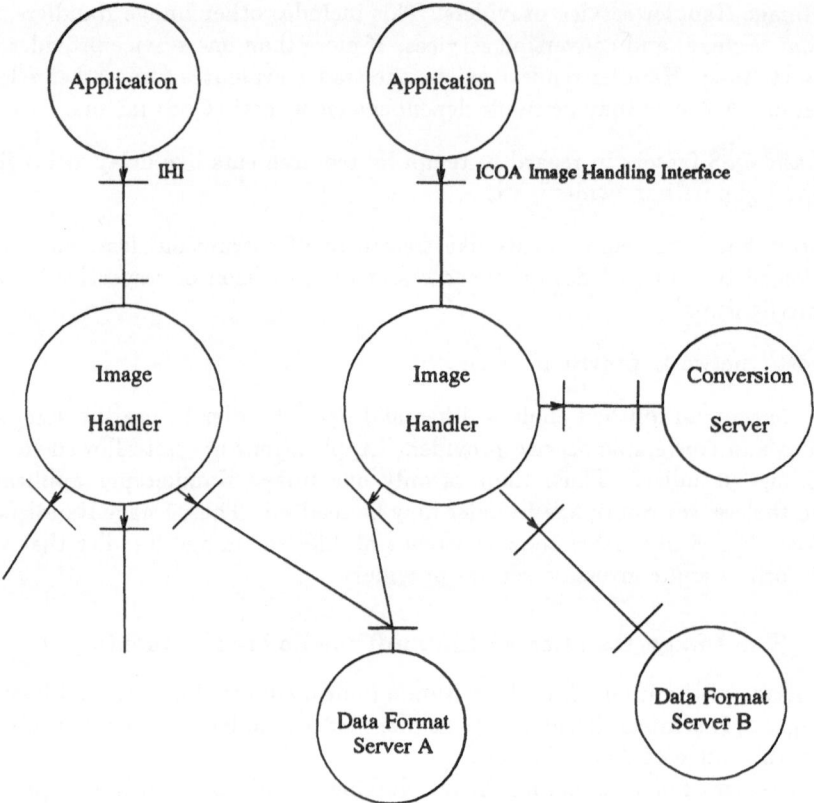

Fig. 8.: Coexistence of Image Handler and sharing of resources.

5.3). As a consequence, a distributed computing environment for the development of distributed systems and services providing trading facilities was chosen for the realization of the Image Handler.

Although several distributed computing environments are available (e.g. DCE[15], OMG CORBA[14], ANSAware[1]), only OMG's *Common Object Request Broker Architecture* (CORBA) and ANSAware provide adequate trading facilities. This encompasses e.g. the evaluation of distinct criteria for the selection of a particular service, for example QoS, by the trader.

Within AMICS, ANSAware was used as the development environment. ANSAware can be briefly characterized as an engineering platform of ODP[3] providing — among other features — client/server concepts, trading and federation.

Within Fig. 7 the decomposition of the Image Handler into specialized ODP objects, namely Image Handler, conversion server, and data format server was illustrated. In regard to interfaces providing communication protocols, the following interfaces have to be distinguished:

---

[3]Many of the concepts of ANSA were incorporated into ODP–RM.

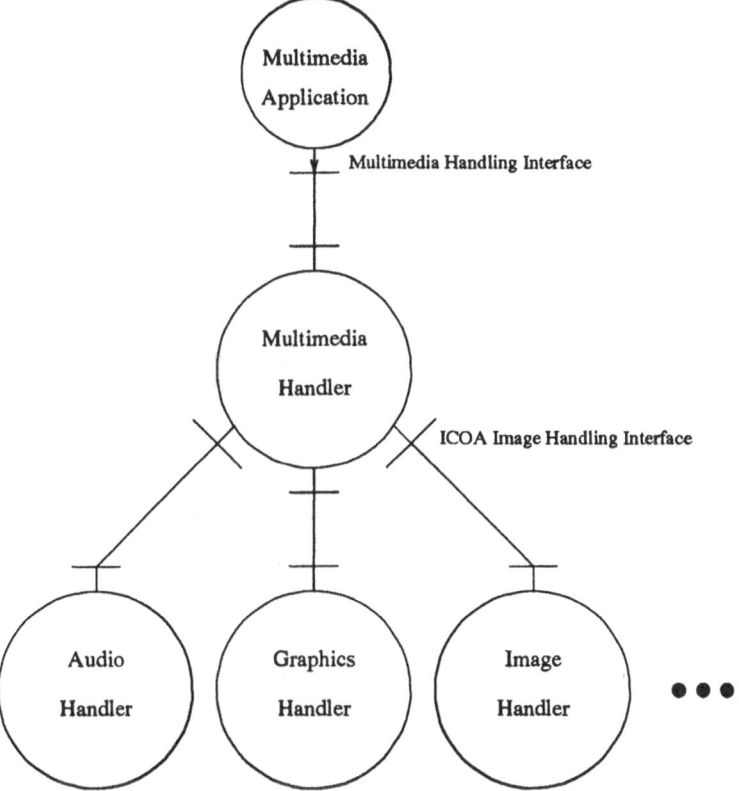

Fig. 9.: The Image Handler within a multimedia environment.

- ICOA Image Handling Interface
- Data format interface(s)
- Conversion interface

The application programmer makes use of the IHI. A C++ language binding of the IHI was established. The data format interfaces represent a subset of the IHI. Only those image data structures, image attributes, and data encodings are supported by these interfaces that are provided by the respective data format(s). The conversion interface consists of one sophisticated function.

The object interfaces — in regard to the communication aspects of the Image Handler — are specified using the IDL of ANSAware. For the realization of the Image Handler, location transparency is provided from the computational viewpoint. This is mapped into an engineering specification where distribution is explicit. This aspect was elucidated in Section 4.2 (see Fig. 3 and Fig. 4).

A *Data Format Access Layer* is defined within the Image Handler object. This layer is responsible to map the Image Handler representations to the respective data format interfaces. This includes means to contact the trader that links to a specific data format service.

Conversion between various compression schemes can be performed by the Image Handler either in software or with the support of specific hardware, i.e. the DIP chip board [3]. For the hardware solution specific algorithms have been developed that are built on top of the DIP–chip board. These are described in [2].

The conversion interface will be realized by means of a pure software solution or the conversion algorithms that run on the DIP chip board. Support of other special purpose chips could be provided in a similar way.

A data format server usually supports one distinct (image) data format. However, the concept of the Image Handler allows that one data format server is not restricted to one file format. A data format server has to provide the specified uniform interface. This is realized by means that the distinct characteristics of the data format(s), i.e. image structures, image attributes and image data encodings, are mapped to the IDM.

For the realization of the Image Handler data formats have been chosen, that provide a variety of digital images, i.e. moving images, multispectral images, binary images, etc.

6 Conclusion

The wide and broad background of the different partners within AMICS enabled the project to explore the huge area of imaging and image communication. Having used this background, the ICOA as a general framework for the areas of imaging and image communication was established.

Based on the ICOA, the Image Handler that supports that framework was developed. The Image Handler provides uniform access to images whether they are stored locally or remotely. The Image Handler can be regarded as a communication service or component able to handle the broad range of images defined in the ICOA Data Model (IDM), thus providing a sophisticated, general handling facility which can be used as a kernel for any application dealing with the handling of digital images. The Image Handler addresses open communication aspects for the broad range of digital images encompassing the handling of various compression schemes and image formats, as well as different conversion facilities.

7 Acknowledgements

The work reflected in this paper has been performed within the RACE II project *Advanced Multimedia and Image Communication Services* (AMICS) supported by the Commission of the European Community (CEC).

AMICS is performed by the following partners: Fraunhofer Institute for Computer Graphics (IGD), Darmstadt, Germany; Rutherford Appleton Laboratory (RAL), Chilton, United Kingdom; Tampere University of Technology (TUT), Finland; Telenorma GmbH (TN), Frankfurt, Germany; Universidad Politècnica de Madrid (UPM), Spain; and University of Sheffield (US), United Kingdom.

Many colleagues namely Ralf Cordes (TN), John Cullan (RAL), Irek Defée (TUT), Julian Gallop (RAL), Robert Maybury (RAL), Luc Neumann (IGD), María J. Pérez–Luque (UPM), Hauke Peyn (TN), and Rob Yates (US) from the AMICS project have contributed to this paper in technical discussions.

References

[1] *ANSA: object pioneers*, volume 7. Technology Appraisals Ltd., February 1993.

[2] I. Defée, editor. Strategies and Architectures for Conversion in ICOA. Deliverable R2056/TUT/DS/P/006/b1, RACE Project R2056 Advanced Multimedia Image Communication Services (AMICS), December 1993.

[3] S. Evans, N.A. Thacker, R. Yates, and P.A. Ivey. A Massively Parallel Vector Processor for Image Communications. In *Proceedings of the 2nd International Conference on Image Communication (IMAGE'COM 93)*, pages 303–308, Bordeaux, March 1993. SEE, IREST, ADERA.

[4] *FTP (File Transfer Protocol)*, Request for Comments (RFC) 959. Internet Network Working Group, October 1985.

[5] Andrew Herbert. Communication Aspects of ANSA. *Cmputer Standards & Interfaces*, 8:49–56, 1988.

[6] *ISO/IEC CD 10746-2: Information Technology — Information Retrieval, Transfer and Management for OSI — Basic Reference Model of Open Distributed Processing ODP, Part 2: Descriptive Model*. ISO/IEC, June 1993.

[7] *ISO/IEC CD 10746-3: Information Technology — Information Retrieval, Transfer and Management for OSI — Basic Reference Model of Open Distributed Processing ODP, Part 3: Prescriptive Model*. ISO/IEC, June 1993.

[8] *ISO/IEC CD 10746-4: Information Technology — Information Retrieval, Transfer and Management for OSI — Basic Reference Model of Open Distributed Processing ODP, Part 4: Architectural Semantics, Specification Techniques and Formalisms*. ISO/IEC, June 1993.

[9] *ISO/IEC CD 11404: Information Technology — Programming Languages — Common Language-Independent Data Types (CLIDT)*. ISO/IEC, 1991.

[10] *ISO/IEC DIS 12087-1: Information Technology — Computer Graphics and Image Processing — Image Processing and Interchange (IPI) — Functional Specification — Part 1: Common Architecture for Imaging (CAI)*. ISO/IEC, November 1992.

[11] *ISO/IEC IS 8571-1: Information Processing Systems — Open Systems Interconnection (OSI) — File Transfer, Access and Management (FTAM) — Part 1: General Introduction*. ISO/IEC, 1988.

[12] *ISO/IEC IS 11072: Information Technology — Computer Graphics — Computer Graphics Reference Model.* ISO/IEC, 1992.

[13] *ISO/IEC WD 10746-1: Information Technology — Information Retrieval, Transfer and Management for OSI — Basic Reference Model of Open Distributed Processing ODP, Part 1: Overview and Guide to Use.* ISO/IEC, August 1993.

[14] OMG. *The Common Object Request Broker: Architecture and Specification,* December 1991. draft.

[15] W. Rosenberry, D. Kenney, and G. Fisher. *Understanding DCE.* O'Reilly & Associates, Inc., May 1993.

[16] R. Strack, C. Blum, D. Duce, D. Sutcliffe, N. García, M.J. Pérez-Luque, E. Moeller, and H. Peyn. Image Communication Open Architecture. *Computer and Graphics,* 18(1), 1994.

[17] R. Strack editor, C. Blum, R. Cordes, I. Defée, D.A. Duce, N. García, G.R. Hofmann, R. Maybury, E. Moeller, M.J. Pérez-Luque, D.C. Sutcliffe, and R. Strack. Conceptual Building Blocks for an Image Communication Open Architecture (ICOA). Deliverable R2056/FhG/IGD/DS/P/002/b1, RACE Project R2056 Advanced Multimedia Image Communication Services (AMICS), April 1993.

COOLIS: a distributed multimedia object–oriented layer

Nour Didi[*], Maurizzio DeCecco[**], Antoine Rizk
EUROCLID, 12 Avenue des Prés
78180 Montigny le Bretonneux, France
email : rizk@nuri.inria.fr, Tel: ++.33.1.30.44.14.56, Fax: ++33.1.30.57.18.63

Anne Béguin, Eric Pillevesse
SEPT, 42 rue des Coutures
14066 Caen Cedex, France
email : beguin@sept.fr, Tel: ++.33.31.75.91.85, Fax: ++33.31.75.06.31

Abstract. This paper describes the architecture and implementation of a toolkit, COOLIS, for the support of multimedia objects in a distributed object–oriented platform. The design of the toolkit is derived from real user requirements for the implementation of CIDRE[1], a distributed multimedia cooperative system, for the circulation of documents and folders in large companies. Both CIDRE and COOLIS are implemented and fully running on the COOL/Chorus[2] platform at SEPT[3].

In addition to a description of the basic architecture and implementation of COOLIS, a discussion and comparison will be given for the major design issues such as access transparency, quality of service, synchronisation mechanisms and object migration.

COOLIS has been largely inspired from the ANSA[4] computational model within the ESPRIT ISA2[5] project. We give here a brief description of how COOLIS would fit the ANSA computational model.

1 Introduction

This paper describes the architecture and implementation of a toolkit, COOLIS, for support of multimedia objects in a distributed object–oriented platform. The design of the toolkit is derived from real user requirements for the implementation of CIDRE, a distributed multimedia cooperative system, for the circulation of documents and folders in large companies. Both CIDRE and COOLIS are implemented and fully running on the COOL/Chorus platform at SEPT. Before

---

[*] Also with LITP, Université Pierre et Marie Curie, 4, Place Jussieu 75252 Paris, France
[**] Now with IRCAM 1, Place Igor Stravinski, 75004 Paris, France

[1] Circulation Intelligente de Dossiers REpartis
[2] Chorus Object–Oriented Layer
[3] Service d'Etudes communes à la Poste et à France Télécom
[4] Advanced Network Systems Architecture
[5] Integrated Systems Architecture

proceeding to the description of COOLIS, we give here a short background on Chorus, COOL and CIDRE.

1.1 Chorus

The Chorus system offers the fundamental basis services needed for an operating system to support distributed and / or real–time applications. The genericity of these services allows different operating systems to be implemented on their basis. The Chorus kernel [16, 17] provides the following services:

- Management of address spaces. A generic memory management interface is offered, allowing various memory management policies to be implemented, from simple single unprotected scheme to distributed virtual memory.

- Management of execution threads. The Chorus kernel manages the scheduling of independant execution threads, multiple threads being allowed to share a given address space. A simple interface is used to synchronise the threads execution.

- Location transparent IPC (Inter–Process Communication). A single programming interface is used regardless of whether a given communication between threads is to be local or distant. The system optimizes local communication.

- Facilities and sufficient response time for "real–time" programming. A "system" user can program exception handling and interrupts, the mechanisms of low–level I/O, and modify them dynamically.

1.2 COOL

The *Chorus Object Oriented Layer* (COOL) is an extension of the facilities provided by the Chorus distributed operating system with additionnal functionalities for the support of object oriented environnements. These functionnalities are realized by a layer built on top of the Chorus kernel, which extends the Chorus interface with generic functions for object management: creation, deletion, storage, remote invocation and migration.

COOL [2, 12] has been designed for developers of distributed object–oriented applications. COOL applications are written in COOL C++, i.e. C++ with a number of additions. COOL C++ enables programmers to create C++ objects that benefit from the COOL support platform, enabling them to migrate between machines, to be dynamically attached to running programs, stored in persistent memory, and messaged transparently within the distributed system. In addition, COOL C++ supports a notion of active objects enabling parallel applications and grouped migration or messaging of groups of objects.

COOL runs above the Chorus micro–kernel [11] which provides the minimum set of abstractions needed to build distributed operating systems, these include naming, ressource allocation, messaging, threads and memory. COOL builds upon and extends these system abstractions and makes them available to language run–times as an extended system call interface.

The base abstractions that COOL offers are the notion of **Context**, which provides an address space in which objects exist and models a traditional address space; the notion of **Object** which is a system supported generic entity offering higher level object abstractions; a **Message based** communication model that enables objects to transparently invoke other objects both locally and remotely. The message system is further enhanced to allow **Migration** of referenced objects between contexts; and finally a set of mechanisms to support object **Persistence**.

Contexts are created as empty address spaces using the Chorus virtual memory abstractions. Each context can support a variable number of virtual memory regions, sparsely allocated and each backed by a secondary storage entity managed by an external memory mapper.

Objects consisting of an initial code region and an initial data region are created according to a template (the type) and a set of attributes. Such attributes determine if this object will be globally known and whether it is a persistant object.

Object communication is based on the underlying Chorus communication model. Objects created with a global attribute are assigned a port for communication and use this as end–point for messages. Messages, synchronous or asynchronous, are delivred to the target object.

A significant feature of the COOL communication model is that the user is able to specify an object that will be migrated from the calling to the receiving context when a message is sent. The communication facilities are used simply to send the object descriptor, the migration of objects is achieved by the underlying virtual memory mechanisms unmapping the text and data segments from the old context, and re–mapping them into the new context.

COOL allows also system developers to detach objects from the context they reside in and move them to backing store returning a persistent object identifier. At a later point such objects can be re–mapped from store to a context.

1.3 CIDRE

CIDRE (*Circualtion Intelligente de Dossiers REpartis*), the pilot application of the ESPRIT project COMANDOS2[6], provides the circulation of documents between networked workstations. It offers facilities to help office workers participating in office procedures by recording and maintaining circulation rules, and managing

---

[6] **COnstruction and MANagement of Distributed Open Systems**

distributed folders, which coordinate several documents. CIDRE runs on COOL/Chorus platform and is currently undergoing real life user tests at SEPT.

The basic object of CIDRE is the document. CIDRE documents, as described in [1] are composed of:

- **The Content**: the content part of CIDRE documents is structured like ODA[7] documents. A generic logical structure is supported: the document content is a set of logical atoms and each logical atom is composed of the access rights and a set of fields.

- **The circulation scheme**: the circulation scheme allows the semi-autonomous circulation of the document between several workstations.

- **The history**: the history part of the document maintains informations about how the circulation scheme has been realized.

Each system user has access to a library of generic documents and folders. He can use and initialise these items and their transfer by instanciation, depending on his requirements. When the user performs the actions requested by the current document, he validates these actions. Automatically, the document migrates to the next actor in the mailbox flow. Documents from the same distributed folder can circulate independently from each other within different departments of the company, meeting at synchronisation points orchestrated by their folder. This is termed the distributed folder concept.

CIDRE is an intelligent document circulation software in the sense that objects (documents and folders) are active and have their own individual behaviour. Each document and folder has its own circulation schedule, but various situations can occur as a result. Folders and documents solve such situations with the help of basic mechanisms stored in knowledge base containing the hierarchical rights and behavioural patterns within the company.

2 The CIDRE requirements

The goal of the multimedia extension to CIDRE is to add multimedia components to CIDRE documents [1]. The multimedia layer built upon the COOL system abstractions will provide a system call interface and a set of services for the creation and the use of multimedia applications.

The multimedia components that will be added to CIDRE documents are currently still images and sound, as well as real time video in the near future (work is already underway). The sound quality must be sufficient for voice and the fixed images quality should be high enough to represent digitalized documents. In fact, the main

---

[7] Open Document Architecture

purposes for sounds are vocal annotations while for images are the circulation of documents acquired as images like faxes and scanned documents.

CIDRE requires that the multimedia objects be modelled as COOL objects so as to allow their inclusion in CIDRE documents without changing the CIDRE architecture. CIDRE defines also the operations to be performed on these multimedia objects. They can both be acquired by the system by means of specific peripherals (micro for sounds, scanner for images). Images can be shown or sounds can be played as a result of a user action.

The solution chosen is the implementation of a multimedia layer added to CIDRE underlying platform i.e. COOL and Chorus. This layer must offer to the applications programmers the set of multimedia objects as well as the services on these objects.

The multimedia layer should cope with a distributed environment in terms of multiple hosts, multiple users and a distributed implementation. It should be defined as an application independant software layer that it can be used by any other application running on the same platform and having similar multimedia requirements as CIDRE.

The design of the multimedia layer only makes assumptions on the defined platform (COOL and Chorus), avoiding hidden assumptions on other system components like the existence of a Unix file system or the use of a particular hardware.

The definition of the software layer interface should allow the portability of the application source code between different implementations and different hardware platforms in which the COOL and Chorus will be available, including heterogeneous systems.

3 The multimedia layer architecture

The COOLIS layer, (see fig.1), constitutes a platform for the implementation of distributed applications that manipulate media objects such as sounds, still images, graphics and animated images.

This platform offers on one hand, a set of multimedia objects, and on the other hand, a set of associated services for manipulating these objects, such as visualisation, playback, etc... These services are implemented as a set of servers that are accessed by client applications on the network via corresponding proxy objects.

The multimedia services layer is based on a distributed event-handling subsystem that offers the mechanisms for weak synchronisation of multimedia objects, the only kind of synchronisation required for the circulation of multimedia folders applications such as CIDRE.

148

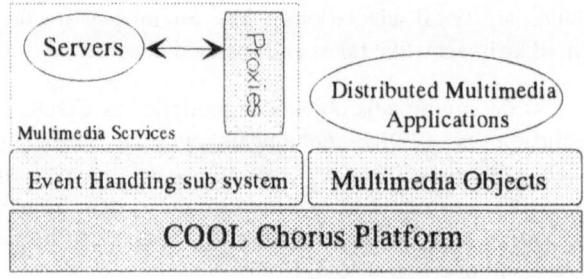

Fig.1. COOLIS Architecture

3.1 The Classes Architecture

COOLIS is designed and implemented as a set of classes, shown in fig. 2, which are used by the distributed application through message communication. These classes inherit all the properties of the subjacent COOL system. The class *cool* defines and implements the behaviour of every COOL object, and mainly offers the primitives for transparency, migration and persistence.

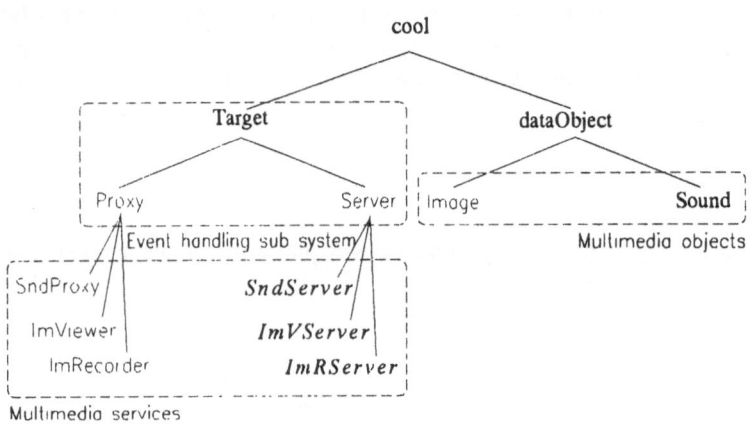

Fig.2. COOLIS Classes Inheritance Tree

The multimedia objects currently implemented i.e., multiformat images and sounds, are viewed as first class objects by the application. They do, however, possess a distinguishing property in that the multimedia data segment is a reference to a separate *dataObject* that implements certain quality of service primitives.

The multimedia services consist of a series of COOL **servers**, i.e. processes running in their separate context, each corresponding to a predefined class of service. On each application context there is a **proxy** object that communicates in a transparent manner with each multimedia server.

Both proxies and servers can handle events and manage event–handlers. The event handling mechanism is provided as an independent subsystem that could be used by the multimedia services or by any other service. Its mechanisms are implemented by the class *Target* that provides primitives for event invocation and transmission as well as handler installation, suspension etc..

3.2 The multimedia objects

A major problem in manipulating multimedia objects is the size of data involved and the resources that it entails for storage, manipulation and transmission. In applications such as CIDRE, multimedia objects are attached to documents and folders, and have therefore to migrate constantly across the network, which could imply heavy overheads.

The solution we have adopted was to make a clear distinction between the multimedia objects as viewed by the application and the actual physical data segment of the manipulated media (image, sound etc. Fig.3). These data segments are manipulated separately from the multimedia objects, and are called upon only when required, for example when the user asks for the effective display of an image. Multimedia objects could therefore accompany folders and documents in their migration without any fear for overhead on transmission resources.

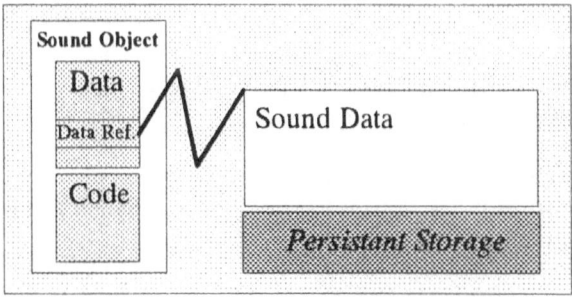

Fig.3. The Sound Object Representation

The *dataObject* class provides the set of primitives necessary for storage, loading and migration of the multimedia data segments. Multimedia objects such as *Image* and *Sound* inherit from this class and contain a full reference to the Chorus segment that actually contains the data. They provide in addition specific primitives for manipulating the actual medium, loading from and saving into segments, format conversion and information access.

Multimedia objects migration is therefore lightweight and takes place as for any other COOL object. When migrating a multimedia object, the application specifies whether it wishes to migrate the data segment as well or to leave it on the original machine. Being based on the Chorus system, access to the data segment remains transparent to the application, independently of its location and of whether it has been migrated or not.

3.3 The multimedia services

COOLIS provides a set of services for manipulating images and sound. This service layer is itself based on an event handling sublayer, necessary for weak synchronisation as required by applications such as CIDRE.

Each constituant server implements a class of services such as image display and capture, sound recording and playback etc...

3.3.1 The event handling sub–system

Synchronisation in COOLIS is event–based. Continuous media synchronisation was deemed unnecessary for the CIDRE application, being itself an asynchronous cooperative system. However, event handling in a heavily distributed environment with frequent migration of objects requires specific treatment so as to insure a minimal quality of service and transparency.

Our event handling system is intricately linked to the server–proxy model we adopted. In this model, the localisation of the server as well as the invocation of its primitives are encapsulated in a special proxy object , that runs in the client's context and represents the server in that context.

The event handling sub–system implements then the dialog between the servers and their proxies and offers primitives for the handlers installation and management as well as for events raising and transmission.

3.3.1.1 The server – proxy model

A multimedia server is an active COOL object that implements a set of services and that could be related to a specific hardware device, for example a sound board in the case of a sound server.

A proxy object represents the server in the application context, see Fig. 4. Each proxy has a global COOL identifier which is unique across the network and which is used by the corresponding server to maintain a table in all its active proxies.

An application should have a proxy running in its context for each server it is client of. Each proxy communicates with its corresponding server in a totally transparent manner with respect to the application. The dialog is established according to a protocol defined in the server and proxy classes.

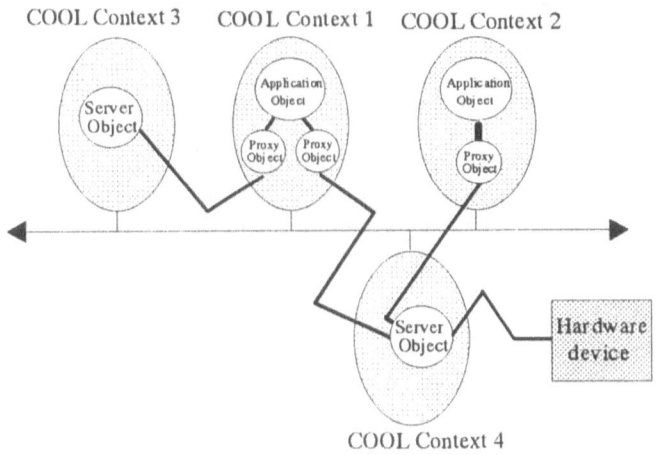

COOL Context 3   COOL Context 1   COOL Context 2

COOL Context 4

Fig.4. The Server – Proxies Communication

3.3.1.2 The handlers management

A handler is an action that is associated to the occurence of a particular event. It takes the form of a method or a function. It could be installed on a target object that could be either a proxy or a server. Each handler carries a status that is set either to active or suspended, in the latter case it is not taken into account when the corresponding event occurs. In addition to its status, a handler carries a priority that defines the execution order of actions in the case where more than one handler are installed for the same event.

The Server and Proxy classes provide the applications with the handler management primitives namely, installation, suspension, reactivation, destruction, priority modification etc..
An application that uses a proxy could install handlers on that proxy. However the actions associated with the handlers could be of two types : action defined in the application and action defined in the proxy itself.

Each server keeps a table that maps the entire set of its proxies to their handlers. The actions corresponding to the handlers of a given proxy are executed in the application context that uses the proxy.

3.3.1.3 The event detection and dispatching

An event is an abstraction that represents a real situation of an object. The meaning of an event is not predefined by the event handling sub-system. The applications must agree at the design level, on the semantics of every event they are going to use; some kind of administration of event numbering might be needed.

An event is detected when it is raised by or on a target object.

Events can be raised on a target object that can be a proxy or a server object. When an event is raised on a target object, all the handlers installed for this event are invoked. To invoke an handler means to call the handler action, which is a C function or a C++ method, in the application context.

When an event is raised on a Server object, it will be dispatched to all its proxies that are interested by the event i.e. that have a handler installed for this event. In turn, when an event is raised on a proxy object, the proxy object will raise it on its server object that may dispatch the event to the others proxies.

This means that raising an event on a proxy object is the same as raising the event on the corresponding server object. This mechanism allows the transparency in the handlers invocation in the sense that it has the same semantics in the local and the remote case.

3.3.2 The Image and Sound Servers

Applications communicate with the Image and Sound servers via their proxy objects respectively. The servers run as separate processes and communicate with their proxies through COOL message passing. At start-up, each server obtains a unique identifier across the network that is subsequently inserted in the COOL naming tree. The client application could then specify to its proxy the site name to which it would like the proxy to connect. It is then the proxy that is in charge of finding its server on that site and opening the connection (fig. 5).

Communication between proxies and servers is synchronous. Messages sent to the server carry their parameters and in certain cases could be accompanied by the migration of multimedia objects to the server context, as in the case where sound is to be played etc. The server acknowledges reception and keeps the proxy informed of the operation status.

Example:

When an application wants to play a sound, it invokes the sound proxy *playSound* method with the sound object and the volume value as parameters. The sound proxy sends then a *play sound request* to the Sound Server. This request contains the request type (*play sound*), the sound object to play and the play volume as optional parameter. Note that in this case, the sound object will be migrated to Sound Server context and that the communication is synchronous. The Sound Server will send a response that will contain an error value if the play request failed.

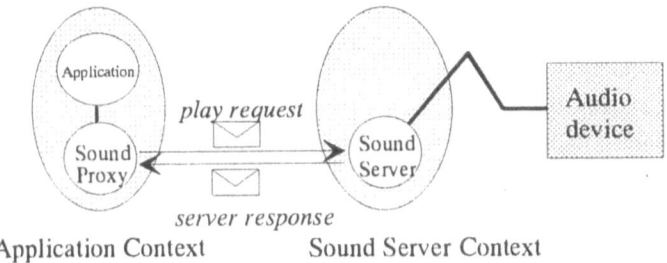

Application Context   Sound Server Context

Fig.5. The Applications – Servers Communication

During execution, the server keeps the proxy informed of the operation status, and invokes events upon their occurence to all the proxies that have declared themselves interested by the event. A predefined (and extensible) set of events has been implemented. Applications could then establish handlers for the various events and tailor their excecution as separate COOL threads for synchronisation.

Weak synchronization support

The weak synchronization relationship has been modeled by the event handling paradigm. The application can install handlers on the proxy object for the interested events to synchronize.

To allow a flexible synchronization between sounds and other events, we define for sounds the concept of marks. A mark is a position in a sound that specifies an event to raise by the sound server when the position is reached during playback.

This mechanism allows the definition of complex interaction between sounds and image events.

Quality of service parameters

Four kind of quality of service parameters have been defined starting from the requirements and the implementation choices. These are the response time for images, the response time for sounds, the maximum delay between sound and image and the sustained throughput from the sound storage to the audio device. From our experimentation error rate is not significant, since the data is considered in relatively secure environment like core or virtual memory.

4 COOLIS and the ANSA/ISA model

Comparison between COOL and the ANSA model has already taken place elsewhere in the litterature [10]. We shall therefore not go into details on the subject in this paper. Only the extensions added to COOL to support multimedia objects will be discussed here, in terms of their eventual support by the ANSA model.

4.1 The computational model

The ANSA/ISA project [3, 4] has developed an abstract model for distributed computation named the "Computational model" which is aimed to be compliant with the ODP[8] reference model [19, 20]. Basically this model defines the unit of separation and of distribution, and the objects as well as their mode of interaction, i.e. invocation with or without a response.

In this model, the objects encapsulate data and have interfaces equipped with operations which other objects can invoke. The data of an object can only be accessed and/or modified via this form of invocation.

Interfaces are identified by references or names. For an object to invoke an operation on an interface, it names the operation in the invocation. The model is inherently transparent in terms of access and location: during invocation, neither the location nor the access interface to the invoked interface are made explicit. That information is contained in storage details hidden in the Engineering model.

One language, IDL[9], enables the description of interfaces, and another, DPL[10] [18], enables to use computational objects via those interfaces.

4.2 COOLIS and the computational model

The following paragraphs discuss the multimedia extensions to COOL and their degree of compatibility with the ANSA Computational model.

---

[8] Open Distributed Processing
[9] Interface Definiton Language
[10] Distributed Processing Language

Image and Sound handling

Adding the various classes required for the management of multimedia objects does not introduce any specific mechanisms likely to change the COOL philosophy. All of the COOL functionalities such as migration, storage, naming etc. are applicable without restriction to these classes, which are encapsulated services. The only difference is on the volume of handled objects and the use of Chorus segments to store the multimedia data .

In the ANSA model this problem is not applicable since object size is supposed illimited. The granularity is an unresolved question in ANSA model, but in ANSAware, it is considered to be 'medium or fine grained'. The engineering choice of using segments could therefore be   adopted by an implementation on ANSAware.

COOLIS is extensible, not only to video, but to any type of data in a linear and coherent manner. The addition of new classes does not have any effect on compatibility with ANSA. COOLIS remains therefore as compatible with ANSA as COOL is itself.

Transparency

ANSA has transparent access and location both of which facilitate the design of distributed applications. Proxy objects in COOLIS which is based on COOL V1 are used to implement this transparency. COOL V2 goes now further into implementing proxy management as a generic concept.

Event Manager

The event manager proposed in COOLIS is a general mechanism which can have other purposes than interactivity management and synchronisation. It adds to COOL a concept which does not exist in the current ANSA model, but that was seen as a requirement by the University of Lancaster [7].

4.3 The University of Lancaster approach

The University of Lancaster approach [13, 14, 15], recommends a solution which does not modify the "computational model" by defining low-level *ad hoc* mechanisms, which are therefore not visible and are not directly accessible at computational level. The transfer of continuous data can take place between ANSA objects, although not between the ANSA interfaces of these objects, but between hidden "interaction points" which may stem from the Engineering level. The object managed at computational level which acts on the low-level mechanisms is the stream. This is a distributed object which can connect media-specific objects. It has quality of service characteristics (throughput, error rate, etc.) which can be accessed and modified on its ANSA interface. It also offers, on this same ANSA interface, connection operations for source and sink objects.

Streams are not useful in COOLIS, but our approach has one same requirement with Lancaster. We both need the ability to express general event–driven synchronisation, and we do it in similar ways.

4.4 The CNET approach

The CNET[11] approach [9], proposes an extension to the computational model with the addition of new entities named reactive objects. These are objects enabling the management of continuous media in terms of real time and synchronisation (notions which lack in the ANSA model). They correspond to finite state machines which react instantaneously to the events produced by their environment, and which then switch back to a wait state for other events. Stream type objects can be part of this environment.

In COOLIS, the management of events attached to a COOL object can be considered as a simplified version of the notion of reactive objects put forward in the conclusions of the CNET research paper. The two notions can also be used for purposes other than intermedia synchronisation (e.g. man–machine interface, process control, etc..).

4.5 The APM approach

The APM approach [3, 4] is exclusively dedicated to the management of continuous media. The identified requirements on which the APM work is concentrated are quite different from those of applications such as CIDRE Multimedia. The notion of streams and their synchronisation are quite foreign to the approach adopted in COOLIS.

5 Conclusions

We have described in this paper the architecture and implementation of the COOLIS layer, for support of multimedia objects in a distributed object–oriented platform. Although the toolkit does not allow yet for video services, the design of its architecture is such that the addition of new media should occur smoothly and in a coherent fashion.

COOLIS does not support continuous media synchronisation (lip synching etc.). Instead, it goes into great depth towards the design and implementation of an elaborate event–driven synchronisation. This kind of synchronisation was felt more useful for cooperative office applications. Moreover, the event mechanism has been

---

[11] Centre National d'Etudes en Télécommunications

designed as a separate general purpose layer that could be used independently of whether multimedia objects are involved.

Both CIDRE and COOLIS are implemented and fully operational on the COOL/Chorus platform at SEPT. CIDRE has been extended using the COOLIS facilities and currently is undergoing real life tests with end users. Work is already underway to provide more multimedia services to the COOL toolkit, starting with real time video for video conferencing during cooperative work on documents.

Acknowledgments

COOLIS has been a two years effort funded by the SEPT. The authors would like to thank all those who provided positive criticisms to its design : Jean–Bernard Stefani, François Horn, Laurent Hazard, Elie Najm and Jean Pierre Martin.

References

1. Béguin, A., Rizk, A.: Multimedia document support. ISA Esprit 2 Project. Technical report T.32. (1992).

2. Lea, R., Jacquemot, C., Pillevesse, E.: COOL : System Support for Distributed Programming. *CACM* Vol.36 N° 9, (1993).

3. The ANSA Computational Model. AR 001.01, APM Ltd., Cambridge UK. (1993).

4. An Overview of ANSA. Architecture Report AR.000.00, APM Ltd., Cambridge UK. (1993).

5. Béguin, A., Bourdon, F., Deshayes, J.M., Gérard, M., Touzeau, P., Tourrade, D.: CIDRE: Intelligent Circulation of Distributed Folders. International Workshop on Telematics, Denver, Co. (1989).

6. Bourdon, F.: Enterprise Modelling in the Office Area: A Point of View. SEPT/ISA/FBo/08.91, (1991).

7. Coulson, G., Blair, G.S., Davies, N., Williams, N.: Extensions to ANSA for Multimedia Computing. Lancaster University, Computer Networks and ISDN Systems (25), (pp 305–323).

8. Deshayes, J.M., Abrossimov, V., Lea, R.: The CIDRE distributed object system based on Chorus. TOOLS 1989, Paris, CS/TR–89–44.1. (1989).

9. Hazard, L., Horn, F., Stefani, J.B.: Notes on architectural support for distributed multimedia applications. ISA project W01 Technical Report, (1991).

10. Lea R.: COOL: Aligning the COOL platform with the ANSA model. T 37.01 Task, CS/TN–90–20 Chorus Systemes, (July 1990, Updated December 1992).

11. Rozier, M.: CHORUS. In Proceedings of Usenix Micro-Kernels and Other Kernel Architectures. Seattle, Washington, Apr. 27-28, Usenix Association (1992).

12. Lea, R., Weightman, J.: Supporting object-oriented languages in a distributed environment: The COOL Approach. In Proceedings of TOOLS USA'91, (1991).

13. Blair, G., Coulson, G., Davies, N., Williams, N.: The Role of Operating Systems in Object-Oriented Distributed Multimedia Platforms. Proceedings of the 2nd ACM/IEEE Workshop on Object Orientation in Operating Systems, Dourdan, France, (1992).

14. Coulson, G., Blair, G., Robin, P., Shepherd, D.: Extending the Chorus Micro-Kernel to Support Continuous Media Applications. 4th International Workshop on Network and Operating System Support for Digital Audio and Video, Lancaster, UK, (1993).

15. Blair, G., Davies, N.: Incorporating Multimedia in Distributed Object-Oriented Systems: The Importance of Flexible Management. 2nd International Workshop on Object Orientation in Operating Systems, Palo Alto, California, (1991).

16. Chorus Systèmes: An Overview of the Chorus/MIX v3.2 Distributed Operating System. Chorus Systèmes CS/TR-92-19, Saint Quentin en Yvelines, France, (1993).

17. Chorus Systèmes: Chorus Kernel v3 r4.0 Specification and Interface. Chorus Systèmes CS/TR-91-69, Saint Quentin en Yvelines, France, (1992).

18. Najm, E., Stefani, J.-B.: A formal semantics for DPL. Esprit/ISA project report, CNET/RC.V01.ENJBS.004, CNET, France, (1992).

19. ISO/IEC JTC1/SC21/WG7: Basic Reference Model of Open Distributed Processing - Part 3: Prescriptive Model. WG7 Draft International Standard, ITU-T Recommendation X.903, ANSI, (1994).

20. Najm, E., Stefani, J.-B.: Towards a formalisation of the ODP Computational Model. To appear in Computer Networks and ISDN, Special issue on Open Ditsributed Processing, (1994).

Hypermedia
and
Authoring

A proposed framework for predicting the development effort of multimedia courseware

I.M. Marshall, W.B. Samson and P.I. Dugard

Department of Mathematical & Computer Sciences
Dundee Institute of Technology
Bell Street, Dundee DD1 1HG

Abstract. Multimedia is increasingly popular in education and training for the delivery of courseware. Unfortunately the costs of developing multimedia courseware is very high. Even with limited use of video, audio and animation, development to delivery times in excess of 800:1 have been reported by various authors. The paper discusses a framework proposal for the development of a metrics based model for predicting the development effort for multimedia systems. It examines the waterfall multimedia courseware development model as the basis for large project developments and proposes a composite multimedia effort development model which makes use of a Rayleigh curve and cost drivers. The Average Number of Training hours is used as the basis for the effort estimate. The proposed cost drivers act on the Average Number of Training hours to tailor it to the type of multimedia project being developed. Initial analysis of cost drivers and delivery time are described. Finally the future development of such a framework is discussed.

1 Introduction

Multimedia has been used in education and training for over 10 years to deliver instruction using computers to control interactive video and other media [1]. From these primitive beginnings to the development of commercially available multimedia computers controlling CD-ROM or interactive video the major constraint on widespread use has not been the hardware but rather the development of courseware. The availability of low cost multimedia production and delivery systems [2, 3] has resulted in an increase in interest in the use of learning materials based on this technology. However, despite the reduction in cost of hardware and improved functionality of authoring software, the development effort required to produce multimedia courseware is still substantial.

Merrill, Li and Jones [4] suggested that traditional Computer Based Training (CBT) requires 100 hours of design and development for every one hour of instruction. The inclusion of high quality, sound, animation and video or intelligence, can increase the development to delivery time ratio to 800:1 and beyond [5, 6, 7, 8]. With development to delivery ratios of this magnitude there is a requirement on the part of the developer to make realistic estimates of the development effort required to produce courseware as early in the development process as possible.

De Diana and van Schaik [9] argue that "In most educational software development projects the effectiveness of the final product and the efficiency of development work are of paramount importance, if not the major goals". To support these goals there is a need for the development of Courseware Engineering [9, 10, 11, 12, 13] which mirrors the call for the development of Software Engineering. Within Software Engineering, metrics are evolving from an informal to a formal framework for the "rigorous approach to measurement extracted from basic ideas in measurement theory and a classification of entities of interest in software development in terms of products, processes and resources"[14].

Early research has indicated that although multimedia development effort estimating systems exist within companies, these tend to be specific to the company concerned. In this paper a proposed framework for research in to multimedia courseware metrics to support the planning and production of cost effective multimedia systems for educational purposes will be discussed. In addition, initial validation of the framework with courseware data will be analysed. While the proposed models are targeted at educational and training use, the method could be extended to the development of commercial multimedia for information systems.

2 The scope of software metrics

The development of Software Engineering led to both the formalisation of the development method and the science of measurement of software. Metrics are an attempt to quantify various aspects of software development. Fenton [14] described software metrics as an all embracing term used to describe a wide range of diverse activities including:

- Cost and effort estimation models and measures
- Productivity measures and models
- Quality control and assurance
- Data collection
- Quality models and measures
- Reliability models
- Performance evaluation and models
- Algorithmic and computational complexity
- Structural and complexity metrics

The original motivation for the development of software measures, models and metrics was managerial with the aim of predicting project costs at early phases in the software development life-cycle [14]. There are a number of alternative models for predicting software development efforts and costs available to help both software engineers and managers predict the development effort and cost of a project. Boehm's COCOMO [15], Putnam's SLIM [16] and Albrecht's function points [17] models are in common use.   These and other models attempt to predict the development effort in terms of person months of development time.

Boehm's COCOMO or COnstructive COst MOdel is a composite model [18] which was developed using a combination of analytical equations, statistical data fitting and expert judgement. COCOMO is one of the best known and widely documented of the composite models.   The basic equation for estimating the software development effort is given by:

$$\text{Effort} = a_i(\text{Size})^{b_i} m(X)$$

The Effort is measured in person months while Size represents an estimate of the thousands of delivered source code instructions and $m(X)$ is a composite multiplier which depends on 15 main cost driver attributes. The values of a_i and b_i depend on the mode of development. COCOMO uses three development modes; Organic, Semi-detached and Embedded.   Organic mode is used with small experienced development teams working on a well understood application area.   Semi-detached mode is used with project teams which have a mixture of experienced and inexperienced personnel working on a new application area.   Embedded mode projects are used to describe software development projects which are being developed under severe constraints of time, reliability or quality.   While there is some criticism of COCOMO concerning the subjectivity and independence of the cost drivers, [19, 20, 21, 22] it still forms the basis for a number of metric based estimating and planning tools.

3 Multimedia courseware engineering models

The development of effort metrics is only possible within a well defined model which carefully describes the phases in software development [18].   One commonly accepted model of the software life cycle is the waterfall model [15].

Similar models have been proposed for multimedia and computer based learning courseware development [23, 24, 25, 26].   Figure 1 describes a waterfall model for multimedia courseware development.   The model starts from the courseware specification phase in which the detailed objectives of the course are defined, along with target audience and the average training hours to be delivered by the courseware. Discussion with developers indicates that on custom development this is the minimum information they require to begin the development process. Following this phase the overall instructional design is developed based on discussions with subject matter experts, courseware designers and the client.   Once this phase has been agreed with the client, then detailed design is undertaken for the media to be used in the final course.   Additional experts such as media specialists, graphics artists, design editors and programmers may be added to the team at this point [25].

164

In the multimedia development phase the graphics, audio, video, sound, simulation and courseware structure is developed. The courseware integration phase brings the various multimedia elements together on one platform. In this phase, the courseware is fully developed and rigorously tested. The testing phase involves pilot testing of the courseware with learners. Problems identified by the evaluation of the courseware during the testing phase are fedback in to the model to improve the quality of the final product. Once the product finishes the testing phase it is published. In the maintenance phase the courseware is only change or altered when serious problems are detected or the client requires changes to update the content.

Fig. 1. The waterfall model of multimedia courseware development

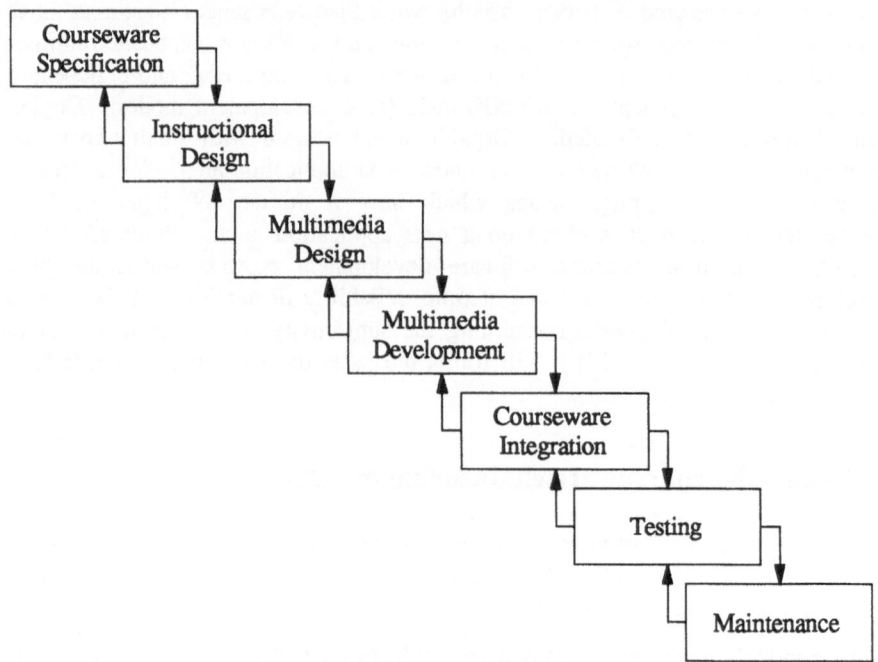

4 The development of multimedia metrics

Using this model, it then becomes possible to develop multimedia metrics to describe multimedia courseware processes, products or resources. While COCOMO and the other metrics measures could be used to measure and analyse multimedia courseware development, it is unlikely to exactly match the development conditions. While it can be argued that the software programming aspects of multimedia courseware could use existing metrics, the instructional aspects, complexity of media development and interfacing do not match the characteristics of normal software development. Software Engineering Metrics were originally developed using data processing or, in some cases, real time development systems data and development models. The incorporation of media design, development and integration into the normal software development life cycle reduces the likelihood that straight transfer of the software metrics will provide useful information on the various aspects of multimedia processes, products or resources.

At present there is very little literature on the metrics or reliability analysis related to educational software production [9]. There would appear to be an opportunity to establish multimedia courseware metrics to objectively measure various aspects of the development process, product or resources. To indicate the potential for the development of general multimedia courseware metrics, a multimedia effort estimation method is proposed.

4.1 Multimedia effort estimation method

The proposed Multimedia Effort Estimation Method (MEEM) is based on an underling assumption that staff utilisation during multimedia development can be modelled to a Rayleigh curve. Figure 2 describes a Rayleigh curve which is used as the basis for Putnam's SLIM [16, 27] and Boehm's COCOMO [15] models for software development effort estimation.

Fig. 2. Rayleigh manpower loading curve

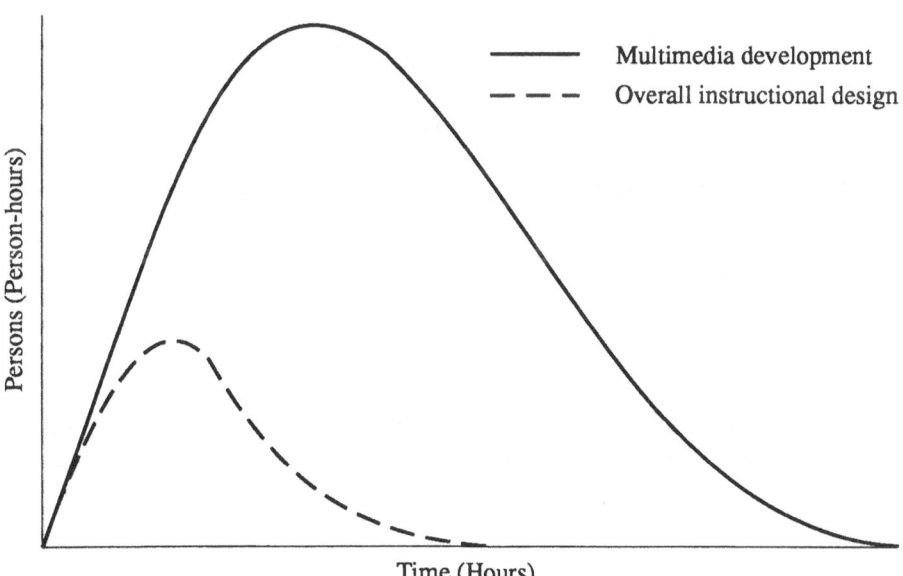

As shown in Figure 2, the overall duration of the project can be made up from a number of individual Rayleigh curves which represent the individual phases of the multimedia project development. While several researchers have criticised the Rayleigh curve assumption for software development, [28, 29] it is a reasonable starting point for this model. The proposed formula for development effort is based on a composite model which incorporates a combination of analytic equations, statistical data fitting and expert judgement [18].

$$\text{Effort} = \text{a (Average Training Delivery Hours)}^b \text{CD(X)}$$

where Effort is measured in person hours and Average Training Delivery Hours is an initial estimate of the number of hours of training required. The reason for suggesting that the relationship should be based on the average number of hours is primarily because it is the one variable which is well defined in most multimedia developments. Normally the commissioning brief for multimedia development will state target training delivery hours. The value of constants a and b are used to map data on to the proposed model and to convert average student hours into development staff hours. Cost driver CD(X) is dependent on a number of factors which affect the development of multimedia courseware. These factors are based on either expert judgement or are dependent on the development project.

4.2 Proposed cost drivers in multimedia development

Tables 1 and 2 lists the proposed cost drivers which have been identified as potentially contributing to the overall development effort of multimedia courseware. It is likely that some of these variables are not independent and they will be eliminated from the final effort estimation model. Currently the cost drivers are defined in terms of ordinal scale which will be validated through the collection of experimental data and statistical analysis. The values of each cost driver range from CD (Very Low) to CD (Very High). Each set of cost drivers will have its own independent range of values to be determined by data collection and analysis but for compactness the values are listed under common headings in Table 1 and 2. The proposed cost drivers are discussed in the following sections.

Number of course objectives

The number of objectives to be achieved by the student is normally well defined, or can be defined, prior to the development of multimedia courseware. The proposed scale makes an assumption that as the number of objectives increases, the size of the cost driver increases. Another assumption is that a normal course consists of between 20 and 30 behavioural objectives. It is also assumed that courseware developments contain less than 100 objectives. These values are based on the analysis of a small sample of multimedia courseware.

Level of course objectives

The highest level of objective to be achieved in the multimedia courseware is assumed to contribute to the development effort. Gagne and Brigg's [30] classification of objectives is used as the basis of the cost driver scale. The lowest value is given to objectives which involve concrete concepts, which typically describe physical entities. Defined concepts describe objectives which try to explain ideas such as inflation.   Lower order rules are used to describe objective which involve learning simple rules, such as, the sequence of actions required to save a document in a word processor.   Higher order rules are used to describe objectives which involve the application of complex rules.   This could describe the level of the objectives required to train a student to programme in a high level language.   The largest value of cost driver is allocated to problem solving objectives.   At this level the student would be applying previously learned behaviours in new or unusual situations.   Gagne described the classification in terms of a hierarchy which forms the basis of the classification of the cost driver scale for level of course objective. Figure 3 describes Gagne's hierarchy of behavioural objectives.

Fig. 3. Gagne's hierarchy of behavioural objectives

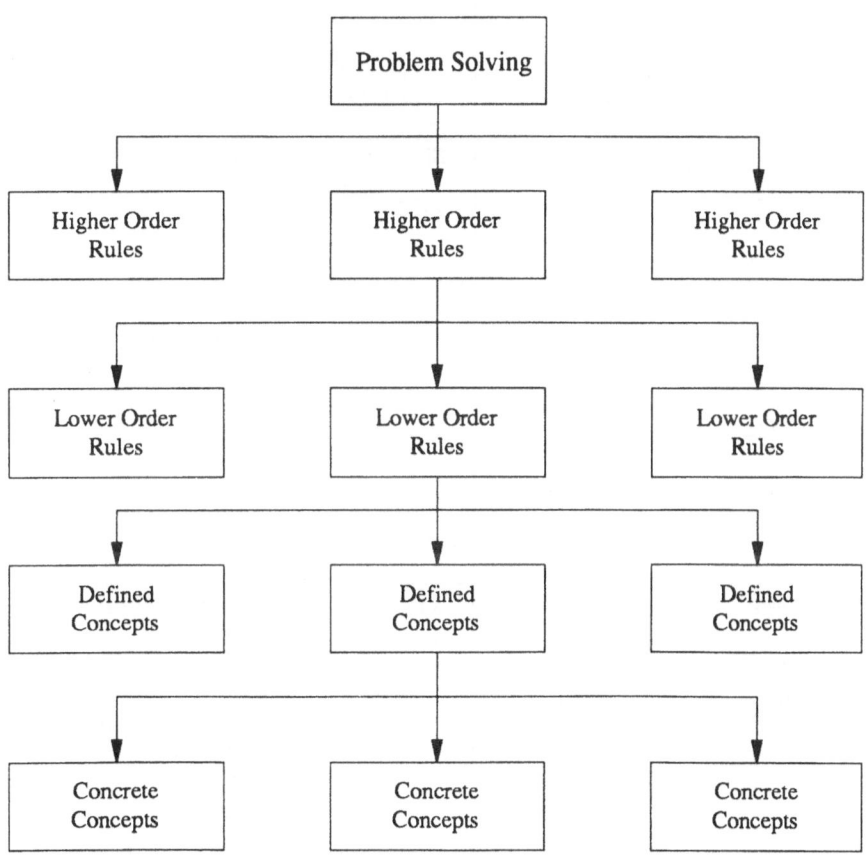

Existing course material

The existence of well prepared course material can significantly reduce the amount of effort required to prepare multimedia courseware.   Rewriting of existing multimedia material for another platform will require less effort than the creation of completely new material.

Table 1 Multimedia cost drivers

Cost Driver	CD (Very Low)	CD (Normal)	CD (Very High)	Group
Number of Course Objectives	Less than 20	41 to 60	Greater than 80	CD
Level of Course Objectives	Concrete Concepts	Lower Order Principles	Problem Solving	CD
Existing Course Material	Rewrite of Existing Multimedia Material	Rewrite of Written Material	New Course	CD
Complexity of Interface	Simple Text Based	Simple Graphical Based	Windowing Graphical Based	IN
Level of Interactivity	Linear	Complex Branching	Complex Adaptive	IN
Type of Question Feedback	None	Right/Wrong with Right Feedback	Remediation on each Wrong Answer	IN
Majority Question Style	True/False	Single Words	Other	IN
Graphics Requirements	None	Simple Original Artwork	Extremely Complex Artwork	IN
Graphics Density	Less then 1 per 20 frames	1 per 10 frames	More than 1 per frame	IN
Animation Requirements	None	Simple Animation	Mathematically Accurate Animation	IN
Animation Density	Less then 1 per 20 frames	1 per 10 frames	More than 1 per frame	IN
Audio Requirements	None	Simple Original Audio	Extremely Complex Audio	IN
Audio Density	Less then 1 per 20 frames	1 per 10 frames	More than 1 per frame	IN
Video Requirements	None	Simple Original Linear Video Clips	Complex Original Interactive Video Clips	IN
Video Density	Less then 1 per 20 frames	1 per 10 frames	More than 1 per frame	IN
Simulation Requirements	None	Simple Original Simulation	Realistic Simulation	IN
Simulation Density	Less then 1 per 20 frames	1 per 10 frames	More than 1 per frame	IN

Table 2 Multimedia cost drivers

Cost Driver	CD (Very Low)	CD (Normal)	CD (Very High)	Group
Production Environment	Authoring Environment	Authoring Language	Low Level Language	DE
Instructional Design, Development and Delivery Methodology	None	Formal First Generation	Formal Third Generation	DE
Size of Proposed Development Team	More than 15	5-9	1	DE
Development Team's Subject Matter Experience	Expert Knowledge of the Subject	Some Knowledge of the Subject	No Knowledge of Subject	DE
Development Team's Multimedia Experience	Extensive Multimedia Development Experience	Extensive Computer Aided Learning Experience	None	DE
Subject Matter Expert's Multimedia Experience	Extensive Multimedia Development Experience	Extensive Computer Aided Learning Experience	None	SE
Availability of Subject Matter Expert	Unrestricted Contact	Weekly Contact	Restricted Contact	SE

Complexity of interface

The complexity of the user interface is also considered to be important in determining the amount of development effort required to create multimedia courseware. A simple text based interface will typically require less effort to develop than a simple graphical interface or windowing environment.

Level of interactivity

Cohen describes interactivity in terms of the richness of the "dialogue" between the learner and the instructional programme [31]. The level of interactivity expected in the final courseware product will affect the development effort. Five levels are used to describe the various types of interactivity found in multimedia courseware. The simplest level describes presentation in a linear sequence with little or no interaction. Complex branching is used to describe programmes in which feedback loops and a significant number of pre-programmed sequences are included. Adaptive is used to describe programmes which include elements of intelligence and perhaps models of the student [8, 32, 33].

Level of question feedback

The level of feedback provided by the multimedia has an effect on the development effort. No feedback on questions requires less development effort than questions which provide relevant feedback and remediation on each wrong answer [31].

Majority question style

Early analysis indicates that the complexity of the questioning style affects the development effort required to produce multimedia courseware. The proposed range of question style varies from simple true or false through limited free text input to other. The other category is used to describe complex interactions such as the definition of touch click areas.

Graphics requirements and density

The graphical requirements cost driver attempts to describe the development effort required to produce graphical images for the multimedia courseware. The existence of suitable artwork considerably reduces the development effort required compared to the production of extremely complex artwork. Extremely complex artwork is used to describe the production of full colour photo realistic images. The scale is used to describe the average level of the artwork required in the proposed multimedia package. The graphical density is used to describe the average requirement for graphical images in the final multimedia product.

Animation requirements and density

The animation requirements cost driver describes the development effort required to produce animation sequences for multimedia courseware. A lower value cost drivers is allocated if a suitable animation already exists. A higher value of cost driver would be given to the production of extremely complex animations. The graphical density is used to describe the average requirement for animations in the final multimedia product.

Audio requirement and density

The audio requirements cost driver describes the development effort required to produce sound for inclusion in multimedia courseware. The existence of suitable sound clips considerably reduces the development effort and would result in a low value of cost driver. Extremely complex audio clips with multiple voices and background sound effects would take more development time and is allocated a higher cost driver. The audio density is used to describe the average requirement for sound in the final multimedia product.

Video requirement and density

The video requirements cost driver describe the development effort required to produce video sequences for the multimedia courseware. The scale is used to describe the average complexity of the video required in the proposed multimedia package. The video density is used to describe the average requirement for graphical images in the final multimedia product.

Simulation requirement and density

Simulation can add considerably to the development effort required to produce multimedia courseware. The simulation requirements cost driver attempts to describe the development effort required to produce simulation for the multimedia courseware. Realistic simulation involving realistic movement, sound and response to student actions is more difficult to produce than a simple animation which simulates the movement of the planets around the Sun. The density cost driver is used to describe the average requirement for simulation in the final multimedia product.

Production environment

The type of production environment used to produce the courseware is assumed to have an effect on the development effort. The scale ranges from an intelligent authoring environment [34] which fully supports instructional design, development and delivery (ID^3) of multimedia courseware to the hand crafting of software using a low level language such as assembler.

Instructional design, development and delivery methodology

This cost driver is designed to measure the effect of a formal instructional design, development and delivery methodology to support the production of multimedia courseware. The existence of a formal methodology improves the effectiveness of courseware production although as De Diana and van Shaik [9] indicate "...very few studies are available that demonstrate that the use of specific design and development methods can in fact improve efficiency". One of the goals of this research is to attempt to accurately determine the effect of a ID^3 methodology on the overall development.

Size of proposed team

The size of the development team is assumed to have an effect on the overall development effort. In software development, small teams are more productive than larger teams because less time is spent in communication between team members [36]. It is assumed that similar effects will be found in multimedia development.

Development team's subject experience

Experience in developing courseware in the same subject area or in related subject areas is assumed to assist in the development process. The team members do not have to spend time learning the terminology used in the subject area.

Team multimedia development experience

Discussions with multimedia developers indicate that the team's experience in developing multimedia can affect the development effort. The scale ranges from no experience in which case the team will spend time on the current project learning from their mistakes through to extensive multimedia experience.

As indicated in the introduction, a number of these cost drivers are not independent of each other. For example, the level of course objective and level of interactivity may be related. Once an adequate data set has been collected, step wise linear regression or principle component analysis will be used to identify the main cost drivers.

Subject expert's multimedia development experience

If the subject matter expert is able to provide the development team with the information in a sequence and in a form which is suitable for multimedia delivery, then the development effort is reduced. The best indicator of the likelihood of an author to provide the subject information in the required format is the author's past experience of multimedia development.

Availability of subject matter expertise

Discussions with multimedia developers indicate that the availability of the subject matter expert for consultation can significantly affect the overall development effort.

4 Initial study

Data on 14 courseware development projects were used to investigate the cost drivers. These were considered to few to yield detailed information on individual cost drivers. The individual cost drivers were grouped under super headings for Course Difficulty (CD), Interactivity (IN), Development Experience (DE) and Subject Expertise (SE). For each of the super cost drivers a simple score was calculated by summing the ratings on each cost driver in the group. This assigns equal weights to all cost drivers in the group, and also assumes that the scale, which is a set of ordered categories, may be considered to be approximated by an interval scale. It may be possible to improve on both of these assumptions when more data is available. The 4 super cost driver group scores, together with the delivery time and development time, are given for the 14 projects in Table 3.

Table 3 Multimedia projects

Development Time (hours)	Course Difficulty (CD)	Interactivity (IN)	Development Environment (DE)	Subject Expertise (SE)	Delivery Time (hours)
28	7	22	16	7	0.167
80	8	18	19	7	1.000
100	9	17	17	7	1.000
100	8	25	18	7	1.000
180	9	21	18	7	2.000
180	9	23	15	6	1.000
200	9	18	19	8	1.000
220	8	18	19	8	1.000
250	10	24	16	6	1.000
320	10	26	17	6	1.000
400	10	19	19	7	1.000
435	7	19	18	6	1.000
500	11	37	19	8	1.000
590	9	37	16	6	3.000

As can be seen from Table 3, 11 of the 14 projects have a delivery time of 1 hour, but the development time for these vary by a factor of more than 5. As a first step, these 11 projects were considered to see whether if the variance in development time could be explained using the four super cost driver scores. There is little variation in the Subject Expertise scores for these projects (all lie between 6 and 8). Plots of delivery time against Course Difficulty, Interactivity and Development Environment are shown in Figures 4 to 6.

Fig. 4. Delivery time against course difficulty

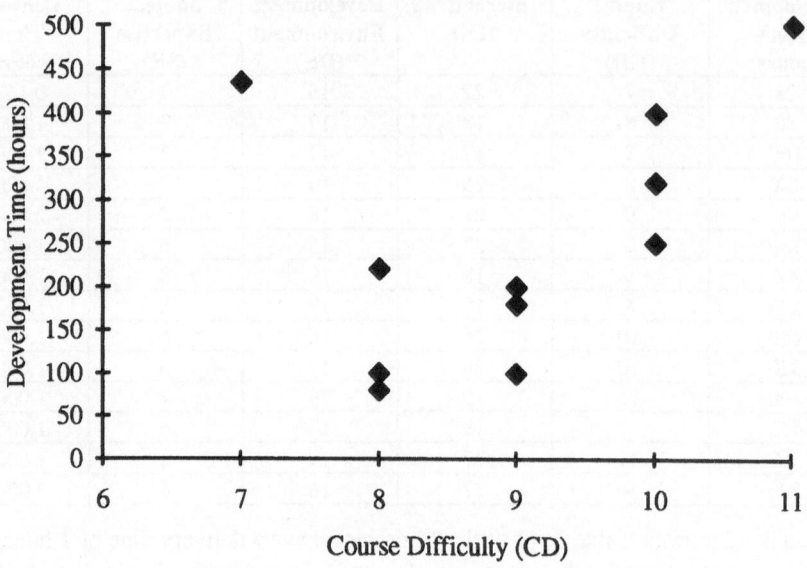

Fig. 5. Development time against interactivity

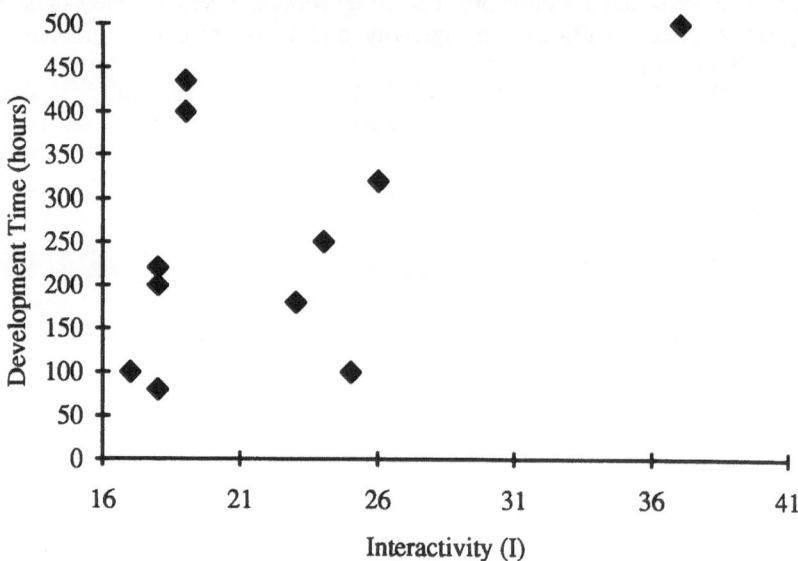

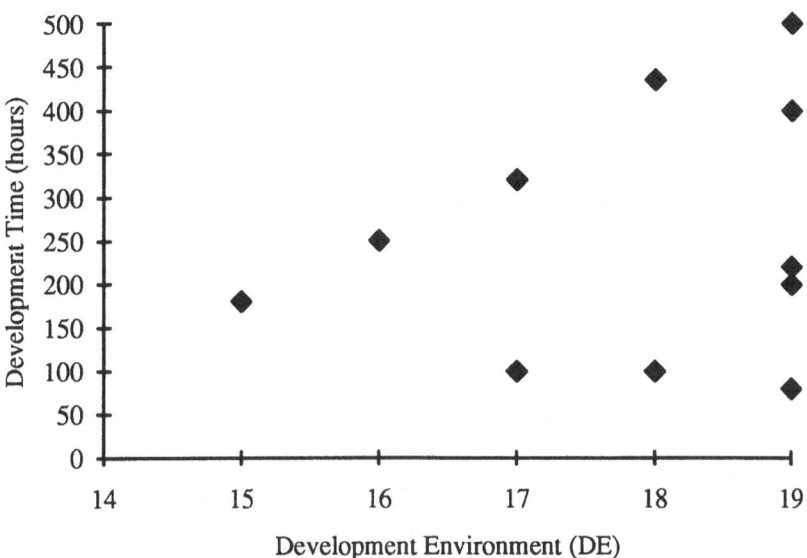

Fig. 6. Development time against development environment

Figure 4 suggests that there is an approximately linear relationship between development time and Course Difficulty, except for the project with Course Difficulty = 7, which has a development time which appears to be much too high. The Interactivity and Development Experience scores for the project are not exceptionally high and it appears that nothing in the data available explains this project. For the other 10, a simple linear regression of development time on Course Difficulty explains nearly three quarters of the variance. Adding Interactivity to the regression barely improves it. This is partly because the correlation between Course Difficulty and Interactivity is high at 0.65. However, adding Development Environment to the regression allows explains 85% of the variance. The actual and predicted values of the development time are given in Table 4.

Table 4 Actual and predicted values of development time

Actual Development Time	Predicted Development Time	Percentage Error
80	128.190	-60.2371
100	186.509	-86.5086
100	97.500	2.5
180	125.129	30.4837
200	247.888	-23.9440
220	128.190	41.7320
250	275.517	-10.2069
320	306.207	4.3103
400	367.586	8.1034
500	487.284	2.5431

Addition of Subject Expertise to the regression does not improve it. The ability to predict the development time for most projects as well as this would certainly be useful, and with more data it may be possible to improve upon it.

4.1 Discussion of results

The limited number of projects in the data set could be unrepresentative of multimedia development. Table 5 shows the maximum and minimum and mean estimated development time for projects with delivery times between 1 and 20 hours [37]. Senbetta collected this data from 21 experienced developers of courseware. In common with the data in Table 3, the development time estimates vary by a factor of about 5 for each delivery time.

Table 5 Expert estimation of courseware development time

Delivery Time (hours)	n	Estimated Development Time		
		Minimum (hours)	Mean (hours)	Maximum (hours)
1	21	90	240	365
2	21	150	380	700
5	21	250	800	1625
10	21	500	1400	2550
15	21	750	1950	3750
20	21	1000	2400	5000

In the data set analysed, there are only 3 projects with delivery times other than 1 hour, so the observations can only be tentative. However, again omitting the outlier with development time 435 and using the other 13 projects, 80% of the variance in development time can be accounted for by a regression on Course Difficulty, Interactivity and Delivery Time. Addition of Development Experience does not improve this result. With a larger data set and more projects with long delivery times it may be possible to attempt to predict development time using Course Difficulty, Interactivity and Development Experience along with delivery time, or it may be possible to do better by developing separate predictors based on Course Difficulty, Development Experience and perhaps Interactivity for Delivery Times in each of several narrow ranges. The use of data with a greater range of values for Subject Expertise may also improve the result. These preliminary results are promising and suggest that even with the unweighted scoring of cost drivers used here can achieve useful predictions. A large and rich data set would allow more detailed investigations which would almost certainly lead to improved results.

4.2 Future work

Given enough data the aim is to produce a software tool version of MEEM. The current model is, of course, simply a framework and cannot yet be used for estimation. It requires to be calibrated to determined the appropriate:

- coefficients

- cost driver values

Boehm [15] used data from 63 projects to calibrate his original COCOMO model and it is anticipated that data from a similarly large number of multimedia projects will be needed. Work is currently underway to identify, collect and analyse such data from multimedia projects. In addition, other potential cost drivers are being identified with the assistance of multimedia developers. Using data from a representative sample of projects, statistical analysis will help to show which cost drivers are more significant.

Experience with stepwise linear regression techniques would suggest that, in any development environment, only three or four of the cost drivers will have a significant bearing on the effort prediction. Other possibilities include the use of appropriate statistical techniques to produce predictions. Robust statistics [38] look promising in this respect. Another possibility which has been explored by Samson, Dugard and Ellison [39] is the use of neural nets to 'learn' how to predict effort from cost driver values. Once these cost drivers have been determined, it may be possible to further simplify data collection.

References

1. Stewart, A.M., Bryce, C.F.A.; Multimedia multipurpose: Is the quality of the learning experience being well served by the use of educational media? In: Percival, F. Ellington, H. (eds.): Distance learning and education. London: Kogan Page, pp. 256-266 (1981).

2. Baron, L.J., Abrami, P.C.: The effect of group size and exposure time on microcomputer learning. Computers in Human Behaviour 8, pp. 353-365 (1992).

3. Stack, P.: Interactive video - the barriers have fallen. Tech Trends Vol. 35, No. 2, pp. 38-40 (1990).

4. Merrill, M.D., Li, Z., Jones, M.K.: Limitations of first generation instructional design. Educational Technology Vol. 30 No. 1, pp. 7-11 (1991).

5. Bourdeau, J., Marshall, I.M., Junginger, S., Sorg, B., Kuyper, M., Schwab, S.: Automating instructional planning. Grimstad, Norway: Proceedings NATO ASI 1993 - Automating Instructional Design, Development and Delivery (In press).

6. Beautement, P.: Review of interactive video systems and their possible application to training in the 90's. Interactive Learning International Vol. 7, pp. 45-54 (1991).

7. Clark, R.: Getting out of the classroom. Data Training Vol. 10 No. 2, pp. 26-34 (1991).

8. Orey, M., Trent, A., Young, J.: Development efficiency and effectiveness of alternative platforms for intelligent tutoring. Edinburgh, UK: Proceedings AI in Education 93 pp. 42-49 (1993).

9. De Diana, I., van Schaik, P.: Courseware engineering outlined: An overview of some research issues. Educational Technology Training International, Vol. 30 No 3, pp. 191-211 (1993).

10. Burkhardt, D., Chicken, P., Hendley, B., Jarratt, P., Jurascheck, N., Stoner, M., Weston, G.,Yandle, J.: The exploration of fourth generation language program generation to assist in the production of multimedia computer aided learning. Computer Education Vol. 12 No. 1, pp. 253-256 (1988).

11. Chen, J.W., Chen, M.: Towards the design of an intelligent courseware production system using software engineering and instructional design principles. Journal of Educational Technology Systems Vol. 19 No. 1, pp. 41-52 (1990).

12. Costello, G.: Developing computer-based instruction: the systems design approach. Training Officer Vol. 28 No. 2, pp. 48-50 (1992).

13. Jones, M.K., Li, Z. and Merrill, D.M.: Rapid prototyping in automated instructional design. Educational, Training Research and Development Vol. 40 No 4, pp. 95-100 (1993).

14. Fenton, N.: Software metrics: A rigorous approach, London, UK: Chapman-Hall, pp. 1-50 (1991).

15. Boehm, B.W.: Software engineering economics. Englewood Cliffs, NJ, USA: Prentice-Hall, pp. 1-30 (1981).

16. Putnam, L.H.: A general empirical solution to the macro software sizing and estimating problem. IEEE Transactions Software Engineering Vol. SE-4 No 4 pp. 345-361 (1978).

17. Albrecht, A.J.: Measuring application development productivity. Monterey, CA: USA: Proceedings of IBM Application Development Joint SHARE/GUIDE Symposium pp.. 83-92 (1970).

18. Conte, S.D., Shen, V.Y., Dunsmore, H.E.: Software Engineering Metrics and Models, Menlo Park, CA USA: Benjamin/Cummings Publishing Company, pp. 1-20 (1986).

19. Subrahmania, G.H., Brelawski, S.A.: A case for dimensionality reduction in software development effort estimation. Philadelphia, USA: Department of Computer Science, Temple University, Internal Report TR-89-02, 1-40 (1989).

20. Kitchenham, B.A. Taylor, N.R.: Software project development cost estimation. Journal of Systems and Software Vol. 5 No. 4, pp. 267-278 (1985).

21. Kemerer, C.F. An empirical validation of software cost estimation models. Communications of the ACM Vol. 30 No. 5, pp. 416-429 (1987).

22. Cuelenaere, A.M.E., van Genuchten, M.J.I., Heemstra, H.J.: Calibrating a software estimation model: why and how. Journal of Information and Software Technology Vol. 29 No 10, pp. 558-567 (1987).

23. De Diana, I., Collis, B.: Adaptable educational courseware: An antidote to several portability problems. Journal of Research on Computing in Education Vol. 23 No 2, pp. 225-241 (1990).

24. Friedler, Y., Shabo, A.: An approach to cost-effective courseware development. British Journal of Educational Technology Vol. 22 No. 2, pp. 129-138 (1991).

25. Phillips, W.A.: Individual author prototyping desktop development of courseware. Computers in Education Vol. 14 No. 1, pp. 9-15 (1990).

26. Maher, J., Iugrahem, A.: Software engineering and ISD: similarities, complementaries and lessons to share. Dallas, Texas, USA: Proceedings Annual Meeting of the Association for Educational Communications and Technology, pp. 234-245 (1989).

27. Putnam, L.H., Putnam, D.T., Thayer, L.P. A tool for planning software projects. The Journal of Systems and Software Vol. 5, pp. 147-154 (1984).

28. Parr, F.N.: An alternative to the Rayleigh curve model for software development effort. IEEE Transaction for Software Engineering Vol. SE-6 No 3, pp. 235-245 (1980).

29. Jeffery, D.R.: Time sensitive cost models in commercial MIS environments. IEEE Transactions in Software Engineering Vol. SE-13 No. 7, pp. 852-859 (1987).

30. Gagne, R.M., Briggs, L.J.: Principles of instructional design (2nd ed.), New York, USA: Holt, Rinehart & Winston, pp. 46-69, (1979).

31. Cohen, V.B.: Interactive features in the design of videodisc materials. Educational Technology Vol. 24 No. 1, pp. 16-20 (1984).

32. Iuppa, N.V., Anderson, K.: Advanced interactive video design, New York, USA: Knowledge Industry Publications, pp. 50-89 (1988)

33. Spohrer, J.C.: Integrating multimedia and AI for training - examples and issues. Los Angeles, USA: Proceedings IEEE International Conference on Systems, Man and Cybernetics 1990, pp. 663-664 (1990).

180

34. Tennyson, R.D., Elmore, R.L. Integrated courseware engineering system. Grimstad, Norway: Proceedings NATO ASI 1993 - Automating Instructional Design, Development and Delivery, (In press).

35. Cohen, V.B.: A re-examination of feedback in computer based instruction: implications for instructional design. Educational Technology, Vol. 25 No 1 pp. 33-37 (1985).

36. Brooks, F.P.: The mythical man-month, New York, USA: Addison-Wesley, pp 27-28 (1975).

37. Senbetta G.: CBT Time and cost estimation: What do the experts say? USA: 10th Annual CBT Training Conference and Exposition, pp 345-356 (1992).

38. Kitchenham, B., Mellor, P.: Data collection and analysis' In Fenton, N.E. (eds.) Software metrics: A rigorous approach. London, UK: Chapman & Hall, pp. 89-110 (1991).

39. Samson, W.B., Ellison, D.G. Dugard, P.I.: Software cost estimation using an Albus Perceptor (CMAC). Pittsburgh, USA: Proceedings Eight International COCOMO Estimating Meeting, (In press).

Soaring through hyperspace:
A snapshot of Hyper-G and its Harmony client

Keith Andrews and Frank Kappe

Institute for Information Processing and Computer Supported New Media (IICM)
Graz University of Technology
A-8010 Graz, Austria.

Abstract. This paper describes the current status of work on Hyper-G and its new viewer, Harmony. Hyper-G is a general-purpose, large-scale, distributed hypermedia information system under development at Graz University of Technology. It is based on the client-server model across the Internet and is interoperable with both Gopher and World Wide Web.

Harmony is the new native Hyper-G client for X Windows on Unix platforms. It takes advantage of Hyper-G's structuring and retrieval features to provide both intuitive navigational facilities and informative feedback about the location of information.

1 Introduction

The requirements of a large volume of information impose certain design decisions on the implementation of a large-scale hypermedia information system. An important issue is support for automatic structuring and maintenance of a dynamically changing body of information. Another aspect of the size of hypermedia datasets is that orientation and navigation become more difficult as size increases. Problems of users of such systems include: becoming "lost in hyperspace", having difficulty gaining an overview, not being able to find information that is known to exist, determining how much information on a given topic exists, how much of it has been seen, and how much is left. These issues have been identified as crucial for the acceptance of hypermedia and have been intensely discussed in the literature (see for example [5, 13, 14]). However, solutions which work well on small systems fail completely when applied to large-scale hypermedia (such as global maps [20]). The Hyper-G project was started in 1990 in order to explore these issues as applied to a large-scale, distributed hypermedia information system.

The first Hyper-G client was a simple terminal viewer[1], which is now a stable, universal point of entry to any Hyper-G server. In October 1992 work started on Harmony, a Hyper-G client for X Windows on Unix platforms. Harmony is a

---

[1] The terminal viewer can be tried out by `telnet`'ing to `hyperg.tu-graz.ac.at` which starts a session on Graz University of Technology's main Hyper-G server.

modern, Motif-style graphical interface for Hyper-G with Version 1.0 scheduled for release in mid-1994.

This paper presents a snapshot of the current status of Hyper-G and Harmony, emphasising particularly interesting and original features not found in comparable systems.

2   Hyper-G

Hyper-G is designed as a general-purpose, large-scale, distributed, multi-user, hypermedia information system, similar in scope to Xanadu [12], Intermedia [8], WAIS [18], Gopher [1], and World Wide Web (WWW) [3]. Based on previous experience with large-scale videotex information systems, the aim of Hyper-G is to develop a flexible hypermedia framework in order to study and possibly eliminate the problems typically associated with large-scale hypermedia systems. The basic concepts underlying Hyper-G have been presented elsewhere [11, 10, 9], here we provide a general overview of current functionality.

At the server level, Hyper-G provides a number of orthogonal structuring and retrieval facilities:

- Structuring of documents into so-called *collections*, which may themselves belong to other collections. Navigation may be performed down through the collection hierarchy, access rights assigned on a collection-by-collection basis, and searches restricted to particular collections.

- Hyperlinks from a *source anchor* within one document to either a *destination anchor* within another document, an entire document, or a collection. Links are not stored within documents (as in WWW) but in a separate database, which has the advantage that they are bidirectional and may be added to read-only documents.

- Attribute and full text search. Documents have an associated set of attributes (author, title, keywords, etc.) which may be searched for, including boolean combinations. Full text search facilities include fuzzy boolean queries [16] and WAIS-like nearest-neighbour searches based on the vector space model [17]. Every document and collection is automatically added to the full text index on insertion into the database. The scope of a search may be as narrow as one collection on a single server or as wide as all collections on all Hyper-G servers worldwide.

Other features supported by Hyper-G and not found in comparable systems such as Gopher and WWW include:

- Four user identification modes: from anonymous to fully identified.
- Support for user groups.
- Access rights per user group for documents and collections.
- Support for multilingual versions of documents and language preferences.

- An underlying object-oriented database to guarantee the consistency and integrity of data (for example the updating of links when a document is moved or the elimination of dangling links when a document is deleted).

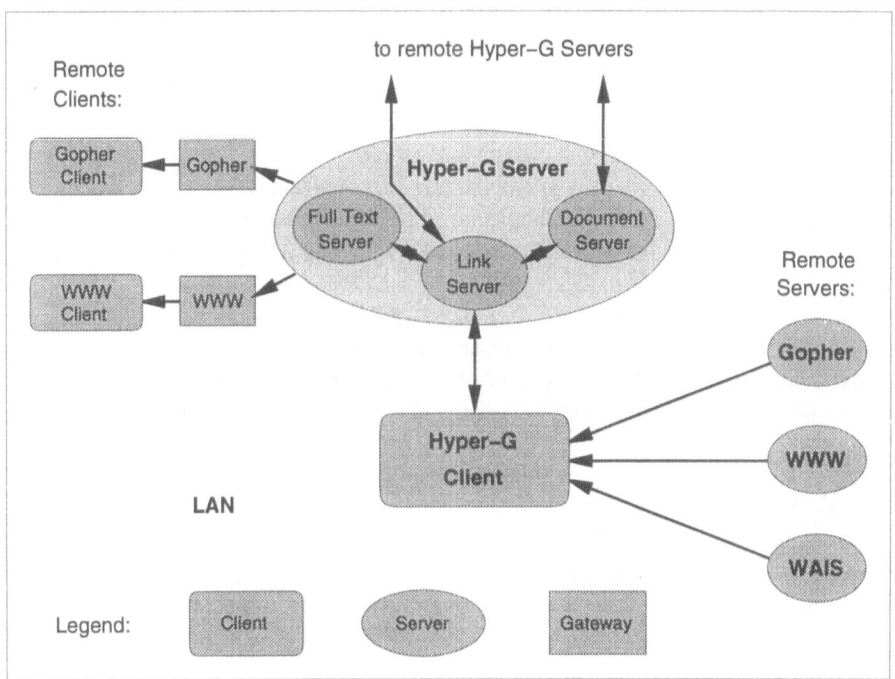

Fig. 1.: The architecture of Hyper-G

Hyper-G is based on a client-server model across the Internet. Figure 1 shows the architecture of Hyper-G. Unlike Gopher or WWW clients which connect to many servers during a typical session, Hyper-G clients talk to a single Hyper-G server for the entire session. Should information from a remote server be needed, the local server fetches it and passes it on to the client. This approach has the following advantages:

- Clients are kept simple.
- An efficient, connection-oriented protocol can be used.
- Remote information can be cached in the local server.
- User accounts and access rights have only to be maintained in the local server (the user has to identify to one server only).
- Statistics and user profile information can be gathered on a per-session basis.

Also apparent from Figure 1 is the interoperability of Hyper-G with Gopher and WWW clients and Gopher, WWW, and WAIS servers. When accessed by a Gopher client, the Hyper-G server maps the collection hierarchy into a Gopher menu tree (hyperlinks cannot be represented in Gopher). A synthetic search item is generated at the foot of each Gopher menu to allow searching the corresponding collection. When accessed by a WWW client, each level of the collection hierarchy is converted to an HTML [4] document containing a menu of links to other sub-menus. The menus are marked as searchable. Hyper-G text documents are transformed on-the-fly into HTML documents, including any links they might have.

In the other direction (the right hand side of Figure 1), Hyper-G clients can contact Gopher, WWW, and WAIS servers in order to retrieve information from them. The Hyper-G server is able to store pointers to such remote objects. This allows the incorporation of information on remote non-Hyper-G servers (almost) seamlessly: Gopher menus are transformed into Hyper-G collections, WWW text documents into Hyper-G text documents, and WAIS queries and responses into Hyper-G queries and responses. We are in the process of moving the knowledge of external protocols from Hyper-G clients to the Hyper-G server, in order to make clients simpler and enable caching of external documents.

3   Harmony

Harmony is the native Hyper-G client for X Windows on Unix platforms. It takes advantage of Hyper-G's structuring and retrieval features to provide both intuitive navigational facilities and informative feedback about the location of information. A number of interesting and novel features, including several kinds of dynamic overview and hierarchy maps, a three-dimensional scene viewer, and three-dimensional navigational aids, have been implemented.

Harmony is a multi-process Unix application (see Figure 2), written in C++, using the InterViews X11 user interface toolkit, and (for its 3D features) Silicon Graphics' GL graphics library. The primary process is the *session manager*, which communicates with the Hyper-G server, provides navigational facilities, and coordinates all other activities. The session manager starts secondary processes, so-called *document viewers*, as necessary to display particular documents.

Native Harmony viewers for text, images, 3D scenes, and MPEG films are currently available. External applications are started to display other document types, such as audio clips and PostScript files. Harmony may optionally be configured to run external programs instead of any native viewer (the document is piped to standard input), but with the restriction that link activation and editing are no longer possible.

Figure 3 shows an example Harmony session. The session manager (left), text viewer (right) and image viewer are visible. Note how the session manager provides for navigation through the collection hierarchy. Collections may be opened and closed and documents activated by double-clicking. Collections or documents which have already been visited are marked with a tick. In this

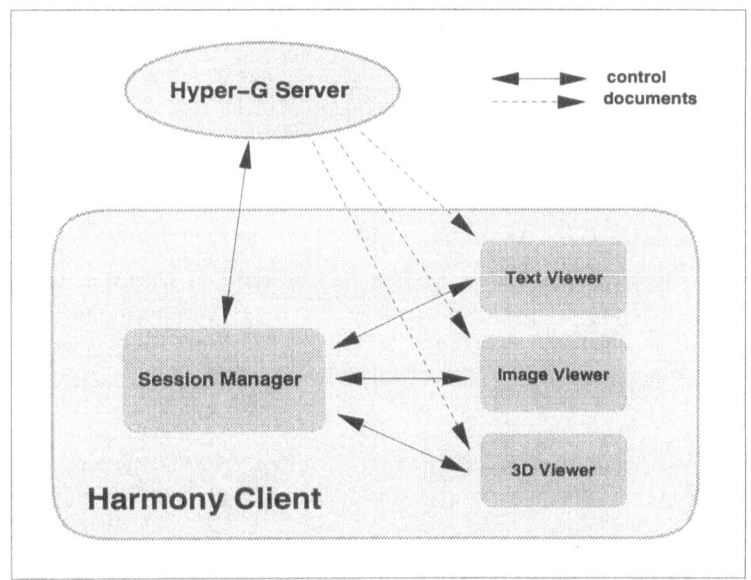

Fig. 2.: The architecture of Harmony

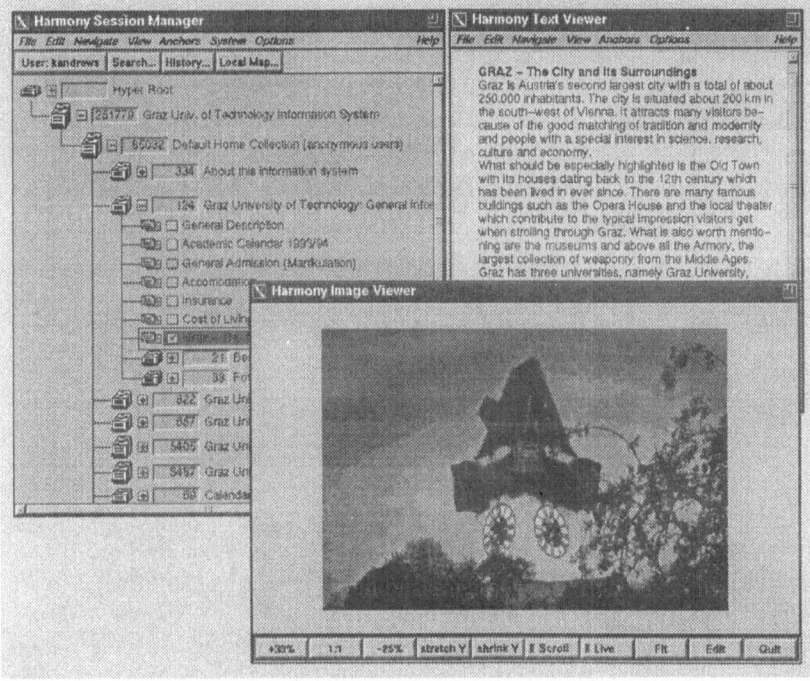

Fig. 3.: Example Harmony session

example, a descriptive text and an image about the city of Graz have been accessed.

The Harmony text viewer displays marked-up (SGML) text documents, and has the usual facilities for scrolling, searching, selecting, etc. The display styles of the various attributes (title, bold, anchor, etc.) are user-configurable. Link activation is accomplished by double-clicking a text anchor and implemented by passing a message back to the session manager.

The image viewer accepts raster images in a variety of common formats (TIFF, GIF, etc.). Common operations such as zooming and panning are available. Link anchors in an image may be of a variety of formats: polygonal areas upon the image, buttons positioned at a particular location, etc.

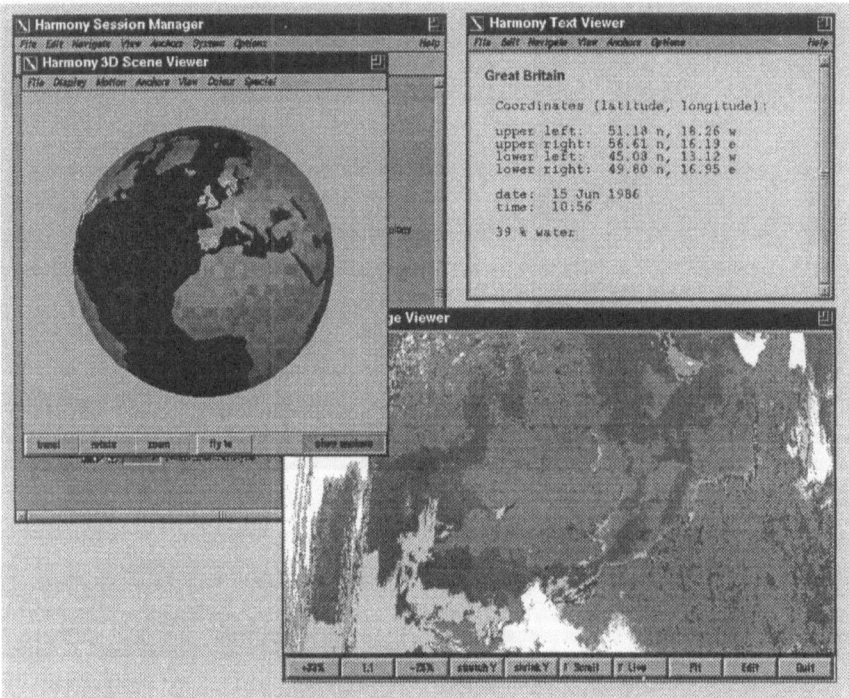

Fig. 4.: Harmony scene viewer

A unique feature of Harmony is its support for 3D scene documents. Scene description files representing arbitrarily complex three-dimensional models of scenes or objects are displayed by the Harmony 3D scene viewer. Figure 4 shows the scene viewer displaying a model of the globe. The anchor representing Great Britain has been clicked to retrieve the corresponding satellite image. Users can manipulate an object (translate, rotate, zoom) and navigate (walk, fly, fly to, heads-up) within a scene, in a fashion similar to the Information Visualiser [15]. Hypermedia links may be attached either to individual objects within a scene or to groups of polygons within an object.

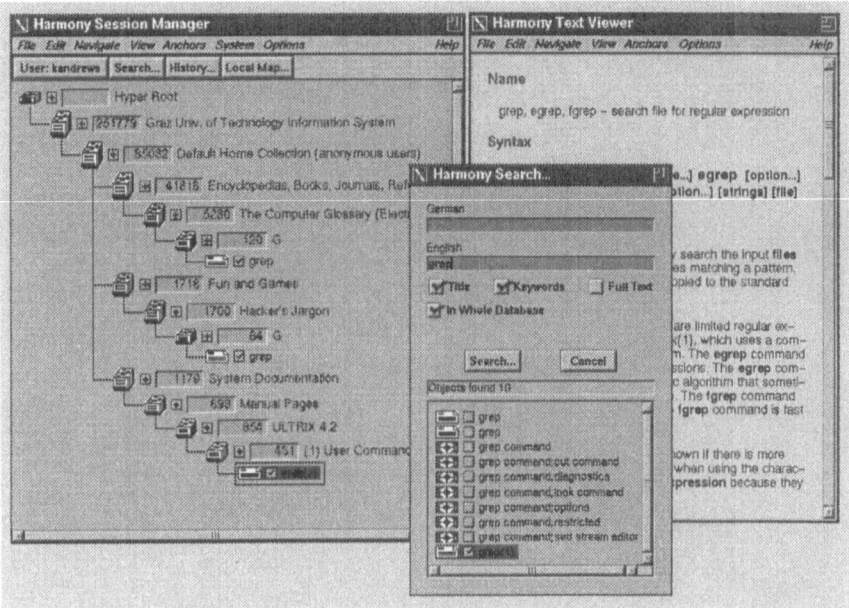

Fig. 5.: Harmony search dialogue

Harmony supports title, keyword, and full text search. The search is per-formed in the current collection by default. The output is an ordered list of matching documents. This list is of course active, so that documents may be ac-tivated by double-clicking within the search output list. Figure 5 shows a search dialogue for the word "grep" in the titles and keywords of all documents and anchors on the local server. Three text documents and a number of anchor ob-jects have been found. Clicking on the three text documents in turn has caused the session manager to open up the path to each of them in the collection hi-erarchy. Having seen that the bottom-most document belongs to the collection "User Commands" in collection "ULTRIX 4.2" in "Manual Pages", the user has activated this document in preference to the Hacker's Jargon or Computer Glos-sary entries. This *location feedback* is an important feature of Harmony – it en-ables users to make intelligent choices about search results before committing to fetch a particular document. Furthermore, it allows users to build up a mental picture of the locations of documents.

The *local map* facility, similar to the local map of Intermedia, provides a kind of short-range radar, generating on request (dynamically) a map of the vicinity of a document. By default, two levels of incoming and outgoing hyperlinks are represented. Figure 6 shows the local map for the "grep" manual page. Of course the local map is active; documents may be activated by double-clicking their icons.

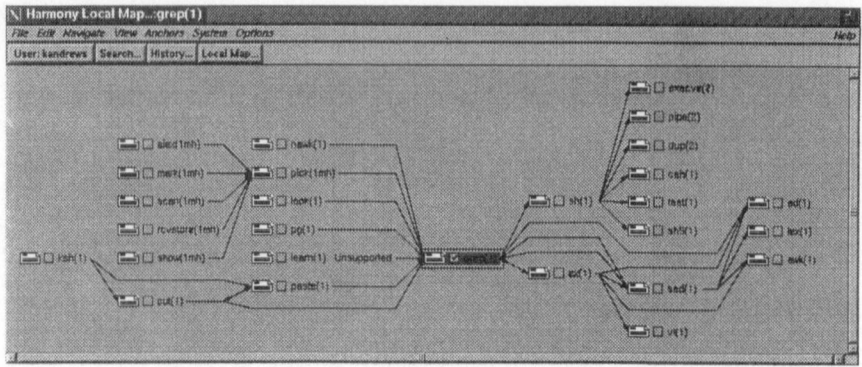

Fig. 6.: Harmony local map

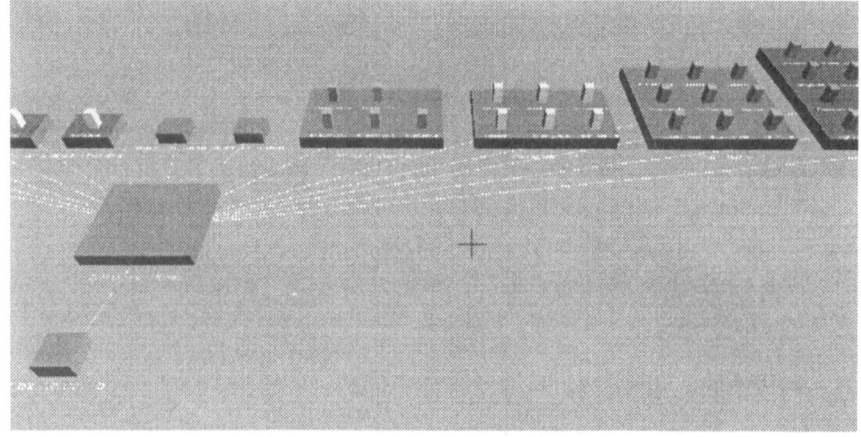

Fig. 7.: Harmony information landscape

Work is currently under way on a three-dimensional graphical overview map, called the *information landscape*, a prototype of which is shown in Figure 7. The collection hierarchy is mapped out onto a plane and the third dimension used to encode size. Users can "fly" over the hyperspace landscape looking for salient features, like flying over a file system with FSN [19]. The information landscape is an alternative to navigating with the session manager's built-in collection hierarchy browser. In the coming months, truly three-dimensional layouts will be investigated [6, 7] and work towards an immersive (virtual reality) interface is planned [2].

Authoring features currently under implementation in Harmony include a drag-and-drop interface to the local file system, allowing documents to be simply pulled into collections in the session manager, and a link editing facility supported across all Harmony viewers.

4 Concluding Remarks

We have pesented a snapshot of the current status of Hyper-G and its Harmony client for X Windows. More detailed information and a number of technical reports are available by anonymous ftp from `iicm.tu-graz.ac.at` in directory `pub/Hyper-G/papers`.

5 Acknowledgements

Partial Support of the Hyper-G project by the Austrian Ministry of Science, Joanneum Research, and the European Space Agency is gratefully acknowledged.

References

[1] Bob Alberti, Farhad Anklesaria, Paul Lindner, Mark McCahill, and Daniel Torrey. The internet gopher protocol: a distributed document search and retrieval protocol. March 1992. Available by anonymous ftp from boombox.micro.umn.edu in directory pub/gopher/gopher_protocol.

[2] Keith Andrews. Constructing cyberspace: virtual reality and hypermedia. December 1993. To appear in Proc. of Virtual Reality Vienna '93.

[3] Tim Berners-Lee, Robert Cailliau, Jean-François Groff, and Bernd Pollermann. World-Wide Web: the information universe. *Electronic Networking: Research, Applications and Policy*, 2(1):52–58, Spring 1992.

[4] Tim Berners-Lee and Dan Conolly. Hypertext markup language (HTML). June 1993. Version 1.2. Available in hypertext on the World Wide Web as http://info.cern.ch/hypertext/WWW/Markup/HTML.html.

[5] Deborah M. Edwards and Lynda Hardman. Lost in hyperspace: cognitive mapping and navigation in a hypertext environment. In R. McAleese, editor, *Hypertext: Theory into Practice*, pages 105–125, Blackwell Scientific Publications Ltd., 1989.

[6] Kim Michael Fairchild. Information management using virtual reality-based visualizations. In Alan Wexelblat, editor, *Virtual Reality: Applications and Explorations*, pages 45–74, Academic Press, 1993.

[7] Kim Michael Fairchild, Luis Serra, Ng Hern, Lee Beng Hai, and Ang Tin Leong. Dynamic fisheye information visualizations. In Rae A. Earnshaw, Michael A. Gigante, and Huw Jones, editors, *Virtual Reality Systems*, pages 161–177, Academic Press, 1993.

[8] Bernard J. Haan, Paul Kahn, Victor A. Riley, James H. Coombs, and Norman K. Meyrowitz. IRIS hypermedia services. *Communications of the ACM*, 35(1):36–51, January 1992.

[9] Frank Kappe. Hyper-G: a distributed hypermedia system. In Barry Leiner, editor, *Proc. INET '93, San Francisco, California*, pages DCC–1–DCC–9, Internet Society, August 1993.

[10] Frank Kappe and Hermann Maurer. Hyper-G: a large universal hypermedia system and some spin-offs. *ACM Computer Graphics, experimental special online issue*, May 1993. Available by anonymous ftp from siggraph.org in directory publications/May_93_online/Kappe.Maurer.

[11] Frank Kappe, Hermann Maurer, and Nick Sherbakov. Hyper-G – a universal hypermedia system. *Journal of Educational Multimedia and Hypermedia*, 2(1):39–66, 1993.

[12] Theodor Holm Nelson. *Literary Machines (Edition 87.1)*. The Distributors, South Bend, IN 46618, USA, 1987.

[13] Jakob Nielsen. The art of navigating through hypertext. *Communications of the ACM*, 33(3):296–310, March 1990.

[14] Jakob Nielsen. *Hypertext & Hypermedia*. Academic Press, San Diego, CA, 1990.

[15] George G. Robertson, Stuart K. Card, and Jock D. Mackinlay. Information visualization using 3D interactive animation. *Communications of the ACM*, 36(4):56–71, April 1993.

[16] Gerard Salton, E. A. Fox, and H. Wu. Extended boolean information retrieval. *Communications of the ACM*, 26(12):1022–1036, December 1983.

[17] Gerard Salton, A. Wong, and C. S. Yang. A vector space model for automatic indexing. *Communications of the ACM*, 18(11):613 ff., November 1975.

[18] Richard Marlon Stein. Browsing through terabytes – wide-area information servers open a new frontier in personal and corporate information services. *Byte*, 16(5):157–164, May 1991.

[19] Joel Tesler and Steve Strasnick. *FSN: The 3D File System Navigator*. Silicon Graphics, Inc., Mountain View, CA, 1992. Available by anonymous ftp from sgi.com in directory fsn.

[20] Kenneth Utting and Nicole Yankelovich. Context and orientation in hypermedia networks. *ACM Transactions on Information Systems*, 7(1):58–84, January 1989.

The Development of a Multimedia Distributed System for Education

Olga M. Beltcheva, Ilia K. Georgiev

Technical University of Sofia, FETT (room 1332A), Student Town H.Botev, Sofia
1156, Bulgaria
Email: olga,ilgeorg@bgcict.bitnet

Abstract. This paper presents some development methods used for multimedia processing in a distributed education system. Multimedia documents are described in HyTime-compliant form to provide network information interchange. An interactive structure-oriented editor helps the user to combine multimedia objects in a document. These documents are used to design education sessions. The proposed abstract model of an education session is intended for rapid development of education software. A time managing mechanism applicable both to multimedia documents and education sessions is elaborated. The paper outlines the architecture of an experimental client-server system for education and the data organisation.

1 Introduction

1.1 Trends in Education and Learning via Multimedia Computers

It is widely recognised that multimedia offers means of improving education and learning environments. First it provides more objective and expressive presentation of knowledge. Second it makes possible simulation-based learning [8].

However multimedia incorporation proves not sufficient for education system implementation. Unlike the computer-aided instruction and intelligent tutoring systems the contemporary education systems are to be developed as interactive learning environments [13] used by students for active interpretation and construction of ideas and products.

It is also important that students could not only conduct and record but also communicate their work. Isolated multimedia computers function in a quite different way than the ones connected in network environments. Advantages of education over LANs are enumerated in [8] and mainly concern the shared databases, the improving of collaborative work, interdisciplinary links and individualised learning.

Documents created with such systems are to be portable and accessible for different purposes. They have to specify in a standardised manner how the information of diverse media and origins is intended to be rendered for human perception in space and time. This specification must not depend on specific characteristics of systems or output devices.

1.2 Previous Research & Development Activities

Some years ago we implemented a stand-alone education microcomputer based on a speech processor with text, graphics, speech and image-based animation output. The software included low level driving modules for the specialised hardware, applications for teaching and examining children on spelling and solving simple mathematical problems, tunes guessing, composing of simple melodies and drawing.

In the process of work many problems grew up. We had not any special mechanism for graphics, speech and text synchronisation. This imposed multiple verification runs to find out the right dynamics. Time dependencies were firmly built in the procedures. The data itself was represented in a device independent manner but the multimedia compositions had some elements of procedural markup which meant dependency on the output process.

After this implementation we turned to another goal - to develop an interactive environment with some authoring functions [7] for combining graphics, speech and text into multimedia documents. We experimented to use the constructs of the Standard Generalised Markup Language (SGML) [2,3] due to their convenience for incorporating information of diverse origins in a single document. The non-text material was included in the SGML document mainly through references to specially coded graphics and speech entities.

We gave up using uniformly SGML markup representation of text, graphics and speech for some reasons. There was no standard widely recognised SGML representation of graphic and speech semantics. It would be almost impossible to cover through SGML markup expressions the whole set of graphic semantic constructs. Character notations of speech data can not be used for some schemes of speech coding (e.g. PCM, ADPCM, LPC). However this approach does not exclude the usage of equivalent SGML markup for some graphic and sound (MIDI coded) objects.

We have considered the Hypermedia/Time-based Document Structuring Language (HyTime) [4,9] as well suited for our application system. The advantages concern mainly the possibility to cover a limitless number of semantics corresponding to any sort of information and the flexible mechanism of defining abstract time dependencies and rendition control.

1.3 Goals and Structure of the Paper

This paper presents decisions taken during the architectural and structural design of a computer assisted education system organised on a client-server platform.

The basic concepts are structure-oriented creating of multimedia documents, education session models interpreting, time managing mechanism, interaction and client-server implementation.

Nowadays multimedia document structure is a topic touched by many research and standardisation teams. We have explored the promising advantages of SGML and

HyTime using a subset of their facilities.

Main efforts have been concentrated on the abstract presentation of the education process. The basic component is an education session which consists of scheduled multimedia documents and their interconnection.

Time managing is organised on the basis of a circular time list controlling the scheduling of multimedia documents.

The organisation of this paper is as follows. Section 2 describes the structure of the multimedia documents and how this structure can be used in the editing process. Section 3 explains the model of a multimedia education session and the elaborated mechanism of time managing. Section 4 outlines the client-server system architecture describing the functionality of the applications and the data organisation. Section 5 presents the experimental configuration. Finally, recommendations for further research are given.

2 Multimedia Document Structure

2.1 Using HyTime Categories

In the world of descriptive markup the content of a multimedia document is always interpreted according to a specific data type definition (DTD) which includes a set of structure elements and the rules for using them.

In order to create a HyTime-compliant DTD we have used our previous SGML description containing already designed entities, elements and attributes.

Figure 1 shows an exemplary simplified SGML DTD including some structure elements for multimedia document description. This exemplary DTD contains two non-SGML data content notations, namely HPGL and LPC. The non-SGML data entities are stored in separate files external to the SGML markup file.

The *entity* is a list of elements grouped together due to their similar properties. The element type *figure* in the entity declaration contains a *picture* followed by an optional *figcap*, and further an optional speech element *sp_elem*. A speech element *sp_elem* contains one or more speech items *sp_items*. The attribute list of the element *picture* includes the attribute *window* which defines the clipping area to be applied to the picture in its own coordinate system and the attribute *width* that controls the picture size when imbedded in the document.

In order to map the existing SGML DTD into a HyTime DTD we have first determined the set of *architectural forms* (object classes) corresponding to the semantics needed. This set includes:

- architectural forms for the information units of media types (speech segments, pictures and text) stored in different widely recognised formats. In this way standardised encoding of the different media is supported;

- architectural forms providing structures of information units (e.g. lists of speech items; figures including pictures, text to the picture and speech elements, pages including figures and written text, image-based animation, etc.). Such architectural forms are for all structure elements of the multimedia documents.

- hyperlinks architectural forms for independent and contextual links.

After the definition the correspondence of the architectural forms to the SGML DTD elements can be established by fixing the value of the *HyTime attribute* of each element to the name of the relevant architectural form.

This approach allows to extend easily multimedia documents with yet another medium - the digital video by elaborating the appropriate architectural forms.

```
<!NOTATIONS HPGL PUBLIC "HP Graphic Entities">
<!NOTATIONS LPC PUBLIC "Linear Predictive Code">

<!ENTITY % blocks    "list | figure | para">
<!ENTITY % phrases  "#PCDATA | unit_ref">

<!ELEMENT list        - -  (item)+>
<!ELEMENT item        - 0  (%phrases; | %blocks;)*>
<!ELEMENT para        - 0  (%phrases;)*>

<!ELEMENT unit_ref     0  EMPTY>
<!ATTLIST unit_ref         idref IDREF #REQUIRED>

<!ELEMENT figure       - -  (picture, figcap?, sp_elemt?)>
<!ELEMENT figcap      - 0  (%phrases;)*>
<!ELEMENT sp_elem     - -  (sp_item)+>

<!ELEMENT sp_item    - 0  EMPTY>
<!ATTLIST sp_item          entity ENTITY #REQUIRED

<!ELEMENT picture     - 0  EMPTY>
<!ATTLIST picture          entity ENTITY #REQUIRED>
                           window CDATA "0,0;1000,1000"
                           width  CDATA "5I">
```

Fig. 1. Extended DTD for non-SGML entities

The above SGML DTD contains no time dependencies. Start time and duration intervals could be included as attributes in the element attribute list. However to obtain an overall plan of the real-time behaviour and synchronisation with other objects, additional processing of the SGML description is needed. Rendering information concerning positions transformation of graphic objects has also to be presented in the attribute list.

HyTime offers a mechanism to define more abstract time dependencies. Information concerning the rendering in time and space is separated and made more easily accessible.

To provide rendering of HyTime objects in space and time they are represented in

Finite Coordinate Space (FCS). Our FCS consists of a time axis and a two dimensional coordinate space. Virtual measurement units of time and space (quanta) are used whose rate of exchange to real measurement units has to be application defined.

Rendered objects occur as *events*. Each event is considered as a bounding box with space dimensions specifying positions on each coordinate axis of the FCS and relative time dimensions specifying the start time point and duration interval.

Projectors determine how the positions and extents in the source FCS (the objects own coordinate system) are to be mapped onto a target FCS (e.g. the device coordinate system) and what is the rate of conversion of virtual time units into real time ones. Thus time based event schedules and projector schedules are supported.

2.2 Structure-Oriented Editing

Supporting of a Hytime-compliant DTD allows to bring the advantages of structure-oriented editing to multimedia documents.

The user has to define the structure elements to be included in the document, the content of the elements or subelements, the projectors to be applied to them during the rendering process.

Through menu selection the user points out the type of element he wants to include in the document. Because the editing program is aware of the HyTime-compliant DTD it provides a menu of the permitted optional subelements and cancels any attempts to include subelements that are not permitted. The content of elements (objects) can be accessed by identifier but also in a navigational and descriptive way.

The editing process includes displaying of *acyclic directed graphs* along the time axis. The nodes of the graph contain structure elements of the DTD. Picking of objects and their association with time is supported. Attributes of objects concerning rendering in space are interactively defined. Editing actions (copy, move, cut, paste, substitute) are provided on the graph. A "zoom" function controls the concealing and revealing of successive levels of detail.

On the exemplary graph on Figure 2 the following multimedia document is built up. At t_0 a *picture* and a *figure caption* form a *figure* on the display. At $t_1 = t_0 + \Delta t_0$ *text* is added to build the element *page*. At $t_2 = t_1 + \Delta t_1$ the message *sp_elem* is pronounced to comment the page content. At $t_3 = t_2 + \Delta t_2$ a new *picture* is rendered thus completing the whole multimedia document.

The output of the editing process is a HyTime-compliant document that represents various types of objects in SGML syntax. HyTime is used only as a network interchange format for revisable multimedia documents. Since HyTime does not provide for run-time efficiency there is yet another editor output. It is a multimedia document linked list of objects with their projection functions.

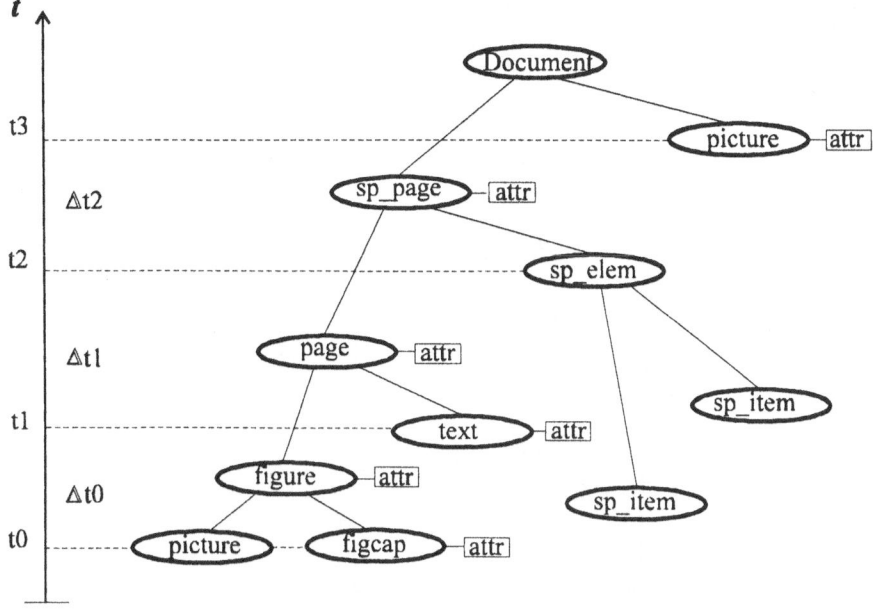

Fig.2. Multimedia Document Constructing

3 Modelling and Processing Framework

The paradigm for good education software is a simulation of the solution of problems. Simulation-based software is aimed not only to project multimedia documents, but also to simulate some activities according to logical conditions resulting from the interaction with the student.

We decided to present the education process in a unified manner forming an abstract model of the education task. The objective is to aid the programmer of the education software. This model should present the sequence in time of the multimedia documents and permit control by conditions that are formed by the interaction or by the education software. The model should have a simple structure allowing easy defining and editing.

Figure 3 shows schematically the modelling and processing framework.

Each multimedia document is presented as a list where the order of objects follows their appearance in time. This list is preliminary constructed using the described structure-oriented editor. It contains pointers to the functions that are to project the multimedia objects.

The programmer makes a task decomposition into *education sessions*. Each education session consists of multimedia documents that are projected under different conditions. These conditions are transformed into *flags*. An education

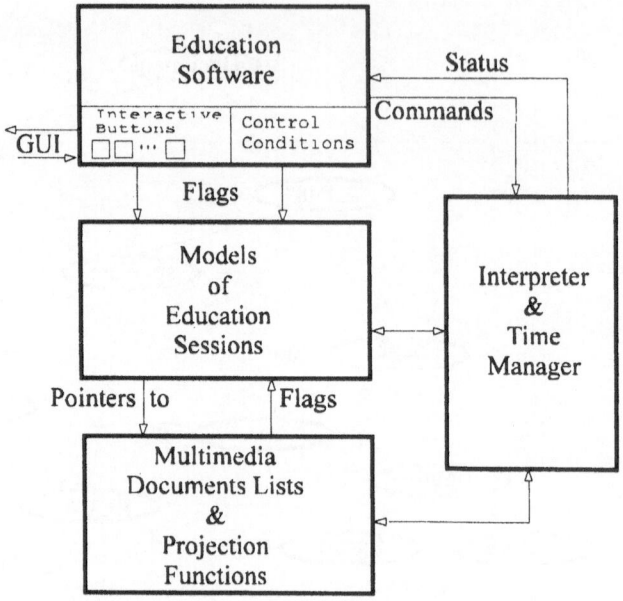

Fig.3. Modelling and Processing Framework

session is presented by a simple *isomorphic (structure-like) model,* that could be easily modified. The flags can start, stop or delay the multimedia sequence and also change the sequence under logical relationships.

Time-dependent running of education sessions is performed by an *interpreter.* It extracts the models of the education sessions from the memory, controls their decoding and execution, and performs the time managing. The interpreter receives commands from the education software and returns status information.

3.1 Model of the Multimedia Education Session

The isomorphic model of an education session presents the building blocks and the interconnections between them. The former are multimedia documents projected in a specific way and sequence depending on some logical conditions. Most of the logical conditions depend on the practical education problem and are out of our consideration.

Each multimedia document has attributes which determine its characteristics. A general characteristic is the *duration interval.* Each multimedia document has many input flags and one output flag (Figure 4).

The occurrence of the input flags i_i can cause scheduling of the document, i.e. the multimedia document becomes an event. There are mainly two logical relations be-

Fig.4. Multimedia document and its flags

tween the input flags. The first one is a conjunction which means that all flags should occur to run the multimedia document. The other one is a disjunction - the occurrence of one flag makes the multimedia document to be projected. The output flag o is set on, when the document is fully projected.

The data structure of a multimedia document is a circular linked list. Figure 5 shows the contents of such a list.

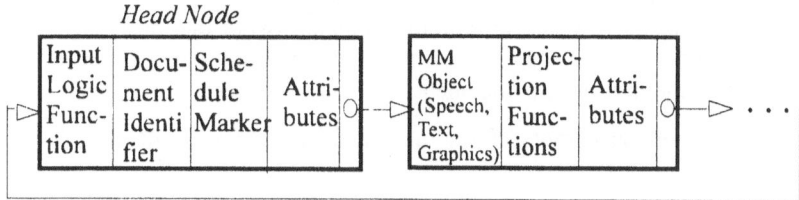

Fig.5. Circular linked list of a multimedia document

The head node consists of the multimedia document identifier, the input logical function (disjunction or conjunction of the input flags), a schedule marker that contains the moment when the document becomes active, attributes of the document (duration interval etc.).

Each following node represents an object (text, speech element, picture etc.) The node consists of an object identifier, pointers to the projection functions, attributes (time distance relative to the projection start moment, duration interval). The order of the object nodes in the list follows the advancing of their projection time.

The model of an educational session is sufficiently defined in terms of multimedia documents and their interconnections. Figure 6 shows a schematic diagram of an education session consisting of four multimedia documents and several flags.

The interconnections between the inputs and outputs of the multimedia documents carry out the flag transfer. These flags control the sequence of the multimedia processing in the education session. The state of the education session at any given time is specified by the state (active or not) of the multimedia documents and the flags at that time.

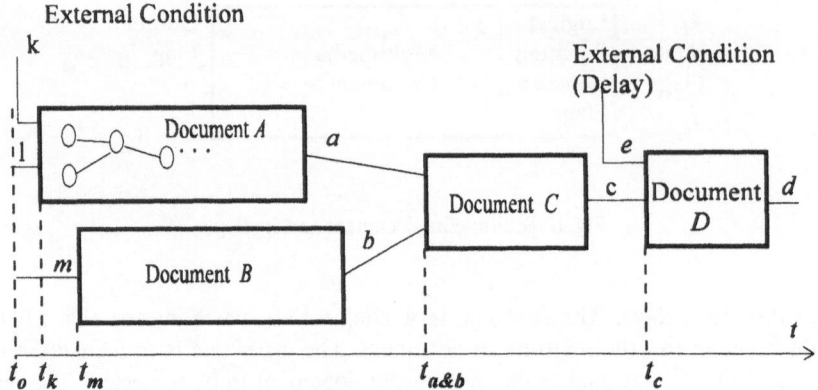

Fig.6. Scheme of an education session

Table 1 presents the isomorphic model of the simple education session shown in Figure 6. Every row describes a multimedia document. The items in the row include multimedia document identifier, duration interval, list of the input flags, the logical function between input flags, the destination of the output flag, pointer to the circular linked list of the multimedia document.

The flags might be outputs of multimedia documents or generated from external conditions.

Table 1. Isomorphic model of an education session

Document Identifier	Duration Interval	Input Flags	Input Logical Function	Destination of the Output Flag	Pointer to Multimedia Document
A	8	k.l	Disjunction	C	
B	10	m	None	C	
C	6	a,b	Conjunction	D	
D	4	e,c	Disjunction	Out	

3.2 Time Managing in Multimedia Processing

The main requirement for processing of multimedia documents is a sufficiently precise emulation of the passage of time. Each media object has its time parameters. These parameters are valid (active), when the event is scheduled. The duration of an event is used to predict the points in time when the next event in the session should be rendered. The next event is recorded as future event, which is included into a time-dependent *event queue*. The concept of the event queue [6,15] can be defined in terms of a set of events ordered along the time axis. The event queue is used to simulate the passage of time by advancing of current time from event to event. In the right time each event is projected, i.e. it is processed at the very moment it becomes the current event.

The data structure for implementing an event queue is a *circular time list*. The passage of current time is simulated in discrete, regular time increments Δt. The circular list contains a node for every time t_i. The size of Δt could be in real or in virtual units. Time normally advances from node to node without skipping, and the location of the node addressed by the scanning process is the precise numerical value of current time.

Nodes in the circular list are either empty or contain an output flag of an event. A flag appearing in this time list represents the moment when the projection of the event ends and following events could start if their input logical condition is satisfied. The scheduling process of the active multimedia event is the inserting of a schedule marker in its header node and of its output flag in an appropriate node in the time list.

The duration intervals of the events are expressed as integer multiples of Δt. The projection of a current event activated by a flag at time t_e, leads to the prediction of its end at $t_e + d_i$, where d_i is the duration interval of the event. The result is not only the moment of the predicted event end but also the address of the time list node where the event output flag must be inserted.

The length L of the list is a time interval specified by the number of time increments Δt. The time increment and the time list length could be set by the interpreter. The selection of these values depends on the duration of the projected multimedia events. The relationship between the events duration and these two values is based on a simple rule. All events duration intervals must be presented as an integer d_i. The real duration is a multiplication $(d_i \times \Delta t)$. The length L can be normally chosen greater or equal to d_{max} which is the maximum duration of a multimedia event in the current education session. The increment Δt could be calculated as a greatest common divisor of the multimedia events duration interval.

This mechanism is illustrated in Figure 7. An input flag has activated multimedia event A at current time t_1. This has caused the insertion of output flag a into a time slice t_9 ($T_A = 8$). The scheduling process has been accomplished by changing the content of node t_9 and by putting a schedule marker in the head node of the list presenting document A. The insertion is a simple placement of the value of the present time (equal to 1) into the head node of the list of A. This schedule marker shows the start time of A. Next, current time is t_4. An input flag has been processed and has caused the scheduling of event B and the inserting of its output flag b in t_{14} ($T_B = 10$). Further, current time is t_{10}. Multimedia event C ($T_C = 6$) has been activated and its output flag (future event) has been inserted into t_1. In this example the length L of the time list was chosen $L = 15 > T_B$, where T_B is the maximum duration interval.

202

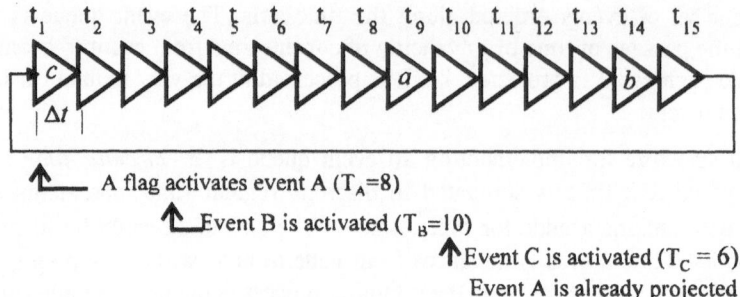

t_1 t_2 t_3 t_4 t_5 t_6 t_7 t_8 t_9 t_{10} t_{11} t_{12} t_{13} t_{14} t_{15}

A flag activates event A (T_A=8)

Event B is activated (T_B=10)

Event C is activated (T_C = 6).
Event A is already projected

Fig.7. Circular Time List

In case when only one time list is used the fixed length and resolution prove a disadvantage. In the above example it is possible that the time increment Δt is too rough to proceed the multimedia event A which is a combination of different time dependent procedures manipulating text, graphics and speech. In this case the described time list technique could be used by attaching of another time list local to A. The schedule marker of A contains a pointer to the local time list of A. The opposite case is the handling of an event of a very long duration. The time list should be extended by connecting an extension list to node t_1. Every multimedia event not fitting into the main time list would be scheduled by inserting it into its proper place in this higher time list. The time increment of this new list is equal to the length L of the normal list. The higher time list should be investigated before each scan of the normal list, and all events belonging to the subsequent scan should be removed from the higher time list and scheduled in the normal time list. In a most complicated case a local time list could be attached to each multimedia document.

Consider now the interpretation sequence and the time managing of the presented simple education session shown in Figure 6. Table 2 follows the content changing of the time list. The point "• " indicates the current moment. The length L is now chosen equal to $13 > T_B$. At current time t_3 the flag k is coming from certain external condition. The logical input function of the event A is disjunction which causes the insertion of k in the time list and the placement of a schedule marker in the head node of A. The event A has been activated. The duration interval $T_A = 8$, the output flag a is inserted into t_{11} as a future event At time t_4 the event B is being scheduled and becomes active. The future event b has been inserted into node t_1 (the duration interval $T_B = 10$). The time advances to t_{11} without changing the content of the time list. During this period the events A and B have been processed. At t_{11} the output flag a becomes current event. The input logical function of C is conjunction. The event C could not be scheduled because flag b is not active. At t_1 the event C becomes active. The value of t_1 is being stored into its head node as a schedule marker. The flag c (future event) is being inserted into the node t_7. At this time event D is being scheduled. The external flag e has no influence. But if the programmer changes the input logic function of D from disjunction to conjunction, then the flag e could be used for delay.

Table 2

t1	t2	t3	t4	t5	t6	t7	t8	t9	t10	t11	t12	t13
•												
	•									a		
		k •								a		
			m •							a		
b				•						a		
b					•					a		
b						•				a		
b							•			a		
b								•		a		
b									•	a		
b										a •		
b											•	
b												•
b•						c						
	•											

This sequence could be interrupted by an interaction condition. Then time advancing is being stopped. New condition could start the time managing again.

3.3 Interaction

In the research it has been found that the interaction is the most difficult part of the whole project.

The dynamics of the interaction is application dependent. Creating an interactive algorithm requires the programmer to comprehend the unpredictable reaction of the students and the processing of multiple variants of control conditions.

Then, once the educational program executes in real interactive mode and does not function correctly, the debugging is a complicated problem. The debugging software requires systematic attention to details as well as knowledge what questions to ask, the ability to analyse the answers received and to formulate the best next questions. To obtain exhausting information about the interaction in an active education process the programmer needs data about the run-time behaviour of the program. And here comes the greatest difficulty. It is almost impossible to formulate a hypothesis of possible interaction events, collect data and experience and review traces of execution or check aspects of the process state.

Our work is not aiming too high, we have had the objective to facilitate the programmers efforts in rewriting complicated programs in case of incorrect interaction behaviour.

First, an attempt is made to create a mechanism for easier changing of the education process when the interaction needs it. The word here is "attempt", since it is impossible to create an general purpose model and processing of the application-dependent interaction. This mechanism is based on the presented simple model of the education session. The interaction can change the behaviour of the education session by forming appropriate flags, by inserting new primary flags and changing the logical input function of multimedia events.

The interactive buttons form the basis for mapping student interaction to application behaviour and to education session functionality. The interactive buttons are a generalisation of the interactions. The buttons are used for a variety of purposes, such as movements, new interface building blocks, and learning control. A button has an image representation and a procedure to execute when pressed. In this meaning buttons are abstractions that can enable students to be in control of their own educational process.

Second, some requirements for a reliable dialogue have been formulated. This reliable dialogue keeps the operational capacities of the learning process irrespective of the wrong student actions and eventually prevents these actions in some limits.

The possible back level after a wrong action should be estimated for every menu item. The experience shows that after a wrong answer students tend to undertake new wrong actions. Sometimes the program branch must be to the most upper dialogue level, sometimes not. Realisation of such branch back is difficult because one must save the state of the educational example before and after every modification.

The cursor should become active only when its use is foreseen. It should appear in that screen areas where student's actions are expected. Depending on the button meaning and the student's answer the warning and highlighting actions should be made.

4 System Architecture

4.1 Distributed Processing

Distributed processing is based of the client-server computing paradigm [14]. One server and multiple clients along with the underlying operations system and interprocess communication allow distributed computation, analysis and presentation.

The configuration of the client-server system is shown on Figure 8.

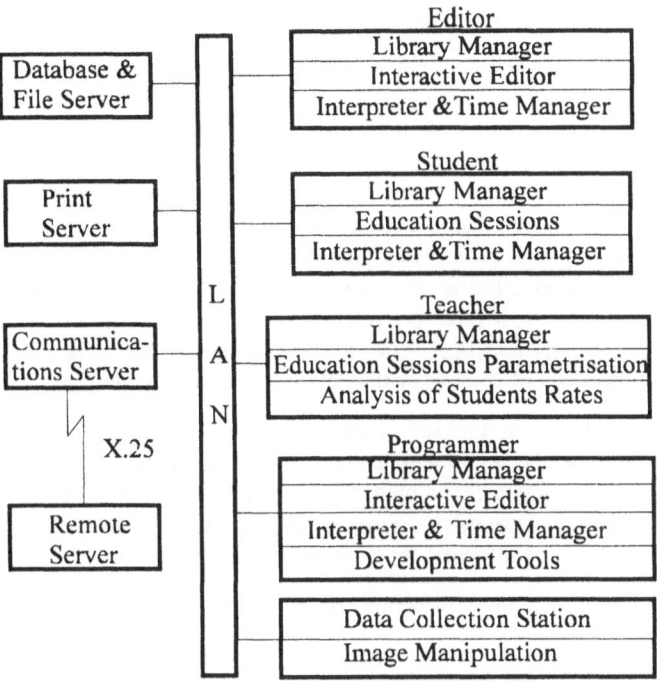

Fig.8. Client-server system configuration

Clients share the server data storage. The server has the functionality of both a file server and database server. The client processes interact with the user and do presentation and some analysis. They have one or several of the following characteristics. They present the user interface. The latter comprises the graphical user interface (GUI) and the audio output. By means of the GUI users queries for data retrieval and analysis are defined. Each client has to have a single consistent graphical and audio interface although in the system multiple interfaces may be supported. Client processes form queries or commands for presentation to the server. They determine whether it is necessary to send the query to the server or the data processing required may be performed by the client itself. Further client processes transmit the queries/commands to the server via the underlying communication methodology. They analyse the query or command results from the server and present these results to the user.

The server-based process provides security management of the shared data and responses to the queries or commands from the clients.

4.2 System Functionality

The set of application tasks includes an interactive multimedia document editor, interpreter and time manager, education software, network record management system, library manager, image manipulation software.

The interpreter & time manager performs rendering in time and space of multimedia documents. It can be activated by the education software or by the interactive multimedia document editor with the purpose of estimating. The education software is built upon already programmed teaching, self-training and examination sessions. An education session can be parametrised by selecting from the network library the appropriate data that the session will be run with. The library manager provides the interface to the network record management system. It maintains the libraries by creating, updating and deleting of records through sequential or random access. The image manipulation software converts between various graphics file formats, performs compression/decompression, makes changes in an image as re-sizing and changing the numbers of colours or the colour space the image used.

A task division between the server and the clients is proposed as follows. The interactive multimedia document editor, the interpreter & time manager, the education software and library manager are client-based processes. The network record management system is a server-based process. It provides centralised processing at the server allowing for efficient multi-user control.

The system comprises the following types of users: editor, programmer, student, teacher.

Users have specific access rights to the distinct applications and data files. Additional control to data is provided through access keys associated with each data file individually.

The editor is allowed to run the interactive multimedia document editor. The session programmer uses the already generated multimedia documents to program education sessions (teaching, self-training and examination). The student only runs these sessions. During the examination session his responses are recorded in a protocol which can be inspected with a normal text editor. The teacher can parametrise the education sessions thus individualising the process. He can also inspect student protocols and run programs for analysis of students rates.

4.3 Data Organisation

Data organisation aims at improved server utilisation and relative rare downloading (initial or run-time) of large data files from the server to the clients, i.e. reduced network traffic.

The data needed by the user interface of the client-based processes reside on the local clients disks. The data used to build up the multimedia documents and to program the education sessions are stored on the shared network disks.

So local databases and local libraries of data files are distinguished from network databases and network libraries (Figure 9).

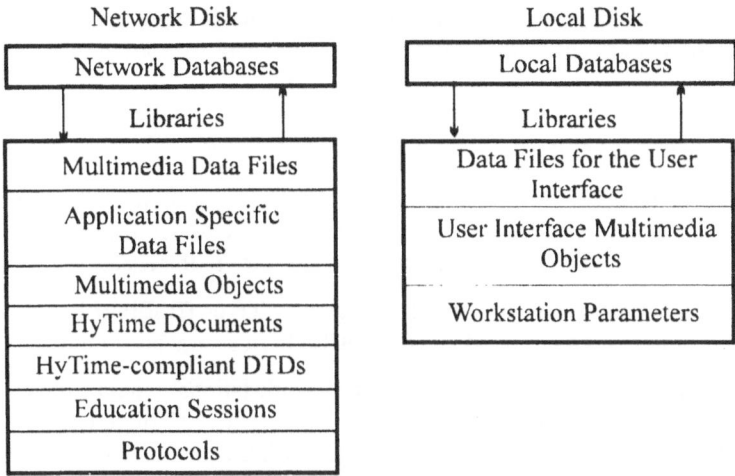

Fig. 9. Data organisation

This approach leads to network traffic reduction since data files servicing the clients user interface have not to be transported each time from the server to the clients local disk memory.

In the system a specialised workstation collects data for the multimedia documents. It combines the characteristics of a speech development and an image scanning station. To each image or sound segment indexing information is entered. When indexing is completed the image or sound segment is stored on the file server disk (in the relevant network library) while the indexing information (media type, media encoding, duration interval, relations to application specific data, comments) is written to the shared media database. The media database holds only the indices as opposed to the images and sound segments themselves thus saving the database from storing of huge amounts of information. In this way the shared media database offers indexing and content addressability of images, image-based animation, texts, speech or other sound segments.

The shared application specific database contains indexing information about application specific data types as tabular scientific data, mathematical equations, chemical data types etc. as well as teaching and examination exemplary data relating to different topics.

Image conversion procedures are executed on the specialised workstation, i.e. they manipulate the scanned-in images and store their results to the file server.

The interactive multimedia document editor can be run without downloading the large image and speech files to the client. The interpreter and time manager can operate in two modes. In the first one, the image and speech files are not locally available. In this case the rendering still incorporates some form of blankness - darkness, silence or an appropriate dummy image or message - so that the space and time relationships of the rendered and unrendered objects is preserved. In the second mode, which is entered during education sessions, data files are downloaded to the clients in real time.

5 Experimental Configuration

Our platform is a PC-based system on a Netware 3.11 LAN. The experimental configuration consists of a Btrieve database server and workstations. The client processes present a Microsoft Windows-based interface to the user.

The database architecture consists of a Requests Server (BSERVER) in the server and a copy of a Requests Supervisor (BREQUEST) in each workstation.

The speech processing devices in the workstations could have different implementation. The simple solution is to use commercial digital telephone PCM coding. We have used speech synthesis devices with Linear Predictive Coding (LPC). The latter provides digital storage and recreation of real speech on the basis of preliminary elaborated mathematical model of the human vocal tract. Speech is represented in a more compressive and editable manner.

6 Future Work

There are some directions in which we would like to follow this research.

The prestigious, but expensive goal is to enhance the range of the multimedia documents. The integration of video will expand the teaching features, but it will increase difficulties in the database managing.

Developing methods for interactive speech editing is one of the next directions that we want to pursue. It is not simply a piece of speech to be speeded up or slowed down, although there are signal-theoretic methods to do it. This will allow to change the dynamic acoustic parameters of the speech which assures intonation control.

Another serious problem grows up together with multimedia database loading. This is the navigation through the information space according to some specific relationships. Presently we are designing a hyperlinking capability upon tree classes. A network database on the server will maintain the linking information (links and their attributes) and use the features of those classes. Additional structure above the underlying hyperlinked data will allow the same data to be easily used in different education sessions.

So far our effort was concentrated predominantly on the multimedia processing. During the implementation it turned out that the sophisticated educational software is the bottleneck of the system.

7 Conclusion

Research and development activities in creating multimedia education applications over a network have been presented. The multimedia document structure is substantiated using HyTime constructs. We have described our innovative approach for presenting the education process as a set of education sessions. These sessions consist of multimedia documents interconnected via flags. The interpretation and time managing of these sessions are based on their isomorphic model.

The interaction and the conditions from the education software control the sessions by forming flags.

Significant amount of work needs to be done to create a usable education system. It is an extremely difficult development problem and we hope that our methods will be helpful to generalise the problem understanding and solving.

This approach is expected to help the ability to specify complex education multimedia functionality in concise, device-independent manner.

Acknowledgements

This research has been partially supported by the Ministry of Science and Education, Bulgaria.

The authors are grateful to Ch.Hornung (Fraunhofer-IGDV, Darmstadt) and to Michael Gervautz (TU Vienna) for the hospitality and fruitful discussions.

References

1. Adie, Ch.: Distributed Multimedia Information Systems. Computer Networks for Research in Europe, Elsevier, vol. 25, 1993, Suppl. 2.

2. Chamberlin, D.D., Ch.F. Goldfarb: Graphic Applications of the Standard Generalized Markup Language (SGML). Computer & Graphics Vol.11, No.4, pp.343-358, 1987.

3. ISO 8879: Standard Generalized Markup Language (SGML), 1986.

4. ISO 10744: Hypermedia Time-based Structuring Language (HyTime), 1992.

5. Coombs, J.H., A.H. Renear, S.J. DeRose: Markup Systems and Future of Scholary Text Processing. Communications of the ACM, vol. 30, No.11, pp. 933-947, Nov. 1987.

6. Georgiev, I.: Speeding Up of Simulation. Proc. of the 10-th International Conference FTSD'87, Varna, 1987.

7. Georgiev, I., O. Beltcheva: Interactive Environment for Multimedia Processing. Proceedings of the International Conference CAD/Graphics'93, Peking, China.

8. Hawkins, J.: Technology and the Organization of Schooling. Communications of the ACM, vol. 36, No.5, pp. 30-34, May 1993.

9. Newcomb, S.R., N.A. Kipp, V.T. Newcomb: The "HyTime"- Hypermedia/ Time-based Document Structuring Language. Communications of the ACM, vol. 34, No.11, pp. 67-83, Nov. 1991.

210

10. Novell, Inc.: Professional Development Series, Austin, Texas.

11. Phillips, R.L.: MediaView - A General Multimedia Digital Publication System. Communications of the ACM, vol. 34, No.7, July 1991.

12. Proceedings of the Eurographics Workshop on Multimedia, Dagstuhl, Nov. 1992.

13. Schank, R.: Learning via Multimedia Computers. Communications of the ACM, vol.36, No.5, pp.54-56, May 1993.

14. Sinha, A.: Client-Server Computing: Current Technological Review. Communications of the ACM, vol. 35, No.7, pp. 78-98, July 1992.

15. Thompson, E.W., S.A. Szygenda: Digital Simulation In a Time-based, Table-driven Environment. Computer, vol.8, No 3, March 1975.

DDD - Dynamic Distributed Documents

Matthias Kummer
Wolfgang Herzner

Department of Information Technology,
Austrian Research Centre Seibersdorf,
A-2444 Seibersdorf, Europe

Abstract. A script-based and object-oriented model for extending Digital's CDA/DDIF for multimedia/hypermedia (mm/hm) and other dynamic aspects in distributed environments is presented, hence the term dynamic distributed documents rather than multimedia documents. Based on that model, a prototype for the presentation of multimedia documents has been developed, which is also presented in this paper[1].

1 Introduction

The extension of conventional document processing (dealing with static contents like text, graphics, and raster images) by dynamic media (like video, audio, or animation) raises a number of problems and aspects reaching beyond the generation and presentation of multimedia contents.

Multimedia documents cannot be printed as simply as conventional documents, they have to be presented by the computer environment directly. But this magnifies the importance of how well the user should be able to control the presentation of such documents, that means, in other words, the user interacts with the presentation.

In multimedia documents with a lot of different content portions there is both a need to select information of specific interest (either by position or by content) and a need to synchronize that information (i.e. describe temporal relationships).

Often authors of multimedia documents want to synchronize the whole presentation flow of a document. This can be done by so-called (multimedia) authoring tools (like Authorware Professional [4]), the counterpart to desktop publishing tools.

When adding input methods, like those supported in conventional windowing environments (buttons, menus, sliders) or graphics systems (coordinates, object picking), to the specification of the author's presentation flow and the user's interactions, the distinction between dynamic documents and applications diminishes and consequentially the difference between document authoring and application development.

Regarding applications of distributed documents - like Computer Supported Cooperative Work (CSCW) or workflow control [9] - new aspects arise like isochrony and unpredictable delays.

[1] This project has been funded by Digital's European External Research Project EERP AU-025A.

Finally, animation has to be considered too when the synchronizational aspects include both temporal and spatial issues (e.g., modifying the characteristics of some sound object according to the progression of a visual object along a certain path).

As a result, the extension of conventional documents by dynamic contents leads to the quest for more powerful tools and methods enabling the authors to create dynamic documents.

The remainder of this paper describes our model for the presentation of distributed dynamic documents. Section 2 describes models and systems in this field. Section 3 describes the synchronization model as well as parts of a scripting language based on that model. Section 4 describes our implementation experiences, the representation of the model and the different parts of the prototype, and section 5 summarizes this paper.

2 Related Work

In this section we give a very brief outline of some models and systems in this domain, which are related to our work with respect to their way of specifying dynamic behaviour.

2.1 International Multimedia/Hypermedia Encoding Standards

HyTime. The hypermedia/time-based structuring language 'HyTime,' published as ISO/IEC standard 10744 in 1992 [13], serves for application- and platform-independent (cleartext-) encoding of mm/hm documents. It provides a set of so-called *architectural forms* to embed mm/hm information into SGML-encoded documents [12].

HyTime's basic feature for specifying the dynamics of a document's representation is that of *schedules*. A schedule places *events* in *finite coordinate spaces* ('fcs'), which are defined as *axes* [7]. An event defines the *extent* of a (document) object within the schedule's fcs. The final mapping of schedules to real presentation is not fully defined by HyTime (nor is user interaction), though it can be guided by *rendition* modules, which actually serve for transformations between fcs.

In addition, HyTime supports hyperlinks and allows for addressing objects by name, position, and semantics.

MHEG (Multimedia/Hypermedia Expert Group). This standard is currently in the status of a committee draft (CD 13522), and expected to be published in 1995 [14]. MHEG serves for ASN.1-encoding [11] of mm/hm documents and applications. By using an object-oriented approach, MHEG knows *content* objects and *composites* for describing the logical architecture of documents, while the dynamic behaviour is specified by the object classes *link*, *action*, and *script*, where the latter is intended to describe control beyond that provided by MHEG itself. It clearly distinguishes between content objects and their representation: *presentables* handle all presentation-related aspects of document components, including user interaction and event handling. Hence, MHEG supports encoding of mm/hm representation and uses an event-driven processing model.

2.2 Script-oriented Authoring Tools

There is a number of so-called multimedia authoring tools available on the market, which allow the development of mm/hm documents and applications, and which provide so-called scripts for the specification of presentation dynamics. Examples are HyperCard, ToolBook, and MacroMind Director.

HyperCard / HyperTalk. HyperTalk [2] is the scripting language of Apple's hypermedia development tool HyperCard [1]. HyperCard uses the metaphor of the "ordered stack of cards" for structuring information, where only one card may be visible at a time, and provides *buttons* as input- and *fields* as i/o-objects. The basic characteristics of HyperTalk are:

- For each object within a stack a script can be defined (not all elements are objects, though). Scripts, bound to visual objects only, may contain a number of handlers, where each one is responsible for the reaction upon the arrival of a specific message.

- For encoding the body of handlers, a rather conventional programming language (though powerful with regard to presentation control) is provided.

- Handlers may not be nested.

- HyperTalk is extremely event-oriented. Without receiving a message by a handler, nothing happens.

- A message sent to an object which doesn't have a handler is automatically forwarded to the next higher level in the hierarchy.

- Application specific messages may be defined.

- Besides message boxes, no objects can be created at presentation time, but a variety of property modifications are possible.

(Multimedia) ToolBook / OpenScript. OpenScript is the scripting language of the multimedia authoring tool (Multimedia) ToolBook by Asymetrix Corp [3]. The main differences to HyperCard/HyperTalk are:

- In ToolBook, the metaphor for structuring information is called the book, consisting of a sequence of pages, where one page may be visible at a time. Several pages in a book may share a common background, which may contain anything a page may contain. Like HyperCard, ToolBook is limited to single-user and one-'window'-at-a-time representations.

- In OpenScript, three kinds of handlers are provided: for accepting messages, for accepting and setting variables, respectively.

MacroMind Director / Lingo. Lingo is the scripting language of the multimedia authoring tool MacroMind Director [16] by MacroMind Inc. Again, this tool resembles HyperCard with respect to the usage of objects, scripts, and event handlers. Characteristic differences to HyperCard and ToolBook are:

- The used metaphor is a (movie) performance including the 'score' (a spreadsheet like structure, where the columns are called frames, the rows tracks, and their intersections cells, respectively), 'casts' (containing the actors), and 'events.'

- Four kinds of scripts are provided: movie scripts, score scripts, cast scripts, and event scripts.

- Synchronization is provided by and limited to frames. (Frames depict the progression in time; each frame has a finite, but individual duration, depending on its content.)
- Factories (a template for author defined objects) allow the creation of an arbitrary number of instances of some object class at presentation time.

2.3 Icon-based Authoring Tools

Besides the previous mentioned authoring tools using a script language, there are a number of other authoring tools using a graphical programming interface to describe the behaviour of a presentation ([17, 20, 21, 22, 23]). An example is

Authorware Professional [4]. Here, icons are used to present content objects as well as control elements like loops or alternatives. By arranging these icons in a flowchart, called 'flow line', the author specifies the control flow of a presentation. Sections of the flow line can be condensed into single icons. Additional control information, e.g., durations or menu strings, is edited in special menus popped-up when the corresponding icon is selected, or in separate windows. In addition, a script-like feature is supported for fine-grained control. And, like most of the other authoring tools, IconAuthor provides tools for directly editing of still contents and simple animations, and calls other tools for editing of dynamic contents.

2.4 Extended Programming Languages

Visual Basic [5], by Microsoft Corp., has been developed for the fast development of graphical user interface applications (including mm/hm) under Windows.

It provides similar features as the script-based authoring systems, with two significant differences:

- it uses Basic (extended for event-handling) as scripting language, and
- it allows to write multiple-windows-at-a-time applications.

Visual C++ ([18, 19, 24]) differs from Visual Basic mainly in the different programming language used.

2.5 Summary

A comparison of the mentioned standards and tools shall help to identify the basic characteristics and differences.

Document structure. Hierarchical structures are generally supported, although sometimes restricted to predefined levels. HyTime does not prescribe certain relationships between document objects.

Separation of document and its presentation. Only MHEG makes a clear distinction, thus allowing to have an arbitrary number of presentations of a single object at a time. A similar effect is supported by HyTime's rendition module and Lingo's factories.

Schedules versus events. Only HyTime and – to some extent – MacroMind Director use schedules, while all other systems are strictly event-oriented. Hence, only HyTime can express end-synchronization.

Scripts. All authoring tools provide certain script languages. Scripts are generally written for individual objects and define their reactions upon certain events. MHEG does not support a specific scripting language, but provides a hook for including arbitrary scripts by means of the script object. In addition, its link and action objects provide a rich functionality for expressing presentation behaviour, which is intended to make scripts unnecessary for not too complex applications. HyTime is more unconcerned about scripts.

Interaction. All authoring tools provide specific interaction objects, usually derived from windowing environments. MHEG provides interaction behaviour for conceptually all content objects; for instance, a video presentable could raise a trigger event when selected by the user. HyTime does not deal with interaction, because this is considered to be described in DTDs (see also the contribution by J.Buford et alii in this book).

Multiple-user and distributed presentation. MHEG is dedicated for these purposes, and HyTime is also suitable for that. However, all presented authoring tools are currently limited to the production of single-user stand-alone presentations.

3 The Synchronization Model and the Scripting Language

3.1 Motivation

In contrast to the approaches described in the previous chapter, our initial goal was the extension of an existing document processing system for dynamic contents and presentations, so that existing, conventional documents could be smoothly integrated into the new environment. On the assumption that Digital's CDA [6] is a main strategy for making documents computable across applications and platforms, it has been chosen as starting point. However, it was decided to choose a model general enough to be applicable to systems other than CDA.

Based on results of earlier investigations [8, 15], a general (object-oriented) model for the presentation of documents is therefore described in this chapter, treating the following concepts:

* *Document structure* - specification of the document architecture.
* *Presentation units* - specification of the default behaviour of documents or their parts.
* *Directives* - description of specific behaviour.
* *Input* - mechanisms to let the user interact with the presentation.

3.2 The Document Structure

To provide the applicability of the model to a variety of document architectures and to ease the specification of simple synchronization types (like 'loop'), the following structuring of a document's content is assumed:

- A document consists of a set of named or unnamed *content objects* or *components*, respectively. The document itself is represented by a top level component.
- Each content object is either a basic or a composite one. Basic content objects are either output or input objects, whereas composite ones consist of a set of subordinate components, which again can be basic or composite.
- Within each set, each component can be presented independently from each other, but only when its parent content is presented.
- Each such set may be ordered.
- For identifying parts of basic content objects (e.g., frames of videos), these objects use their individual 'finite coordinate space.' If sets of content objects are ordered, then this applies to them as well, by implication.
- Components may be shared by several documents.
- For each component, so-called *presentation units* can be defined, which describe the behaviour of the selected content object at presentation time.

This leads to a hierarchical multi-level architecture.

3.3 The Presentation Units

Presentation units (or 'pUnits', for short) serve for the description of content objects' behaviour at presentation time. To present a content object, a controlling pUnit must exist for that object. That implies that a component not controlled by any pUnit will not be presented. (It may, however, be assumed that each document component, including the document itself, has an appropriate pUnit assigned to it by default.)

A content object may be controlled by more than one pUnit. Since an arbitrary number of pUnits may be active at the same time, this could imply that several instances of a content object may be presented simultaneously. But the primary purpose of that concept is to allow one content object to be presented in different contexts (e.g., a slide could be used in several lectures of a course).

Basic characteristics of a pUnit:

- Each pUnit has a 'sync-type' (given by its *class*), specifying default behaviour.
- It can have a *name* for identification.
- Its *scope* is always a content object or a subset of its components.
- A *state* model controls its life cycle.
- *Attributes* control additional aspects (e.g., the maximum number of iterations).
- *Variables* defined by the author provide further control.
- It communicates with other pUnits by emitting *signals* and receiving *messages* or applying commands, respectively. This is specified by means of so-called *directives*.
- A pUnit can have nested pUnits whose activities are restricted to that of their parent pUnit.

pUnit classes. pUnit classes are templates for synchronization types from which pU-nits are instantiated. They can be predefined or specified by the author. All pUnit classes are derived from the most general one, *simple*. Several classes are considered to be of general usage, and should therefore be predefined, as illustrated in Figure 1.

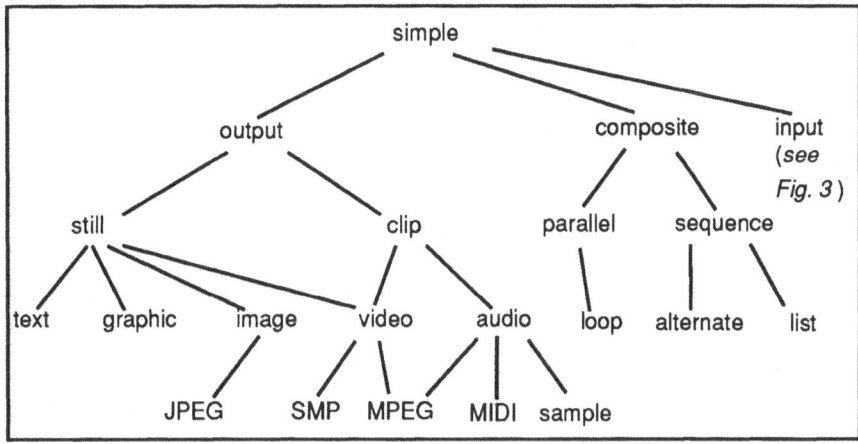

Fig. 1. pUnit classes hierarchy

Characteristics of the pUnit classes:

simple: defines general pUnit behaviour

output: collector class for basic content objects

still: provides color and specific geometric transformation handling

clip: provides general handling of dynamic content (e.g., pacing)

composite: general handling of composite pUnits, namely
- propagation of attribute values to its components
- synchronization of / communication with components

parallel: presents all components in parallel

loop: general iteration handling; this class specifies that the components are presented in parallel and in an iterated way (automatic restart after termination of all components)

sequence: sequential presentation of the components; the order is either predefined or given together with the pUnit

alternate: like sequence, but presents each component at the position of the first component

list: like sequence, but terminated visual components are not removed.

The life-cycle model. During presentation, any pUnit passes through a sequence of states. State transitions occur either due to the reaction upon receipt of messages, or due to internal events. In each state, the pUnit performs certain actions, and reacts only to specific messages. Upon certain state transitions, signals are emitted to indicate the completion of corresponding actions.

218

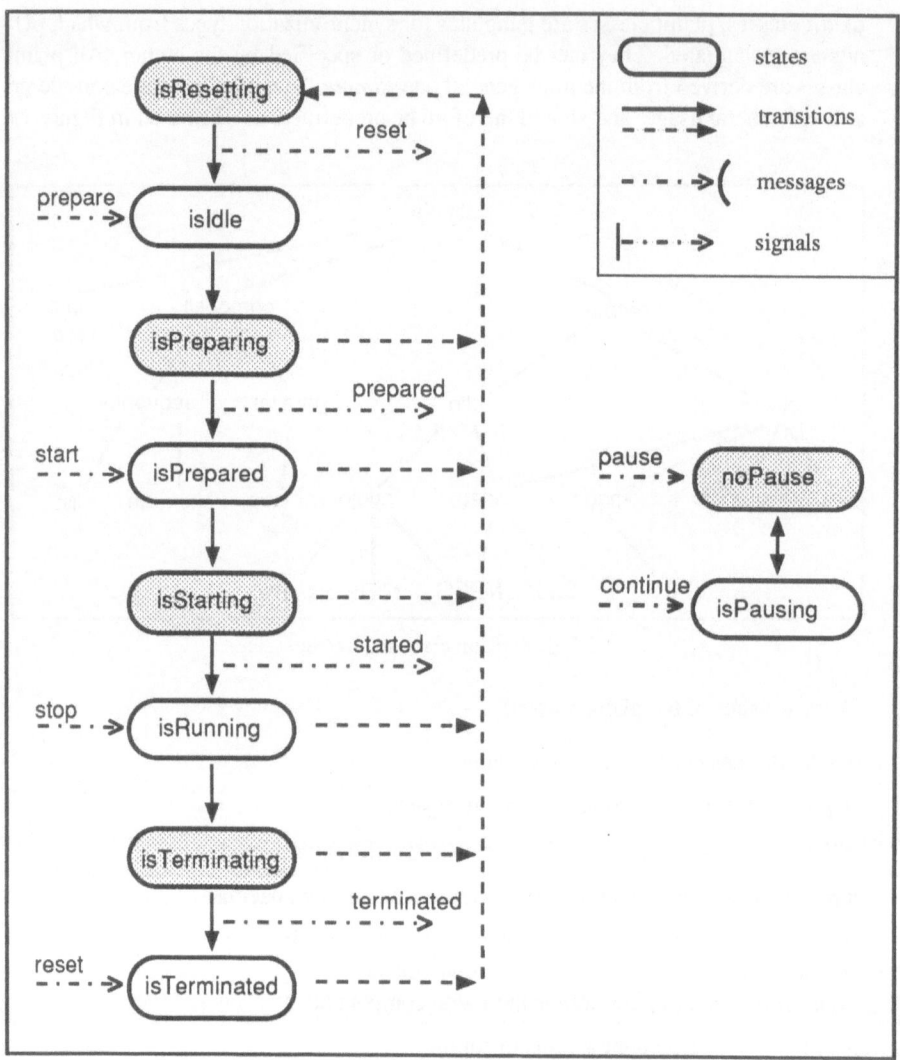

Fig. 2. Life cycle state diagram

This life cycle (see Figure 2.) shows that the messages (**prepare** ... **reset**) are accepted only in white states not later than the one indicated. Once a pUnit arrives at state isTerminated, it cannot be presented anymore, as long as it is not reset, either implicitly or explicitly by receiving a reset message, which is accepted in any white state other than isIdle.

In addition, a pUnit's state contains one further component, noPause/isPausing, which is controlled by the message pair pause/continue. These messages are accepted at any time, but take effect only in the isRunning state.

The shaded states allow for adjustment of hard/software caused delays.

Signals are to be considered as some kind of boolean pUnit attributes which are initialized to false and causing its pUnit to send a message to all that are waiting for it when switching to true. Setting a signal once more when already true doesn't cause anything to happen. And resetting a signal sets its value back to false. Since predefined signals are reset only when a reset-command is executed, they can be used to identify that phase of a life cycle from their setting to the moment the object gets reset.

Application defined signals behave in the same way, but can be set and unset explicitly by the application.

A reset command implies that the following actions have to be performed: first, the pUnit's state is set to isResetting; second, any actions necessary for terminating the presentation are performed; third, all signals (predefined as well as application-defined ones) are set to false; fourth, all attributes are re-initialized and updated respectively, depending on their meaning; and fifth, the object state is set to isIdle.

Besides those messages shown in Figure 1, pUnits may accept further messages and emit additional signals. For example, iterating pUnits will stop the current iteration and start the next or previous iteration when receiving next or previous, respectively. Also, input objects may emit the signal triggered for indicating a corresponding user action.

Scope. A pUnit is always defined for a particular content object. For composite objects, alternative pUnits may select different subsets of its components. These are then called the *scope* of the pUnit. The purpose of scopes is that pUnits apply their default behaviour to exactly this set of components. In other words, a content object which is within the scope of a pUnit is seen as being part of or controlled by this pUnit.

Scopes can be ordered, which is necessary for certain sync types like sequence, alternate, or list.

Since pUnits actually deal with pUnits rather than with content objects, scopes are built of pUnits. And since for lower-level components alternative pUnits may be defined as well, it is possible to include these in a scope.

A pUnit X within the scope of some other pUnit Y is regarded as being subordinate to Y. Subordinate pUnits describe the behaviour of the components within their scope under the scope of their higher pUnits.

A pUnit of composite class may contain nested pUnits. In opposition to subordinate pUnits, they serve for additional behaviour specification within a pUnit. Therefore, their scope must be a subset of the scope of their parent pUnits, and they override the default behaviour defined by their parent's class.

Each pUnit can send messages to only those pUnits which it 'sees': itself, all its named nested pUnits, its scope, its parent, and all named top level pUnits, in that order in case of name clashes.

Attributes. Each pUnit possesses a number of attributes according to its class or sync-type, which describe or control special characteristics. Some examples of attributes are:

autoreset: indicates whether the object shall be reset automatically after termination

round_robin: indicates that the scopes of iterating pUnits other than loops are treated as closed lists (i.e. first element after last and vice versa)

max_rep: limits the number of repetitions of iteration pUnits

pacing: initial value for a pacing factor for all affected dynamic components

duration: limits presentation time

device: allows the use of different devices within one presentation. At presentation time, logical channels are assigned to appropriate physical devices (e.g., displays or loudspeakers). Supports distributed applications.

Variables. Variables can be bound to pUnits. They can be set and queried by directives. They can either be private to the pUnit, or public, which makes them visible to other pUnits. A special kind of variables are application-defined signals. They are controlled by the messages set and unset, and can be used like the predefined signals.

3.4 Directives

Directives are the fundamental tool for specifying additional constraints overriding the default behaviour. A directive describes *what* shall be done in its *operation* part, and *when* or *while* this shall be done in its *condition* part. Directives are always bound to pUnits.

Conditions. Conditions serve to describe under which circumstances the operation(s) of a directive shall be executed. They are boolean expressions covering signals, states, attributes, and variables. Such boolean expressions may contain relational expressions, which again can be built from arithmetic, string or other appropriate expressions. Finally, 'time offsets' may also be specified within conditions (e.g., 'X.started + 10 sec' would denote a moment 10 seconds after X emitted the signal started).

This results in condition values which may switch between false and true repeatedly during a presentation. How these switchings control the associated operation(s) depends on the mode of the directive.

In the *when* mode, the directive executes its operation(s) whenever the condition switches from false to true, whereas in the *while* mode, the directive executes its operation(s) as long as the condition is true; that means it starts to execute whenever a false->true change occurs, and it terminates the execution whenever a true->false change happens.

Operations. Several kinds of operations are distinguished:

Simple commands. Send the messages prepare, start, stop, and reset to target objects, or set resp. unset to application defined signals; only usable in *when*-conditions.

Pause command. May be used also in conjunction with *while*-conditions, such that they send a pause message when the condition becomes true, and a continue message when the condition's value switches back to false.

Modify command. Allows to change values of attributes or variables. If controlled by a *when*-condition, then the corresponding message is sent to the target pUnit whenever the condition becomes true. Under a *while*-condition, this allows for continuous updating.

Play command. Starts some pUnit, but also allows providing special initial values for attributes. In combination with a *while*-condition, it also sends a stop message when the condition turns to false.

Sync command. Informs pUnits that they have to synchronize themselves to some master pUnit. In conjunction with a *while*-condition the target process is terminated when the condition switches back to false.

Input command. Informs an input object about how it has to perform. Needed mainly for overriding defaults. In conjunction with a *while*-condition the target process is terminated when the condition switches back to false.

Execute command. Informs the owner pUnit of the directive to execute a method. In addition, it allows establishment of a permanent connection between variables/attributes and the method's arguments. Conceptually, that enables the pUnits' values to be manipulated continuously according to the method. In conjunction with a *while*-condition the target process is terminated when the condition switches back to false.

A directive may have a list of operations, which are then executed either in parallel, which means that no assurance can be given about their mutual concurrence, besides the general rule that messages are sent and received immediately. Or, they can be executed in a given order. That means that a single operation is not executed, until the execution of the previous one has been finished. When controlled by a *while*-condition, this may imply that not all of the operations will actually be performed.

3.5 Input

User interaction at presentation time is modelled by means of so-called input objects adhering to the following concepts:

- Several *classes* of input objects are provided.
- For each input class specific *attributes* describe appearance and behaviour.
- Each input class provides a certain attribute reflecting associated user actions, called *measure*.
- Input objects can be driven in one of four *modes*; each class has a 'natural' mode, which is also the default.
- Input objects have the same life-cycle states as pUnits, and therefore are controlled by the same commands as output objects.

The input mode is a special attribute, which selects the general form of behaviour:

single: the measure value is released when the input object is explicitly activated by the user. Then, the input object's state automatically switches to isPausing; hence, no further input is possible until it is reset to noPause.

multiple: like single, but the input object switches back to noPause immediately.

exclusive: like single, but the rest of the whole presentation is paused, while the input object is in the isRunning state. Forces the user to do the requested input (for example to confirm an error notification).

continuous: the measure value is continuously sampled, without the need of explicit activations by the user. Allows for smooth changing of 'output' attributes (e.g., pacing factor or position) by user actions.

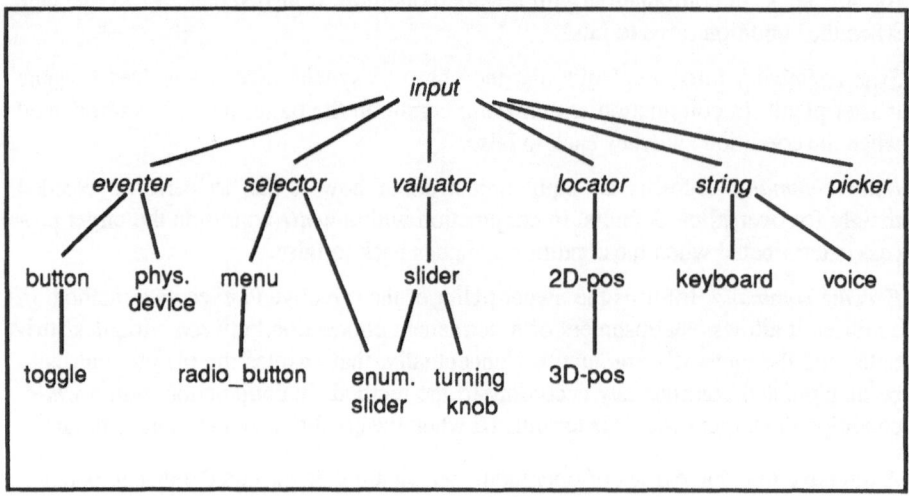

Fig. 3. Input classes hierarchy

Figure 3 shows a possible class hierarchy for input objects. It is an extension of the class hierarchy of pUnits (see Figure 1):

Input: provides input modes and 'triggering' behaviour, but does not define how triggering occurs. Sets default mode to multiple.

The following 'meta-classes' define when this state transition occurs:

Eventer - metaclass for button-like input devices. Provides 'press/release' functionality.

Selector - metaclass for pulldown-menu like input objects. Provides 'selection' functionality.

Valuator - metaclass for input objects providing single numerical values.

Locator - metaclass for input objects providing coordinates.

String - metaclass for input objects providing text strings.

Picker - allows to select ('pick') content objects by the user.

Generally, trigger signals can be used like ordinary signals. In addition, specific measure values can be used in expressions and/or assigned to attributes and variables.

It should be noted here that this input model has been influenced by that of GKS [10]. So, the input classes *valuator ... picker* can be found in GKS as well, and input mode *continuous* has some similarity with GKS' *sample* mode.

4 Experimental Implementation

In a prototype, the described model has been partially implemented. (What has not been included, are variables other than signals, input classes other than buttons and sliders, and several attributes and operations.) That protoype is described in this section.

Since the presented model is suitable for a wide variety of document architectures, clause 4.1 outlines the adopted one, together with some general implementation aspects. Clause 4.2 deals with the architecture of the implementation itself, while 4.3 illustrates how default behaviour is handled. Finally, 4.4 summarizes the used environment.

4.1 Model Representation

The basic metaphor in our prototype implementation to describe a presentation is a *slide*. A slide is a window with arbitrary size and behaviour. Each slide contains a number of objects (output as well as input objects). We decided to use only four types of output objects and two types of input objects (see the Slide Editor for more details).

As discussed before, each document consists of a set of identifiable content objects. But we are interested in those content objects associated with pUnits, that means, strictly speaking, we are interested only in pUnits.

For the internal representation we define that all pUnits which have no parent pUnit are instances of a slide if they are of the simple or composite class (parallel, loop, sequence, alternate, and list). All other pUnits - of class output (and sub-classes) or input (and sub-classes) - are to be regarded as basic content objects of a slide, and may be referenced by each instance of a slide. These basic objects will be called i/o components for the rest of the paper.

To present a slide generated in that way, it is necessary to create scripts by using the Script Editor.

The simplest script of a slide is

simple(*);

which specifies an unnamed pUnit without any sub-pUnits or directives, where all the i/o components specified for that slide are presented at the same time.

Each such pUnit or i/o component has a default behaviour. Therefore, a set of rules determines what has to be done when a particular state of the pUnit's or i/o component's life cycle is entered. That means there is a description of when to prepare, start, stop, or reset a pUnit or an i/o component (see 4.3).

If there are explicit directives, they may alter the behaviour of the presentation, because they override any rule stated in the default behaviour (e.g., an explicit start directive implies that the same directive in the set of rules for the default behaviour will be ignored).

In most cases the execution of a directive implies the setting of signals to true or false, the state change of pUnits or i/o components, or the change of attribute or variable values. Because other conditional directives may depend on those signals, states, or variables, it has to be guaranteed that the conditions of these directives get the right information at the right time. Therefore a certain propagation model is used.

Propagation of events. Each object / pUnit or i/o component - is in a well-defined state during the presentation. When a state change occurs (depending on any directive) a two step propagation is done. First, all the (sub) conditions where the old state is referenced are set to false, and second those where the new state is referenced are set to true. In the internal tree representation (of a condition), these conditions are leaves, thus a re-evaluation of the entire condition tree is necessary. The propagation of signals and variables is done only in one step: all conditions where signals or variables are addressed are re-evaluated.

Activity of pUnits. For the sake of simplicity we decided that the directives of a pUnit will only be regarded when it is active, that means it has to be in a status other than *isIdle* and *isTerminated*. But before the presentation starts, a pass over the whole document will show the dependencies of the slides (the presentation order) as well as those pUnits which have to be set to active.

Life cycle of signals. The value of the signals prepared, started, and terminated of a pUnit resp. an i/o component remains true until the pUnit or i/o component is reset. (An explicit setting to false is not possible.) Then the values of all those signals are set to false except the reset signal, where the value remains true until the next reset directive occurs.

The triggered signal of input components have to be handled differently. When in the single mode, only the first button click is accepted and propagated, whereas all further ones are ignored. In the multiple mode, all button clicks have to be accepted and propagated; that means each trigger event can be addressed separately.

4.2 The Prototype Architecture

The prototype consists of five parts:

- the *Slide Editor* for the object generation,
- the *Script Editor* for the script generation,
- the *Script Parser* for parsing the script (syntax check),
- the *Logical Device Editor* (for distributed presentation), and
- the *Presentation Tool*.

The Slide Editor. This editor serves to create slides with arbitrary size and behaviour (display priority, attributes for resizing, iconizing, moving, and naming), and to create objects within these slides.

Currently, a slide can be filled with two different types of objects, the i/o components:

output objects of type *still* (pixmap), *text*, *audio* (sampled sound), and *video* (Software Motion Pictures),

and input objects of type *button* and *slider*.

The Script Editor and Script Parser. To present a slide it is necessary to produce a script for that slide, because only slides equipped with a script are presentable.

For each document object (that means for each slide), a script can be generated. After finishing script editing, the tool parses the script (plain ASCII code), checks for syntax errors and produces a file where all the information of the document (object description and script) is stored in an optimized way. Users are notified in user-friendly fashion of errors occurring when compiling the document.

The Logical Device Editor. To enable distributed presentation, it is necessary to specify where to present either the whole document or parts of it. Therefore, the node and the display information as well as the transport information are stored in a separate file. This file is handled like a lookup table, where each entry is associated with a predefined number. Thus, in the script editor it is only necessary to refer to that entry number.

The Presentation Tool. The most important and most sensitive part of the engine is the so-called *conductor*, a process which has to do the following tasks:

- to read in those files created by the Script Editor and updated by the Script Parser
- to add information describing the default presentation behaviour
- to merge the presentation information obtained by the two previous items
- to evaluate this merged presentation data for the first pass
- to handle activities of the window system (optional)
- to send data to presenter(s) (if necessary)
- to receive data from (a) presenter(s) (if necessary).

Additionally, besides the conductor, a process called *presenter* has to be started when i/o components like pixmaps, video, or audio objects have to be presented. The presenter engages a number of subpresenters for the previously mentioned object types. Each object has its own presenter (of course only for its lifetime). The communication between conductor and presenter is performed by message queues, whereas the communication between presenter and subpresenters is performed by pipes.

The success of the execution of each directive is sent from the presenter to the conductor.

4.3 Example for Integrating Default and Specific Behaviour

Set of rules: For merging specific behaviour (described by directives) and default behaviour, the following approach has been taken:

- First, rules describing the default behaviour (i.e. directives) are generated for each unnested pUnit according to its type, scope, and nested pUnits.
- Then, the directives specified by the author are added under removal of overridden default rules.

An example shall illustrate how this works: specification of a pUnit named A and of the simple type with n components and m nested pUnits.

Syntax:

$$A : simple (c_1,..c_n) \qquad // A \qquad ... \text{current pUnit}$$
$$begin \qquad\qquad // c_1\text{-}c_n \qquad ... \text{components of A}$$
$$A_1 : ...; \qquad\qquad // A_1\text{-}A_m \qquad ... \text{nested pUnits of A}$$
$$A_m : ...;$$
$$end;$$

Description of default behaviour:

A)   when (A.IsIdle)
          begin
          prepare A, $A_1..A_m$, $c_1..c_n$;
          end;

B)   when (A.IsPreparing AND
                  $(A_1..A_m)$.Prepared AND $(c_1..c_n)$.Prepared)
          set A.Prepared;

C)   when (A.Prepared)
          begin
          start A, $A_1..A_m$, $c_1..c_n$;
          end;

D)   when (A.IsStarting AND $(A_1..A_m)$.Started AND $(c_1..c_n)$.Started)
          set A.Started;

E)   when (A.IsTerminating AND
                  $(A_1..A_m)$.Terminated AND $(c_1..c_n)$.Terminated)
          begin
          set A.Terminated;
          reset A;   /* when the AUTORESET option is used */
          end;

F)   when (A.started + duration) /* if a duration option is used */
          begin
          stop A, $A_1..A_m$, $c_1..c_n$;
          end;

If, for example, this pUnit A has an additional directive,

$$\text{when } (A_1.\text{started} + 5 \text{ secs}) \text{ start } A_2;$$

such that the sub-pUnit A_2 shall start 5 seconds after the start of sub-pUnit A_1, this implies that in C) the implicit start directive for A_2 is overriden, and in D) the started signal of A_2 is also ignored.

4.4 Developmental Environment

The prototype was developed on a RISC workstation (DECstation 5000/133 running under operating system ULTRIX 4.3). The windowing system used was X/Windows (X11R4) furthermore OSF/Motif 1.1. DECaudio was used for presenting audio data, and DEC's SMP (Software Motion Picture) was used to present videos. For the presentation of stills, an adapted version of XView was used to achieve the desired behaviour. And finally, the whole system was written in the programming language C.

5 Conclusion and Future Directions

The presented model is suitable to describe dynamic presentations of multimedia documents in distributed environments. Although distribution has not been the primary goal of the prototype, it allows for distributed presentation of distributed documents with the current restriction to the mentioned hw/sw environment. The used state-model was important in coping with unpredictable command execution durations unavoidable in such computing environments.

The developed scripting language has proven itself as being powerful for the compact description of moderately complex situations. However, authors have to proceed cautiously when generating scripts for more complex applications, because this may lead to unpredictable results. Reasons for that may be:

- thinking in parallel processes has to be thoroughly cultivated and practiced, and
- a plethora of interrelationships have to be considered.

Many logical expressions on variables (variable in time) for the control of actions (as allowed in directives) are very powerful, but they may include contradictions, which are sometimes hard to resolve. But in most applications such complexity isn't actually needed.
Finally, the following activities are intended to be addressed in future:

- Improvement of the protoype and addition of the not yet implemented features.
- Integration with CDA. Currently, an own format is used to store documents created with the prototype. In future, CDA's DDIF could be used as storage format, allowing the usage of documents created with other CDA-tools like DECwrite or DECpresent, e.g., as (static) contents.
- Support of MHEG as output format. Due to a number of significant similarities between DDD and MHEG, it could be envisaged to use DDD as powerful authoring tool for MHEG-objects.
- Migration to other platforms.
- Use of broadband communication services.

References

1. HyperCard Script Language Guide. Apple Computer Inc. (1989).

2. HyperTalk Beginner's Guide: An Introduction to Scripting. Apple Computer Inc. (1989).

3. OpenScript Reference Manual. Asymetrix Corp. (1991).

4. Authorware Professional Handbook, Authorware Inc., Berkshire, UK (1992).

5. Das große Visual Basic Buch. Data Becker (1991) (in German).

6. Blake, J.C. (Ed.): Compound Document Architecture CDA. Digital Technical Journal vol.2 no.1, Digital Equipment Corp., Mass. (Winter 1990).

7. Buford, J., Rutledge, L., Rutledge, J., Keskin, C.: HyOctane: a HyTime engine for an MMIS. In: Multimedia Systems, vol.1, no.4, pp173-185 (Feb. 1994)

8. Herzner, W., Kummer, M.: MMV - Synchronizing Multimedia Documents. Proceedings of 2nd Eurographics workshop on Multimedia, Darmstadt 1992 (Springer Eurographic Seminars 1992).

9. Hornung, Ch. (Ed.): Experiences, Hyperstructure Concepts, and Cooperative Work. Proceedings of the 2nd Eurographics Workshop on Multimedia, Darmstadt 1992, Eurographics Technical Report Series, EG 92 MU, ISSN 1017-4656.

10. Information Processing - Computer Graphics - Graphical Kernel System (GKS), ISO 7942:1985, Genéve 1985.

11. Information Processing – Open Systems Interconnection – Specification of Abstract Syntax Notation (ASN.1), ISO 8824:1987, Genéve 1987.

12. Information Processing - Text and Office Systems - Standard Generalized Markup Language (SGML), ISO 8879:1986, Genéve 1986.

13. Information Technology - Hypermedia/Time-based Structuring Languge (HyTime), ISO/IEC 10744:1992, Genéve 1992.

14. Information Technology - Coded Representation of Multimedia and Hypermedia Information Objects - (MHEG) - CD 13522 (June 1993).

15. Kummer, M., Kuhn, W.: ASE - Audio and Synchronization Extension of Compound Documents. Proceedings of 1st Eurographics workshop on Multimedia, Stockholm 1991 (Springer Eurographic Seminars 1991).

16. MacroMind Director V3.0 - Interactivity Manual. MacroMind Inc. (1991).

17. Schorr, J.: First-Time Authoring. Macworld, March 1993, pp106-113.

18. Siering, P.: Stelldichein - Neue C++-Compiler für DOS, Windows & Co. c't Magazin für Computertechnik 8 (1993), p22 (in German).

19. Siering, P.: Nachschlag - Microsofts 'Visual C++ 32 Bit Edition'. c't Magazin für Computertechnik 12 (1993), p80 (in German).

20. Steinbrink, B.: Multimedia-Baukasten - Autorensysteme und -werkzeuge im Vergleich. c't Magazin für Computertechnik 5 (1992), pp70-79 (in German).

21. Steinbrink, B.: Multimedia-Regisseure - Autorensysteme und -sprachen im Vergleich. c't Magazin für Computertechnik 10 (1993), pp168-179 (in German).

22. West, N.: Multimedia Masters. Macworld, March 1993, pp114-117.

23. Yager, T.: Build Multimedia Presentations with MacroMind's MediaMaker. BYTE, September 1991, pp302-304.

24. Zerbe, K.: Faul Zaubern - Microsoft Visual C++ und die Foundation Classes 2.0. c't Magazin für Computertechnik 9 (1993), p96 (in German).

Authoring a Large Distributed Hypermedia System: Document Linking and Embedding (DLE) concept

H. Maurer, F. Kappe, N. Scherbakov

Institute for Information Processing and Computer Supported New Media,
Graz University of Technology, Schieszstattgasse 4a,
Graz, A-8010 Austria.

Abstract In this paper we examine issues of collaborative authoring of large distributed hypermedia systems. We contend that there exists a certain discrepancy between the needs of local users engaged in hypermedia authoring tasks and the functionality provided by the distributed hypermedia system which creates and maintains a global view of the network. In this context we offer a so-called Document Linking and Embedding (DLE) concept. In accordance with this concept a number of documents can be gathered together into a new document, which can be embedded into other documents in turn. There exist two different dimensions of such logical structure: logical structure of a particular document (i.e. number of other documents related by means of computer navigable links); and global structure of a hypermedia database as such where documents are related by means of semantic relationships "is-a-part". The DLE concept strongly separates authoring of these two logical structures. An experimental prototype system based upon this approach has been developed, the demonstration version is available via anonymous ftp from "iicm.tu-graz.ac.at" in direcory "pub\hmcard".

1 Introduction

Hyper-G [18] is a large distributed hypermedia system suitable for a wide range of applications. Hypermedia objects of different types (text, graphics, raster images, video- and audio clips) can be stored and associated with each other using the well-known concept of computer-navigable links, but also other more sophisticated methods. Thus, Hyper-G permits the structuring of information into hierarchies of so-called collections to present the user with a rough feeling of what might be found where and supports advanced techniques such as fulltext and "fuzzy" search in domains defined by the user. Hyper-G is designed to handle not just megabytes of data but mega-quantities of hypermedia objects which have to be integrated into one database. This necessitates some new methods of collaborative creation (i.e. collaborative authoring) of very large hypermedia databases .

On one hand, many authors now distinguish between stand-alone small hypermedia applications built by means of a particular hypermedia tool (say, for instance, HyperCard, ToolBook, etc.) and large multi-users hypermedia systems which allow remote access, sharing and reusing of distributed hypermedia resources [3], [28], [37].

On the other hand, authoring concepts developed for such stand-alone systems are considered to be applicable for large distributed systems. Taking into consideration collaborative authoring of a very large hypermedia database, we face the following paradoxical situation: any chunk of hypermedia information is created by a particular author who is responsible for this information, but the whole database has no particular author because no one person or particular group of persons (i.e. no one team) can embrace the whole scope of information available within such a system [3], [34], [37].

In this paper we contend that there exist at least two different types of authoring activity dealing with such a large hypermedia database - local authoring and global administering of the database as a whole. Local authoring deals with a well-defined unit of hypermedia information, and the author is personally responsible for such a unit (say, for a particular document). In other words, local authoring focuses on information content of documents (i.e. on units of multimedia information - text, picture, movie clip, etc.) and the local connection between such units (say, a picture should be shown, if a certain "hot" area is clicked on) [3], [8], [16], [22]. In Database Administering task it is important to maintain a global distributed database. Thus, Database Administering provides users with possibility to access information of interest independently of a particular author who creates such information. Administering allows also to reuse chunks of hypermedia information created by different authors in order to create new chunks [28].

In this context, we describe a so-called Document Linking and Embedding (DLE) concept which is now under development as a part of the Hyper-G project. The DLE concept can be seen as a combination of data structure types, navigational paradigm and integrity constraints which control modifications of the data base. The second part, we believe, forms a basis for collaborative authoring of large distributed hypermedia databases.

2 Data structuring on the basis of the DLE concept

In accordance with the DLE concept, there exist two levels of logical data representation within a hypermedia system. On the first level which is called Basic

Level henceforth, a hypermedia database can be simply seen as a large number of documents which can be combined into collections (see [18] for more details). Documents which are available on the Basic level are called *Registered Documents.* All registered documents can be accessed by means of basic navigational paradigms available in Hyper-G (i.e. as a member of a particular collection or via document retrieving mechanism using keywords or full-text search).

Each registered document has a unique identifier (used by other documents for addressing) and a so-called *data unit.* Accessing a document implies executing its data unit: this will ordinarily cause some information to be presented (text, pictures, audio, video-clips).

Additionally, registered documents can encapsulate a so-called *embedded navigable structure.* In this paper, we consider the case when a registered document is devoid of such an internal structure, as an exception. Such embedded navigable structure can be seen as a small stand-alone hypermedia database encapsulated within a certain registered document. More precisely, the navigable structure is a set of other documents (called *members* henceforth) related by a number of computer-navigable links (see Fig. 1). Note that we connect documents including navigable structures (i.e. entities) and not data units.

It is very important to understand that registered documents can be reused within different embedded navigable structures and hence accessed during navigation through different embedded structures. For instance, a CBL lesson can be seen as such an embedded navigable structure, if such a lesson "refers" to other registered documents (say, relevant articles of an encyclopaedia), then these documents should be explicitly "inserted" into the embedded navigable structure and provided with relevant links by the author of this lesson (see below). In analogy, the author of another document (i.e. of another embedded navigable structure) can reuse such a CBL lesson and create, for example, a library of courseware.

Thus computer-navigable links are encapsulated within a particular document. In other words, links may be defined only between members of a certain document; and in this sense, they belong to the document (i.e. they are a part of hypermedia description of an entity), but they do not belong to a hypermedia database or to members that are related by means of links (see, for instance, Fig. 1 where different links between documents "a" and "b" are encapsulated within different documents "d" and "c", and have different context therefore). A document devoid of such an internal structure is called a primitive document (see, for instance, documents "a" and "b").

At any particular moment in time the user can navigate on the Basic Level of data representation or through a concrete document which is called a *current container,* by means of links defined within this particular document. The current container confines the user to a particular navigational paradigm. As we shall see this neither limits the access nor the scope of information available within the hypermedia database. The navigation consists of a certain number of steps. A concrete document is the current one for each particular navigation step. More precisely, on each navigation step the user can access a certain document within the database or a particular current container. To "access" means to visualise the document. The document most recently accessed (visualised within the current container) is called the *current document*.

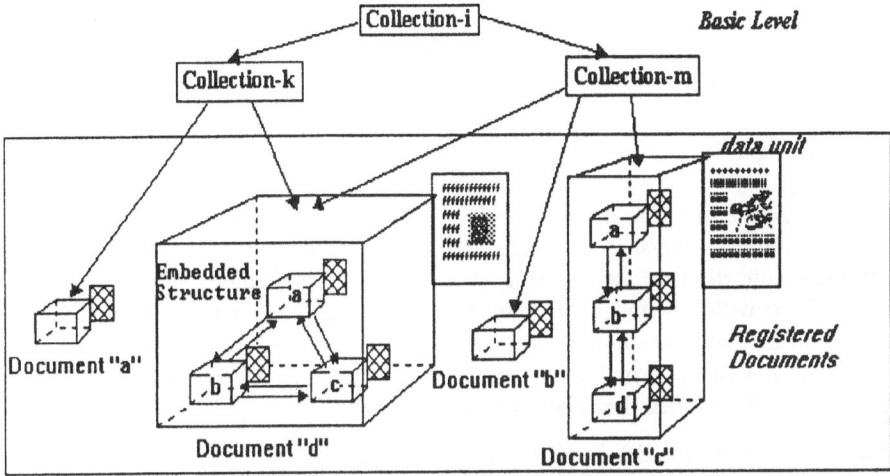

Fig. 1: Hypermedia database

For instance, consider the navigation through the previously defined document "d" (see Fig. 1). In this case, the user can access the documents "a", "b" and "c" by means of links available within the current container (i.e. within the document "d").

More precisely, if the document "a" is the current document, then it is visualised (i.e. a corresponding data unit is displayed by means of a particular procedure of visualisation), and the user has the links to the members "b" and "c" available (i.e. the user can access the document "b" or the document "c" on the next step of navigation).

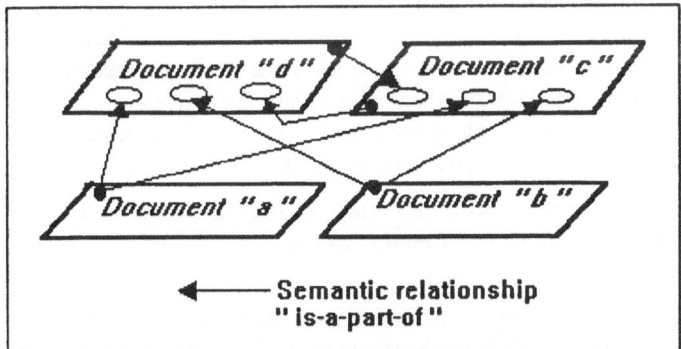

Fig.2: Semantic relationships on Global Level of Hypermedia Database

Note that the links can be seen as a mechanism in order to create a description of a new entity (say, the entity "d") as a composition of descriptions of its sub-parts (say, the sub-parts "a", "b" and "c"). In this sense, we distinguish between computer-navigable links that exist only within definition of a particular entity (i.e. within a particular document) and semantic relationships which exist on the global level of a hypermedia database (see Fig. 2).

In accordance with [22], we can also say that an embedded navigable structure consists of so-called slots which are filled with other documents registered on the global level of data representation.

3 Browsing a hypermedia database

The user starts a browsing from the basic level of Hyper-G and has all navigational tools available (i.e. he/she can access any registered document as a member of a particular collection or as a result of a searching procedure). Since links are encapsulated within a document, they become available (or become activated) for navigation only if the document has been "entered". Such an *entering* of a document to activate the encapsulated links (and thereby changing the current navigational paradigm) will be called the "zoom in" operation.

Thus, at any moment the "current" document can be "entered". In this case an encapsulated navigational paradigm becomes available. During the navigation by means of this navigational paradigm, another registered document can be accessed and optionally "entered" activating new navigational paradigm and so on.

At any point of browsing a particular embedded navigable structure, it (i.e. embedded navigable structure) can be "closed", this action leads to reactivating of the most recently used navigational paradigm (i.e. the system supports a stack of active embedded navigable structures). In other words, if the current document is a complex document (i.e. the most recently accessed member of the current container is a complex document) then the user can apply the operation "zoom in" in order to make this member a new current container. In analogy, the current container can be "closed", in this case, the system "undoes" the most recent "Zoom In" action. Additionally, for each registered document there exists a list of embedded navigable structures where this particular document has been used as a member, and the user can "switch" to one particular embedded navigable structure from this list [30]. For instance, if the user accesses the document "b" (see Fig. 2) in some way, he/she may switch to browsing of internal structures of documents "d" or "c".

Of course, at any point the user can return to the basic level and apply key word search or other navigational tools available on this level.

Consider, for instance, an asynchronous electronic conference being carried out in the form of a multi-user hypermedia database. The users can submit, discuss and comment on particular papers in electronic form. To be more specific, let us assume that we have a number of papers prepared in the form of documents (say, "paper-1" and "paper-2" in Fig. 3). Each submission has a title page as data unit and a number of members corresponding to electronic pages. If such a paper refers to another paper, the subject of reference (in this case the paper that is referred to) has to be inserted into the same document as a member (see Fig. 3).

Above discussion has indicated how primitive chunks (i.e. pages) may be gathered into more complex structures (in this case, "papers"). The documents corresponding to papers can be further used as members of other documents. For instance, the document "paper-1" can be used as a member of the document "Discussion on paper-1" which also includes members representing comments on this paper. Once again the comments on this paper can also be complex documents (see Fig. 3) and, thus, include other cited papers or comments as members.

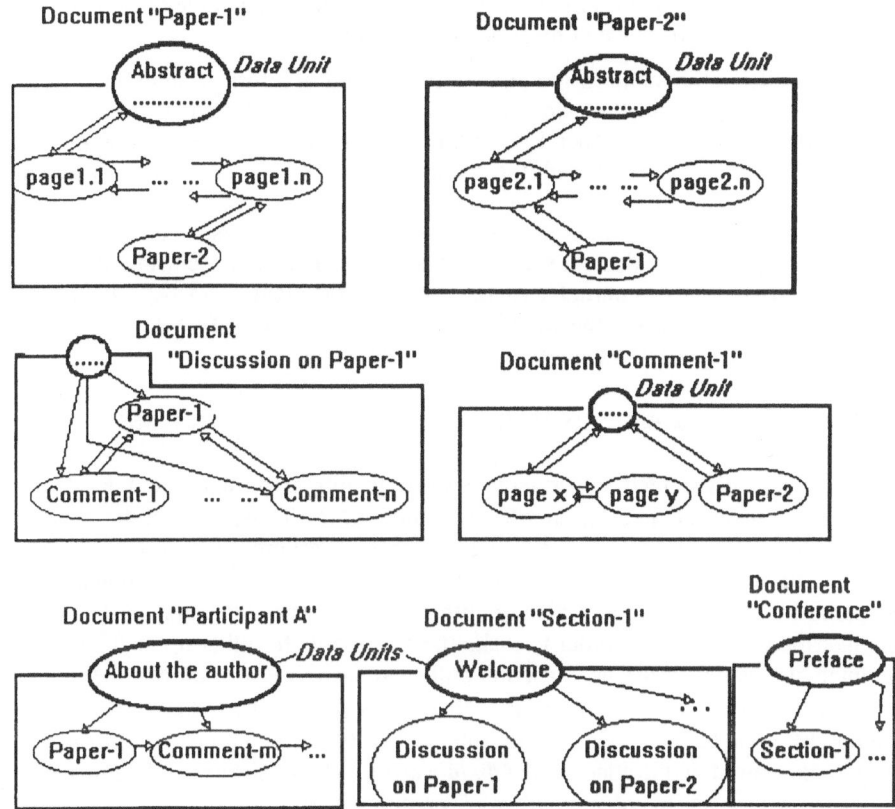

Fig. 3: A sample hypermedia database

Furthermore, there can exist documents containing certain information on the participants. For instance, the document "Participant-A" has a short description about the author as data unit and his papers (document "Paper-1"), (document "Comment-m"), etc. as members. To conclude our example the documents representing discussions may well be combined into documents "Sections" dealing with particular topics (say, "Section-1: hypermedia databases", "Section-2: CAL" etc.). Finally, one could combine all the "Sections" documents into a document "Conference".

To understand the basic properties of the DLE concept let us simulate the steps of a typical user session. The user starts navigation from the document "Conference" (see Fig. 3). The data unit of the document displays a "chairman's preface". If the document "section-1" becomes the current document (i.e. the user activates link to the document "Section-1" within the document "The conference") a "welcome message" defined within the data unit of document "Section-1" is displayed. Note that the navigational paradigm associated with the document "The conference" is still active. The user has the possibility to access another section by clicking at it. After selecting a particular section, the user can "enter" this document. Once a document is "entered" the user obtains links encapsulated within the document (say, a menu indicating the choice of discussions on papers).

Each choice from the menu results in the presentation of information defined by the data unit of thecorresponding document. If the user has selected and entered the document "Discussion on Paper-1" and then selected the document "Paper-1", the abstract of the article is visualised (the document "Paper-1" is the current document) and links to members (i.e. to the comments) become available. The user can either read the article (i.e. to open the document) or browse comments. The user can also "switch" to such other documents that "refer" (i.e. reuse) the current document "Paper-1" (say, to the internal structure of the document "Paper-2" where this document is used as a reference). If the user decides to browse comments, other papers can be accessed as members of the document "Comment".

4 Authoring and Administering of Hypermedia Databases

Hyper-G is a distributed hypermedia system having a primary goal to deliver Hypermedia materials to a big number of remote users. Thus, we face the classical situation of local authoring of integrated information resources (i.e. of an integrated hypermedia database). More precisely, chunks of information (i.e. documents) are prepared locally and have a particular author, and they are integrated further into a big distributed database in order to make them available for other users. Thus, such an integrated database has no particular author as such, it is a result of collaborative efforts of many users and number of such users is permanently changing (i.e. they cannot be seen as a certain team). Integration of locally prepared information resources is based on the concept of *Administering* a shared database. Administering can be seen as stating of a number of predefined rules or integrity constraints (combination of such rules can be called a database metastructure or conceptual schema) and all potential users (i.e. authors) have to follow these rules if they want the materials to be available to other users. More precisely, the Hyper-G system automatically checks these predefined constraints.

Thus, authoring in a conventional sense does not exist on the basic level of a large distributed hypermedia system. The Hyper-G system as such supports only a procedure of registration of documents including insertion of them into relevant collections and providing keywords. In other words, a large distributed hypermedia system directly supports data administering, which corresponds to its primary goal of integrating and sharing of hypermedia resources.

Actually, authoring exists on the document level including, of course, authoring of internal navigable structures. Authoring is based on the concept of modularity of hypermedia resources. Thus, each document has a particular author, date of registration and optionally a number of versions. Such composite documents including embedded navigable structures are created by means of a special authoring system called HM-Card which provides dynamic access to currently registered documents within the main Hyper-G database in order to allow reusing of all hypermedia resources available at the current moment of time.

4.1 Local Authoring using DLE concept

Let us summarise the features of embedded navigable structures which are of interest from the Local Authoring point of view:

(1) Each embedded navigable structure belongs to a particular type which defines the navigational paradigm available for the browsing of its contents (say, menu using push-buttons, freelink using "hot" words, menu using "hot" areas, stack, multi-sorted stack, etc.). Due to the notion of typed structures most of the link maintenance disappears from local authoring (see also [29]). Thus, the author just selects a desired type of a created document, and insertion of a new member into the document (say, a new comment on a particular paper) requires just a statement to that extent: the necessary link adjustments are carried out automatically. In case of "freelink" maintaining links can, of course, not be removed from the author. However, in documents of a composite type involving freelink most links can be created automatically with just some special links to be dealt with manually (see, for instance, Fig. 3 where the documents "Paper-1" and "Paper-2" belongs to such composite type "stack+freelink").

(2) Since the DLE concept does not support "global" references, all information which is referred within a particular document (i.e. internal structure) must be inserted into the same document (see, e.g., "references" to the document "Paper-2" within the documents "Paper-1", "Participant-A" and "Comment-1"). We believe that such "local referential integrity" [19] is a necessary prerequisite of successful local authoring which focuses (let us recollect that) on well-defined chunks of hypermedia information.

(3) In accordance with the DLE concept, we refer complex data objects which describe "entities" (i.e. documents) encapsulating particular navigable structures, but not units of hypermedia information (i.e. *not* primitive nodes). See, for instance, references to the documents "Paper-1", "Section-1", etc. Note also that we refer such complex data objects in a particular local context (i.e. as member of a certain internal structure). For instance, note the references to the document "Paper-2" in the context of "Section-1", and in other contexts "Paper-1", "Comment-1" etc. Thus, we can say that the semantics of the links are captured by the document containing these links [28]. We believe that this kind of references supports "coherence" and "homogeneity" of co-operatively created hypermedia information [4], [27], [32], [36] .

(4) An embedded navigable structure can consist of other registered documents. In this sense, the author can simply reuse existing hypermedia documents (informally speaking, embedded structure includes references to such documents). On the other

hand, the embedded structure may also include non-registered documents (in this case these documents cannot be reused within other embedded navigable structures and cannot be accessed directly from the basic level of navigation). Say, for instance, a particular electronic page of a scientific paper can be registered within Hyper-G and, thus, can be made available for reusing, or it can be defined as just a part of one particular embedded navigable structure. Hence, authoring based on the DLE concept supports such desirable features as "modularity", "reusability", "sharing" and "rapid prototyping" of hypermedia resources. In other words, a hypermedia database is built from independently created but fully compatible hypermedia database modules (i.e. documents). For instance, the documents "Paper-1", "Participant-A", "Paper-2", "Comment-1", "Section-1", etc. can be created by different authors at different moments in time. Such hypermedia modules can be reused or shared by authors of new modules. See, for instance, reusing of the documents "Paper-1" and "Paper-2" by authors of the documents "Section-2", "Comment-1", "Participant-A", etc.

(5) Note that the further editing of a document does not affect its participation within other documents. For instance, initially the document "Paper-1" can be defined as a primitive one (for instance, it includes only the data unit "Abstract of Paper") and then further developed by means of inserting new members (say, the documents "Page1.1", "Paper-2", etc.). The documents "page 1.1" and "Paper-2" in their turn can also be further developed independently.

The last property of the DLE concept, i.e. the possibility to separate the information content of a particular document and participation of the document within other documents, deserves additional discussion, as it can be efficiently utilised for administering of hypermedia databases.

4.2 Administering Hypermedia databases using the DLE concept

In conventional database systems, there exist two levels of data abstraction: information (i.e. database) and meta-information (i.e. database schema). From one point of view, the concept of such "global" database schema is useful for maintaining consistency, integrity and reusability of large-scale, multi-user database systems.

On the other hand, this concept is a firm restriction in the application of database systems for managing ill-structured data (e.g., CAD, CAM, Textual documents etc.) and in supporting evolution and incremental development of database systems.

Initially, hypertext/hypermedia systems had only one level of data abstraction - a hyperweb of nodes arbitrarily connected by means of links (i.e. internal structure of nodes and links were not restricted with some predefined set of types or classes). But it has been recognised very soon that as hypermedia systems become larger, more dynamic, and possibly distributed, it necessitates some kind of meta-information for providing consistency of database creation (co-authoring).

It is interesting to note that while the database community is trying to get rid of strict database schemata [31], [10], the hypertext/hypermedia community is looking for similar two-level mechanisms of data representation [4], [21], [22], [36], [41].

We believe that the number of levels of data representation within up-to-date hypermedia systems should not be restricted or predefined. It is a matter of a concrete application how many levels of such data representation are used. In other words, there can exist any number of levels of logical data representation, and data on each level can be seen as a meta-information for the next level or levels. We contend that data on a certain level of data representation should form a "schema" (i.e. a template) for the next level and so forth. Obviously, this approach makes desirable evolution of meta-information [31] easily applicable.

Observe that the DLE concept provides exactly this kind of functionality where information stored into a database, can be seen as "templates" for newly created data, etc. More precisely, the meta-information is a particular predefined structure of a hypermedia document or a group of such documents including a number of so-called "slots" (i.e. "empty" documents) that should be filled with information on the next level of data representation (for more details see [23]). For instance, let us consider the above discussed example. The document "Conference" can be created in the form of particular internal structure which includes slots corresponding to "sections". Such predefined structure of documents is called a category. Thus, the category "conference" can be defined on the data administering level. In analogy other categories of documents can be predefined (say, category "Section", "Paper", "Comment", etc.). Additionally, slots defined within such a predefined internal structure can be optionally bound to one of existing categories. For instance, previously mentioned slots within the category "Conference" may be bound to the category "Section", slots within the category "Section" to the category "Paper", etc. Such relationships between categories can be seen as a conceptual schema of hypermedia database (see Fig. 4).

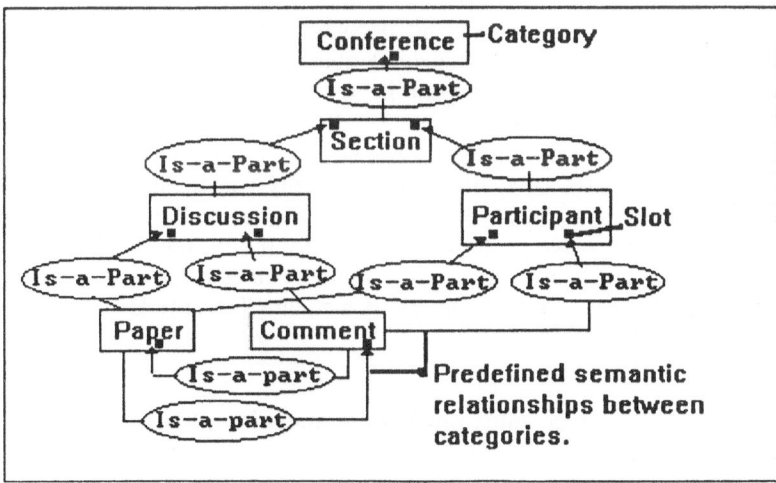

Fig. 4: Metastructure of Hypermedia Database

In Hyper-G such semantic relationships between categories can be provided with options "mandatory" and "optional". Thus, for instance, if the category "Section" is bound to a slot within the category "Conference" with the option "mandatory", the system automatically "inserts" a newly created document of the category "Section" into a particular document of the category "Conference" (of course, the system just automatically asks the local author of the document "Section" to which particular "Conference" this document "Section" belongs).

This situation is a typical case of Administering of large hypermedia databases: The local authors just create documents and register them. The system controls the process of registration (i.e. maintains a semantic integrity of the database) using a number of predefined rules. In the example being discussed, such integrity means a compulsory participation of the documents of category "Section" within a registered document of the category "Conference". In analogy, participants may be also registered for a particular conference, comments for a particular paper and so on.

Thus, data from the basic (i.e. global) level of data representation is perceived as meta-information (i.e. schema) for the second level. Participants of the conference may create papers and comments on papers according to this dynamically defined meta-structure and the hypermedia system automatically maintains this collaborative authoring activity in accordance with the predefined metastructure. Additionally, a new category may be defined in order to carry out discussion "pro and contra" and so forth. It is interesting to note, that local authors may also use slots and bind them to previously defined categories registered on the global level. Thus, for instance, author of a particular paper may "foresee" comments "Pro" and "Contra" and bind them to the category "Comment". In this case, contents (i.e. internal structure) of the paper can be amended by other authors, but this activity is controlled by the original author.

Furthermore, the DLE concept can be enriched with different types of integrity constraints [35]. Some integrity constraints can be *dynamically* bound to a "slot" for checking the internal structure of the document from a higher level of data representation. Say, for instance, maximal number of papers within a concrete section or limit for submitted papers in the form of cardinality constraints, compulsory discussion of invited papers in the form of essentiality constraints, uniqueness of discussion concerning a particular paper in the form of exclusiveness constraints, etc. The issue of application of integrity constraints in administering hypermedia databases is currently under investigation. We believe that the possibility to bind integrity constraints dynamically (i.e. at run-time) to particular data objects (i.e. documents) gives a big area for innovations especially in CAD/CAM applications and in semantic data modeling [1], [14], [26].

Summary

We have discussed some common problems of authoring of large-scale multi-user hypermedia systems.

We advocate two different types of authoring activity: local authoring and administering large distributed hypermedia systems and propose the DLE concept which utilises principles of the E-R [7] conceptual modeling. However, this approach does not obliterate the conventional "node-link" paradigm and this situation is much similar to relationship between assembly-language and high-level programming languages [11], [38]. Thus, the concept can be implemented on the top of existing "node-link" based hypermedia systems as higher level of user view onto a hypermedia database [16].

References

1. Abiteboul, S., Hull, R.: IFO-A formal semantic database model. ACM Trans. on Database Systems., 12 (4) (1987) pp. 525-565.

2. Andrews K., Kappe F.: Strait-Jacketing Authors: User Interface Consistency in Large-Scale Hypermedia Systems. In: Frei, H.P., Schäuble (Eds.): Proc. Hypermedia'93, Springer (March 1993) pp 130-137.

3. Berk, E., Devlin, J. (Eds.): Hypertext/Hypermedia Handbook. McGraw Hill Software Engineering Series, New York (1991).

4. Botafogo R B A, Shneidermann B.: Identifying Aggregates in Hypertext Structures. In Proc. ACM Hypertext'91, San Antonio (December 1991) pp 63-74.

5. Bieber M.: 'Issues in Modelling a "Dynamic" Hypertext Interface for Non-Hypertext Systems' In Proc. ACM Hypertext'91, San Antonio (December 1991) pp 203-217.

6. Casanova M A, et al.: The Nested Context Model for Hyperdocuments. In Proc. ACM Hypertext'91, San Antonio (December 1991) pp 193-201.

7. Chen P.: The Entity-Relationship approach: Toward a unified view of data. ACM Transactions on Database Systems Vol 1 No 1 (January 1976) pp 9-36.

8. Conklin E J.: Hypertext: An Introduction and Survey. IEEE Computer Vol 20 No 9 (September 1987) pp 17-41.

9. Conklin E J, Begeman M L.: gIBIS: A Hypertext Tool for Argumentation. ACM Transactions on Office Information Systems, Vol 6 No 4 (July 1988) pp 303-331

10. Date C.J.: Introduction to Database Systems. 3rd Edition. Addison-Wesley Publ. Company (1981)

11. De Young L.: Links Considered Harmful. In Proc. ECHT'90, Versailles, Cambridge University Press (November 1990) pp 238-249.

12. Furuta R, Stotts P D.: The Trellis Hypertext Reference Model. In Proc. of the Hypertext Standardization Workshop, Gaithersburg, (January 1990) pp 83-93.

13. Garzotto F, Paolini P, Schwabe D.: HDM - A Model-Based Approach to Hypertext Application Design. ACM Transactions on Information Systems Vol 11 No 1 (January 1993) pp 1-26.

14. Hull P., King R.: Semantic Database Modeling: Survey, applications and research issues. ACM Comput. Survey Vol 19 No 3 (October 1987) pp 201-260.

15. Halasz F, Moran T, Trigg R.: NoteCards in a Nutshell. In Proc. ACM CHI'87 (1987) pp 45-42.

16. Halasz F.: Reflection on Notecards: Seven Issues for the Next Generation of Hypermedia Systems. Communications of the ACM, Vol 31 No7 (July 1988) pp 836-852.

17. Halasz F, Schwartz M.: The DEXTER Hypertext Reference Model. In Proc.of the Hypertext Standardization Workshop, Gaithersburg, (January 1990) pp 95-133.

18. Kappe, F.: Aspects of a Modern Multi-Media Information System. IIG Report 308, Graz (1991).

19. Kappel G, Schrefl M.: Local referential integrity. In Proc. Entity - Relationship Approach - ER'92, Karlsruhe, Germany, LNCS 645, Springer (1992) pp 41-57.

20. Kim W, Lochovski F H, (Eds.): Object-Oriented Concepts, Databases, and Applications. Addison-Wesley (1989).

21. Marmann M, Schageter G.: Towards a Better Support for Hypermedia Authoring: the HYDESIGN Approach. In Proc. ECHT'92, Fourth ACM Conference on Hypertext & Hypermedia, Milan (December 1992) pp 232-241.

22. Marshall C C, et al.: Aquanet: a Hypertext Tool to Hold Your Knowledge in Place. In Proc. ACM Hypertext'91, San Antonio (December 1991) pp 261-276.

23. Maurer H, Scherbakov N.: The HM Data Model. IIG Report, Graz (1993).

24. Maurer H, Scherbakov N, Srinivasan P.: A New Hypermedia Data Model. In Proc. DEXA'93, Prague, Czech Rep., LNCS 720, Springer (1993) pp 685-696.

25. Maurer H, et al.: Structured Browsing of Hypermedia Databases. In Proc. VCHCI'93, Vienna, LNCS 733, Springer (September 1993) pp 51-62.

26. Maurer H, et al.: Object-Oriented Modeling of Hyperstructure: Overcoming the Static Link deficiency. Information and Software Technology (Special issue on Hypermedia September 1994) to be published.

27. Nielsen J.: Hypertext and Hypermedia. Academic Press (1990).

28. Panel Session: 'Database Support for Hypertext'. In Proc. of the Fifteenth Int. Conf. on VLDB, (1989) pp 183.

29. Parunak H V D.: Hypermedia Topologies and User Navigation. In Proc. ACM Hypertext'89, Pittsburgh (November 1989) pp 43-50.

30. Parunak H V D.: Don't Link Me In: Set Based Hypermedia for Taxonomic Reasoning. In Proc. ACM Hypertext'91, San Antonio (1991) pp 233-242.

31. Roddick J F.: Schema Evolution in Database Systems - An Annotated Bibliography. ACM SIGMOD RECORD, Vol 21 No 4 (1992) pp 35-40.

32. Schnase J.L., et al.: Semantic Data Modeling of Hypermedia Associations. ACM Transactions on Inform. Systems Vol 11 No 1 (January 1993) pp 27-50.

33. Stotts P D, Furuta R.: Adding Browsing Semantics to the Hypertext Model. In Proc. ACM Document Processing Systems Conf., Santa Fe (1988) pp 43-50.

34. Streitz N, et al.: SEPIA: A Cooperative Hypermedia Authoring Environment. In Proc. ECHT'92, Fourth ACM Conf. on Hypertext & Hypermedia, Milan (December 1992) pp 11-22.

35. Thalheim B.: Fundamentals of Cardinality Constraints. In Proc. Entity - Relationship Approach - ER'92, Karlsruhe, Germany, LNCS 645, Springer (1992) pp 1-16.

36. Thuring M, Haake J M, Hannemann J.: What's Eliza doing in the Chinese Room? Incoherent Hyperdocuments-and How to Avoid Them. In Proc. ACM Hypertext'91, San Antonio (December 1991) pp161-177.

37. Tomek I, et al.: Hypermedia - Introduction and Survey. Journal of MCA Vol 14 No 2 (March 1991) pp 63-103.

38. Van Damm A.: Hypertext'87 Keynote Address. Communications of the ACM, Vol 31 No7 (July 1988) pp 887-895.

39. Ullman D.: A Comparison Between Deductive and Object-Oriented Database Systems. In Proc. DOOD'91 (LNCS566), Springer (1991) pp 263-277.

40. Yankelovich N, et al.: Intermedia: The Concept and the Construction of a Seamless Information Environment. IEEE Computer, Vol 21 No1 (January 1988) pp 81-96.

41. Zellweger P T.: Scripted Documents: A Hypermedia Path Mechanism. In Proc. ACM Hypertext'89, Pittsburgh (November 1989) pp 1-14.

Architectures

On the use of extents in distributed multimedia computing environments

Th. Kirste and M. Frühauf

Computer Graphics Center
Wilhelminenstr. 7
D·64283 Darmstadt, Germany
email: {kirste,fruehauf}@igd.fhg.de

Abstract. In this paper a concept is proposed which summarizes both navigation- and query-based retrieval techniques of distributed information systems such as WorldWideWeb or the Wide Area Information System. It is argued that both access strategies are specific forms of *content based retrieval*. Based on an extension of the "anchor"-concept of hypermedia, the modeling primitive *extent* is introduced, whose purpose is to support both retrieval mechanisms. It is then shown, how this modeling primitive can be used to substantially enhance the throughput of a distributed multimedia information management system, based on the mechanism of *server based extent computation*.

Keywords. hypermedia, content based retrieval, distributed multimedia information systems

1 Introduction

Distributed multimedia information systems are an emerging technology. Their main purpose is to provide easy access to multimedia information which is stored in different sites connected by a wide area network. Typical examples of first systems are the WorldWideWeb (WWW [1]) and the Wide Area Information System (WAIS [10])[1]. Incidentally, each of these systems provides one of the two orthogonal retrieval facilities found in modern information systems:

- Navigation (WWW).

- Query (WAIS).

The query retrieval of WAIS accesses data objects, whose contents match a user defined query expressions; the query is executed at the WAIS information servers which keep a fully inverted index of all objects they are responsible for. The navigation retrieval of WWW retrieves objects, which are connected by hyperlinks to a part of the content of the currently displayed object. The distinction between navigation and retrieval is primarily from the user's point of view: A query is started by entering a search expression *independent* from the current position in the document structure (if such

---

[1] See also [5, 19].

structure exists at all), while navigation is triggered by interacting with a specific part of the document structure, causing the display of a different part of the document. This interaction is typically a mouse-click on a highlighted region of the currently displayed document part. In contrary to the user's point of view, the system is free to determine the destination of the hyperlink based on a query-expression stored within that link, therefore using a unified mechanism for query and navigation. (Examples for systems providing such a mechanism are Hyperscript [17] and HyperPicture [15].)

For the purpose of this paper, the interesting fact is that both retrieval activities are based on the *content* of an object: Query retrieval determines the result set of objects based on whether their content fulfills the predicate of the query expression. In navigation retrieval, the object content is used as an index into a set of query expressions; interacting with a certain highlighted part of the object content causes the traversal of a certain hyperlink, whose identity is determined through the identity of the content part.

In this paper we propose a concept which summarizes both of these content based retrieval techniques into one modeling primitive. The model therefore renders the two complementary aspects of content-based retrieval introduced above – use of content as index for navigation and use of content as qualification for query – as two sides of the same coin. Specifically, we take the approach of a straightforward extension of the anchor-concept well established in the field of hypermedia, so that an easy integration into existing hypermedia approaches seems at least possible.

In the next section we give a short summary of the mechanisms an open multimedia system should provide, as far as these mechanisms have an impact on the model. We then discuss the "anchor"-concept of hypermedia, which captures the content based navigation, and identify its weakness with respect to an open environment. In section 4 we develop a model for accessing object contents based on the new modeling primitive "extent". In the following section it is shown how this model can be extended to substantially increase the throughput of a distributed multimedia information management system, by using a mechanism called *server based extent computation*.

2 Distributed multimedia data management

As fundamental assumption, we consider general purpose data management systems which are required to provide the following characteristics:

- Usability of external applications for managing and modifying object contents.

- Dynamic changes of data structures.

- (Run-time) extensibility through introduction of new object types and managing applications.

- Ability to connect parts of objects which are managed by different applications ("inter-application linking").

- System-provided functionality for creating and modifying the information structure.

These are characteristics which define *open hypermedia systems*. Fundamental architectures for such systems are provided by concepts (and implementations) such as Hyperform [21], PROXHY [9] and HB2 [18], and HyperPicture [15]. The typical architecture of an open hypermedia system is shown in figure 1. One basic aspect of an open hypermedia system is the strict separation between content-specific functionality – which is provided by the application – and structure specific functionality, provided by the system itself. The Dexter reference model [8] explicitly calls for this separation.

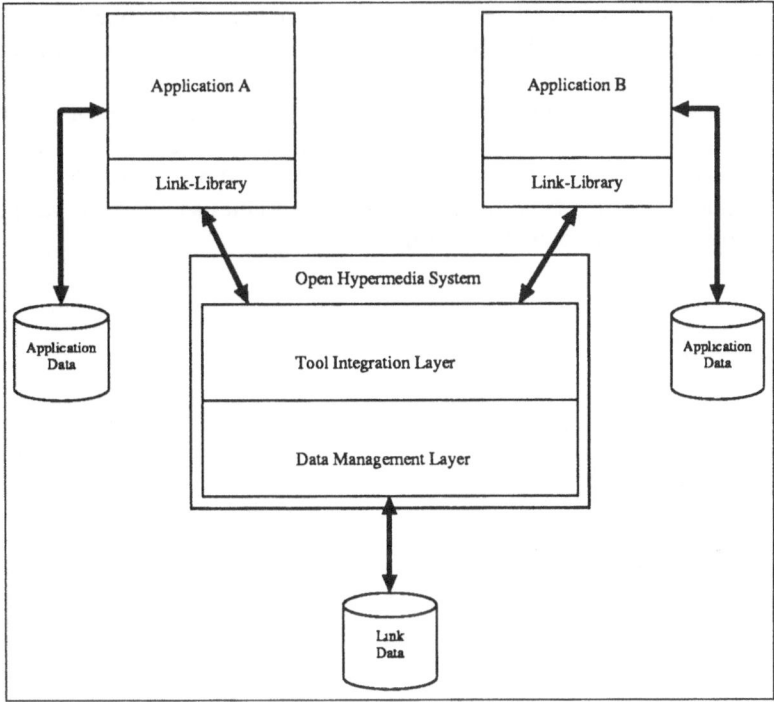

Figure 1: Typical architecture of open hypermedia systems

Systems like WWW do not fall into this system category, as they do not provide general functionality for modifying the data structure and ensuring its integrity: An information structure is created manually by editing an ASCII-File containing HTML source code (Hypertext Markup Language [2]), and making this publicly available. There is no guarantee that referred documents exist or have a content of a specific shape.

If an open hypermedia system is extended to a distributed environment, one arrives at a scenario which may be called a *Distributed Multimedia Computing Environment*. A system for managing data in such an environment will be called a *Distributed Multimedia Data Management System*, $(DM)^2 S$ for short.

A central aspect of an open hypermedia system – and therefore of a $(DM)^2 S$ – is the extensibility of the data structures managed by the system through new content types. This implies that the system in general can not interpret the content of an object, as new applications (managing new types of objects) may be created and attached to the system *after* the system has been built. This fact is mirrored by the separation between content specific and structure specific functionality.

3 Anchors, events and extents

In the area of hypermedia, *anchors* [8] may be used for connecting parts of documents to each other via hyperlinks (see fig. 2). An anchor describes, which interaction with the object content will cause the hyperlink to be traversed. Things like "a mouse-click on the character positions 100-120" for text or "a mouse-click on the pixel rectangle ((10,10),(100,100))" are typical examples (concepts for anchors in time-varying media such as video are discussed in [4]). Implicitly contained in the notion of an anchor is therefore the concept of a *part of an object content*, such as the range of characters or the pixel rectangle in the examples above. This part will now be called the *extent*[2]. In addition to the extent, an anchor also implicitly specifies an *event*, the state change which triggers the traversal of the hyperlink.

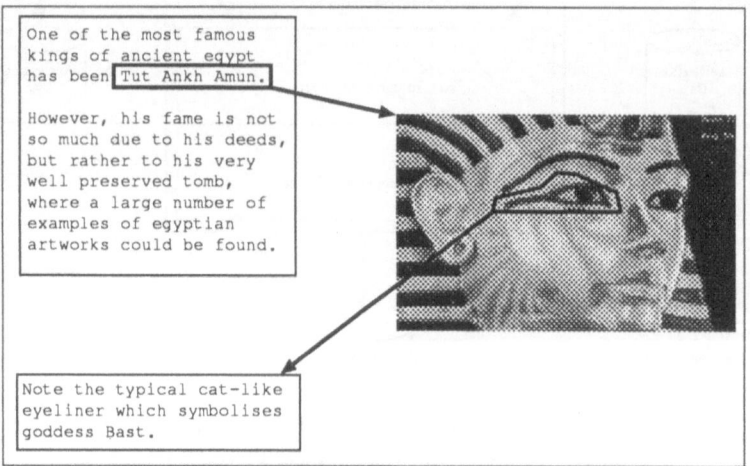

Figure 2: Fragment of a hypertext

The concept of an anchor in hypermedia is – although well established – quite problematic, as it combines the description of interaction behavior and structural relations without explicitly providing events and extents as modeling primitives. In closed systems this is not a problem – the set of content and interaction types is fixed so that an anchor is always interpretable by the system. In open systems however, this is not possible: as content and atomic interactions are managed by external applications, the system can not be assumed to be able to understand an anchor specification. As for extents, so for events too the managing applications are responsible for this interpretation, because it is in general not possible to assume a fixed set of events for interacting with objects, without severely restricting the $(DM)^2 S$' openness towards new object types

---

[2]Other authors – e.g. [18] – prefer to call this concept "Persistent Selections". "Hot Spots" or "Area-Of-Interest" are other names for the same concept.

and applications with unanticipated interaction paradigms. This implies that a $(DM)^2S$ can not know which parts of an anchor specification describe the event and which ones the extent.

Consider now that an anchor may also be used for specifying the *destination* of a hyperlink [8], thereby allowing a hyperlink to point *into* an object's content (e.g., identifying the really relevant part). On the other hand, a managing application is free to request arbitrary changes of anchors of an object it is responsible for. Specifically, it may replace the anchor specification by another one which does only describe an event (such as the selection of a menu item). This now plays games with the original interpretation of the anchor as pointer into the object's content, resulting in an unexpected behavior upon navigation.

Because anchors are a not further specified mixture of interaction and extent, the $(DM)^2S$ can not guarantee that an anchor always defines a part of an object content (likewise, an anchor does not always define an event)[3]. However, if one separates the structural and behavioral elements of anchors (as already suggested in [15]), both are independently available and allow the attachment of specific interpretations and support through the $(DM)^2S$. Events may be used to support a fine grained description of the interaction behavior of objects, independent from their connectivity properties (see [13] for a discussion of these aspects). Extents capture the structural aspects of anchors, the end points of hyperlinks which point *into* an object's content. This paper is concerned with the introduction of extents and their use in a $(DM)^2S$.

4   The basic extent model

Extents have been introduced as parts of an object's content. A somewhat closer look quickly reveals that an extent, to be a useful modeling primitive, can not be a content-part in itself, but rather the *description* of such a part. However, in order to use this description to access the content part, its semantics needs to be defined. This implies that the data management system must understand the object's content. The latter is clearly not acceptable for a $(DM)^2S$ which has to be open to *any* kind of object content, not only the ones which happen to be compiled into the system.

On the other hand, the primary purpose of an extent – as introduced up to now – is to serve as a pointer into the object's content. Only upon object display by the managing application this extent really needs to be interpreted. On the $(DM)^2S$ side it is sufficient to control the *existence* of extents so that the integrity of references to extents can be guaranteed. Therefore it seems sufficient to define extents as entities with an object-locally unique identity. Based on this identity, the system is then able to enforce integrity constraints, without having to understand the extent description itself. It is up to the application managing the object's content to make sure that the content has a shape compatible with all extent definitions for this object. So *extent identity* and *extent definition* provide a clear separation between system and application responsibilities.

As extents – other than anchors – *always* refer to parts of an object's content, it is now possible to exploit this by further detailing the $(DM)^2S$ and application responsibilities

---

[3]Due to this lack of defined semantics, the designers of Hyperform have completely omitted anchors and links; here the user is responsible for implementing them.

with respect to the handling of extents.

We now we give a formal sketch of a model for representing, managing and exploiting extent-information in a $(DM)^2S$.

Formal paragraphs are written using the Z-Notation [20, 3], a specification language based on set-theory which has also been used for the formal specification of the Dexter model [8].

4.1 Fundamental definitions

Objects have unique ids, which are elements of the given set

$[OID]$.

Extents have object-local unique ids, which are elements of the given set

$[XID]$.

There is a set of extent definitions

$[XDEF]$.

As a $(DM)^2S$ is not required to understand extent definitions (this is the responsibility of the managing application), no more detailed description of this set is required.

An *object reference* is an object-id (basic reference) or a pair of object-id and extent-id (extent reference):

$$ORef ::= BRef \langle\!\langle OID \rangle\!\rangle$$
$$| \quad XRef \langle\!\langle OID \times XID \rangle\!\rangle$$

As far as this model is concerned, an object consists of a number of extents defined for it, and a set of $ORef$s, the references introduced by the object.

$$
\begin{array}{|l}
\hline
\_\, Object \_\!\_\!\_\!\_\!\_\!\_\!\_\!\_\!\_\!\_\!\_\!\_ \\
\hline
extents : XID \nrightarrow XDEF \\
refs : \mathbf{P}\ ORef \\
\hline
\end{array}
$$

In a complete model, the content of the *refs* component would be determined by the links of the object. This aspect is omitted here, as it is not relevant for the topic of this paper.

An *information structure* is essentially a function *objects*, mapping object-ids to their respective object data. For all object references in the object data contained in the range of *objects*, the respective objects (together with the extents) must exist in the structure. This is the central referential-integrity constraint defined for the model. It prevents the existence of "dangling links".

$$
\begin{array}{|l}
\hline
\text{\textit{Struct}} \\
\hline
objects : OID \nrightarrow Object \\
\hline
\forall\, r : \bigcup((\lambda\ Object \bullet refs)(\!|\mathrm{ran}\ objects|\!)) \bullet \\
\quad \exists\, o : \mathrm{dom}\ objects;\ x : XID\ | \\
\qquad r = BRef\ o\ \vee \\
\qquad r = XRef(o, x) \wedge x \in \mathrm{dom}\ (objects\ o).extents \\
\hline
\end{array}
$$

We now have introduced the modeling primitive "extent" together with the necessary structural integrity conditions. The next step is the definition of the content-specific interpretation of extents.

4.2 The semantics of extents

Based on the fundamental definitions given above, the semantics of extents in this model are given now. First, the values of object contents are introduced as the given set

$[CONTENT]$.

As for $XDEF$, no further detailing is necessary since the managing application is responsible for the interpretation of an object's content.

The semantics of extent definitions are now defined by introducing the relation ($\_hasExtent\_$) and the function $theExtent$:

$$
\begin{array}{|l}
\_hasExtent\_ : CONTENT \leftrightarrow XDEF \\
theExtent : XDEF \rightarrow CONTENT \rightarrow CONTENT \\
\end{array}
$$

($\_hasExtent\_$) defines whether a given extent definition is contained in a given content value; $theExtent$ maps a content value on the basis of an extent definition to a new content value (which is supposed to be the content part described by the extent definition).

Now the definition of an object value is changed by adding a content and stating the application-sided (content-specific) integrity constraint: an object's content must always have a shape compatible with all extent definitions given for the object.

$$
\begin{array}{|l}
\hline
\text{\textit{Object}} \\
\hline
\ldots \\
content : CONTENT \\
\hline
\forall\, x : \mathrm{dom}\ extents \bullet \\
\quad content\ hasExtent\ (extents\ x) \\
\hline
\end{array}
$$

Note that extent definitions are completely local to an object, so there is exactly one place to look for them. This is a prime requirement when modifiable information structures are considered: once an application modifies an object's content, it has possibly to update extent definitions in order to maintain the object-local integrity condition (which means: make sure that the defined extents are still part of the object's content). If – as it is, e.g., suggested for Hyper-G [11] or WWW – "anchors" are stored distributed, this would require the application to check the anchor definitions at all storage sites. (In Hyper-G and WWW this is not a problem as content modifications are not considered.)

4.3 Content based retrieval

A first observation is that, based on this model, one can now also describe a primitive kind of *content based retrieval* by using the relation *hasExtent*:

$$
\begin{array}{|l}
\hline
retrieveObjects : Struct \rightarrow XDEF \rightarrow \mathbb{P}\; OID \\
\hline
\forall s : Struct;\; xd : XDEF \bullet \\
\quad retrieveObjects\; s\; xd = \\
\qquad \{\; o : \mathrm{dom}\; s.objects \mid (s.objects\; o).content\; hasExtent\; xd\; \} \\
\end{array}
$$

retrieveObjects returns all objects stored in a structure, whose contents contain an extent as described by the extent definition given as argument.

And we may of course define the retrieval of the content part described by a given extent:

$$
\begin{array}{|l}
\hline
getExtent : Struct \rightarrow OID \times XID \nrightarrow CONTENT \\
\hline
\forall s : Struct;\; o : OID;\; x : XID \bullet \\
\quad getExtent\; s\; (o, x) = \\
\qquad (\mu\; obj : \{(s.objects\; o)\} \bullet theExtent\; (obj.extents\; x)\; obj.content) \\
\end{array}
$$

4.4 Summary

The formal model introduced above identifies the description elements required for content based retrieval. Above all, it integrates navigation (that is, hyperlinks between parts of objects) and query retrieval through the explicit introduction of a mechanism for describing extents (*XDEF*) and the definition of its semantics.

However, it does not at all define any implementation strategy for the various given sets and axiomatically defined functions. Thus it serves only as a reference model, which has to be instantiated with concrete values for the unspecified elements. Although it has been claimed that *hasExtent* and *theExtent* define the semantics of extents, this definition is almost void, as for both only the static semantics, the type, has been given.

This means that both functions are implicitly located within the managing applications, since only there functions with unspecified dynamic semantics can exist. But such an assumption is clearly unacceptable for a distributed multimedia information system, as it would require that content based retrieval is carried out by the application which asks for it, so that the bulk data has to be moved across the network. In the next section we will therefore introduce a simple extension using an explicit definition of the object data storage, which then allows extent computations to be carried out at the storage site.

5 Introduction of server based extent computation

5.1 Extensions of the basic model

In order to allow the server side to carry out the extent computation, a concrete representation of object contents has to be defined. It is obvious – on a first glance – that on storage media an object's content may be represented by a function mapping indices to bytes[4]:

$$BYTE == 0..255$$
$$STORAGE == \mathbb{N} \nrightarrow BYTE$$
$$SRESULT ::= data \langle\!\langle STORAGE \rangle\!\rangle \mid nil$$

$SRESULT$ has been introduced to describe the results of operations on $STORAGE$s, the value nil should be interpreted as "there is no fitting data available".

The only point of interest now is, to be able to define arbitrary functions of the type $STORAGE \rightarrow SRESULT$ at the $(DM)^2 S$-side. This, however, is already possible: Since we know the data to operate on, we can easily identify a mechanism for specifying arbitrary (computable) functions on this data. (E.g., the lambda calculus with constants or some other suitable notation.) It is therefore sufficient – as we know that these things do exist – to explicitly state this existence:

$$[SFDEF]$$

$$
\begin{array}{|l}
translate : XDEF \rightarrow SFDEF \\
compile : SFDEF \rightarrow STORAGE \rightarrow SRESULT \\
read : SRESULT \rightarrow CONTENT
\end{array}
$$

$SFDEF$ is the set of definitions of storage accessor functions. $translate$ is the application function for translating an extent-definition into a storage accessor function definition. $compile$ is the $(DM)^2 S$-based function for translating storage accessor function definitions into the respective storage accessor functions (which are executed by the $(DM)^2 S$ too). $read$ is another application-defined function, which translates a flat storage representation into the application's content representation. For completeness, we introduce also a function $write$, which transforms application data into its storage representation:

$$
\begin{array}{|l}
write : CONTENT \rightarrowtail STORAGE \\
\hline
read \circ data \circ write = \text{id } CONTENT
\end{array}
$$

$write$ is required to be an injection (every $CONTENT$ must have a unique $STORAGE$ representation), and the composition of $write$, $data$ (the injection into $SRESULT$), and $read$ is the identity for content values (which means that reading a written content value should return just this value).

Now the definition of an information structure is modified by introducing storage representations for object contents, and stating the relation between storage representations and content values:

$$
\begin{array}{|l}
\_\_Object_____ \\
\dots \\
store : STORAGE \\
\hline
store = write \; content
\end{array}
$$

---

[4]This of course does not cover the difficulties of real-time streams, and other data streams which do not provide random access.

And now we can describe the access of an extent:

$$\forall\, s : Struct;\ o : OID;\ x : XID\ \bullet$$
$$getExtent\ s\,(o, x) =$$
$$\mu\, obj : \{(s.objects\ o)\}\ \bullet$$
$$(read \circ ((compile \circ translate \circ obj.extents)\ x))\ obj.store$$

The following implications for a system architecture hold:

- *translate* and *read* are provided by the application.

- *compile* (and the necessary facilities for executing the resulting storage accessor function) are provided by the $(DM)^2 S$.

- *CONTENT* and *XDEF* are application specific.

- *SFDEF* and *STORAGE* are defined by the $(DM)^2 S$.

Based on the value *nil* we can also redefine the content based retrieval with *retrieveObjects*:

$$\forall\, s : Struct;\ xd : XDEF\ \bullet$$
$$retrieveObjects\ s\ xd =$$
$$(\mu\, sf : \{(compile \circ translate)\ xd\}\ \bullet$$
$$\{\ o : dom\ s.objects\ |\ sf((s.objects\ o).store) \neq nil\ \})$$

Again, *translate* is executed by the client. *compile* and the resulting *sf* are executed at the server side. This means that the computation of result sets of queries – as well as data reduction for extent transfers – is done at the server side, thereby completely avoiding bulk data transfers to the application.

(_hasExtent_), which has been used for defining the local integrity constraints for objects, can now be explicitly described:

$$\forall\, c : CONTENTS;\ xd : XDEF\ \bullet$$
$$c\ hasExtent\ xd \Leftrightarrow (compile \circ translate)\ xd\ (write\ c) \neq nil$$

This definition has the disadvantage of including the application's functions *translate* and *write*, which would be inacceptible in a distributed environment. It is clear that these functions are not required, if we explicitly include the translated extent definition in the object data and slightly modify the integrity conditions for extents, so that we finally arrive at the following definition for *Object*:

```
┌─ Object ────────────────────────────────────────────
│  . . .
│  tr : XID ↦ SFDEF
├─────────────────────────────────────────────────────
│  dom tr = dom extents
│
│  ∀ x : dom extents •
│     tr x = translate(extents x) ∧
│     (compile ∘ tr) x store ≠ nil
└─────────────────────────────────────────────────────
```

5.2 Some remarks on the model

The following observations hold for the extension of the model:

- The introduction of server based extent computation has been based on the following mechanisms:

  - Fixing of a fundamental storage representation of object data.
  - Requiring the storage server to be runtime-extensible through storage accessor function definitions.

- Although the basic storage model is quite simple, it allows the handling of arbitrarily structured contents through the computational completeness required for *SFDEF*: An object's *store* contains a linearized representation of the possibly structured *content*. An *SFDEF* may then be defined to delinearize this representation and construct a content structure isomorphical to *content* at the storage site. The computational properties of *SFDEF* guarantee that this is always possible.

  SFDEF in effect allows the transfer of content semantics from the application to the $(DM)^2S$.

- It is obvious that the query processing strategy implied by the definition of *retrieveObjects* is *very* resource intensive. It should therefore be considered that a preclassification of objects, as they are imported, may substantially increase the retrieval efficiency. For this purpose *SFDEF* needs to contain general functions for operating on information structures – instances of *Struct* –, just as conventional query languages do for databases.

  The Manchester Multimedia Information System [6] for example, addresses several issues which relate to means for enhancing efficiency, such as lazy query evaluation etc.

5.3 An example

As an example for the use of extents and server based extent computation, consider a distributed database of faces (stored in high resolution) which may be used for the creation of phantom faces. In addition we assume that an application presents individual images to the user as low resolution miniatures and allows the identification of interesting areas, such as the eyes, thereby implicitly creating an *XDEF*. The application then requests the corresponding original data from the $(DM)^2S$ by translating the *XDEF* into its corresponding *SFDEF* and sending this to the $(DM)^2S$. The $(DM)^2S$ computes the *SRESULT* from the *SFDEF* and the object's *store*, and sends this result back to the application.

For an example image such as given in figure 3, the transfer of only the eye-section (the extent shown in figure 4) results in a quite noticeable decrease of data volume to be moved from storage site to display: instead of 64000 pixels only 2975 had to be transferred – less than 5 percent of the original data volume.

This technique is used by the SpacePicture application [14], an interactive satellite-image retrieval system for storing and retrieving high-resolution images (e.g., 6000 ×

Figure 3: The original image

Figure 4: The extracted extent

6000 pixels resolution at 7 × 8 bit per pixel) on optical WORM-Jukeboxes. Here, low resolution presentation derivatives (1000 × 1000 pixels) and very-low resolution miniatures (120 × 120 pixels) are used by the system to allow the identification of interesting images, and the definition of the relevant extents on these images. Once an extent has been defined, the server process starts with extracting the respective area out of the original data set stored on the jukebox. Only the extracted area is then transferred to the user's workstation.

A more complex example is displayed in figures 5 and 6. Here, the extent is defined by the areas around significant intensity changes ("edges") in the image (computed using the pythagorean sum of two Sobel gradient operators at 90 degrees to each other – see [7, chapter 7] for more details). Figure 5 displays the resulting area, figure 6 the actual pixels to be transferred. In this case the actual number of pixels to transfer is 18031, about 28 percent of the original data. However, it has to be taken into account that additional coordinate information will have to be included in order for the application to be able to determine the blank spaces between the extent's pixels.

6 Conclusion

In this paper we have proposed the fundamental aspects of a system architecture and a data model which supports the content based retrieval in open, distributed multimedia information management systems. The model has been based on an analysis of the "anchor"-concept of hypermedia and the identification of the two independent modeling primitives "extent" and "event". After the introduction of extents as required for hypermedia anchorage, we observed that the new modeling primitive also provided for content based query-retrieval. Thus we were able to prove our introductory claim by capturing the two content based retrieval paradigms within one modeling primitive.

By an extension of the model we could then show how to avoid unnecessary bulk data

Figure 5: The extent's bit-Mask

Figure 6: The extracted extent

transfers between storage site and application. The main aspects of this extension have been the identification of the concepts of a common storage representation scheme, and the runtime extensibility of the $(DM)^2S$ with storage accessor functions. The interesting fact here is not so much the idea of server-based extent computation in itself, but rather the embedding into the extent model, again demonstrating the use of extents and the expressiveness gained by disassembling anchors.

It is obvious that the model requires a large amount of detailing in order to provide a suitably efficient implementation of the storage system and the execution machinery for storage accessor functions. Although the extensibility by arbitrary computable functions at runtime is a fundamental requirement for a $(DM)^2S$, the research is not finished there – after all, this requirement is also met by, e.g., LISP programming environments. So the question is now: *which* concrete storage representations should such a system provide? It has already been mentioned that the assumption of a random access to storage is not valid in general. Therefore, further modeling facilities to describe different types of storage accesses (such as strictly sequential and isochronal access) are required.

It is especially interesting to identify $SFDEF$ with a query-language, and *compile* – as well as the storage accessor function execution – with the functionality of a database management system. The difference to other DBMS-based approaches to managing hyperstructures is that in this case the DBMS would be used for managing and accessing *content* data instead of structural information. Therefore non-standard DBMS are required which support the efficient storage and access to multidimensional information.

We have implemented parts of the model in the open hypermedia system HyperPicture [15]. The system provides the extension language HCL (HyperPicture Command Language) [12], a LISP-like language developed at the Computer Graphics Center which has been specifically designed for the HyperPicture system.

HCL enables an application to transform its specific format of extent definitions into HCL function definitions, which are then evaluated by HyperPicture in order to retrieve the extent data. HCL is therefor an instance of *SFDEF*; the HCL interpreter is the implementation of *compile*.

However, the system does not include the mechanisms for enforcing object-local referential integrity as defined by the model.

References

[1] Berners-Lee, T., Cailliau, R., Groff, J., Pollerman, B. WorldWideWeb: The Information Universe. *Electronic Networking: Research, Applications and Policy*, 1(2):52–58, Spring 1992.

[2] Berners-Lee, T., Connolly, D. Hypertext Markup Language (HTML). Internet draft, IETF IIIR Working Group, June 1993.

[3] Brian, S., Nicholls, J., editors. *Z Base Standard (Version 1.0)*. Oxford University Computing Laboratory, Programming Research Group, November 1992.

[4] Burrill, V., Kirste, T., Weiss, J. Time-varying Sensitive Regions in dynamic multimedia objects: A pragmatic approach to content-based retrieval from video. *Information and Software Technology, Special Issue on Multimedia Information Systems*, July 1994.

[5] Danzig, P.B., Obraczka, K., Li, Shih-Hao. Internet Resource Discovery Services. *IEEE Computer*, 26(9):8–22, September 1993.

[6] Goble, C., O'Docherty, M., Crowther, P., Ireton, M., Daskalis, C., Oakley, J., Kay, S., Xydeas, C. The Manchester Multimedia Information System. In Kjelldahl [16], pages 244–268.

[7] Gonzales, R.C., Wintz, P. *Digital Image Processing*. Addison-Wesley, 1987.

[8] Halasz, F.G., Schwartz, M. The Dexter Hypertext Reference Model. In *Proc. NIST Hypertext Standardisation Workshop*, Gaithersburg, Maryland, January 16–17 1990. National Institute for Standardisation.

[9] Kacmar, C.J., Legget, J.J. PROXHY: A process-oriented extensible hypertext architecture. *ACM Transactions on Information Systems*, 9(4):399–419, October 1991.

[10] Kahle, B. WAIStation: A User Interface for Wide Area Information Servers. Technical report, Thinking Machines Corporation, September 1990.

[11] Kappe, F.M., Pani, G. The Architecture of a Massively Distributed Hypermedia System. Technical Report IICM 341, Graz University of Technology, 1992 (?).

[12] Kirste, T. HCL Language Reference Manual, Version 1.0. ZGDV-Report 68/93, Computer Graphics Center, 1993.

[13] Kirste, T. Some issues of defining a user interface with general purpose hypermedia toolkits. In Schuler, W., Hannemann, J., editors, *Workshop on Methodological Issues on the Design of Hypertext-based User Interfaces*, Darmstadt, July 13-14 1993. GMD-IPSI.

[14] Kirste, T. SpacePicture – An Interactive Hypermedia Satellite Image Archival System. *Computers & Graphics*, 17(3):251–260, 1993.

[15] Kirste, T., Hübner, W. An Open Hypermedia System for Multimedia Applications. In Kjelldahl [16], pages 225–243.

[16] Kjelldahl, L., editor. *Multimedia: systems, interaction and applications (Proc. 1st Eurographics Workshop on Multimedia, April 18–19 1991, Stockholm/Sweden)*. Springer, 1992.

[17] Sandkuhl, K., Schoepf, V. Issues and Limits of Dynamic Hypermedia Systems – The HyperScript System. In Cordes, R., Streitz, N.A., editors, *Hypertext und Hypermedia '92 – Konzepte und Anwendungen auf dem Weg in die Praxis*, pages 75–86. Springer, 1992.

[18] Schnase, J.L. *HB2: A Hyperbase Management System for Open, Distributed Hypermedia System Architectures*. PhD thesis, Texas A&M University, 1992.

[19] Schwartz, M.F., Emtage, A., Kahle, B., Neumann, B.C. A Comparison of Internet Resource Discovery Approaches. *Computing Systems*, 5(4), 1992.

[20] Spivey, J.M. *The Z Notation*. Prentice Hall, 1989.

[21] Wiil, U.K., Legget, J.J. Hyperform: Using Extensibility to Develop Dynamic Open and Distributed Hypertext Systems. In *Proc. ECHT'92*, pages 251–261, Milano, Italy, November 30 – December 4 1992. The Association for Computing Machinery.

Specification summary

Given sets:

$$[OID, XID, XDEF, CONTENT, SFDEF]$$

Type synonyms:

$$BYTE == 0 \, .. \, 255$$
$$STORAGE == \mathbb{N} \nrightarrow BYTE$$

Structured types:

$$ORef \qquad ::= BRef \langle\!\langle OID \rangle\!\rangle \mid XRef \langle\!\langle OID \times XID \rangle\!\rangle$$
$$SRESULT ::= data \langle\!\langle STORAGE \rangle\!\rangle \mid nil$$

Semantic functions:

$$translate : XDEF \rightarrow SFDEF$$
$$compile : SFDEF \rightarrow STORAGE \rightarrow SRESULT$$
$$read : SRESULT \rightarrow CONTENT$$
$$write : CONTENT \rightarrowtail STORAGE$$
$$\_hasExtent\_ : CONTENT \leftrightarrow XDEF$$

$$read \circ data \circ write = \mathrm{id} \, CONTENT$$

$$\forall c : CONTENT; \; xd : XDEF \bullet$$
$$c \; hasExtent \; xd \Leftrightarrow (compile \circ translate) \, xd \, (write \, c) \neq nil$$

Objects:

```
┌─ Object ─────────────────────────────────
│ extents : XID ↠ XDEF
│ refs : ℙ ORef
│ content : CONTENT
│ store : STORAGE
│ tr : XID ↠ SFDEF
├──────────────────────────────────────────
│ ∀ x : dom extents •
│    content hasExtent (extents x)
│ store = write content
│ dom tr = dom extents
│ ∀ x : dom extents •
│    tr x = translate(extents x) ∧
│    (compile ∘ tr) x store ≠ nil
└──────────────────────────────────────────
```

Information structures:

$$
\begin{array}{l}
\rule{0pt}{0pt}\quad Struct \\
\hline
\quad objects : OID \nrightarrow Object \\
\hline
\quad \forall\, r : \bigcup((\lambda\ Object \bullet refs)(\!|\mathrm{ran}\ objects|\!)) \bullet \\
\qquad \exists\, o : \mathrm{dom}\ objects;\ x : XID \bullet \\
\qquad\quad r = BRef\ o\ \vee \\
\qquad\quad r = XRef(o, x) \wedge x \in \mathrm{dom}\ (objects\ o).extents \\
\end{array}
$$

Content based retrieval:

$$
\begin{array}{l}
\quad retrieveObjects : Struct \to XDEF \to \mathbb{P}\ OID \\
\quad getExtent : Struct \to OID \times XID \nrightarrow CONTENT \\
\hline
\quad \forall\, s : Struct;\ xd : XDEF \bullet \\
\qquad retrieveObjects\ s\ xd = \\
\qquad\quad (\mu\ sf : \{(compile \circ translate)\ xd\} \bullet \\
\qquad\qquad \{\, o : \mathrm{dom}\ s.objects \mid sf((s.objects\ o).store) \neq nil \,\}) \\
\quad \forall\, s : Struct;\ o : OID;\ x : XID \bullet \\
\qquad getExtent\ s\ (o, x) = \\
\qquad\quad (\mu\ obj : \{(s.objects\ o)\} \bullet \\
\qquad\qquad (read \circ ((compile \circ translate \circ obj.extents)\ x))\ obj.store \\
\end{array}
$$

Interaction Objects in the MADE Multimedia Environment

Frans C. Heeman, Ivan Herman, Graham Reynolds

Centre for Mathematics and Computer Sciences
P.O. Box 94079, 1090 GB Amsterdam, The Netherlands

Abstract. In order to support flexible interaction in interactive multimedia systems, we have defined general interaction objects that allow dynamic and transparent coupling of user interaction to media objects and other types of objects. The interaction objects are programmable in that they may use scripting languages for defining their behavior. This mechanism can be used to glue existing application capabilities together to form new end-user functionality.

1 Introduction

The definition of user interaction is often one of the most difficult tasks to perform during the development of an interactive system. Usually an iterative approach is taken, so that different interactions can be tested out and refined. This is best achieved when a flexible means to define and change interaction is provided, independently from an application's functionality. Multimedia systems in particular, are often more complex on the application side because of their need to handle multiple, time-critical streams of high volume distributed data, and consequently they may push aside the user interface as a secondary issue. Having a means to separate the interaction from the application side makes it possible to give the development of the user interface its proper place.

In the European Communities' ESPRIT III project MADE (Multimedia Application Development Environment [3, 7]), a portable object-oriented development environment is being defined and implemented for multimedia applications. The outcome of this work will be a programming environment, based on C++, running on various UNIX platforms and on Windows-NT environments.

A flexible scheme has been defined as part of the MADE project for handling user interaction. Essentially, it consists of general interaction objects based on finite state machines, where the behavior of the state machine can be defined either as part of the interaction object itself or separately in a script. State transitions are triggered by events originating from input devices or from other objects. General software interfaces have been defined, so that interaction objects defined in MADE programs can access scripting languages in a way that is independent of the specific scripting language used, and conversely, scripting languages can invoke application functionality defined in a MADE program.

Section 2 of this paper describes the general considerations that underly our design. The actual architecture is given in Section 3. Some examples in Section 4 show the concrete application of the design to typical multimedia scenario's. Conclusions are given in Section 5.

2   Design Considerations

As discussed in the introduction, we think it is important to be able to separate the definition of user interaction from the actual application functionality. In the design of interactive systems, this requirement comes down to separating the definition of interaction from the objects being manipulated. Furthermore, to be able to iterate quickly over changes in the user interface it must also be possible to change the definition of interaction dynamically, without touching the application in any way. Taking these two points together, we arrive at the notion of *programmable interaction objects*. In addition, we required that the use of interaction objects be supported by some model for defining interaction.

The requirements for separation and programmability of the interaction lead to the use of scripting languages, i.e., interpretative languages used outside of the application. The requirement for an interaction model lead to the use of finite state machines (FSM's), in which events move the interaction from state to state. Each of these design decisions will be described in more detail below.

2.1   Modelling Interaction with Finite State Machines (FSM's)

In order to support interaction several approaches can be used, such as grammars, event handlers or state-transition networks. They differ in flexibility and expressiveness (see [5] for a more detailed comparison):

1. Grammars are not suitable for expressing multi-threaded interaction (such as invoking a help function at arbitrary points in the interaction).
2. The mechanism of event handlers, as found in window systems, consists of sending events to event handlers which can perform arbitrary actions. Although this is a general and powerful mechanism, it imposes little in the way of structure.
3. State-transition networks are often used in user interface management systems. One example is the Generic Window Manager GWM [8], which uses FSM's and a LISP dialect to specify the behavior of a window manager. See [5] for other examples. The main disadvantage of state-transition networks is the danger of state explosion, in which similar state-transition behaviors are to be repeated in several states. This disadvantage can be mitigated by the use of recursive state-transition networks. In addition, augmented transition networks extend these by adding computation facilities (data storage and functions, which are only visible within the network).

All in all, we have chosen the model of finite state machines, because it gives support for modelling interaction in terms of states and transitions. By using it in a programming environment, it becomes general and powerful enough to express even complex interactions.

2.2   Specifying Interaction using Scripting Languages

In order to be able to change the definition of an interaction dynamically, simply separating it from the application functionality is not sufficient. If interaction is defined separately, but changing it still requires reprogramming or recompiling part of the application, then much of the advantages of separation are lost. What is needed in addition to separation is an *interpretative* definition of the interaction. This approach is already used in other systems, such as Tcl [9].

Rather than defining our own scripting language, or relying on one specific scripting language, a general software interface for scripting languages was developed. Through a small set of functions the interaction object can execute files containing scripts, as well as call functions defined in a script. In practice, some requirements are imposed on a scripting language to be used in this way, but these requirements are easily met by most scripting languages (see Section 3.4 for details).

2.3 Programmable Interaction Objects

Having this general mechanism of interaction objects as script based programmable FSM's opens up a way to reuse interaction objects. Interaction objects can be composed into more complex interaction sequences and can be reused as interaction patterns. Also, the mechanism of defining the behavior of an interaction object in a script, separate from the application, makes it possible to combine existing application functionality into new user-level functionality. Interaction objects can then be used to glue together suitable application building blocks into new applications.

The notion of programmable FSM's can also be used in contexts other than interaction. In the current draft of the new proposal for the ISO-standard PREMO (Presentation Environment for Multimedia Objects [4]), general controller objects are defined. The distinctive characteristic of controller objects is that they maintain a programmable state-transition model. In PREMO, controller objects are used for interaction as well as for synchronisation. For example, a controller object may model an OR-synchroniser, which takes some actions as soon as it receives one event out of a set of events, or an AND-synchroniser, which only takes some action after it has received all of a set of events.

One consequence of using programmable interaction objects is that the definition of interaction is separated from an application's functionality. Communication between these two sides is carried out through their respective software interfaces. For example, when using a mouse to drag an object displayed on the screen, the events coming from the mouse are not forwarded directly to the object involved, but rather to an associated interaction object. This interaction object then determines how to perform the dragging operation. It may, for example, call the 'move' method of the object on each event. Alternatively, it may perform the feedback itself by showing an outline of the object, and only call the 'move' method of the object when the drag operation is complete. The point is that direct manipulation and other user interaction now only use the functional interface of the objects involved.

Another point arising from the separation is that an association is set up that forwards events directed to objects to the appropriate interaction object. For this association, we use the notion of sensors (see also GoPATH [2]). A sensor is an object that may be associated to other objects. In addition, it is also associated to an interaction object. Sensors express to the window system an interest in receiving events. In fact, they are the only objects that do this. Whenever an input event is generated, the window system forwards it to the appropriate sensor (see figure 1).

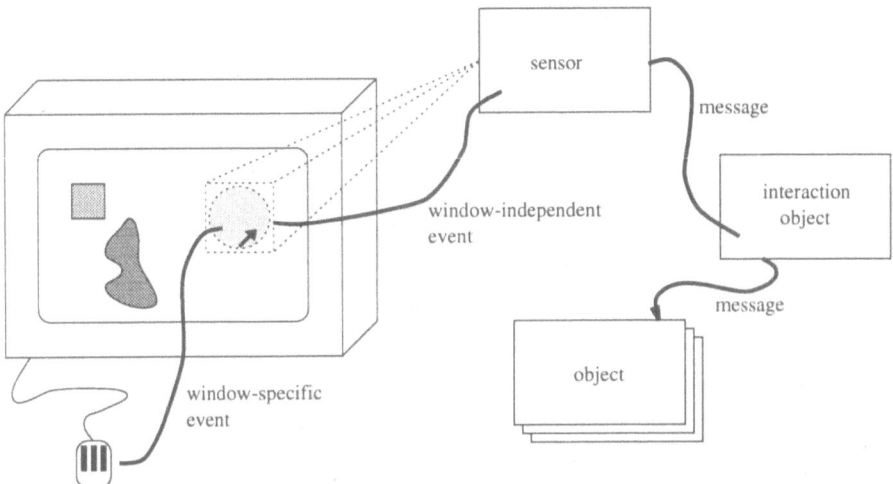

Fig. 1. A sensor in an interactive application

A sensor expresses interest in a event by defining a sensitive 'region' and an event type. For example, if a sensor whishes to receive events directed to a graphical object, it can define its region to coincide with the area covered by the graphic object. Alternatively, a sensor could define a different region, for example, one which covers only the corners of a bounding box for the graphic object. The sensor sends the event to its associated interaction object by calling a specific method defined for the interaction object. The sensor is free to change the event, send another event, or send messages to other objects as well. Typically, the event is translated into a window system independent event, so that the objects receiving events do not depend on the specific window system that is used. This implies that a fixed set of events must be defined. Events are also (of course) objects, so any object could create event objects and send these to other objects, simulating input events.

The mechanism of sensors allows the establishment, dynamically, of a link between an object being manipulated and an interaction object. The object involved is unaware of its associated sensor(s).

3   Architecture

3.1   Overview

Assuming that an interaction object instance has been created, then the architectural structure depicted in Figure 2 will exist for it (details of the instantiation and initialisation of an interaction object are given later):

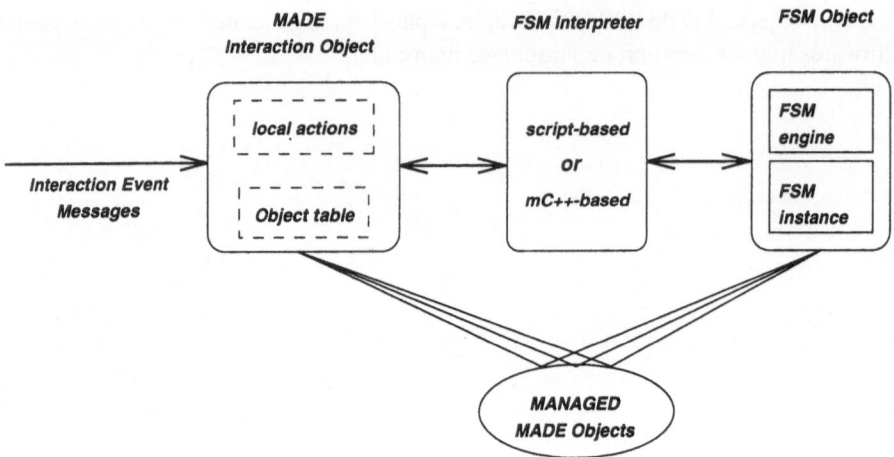

Fig. 2. Interaction object architecture

1. The interaction object itself, which receives messages representing interaction "events", typically from an associated *sensor object*, but also potentially from other interaction objects in an interaction hierarchy.
2. The FSM object, which consists of a general FSM engine and a specialized FSM instance. The FSM engine provides methods for the creation of an FSM and for performing transitions on an FSM. The FSM instance defines local actions to be performed on recognition of a particular event in a specific state of the FSM.

   The entire FSM object is defined either in a scripting language or is C++-based. An FSM object is not required. If none is defined for a specific interaction object, any events sent to the interaction object are redirected using a set of virtual functions defined in the interaction object[1]. The default definitions of these virtual functions is to do nothing. They can be redefined by writing an appropriate subclass of the general interaction object class.
3. If the FSM object is defined in a scripting language, then also a script interpreter object is present. Conceptually, if the FSM object is C++-based, then this interpreter amounts to the C++ runtime environment.

Both the interaction object and the related FSM object maintain equivalent tables of information on the objects that are managed by the interaction object.

The basic operation of an interaction object is as follows:

1. On receipt of an interaction event, the interaction object invokes its FSM object through an appropriate interpreter and passes it the event and any arguments. In case no FSM object is defined for the interaction object, it calls one of its own virtual functions, so that the response on events can be handled by a subclass of the interaction object.

---

[1] In the mC++ programming language used in the MADE environment (see Appendix A), these functions can also be dynamically redirected using *delegation*.

2. The FSM engine determines the action to be performed for the event based upon the transition defined for that type of event in the current state. The engine may call a locally defined procedure within the FSM instance itself. Alternatively, it may either invoke a locally defined action method within the interaction object or invoke a public method of any other MADE object. These later two possibilities rely on the provision of the MADE dynamic call mechanism (see Section 3.3). Of course, a local action defined in an FSM instance may also make use of this dynamic call interface.

In MADE, the FSM that defines the behavior of an interaction object can be specified in three ways:

1. by defining a subclass of a general interaction class;
2. by providing a C++-based FSM;
3. by providing a script-based FSM.

The first alternative is the most restrictive, in that interactive behavior is compiled into the program and the programmer has to code all state manipulations. The second alternative adds support in the form of a general FSM class. The third alternative in addition allows interactive behavior to be defined outside of the compiled program, giving more flexibility in designing user interaction.

The specific approach taken, however, is completely hidden to the rest of the program that uses the interaction object. This means that, for example, one could first use a script-based approach to design some user interaction, and later incorporate a final version into the program so that it may run without the overhead of a script interpreter. All of this is without any change to the rest of the program.

3.2 Class Definition for the Interaction Objects

Figure 3 gives the mC++ class interface for interaction objects (for a short overview on mC++, see Appendix A). The functionality of an interaction object includes the following:

MInteractor(FSMname) :
The constructor's principal task is to create and initialise an FSM object, possibly with a script interpreter. The FSMname argument is used as the basis for locating the FSM to be used. It can refer to a file containing a script definition of the FSM. Alternatively, it may refer to a C++ object implementing an FSM. This second possibility is checked using the dynamic call interface (see Section 3.3). If FSMname does not refer to an FSM definition, the interaction object is supposed to use its hard-wired behavior.

resetInteractor() :
Reset the state of the FSM associated with the interaction object. Because reset-Interactor() is declared as virtual, subclasses can override this function to provide hard-wired behavior.

```
Mutex MInteractor {
public:
    MInteractor(const char * =0);
    virtual void resetInteractor();
    virtual void triggerInteraction(MEvent *, char * ="", MCva_list);

    void manageObject(MObject *, char *, MBool add);
    void delegateUnknownEvent(MObject *, const char *);
    void delegatePassEvent(MObject *, const char *);

protected:
    MSet managedObjs; // general set of ManagedObject instances
    virtual void unknownEventAction();
    virtual void passEventAction();

    ~MInteractor();
};
```

Fig. 3. Interface of the general MInteractor class.

triggerInteraction(event, format, ...) :
Used by other objects to send an interaction event message to an interaction object. The format describes the types of additional parameters that may be present. This method is used primarily by sensor objects. Because this function is declared as virtual, subclasses can override this function to provide hard-wired behavior.

unknownEventAction() :
Method that is called whenever the interaction object receives an event that it can not handle.

passEventAction() :
Method that is called whenever the interaction object receives an event that it wants to pass on.

delegatePassEvent() :
delegateUnknownEvent() :
Methods that use the mC++ delegation mechanism to delegate the two methods unknownEventAction() and passEventAction(), respectively, to another object.

manageObject(object, memberFunction, addOrRemove) :
Method that adds or removes a reference to another object, together with an identification of a member function of that object, to or from the set of objects managed by this interaction object.

3.3   The Dynamic Call Interface

The model of interaction objects has been implemented in the MADE project in a C++ environment (see Appendix A. The main addition made by MADE to C++, relevant to the implementation of the interaction objects, is the *dynamic call interface.*

The dynamic call interface allows methods of C++ objects to be called, given only a string specification of the method to be called, and knowing only a common base type for all MADE objects. This mechanism is essential for allowing general FSM's to call arbitrary methods in arbitrary MADE objects. Also, it is needed in the implementation of the general scripting interface. The C++ language does not offer this ability. Because of its static type checking, all object types and method signatures must be known at compile time. C++'s mechanism of virtual functions allows runtime binding of methods to objects, but only for the set of functions that are defined, at compile time, to be virtual. These restrictions makes it cumbersome to implement applications that require runtime binding. For example, when accessing C++ objects from within a scripting language, the C++-method to be called will always be identified by the script using some interpretable description. In C++, this description then has to be matched with a method. In the MADE C++ environment (called mC++ [1]), we have added support for this. It is interesting to note that in the OMG specification [6] a similar facility is included. In MADE, the dynamic call interface contains the following:

MCallMethod(MObject *obj, const char *signature, ...) :
Call the method specified by signature on obj. A variable number of parameters, to be forwarded to the member function to be invoked, can be supplied. These are handled using the standard C stdarg functionality.

MCallMethodv(MObject *obj, const char *signature, va_list ap) :
This one is similar to the previous function, but takes a reference to a variable number of parameters, rather than the parameters itself. Again, this uses the standard C stdarg functionality.

MInqMethod(MObject *obj, const char *signature) :
Check whether obj defines a member function that has signature as its declaration.

3.4 Requirements on Scripting Languages

As mentioned before, the design of the interaction objects allows for three possibilities: hard coded without an FSM, hard coded but FSM-based, and an external interpreter with an FSM encoded in a script. In the current implementation, the main requirements on a scripting language to be used in this way, are that it is embeddable (i.e. a software interface is defined for it which allows access from within C or C++), and that it contains the notion of functions callable by a name. Candidates for scripting languages that are suitable for use as FSM interpreters include Perl [11] (the latest version is now embeddable), Python [10], and Tcl [9]. Section 4 gives a working example of a script-based FSM using Python. It defines a general FSM class which is specialized into a simple controller for a video player. The example also shows an equivalent FSM written in C++.

4 Examples

Two examples are given that illustrate the use of programmable interaction objects. The first example, a video player, is intended to show the merits of using an FSM to describe the states and transitions inherent to a particular interaction. The second examples is intended to highlight the use of sensors, and to show the ease with which the interactive

272

behavior and end-user functionality can be changed by simply changing a script that is used for the interaction definition.

4.1 Example: A Video Player

The first example implements a video player with the usual play, stop, pause, forward and backward buttons. An FSM can be used to model the behavior of the player. In this example, several entities are assumed which, for brevity, we do not specify further. These are:

1. a user interface with buttons for play, stop, fast-forward, etc.;
2. a sensor associated with each button;
3. a video player object;

In addition to these, an interaction object and an FSM are defined. The interaction object's interface is given in Figure 4. It is defined as a Mutex object, which is an mC++ construction that provides protection against multiple access by several threads at the same time (see Appendix A). The interaction object defines methods for invoking the appropriate actions on the video player. For example, it defines a method void issuePlay() to start up a video player. Although in this example the methods do not have arguments, there is nothing that prevents them from doing so.

```
Mutex Player : public MInteractor {
protected:
    void unknownEventAction();
    void passEventAction();

    void issueStop();
    void issueBackw();
    void issueForw();
    void issuePlay();
    void issuePause();
    void releasePause();
public:
    Player(char * =0); // The parameter contains the FSM name
    // For hard-wired behavior, define the following:
    // void resetInteractor();
    // void triggerInteraction(MEvent *, char *, MCva_list);
};
```

Fig. 4. Interface of an interaction object for a video player.

The FSM definition is given in Figure 5. Figure 5 actually shows two FSM definitions, one written in Python, the other in mC++. The interaction object given in Figure 4 can be used with either of these, without any further changes. As indicated by the comments in Figure 4, it can even be used without an FSM by redefining the interaction object virtual methods resetInteractor() and triggerInteraction().

When one of the buttons in the user interface is pressed, the sensor associated with the button sends an appropriate message to the interaction object. For example, if the

```
# The module 'madeif' interfaces to MADE programs
import madeif
# The module 'MFsm' contains a general FSM class
import Mfsm

# class Video is a subclass of the general FSM class
class Video(Mfsm.MFSM) :
    # local actions, defined by class functions:
    def localInit(self) :
        self.pausedState = 'STOP'

    def stopAndBackw(self,arg) :
        madeif.callmethod(self.iao,'void issueStop()' , 'n')
        madeif.callmethod(self.iao,'void issueBackw()', 'n')

    def stopAndForw(self,arg) :
        madeif.callmethod(self.iao,'void issueStop()', 'n')
        madeif.callmethod(self.iao,'void issueForw()', 'n')

    def stopAndPlay(self,arg) :
        madeif.callmethod(self.iao,'void issueStop()', 'n')
        madeif.callmethod(self.iao,'void issuePlay()', 'n')

    def paused(self,arg) :
        madeif.callmethod(self.iao,'void issuePause()', 'n')
        self.pausedState=self.returnState()
        self.setState('PAUSE')

    def outOfPause(self,arg) :
        madeif.callmethod(self.iao,'void releasePause()','n')
        self.setState(self.pausedState)

    # The definition of the FSM itself:
    initState = 'STOP'
    transTable={
        'STOP' :{'Play'  : ('void issuePlay()' ,'PLAY' ), \
                 'Backw' : ('void issueBackw()','BACKW'), \
                 'Forw'  : ('void issueForw()' ,'FORW' )},\
        'PAUSE':{'Stop'  : ('void issueStop()' ,'STOP' ), \
                 'Pause' : (outOfPause                  )},\
        'PLAY' :{'Stop'  : ('void issueStop()' ,'STOP' ), \
                 'Pause' : (paused                      ), \
                 'Backw' : (stopAndBackw        ,'BACKW'), \
                 'Forw'  : (stopAndForw         ,'FORW' )},\
        'FORW' :{'Stop'  : ('void issueStop()' ,'STOP' ), \
                 'Pause' : (paused                      ), \
                 'Play'  : (stopAndPlay         ,'PLAY' )},\
        'BACKW':{'Stop'  : ('void issueStop()' ,'STOP' ), \
                 'Pause' : (paused                      ), \
                 'Play'  : (stopAndPlay         ,'PLAY' )}}
```

```
Mutex Video : public MFSM {
private: char *pausedState;
public:  Video(MInteractor *anIao);
    void stopAndBackw();
    void stopAndForw();
    void stopAndPlay();
    void paused();
    void outOfPause();
};

MFSMEntry FSMspec[] = { // defintion of a video FSM:
    ("STOP"),  ("Play"  , "void issuePlay()"  ,"PLAY"  ),
               ("Backw", "void issueBackw()" ,"BACKW" ),
               ("Forw"  , "void issueForw()"  ,"FORW"  ),
    ("PAUSE"), ("Stop"  , "void issueStop()"  ,"STOP"  ),
               ("Pause", "void outOfPause()"  ,        ),
    ("PLAY"),  ("Stop"  , "void issueStop()"  ,"STOP"  ),
               ("Pause", "void paused()"      ,        ),
               ("Backw", "void stopAndBackw()","BACKW" ),
               ("Forw"  , "void stopAndForw()" ,"FORW"  ),
    ("FORW"),  ("Stop"  , "void issueStop()"  ,"STOP"  ),
               ("Pause", "void paused()"      ,        ),
               ("Play"  , "void stopAndPlay()" ,"PLAY"  ),
    ("BACKW"), ("Stop"  , "void issueStop()"  ,"STOP"  ),
               ("Pause", "void paused()"      ,        ),
               ("Play"  , "void stopAndPlay()" ,"PLAY"  ),
    0
};

// The name of the start state and a reference to the
// FSM description are passed to the general FSM class
Video::Video(MInteractor *anIao)
    : MFSM(anIao, "STOP", FSMspec) {
    pausedState = "STOP";
}

void Video::stopAndBackw() {
    MCallMethod(iao, "void issueStop()");
    MCallMethod(iao, "void issueBackw()");
}

void Video::stopAndForw() {
    MCallMethod(iao, "void issueStop()");
    MCallMethod(iao, "void issueForw()");
}

void Video::stopAndPlay() {
    MCallMethod(iao, "void issueStop()");
    MCallMethod(iao, "void issuePlay()");
}

void Video::paused() {
    MCallMethod(iao, "void issuePause()");
    pausedState = returnState();
    setState("PAUSE");
}

void Video::outOfPause() {
    MCallMethod(iao, "void releasePause()");
    setState(pausedState);
}
```

Fig. 5. Video player FSM written in Python (left) and mC++ (right)

play button is pressed, the sensor sends a message containing an event with name Play. The interaction object forwards the event to the FSM. The FSM specification in Figure 5 specifies that when a Play event is received while the FSM is in state STOP (which we assume here for the example), then the member function void issuePlay() should be invoked on the interaction object[2]. To continue the example, if next the

---

[2] In the Python FSM specification, member functions of the associated interaction object are denoted by strings, local actions within the FSM are denoted using the local function name. In the mC++ FSM specification, methods defined in an interaction object or in the FSM are both denoted by strings. They are distinguished at runtime: first a runtime check is made to see whether the function given by the string is defined in the FSM, and failing that, whether it is defined in the associated interaction object. The ability to check at runtime the existence of member functions is supported by dynamic call interface defined in the MADE environment.

fast-forward button is pressed, the sensor associated with that button sends a `Forw` event to the interaction object, which forwards it to its FSM. The FSM is now in state `PLAY`, and on receiving the `Forw` event it calls the local function `stopAndForw`. This function first call the `issueStop()` method on the interaction object, followed by calling the `issueForw()` method on the interaction object. This shows how in a script existing application functionality (stop and forward) can be combined into new end-user functionality (stop-and-forward).

The FSM is now in state `FORW`. Suppose the FSM receives another `Forw` event. Because this event is not allowed in the current state of the FSM (only `Stop`, `Pause` or `Play` are allowed), the FSM calls the `unknownEventAction()` method on the interaction object which is supposed to handle any inappropriate events.

4.2 Example: Interaction with Object-Based Animation

Our second example deals with an animation of bouncing lines. In this animation, each line is an autonomous moving object that collides with other lines as well as with the walls that enclose its space. Each line has an equal mass, so that when two lines collide they bounce off equally in their opposite directions. Furthermore, the user may select a line with the mouse and subsequently drag the line through the space. The selected line is bound to the mouse pointer (i.e. it no longer determines its own movement), so that when it collides with other lines the selected line itself remains in its position whereas the other lines bounce away. Of course, the selected line can not be dragged outside of the walls.

This example is implemented by an mC++ class modelling an animated line. This mC++ class is an *Active* class, meaning that is has its own thread of control which calculates the next position for the line and redraws the line. The space containing all lines is implemented as an mC++ *Mutex* class, which means that it is automatically protected against concurrent access by several threads. For this paper, however, the implementation of the interaction is more important. Each line has a sensor associated with it, that listens for mouse events. Each sensor propagates a mouse event to the same interaction object. The interaction object stores which line is currently being manipulated. When the interaction object receives a mouse down event, it sends a message to the line involved that sets its mass to a very high quantity. The FSM associated to the interaction object then makes a transition to a state that takes care of dragging the line. After a mouse up event the FSM returns to its initial state.

Figure 6 shows the FSM for this example, again written in Python. Note that because of the script-based definition of the FSM, it is very easy to change the interaction so that the selected line will get a different mass, changes its color, etc.

5 Conclusions

We have described our notion of interaction objects whose behavior is defined by a programmable finite state machine. The state machine can be either hard-coded (in mC++) or it can be programmed by an interpretive scripting language. This choice is transparent to the interaction object and the rest of the application.

```
# The module 'madeif' interfaces to MADE programs
import madeif
# The module 'MFsm' contains a general base class for FSM's
import Mfsm

# class Dragger is a subclass of the general FSM class
class Dragger(Mfsm.MFSM) :
    mass = 0 # instance variable for storing the mass
    # local actions, defined by class functions:
    def makeHeavy(self, arg) :
        # arg[0] contains the line involved.
        mass = madeif.callmethod(arg[0], 'int getMass()', 'i')
        madeif.callmethod(arg[0],'void setMass(int)', 'n', [10000])
        madeif.callmethod(arg[0],'void makeInanim()', 'n')

    def setPos(self, arg) :
        x = arg[1]
        y = arg[2]
        madeif.callmethod(arg[0],'void setPos(int,int)', 'n', [x, y])

    def restoreMass(self, arg) :
        # arg[0] contains the line involved.
        madeif.callmethod(arg[0],'void setMass(int)', 'n', [mass])
        madeif.callmethod(arg[0],'void makeAnim()', 'n')

    # The definition of the FSM itself:
    initState = 'DEFAULT'
    transTable={'DEFAULT'  :{'MouseDown': (makeHeavy   , 'DRAGGING')},\
                'DRAGGING':{'MouseMove': (setPos      , 'DRAGGING') ,\
                            'MouseUp'  : (restoreMass, 'DEFAULT ')}}
```

Fig. 6. FSM for dragging animated lines.

Interaction objects can dynamically and transparently be bound to application objects through the use of sensors. In this way, the objects are not explicitly aware of user interactions. Sensors forward window system events to interaction objects, which use the functional interface of the application objects to manipulate them.

The combination of interaction objects that are both programmable outside of the application and that can be bound dynamically to application objects makes it possible to separate the definition of user interaction from the application, and allows for rapid prototyping. This is a necessary condition for being able to design user interfaces for interactive applications in an incremental way, which is regarded as a prerequisite for designing good user interfaces. This holds even more strongly for multimedia application, where the technical complexity of the application may overwhelm the proper design of the user interface.

A Short Overview of mC++

mC++ [1] is an extension of C++ that has been developed as part of the MADE project. Features added to C++ include the following:

Active objects These are defined by a regular C++ class definition, except that the C++ keyword class is replaced by the mC++ keyword Active. The active class definition always contains a main() member function that is executed for each newly created instance. This construct allows for active objects that have their own thread of control. Communication between active objects can be achieved using synchronous or asynchronous messages, the type of message being defined by the receptor. Methods of active objects can specify explicit accept statements for receiving messages. An active object handles at most one message at a time.

Mutex objects These are defined by a regular C++ class definition, except that the C++ keyword class is replaced by the mC++ keyword Mutex. Instances of mutex classes are automatically protected against concurrent access by multiple threads.

Prototypes and Delegation The object-oriented model employed by languages such as C++ and SmallTalk is that of classes and instances, in which a class may inherit from one or more other classes. An alternative model, used in languages such as Self, is that of prototypes and extensions. In this model, the concept of a class does not exist. Instead, to create new objects, a copy is made of another *prototype object*, and the copy is then extended with additional data and/or member functions. The new object then handles the extended part of its functionality by itself, and *delegates* the rest to its associated prototype.

In mC++, in addition to the C++ class model, we have defined a more restricted version of the prototype-extension model. In mC++ a class may define a prototype, and exactly one instance of this is automatically created at runtime. Regular instances of the class may define functionality in addition to what is defined in the prototype, and use delegation whenever functionality is used that is only defined in the prototype. Furthermore, any object may delegate one or more of its member functions to other objects. When a member function of an object is delegated to another object, the delegating object is no longer aware of any invocation of its own version of the member function.

References

1. F. Arbab, J. Davy, F.C. Heeman, I. Herman, O. Jojic, G.J. Reynolds, and M.M. de Ruiter. Specification of the MADE object model and of the mC++ language, December 1993. (version 2.0).
2. J. Davy. Go: A graphical and interactive C++ toolkit for application data presentation and editing. In *Proceedings of the 5th Annual X Technical Conference*, USA, January 1991. (also in The X Resource, 1, Winter 1992).
3. Esprit project proposal – MADE I – 6307 – Technical Annex, March 1992. (version 1.1).
4. International Organization for Standardization. Presentation environment for multimedia objects (PREMO). ISO/IEC JTC 1/SC 24/WG 6, OME 61, 1993.
5. M. Green. A survey of three dialogue models. *ACM Transactions on Graphics*, 5(3):244–275, July 1986.
6. Object Management Group. The common object request broker: Architecture and specification, 1991. OMG document number 91.12.1, Revision 1.1.
7. I. Herman, G.J. Reynolds, and J. Davy. MADE: A multimedia application development environment. In *Proc. of the IEEE International Conference on Multimedia*

Computing and Systems (ICMCS'94), Boston, U.S.A, May 1994. IEEE.

8. C. Nahaboo. The X11 generic window manager – GWM manual, 1991. (version 1.7l), Koala Project, Bull Research.

9. J.K. Ousterhout. Tcl and the Tk toolkit, August 1993. Computer Science Division, University of California, Berkely.

10. G. van Rossum. Python reference manual, February 1993. CWI, Amsterdam.

11. L. Wall and R.L. Schwartz, editors. *Programming Perl*. O'Reilly, Sebastopol, 1992. (ISBN 0-93717564-1).

Multiuser and Multimodal Aspects of Multimedia

Hans-Werner Gellersen, Max Mühlhäuser, and Oliver Frick

University of Karlsruhe, Telecooperation Group
P.O.B. 6980, 76128 Karlsruhe, Germany; [+49] (721) 608-4790

Abstract. A set of coordinated approaches is presented, contributing to a software technology suitable for multimedia. In contrast to a separate "niche" technology, the importance of integration is stressed in the multimedia context. This leads to the notion of cooperative media-integrated software and corresponding software technology. Three important elements of a modeling and development framework for such cooperative media-integrated software are motivated, denoted as *ubiquity, modality,* and *synergy.* The latter two elements are elaborated by presenting corresponding approaches for multimodal interaction and for workplace and enterprise integration.

1 Motivation and Overview

Multimedia has come to the desktop - the increasing power of desktop computers and the availability of (increasingly) affordable audio/video extensions lets multimedia document handling and point-to-point audio/video connections smoothly enter the workplace. So, are computer science, telecommunications, and consumer electronics really about to merge, as analysts predict? Many a practitioner doubts it, because the merge of these huge disciplines can only become a reality if it is exposed to and made beneficial for southers in form of an integration on the software side, not only on the hardware side.

In other words: the 'everyday' application development must be enhanced by multimedia aspects, instead of providing multimedia-specific software development support for multimedia-specific 'niche' software. Trying to do so, one can make two key observations early on:

- Multimedia support is orthogonal to any software development concept, i.e. all components of a software development environment have to be multimedia-enhanced.

- Multimedia is one of several challenges to traditional software development, i.e. an intent to enhance software must regard these challenges *together.*

In the remainder of this overview section, we will discuss five major challenges which we regard as important, and we will derive a coarse description and depiction of the software technology aspects which are necessary to respond to these challenges.

1.1 Distribution - Scalability and Limited Transparency

Although distribution is the oldest and most well-understood actual challenge for software development, a widely-accepted software technology for distributed application development is not yet established.

Scalability is in one of the most important issues which are not well resolved in many common distribution concepts such as distributed databases (where, e.g., query optimization algorithms do not scale well) or client/server-systems (which can not very well reflect the irregular, very meshed structure of large distributed systems where clients and servers become blurred). We regard distributed object-oriented approaches (DOO) as an important step forward here, much better suited than pure client/server-approaches based on remote procedure call (RPC) for reflecting the nature of real world objects [16]. DOO allows to abstract from details of the target hardware during design and scales well as organizations, networks, and applications grow.

Transparency: large efforts are made to hide network characteristics ('network transparency') or even the fact that software is distributed ('distribution transparency') from users and even software engineers. There are a several problems inherent with distribution: e.g., risk of partial failure, communication, locality, lack of global state, and heterogeneity. Distributed systems research has much focussed on hiding these unpleasant characteristics from users and software engineers (cf., e.g., distributed operating systems, service traders providing server transparency such as the ANSA-trader, and the distributed object-oriented programming paradigm which provides location-independent message passing and migration of arbitrarily granular objects). These advances take major steps towards abstraction from distribution aspects, and allow users in many instances the illusion of local interaction.

Yet, we argue that despite advances in distributed systems, distribution-related problems can not be encapsulated entirely. Transparency is always limited: problems such as availability and performance may even effect human-computer interaction and cooperation, e.g. consider loss of connection to a cooperation partner. Thus, it is important to properly handle the areas and cases where distribution characteristics become visible to a given layer.

In the context of *multimedia,* both scalability and limited transparency get aggravated. Sophisticated servers are needed for providing network transparent access to distributed multimedia objects [2], but software technology also has to provide means for applications-specific solutions to multimedia handling in large and bandwidth-bound networks, and even user-level decisions have to be foreseen.

1.2 Mobility - New Usage Scenarios and Devices

Computing has lately been challenged by the request for "mobility support". On one hand, physical mobility of users (or even goods) and computers (or peripherals) are investigated in the area of 'mobile computing'. On the other hand, the pressure for ever-increasing human mobility shall be partly compensated via support for 'mobile information'. Mobile information in turn has different facets, such as support for cooperative work, object migration support in DOO systems, and remote access to information kiosks.

New usage scenarios: Many consider mobile computing simply as deployment of distributed systems to mobile networks. They believe that the emerging communication protocols such as 'mobile IP' or more elaborate ones with extended quality of service, and caching techniques will solve the major open issues. But of course sophisticated mobile computing requires additional services and, in particular, "mobility-aware" applications to be developed - again, software technology must meet this requirements by providing support for such mobility-aware programming.

And then, of course, there is much more to mobile computing than simply enabling users to interact with network services and applications outside their offices: many human tasks can not be carried out in offices because they involve human mobility. Many formerly neglected application domains can be addressed by mobile computing, characterized by inherently mobile objects and users, reflecting mobile goods and humans and the involved logistics in real-world tasks. Mobility with these facets will alter computing in general, and human-computer interaction in particular. Driving forces in this direction are new device technology and new usage scenarios.

New devices: Several trends can be observed in mobile device development:

- *Miniaturization of general-purpose computers,* porting traditional ways of computing into mobile environments. The ways of interaction remain the same (keyboard, mouse, display), and so do the applications. The use of traditional interaction techniques poses a limit for further miniaturization, and thus alternative interaction techniques are increasingly investigated.

- *Personalized communicators* (PDAs) can be thought of as mobile terminals rather than mobile computers. They do not strive to provide general-purpose computing but are supposed to provide highly personalized access to network services via wireless connections (e.g. RadioLAN). Interaction with these PDAs is based on a first post-keyboard generation of interfaces employing pens for pointing and writing.

- *Integration of human-human communication,* e.g. FAX. This trend is very much in line with the predicted merge of computing and telecommunications.

- *Tracking devices*: a new class of rather low-tech mobile devices for tracking people and goods is currently emerging. Interaction with these devices is system controlled as opposed to user controlled. E.g. with active badges or monitoring devices in a media space the user interacts with the system merely by his physical presence. Devices such as active badges mark a shift of interaction locus away from terminals into the users' environments [18], but of course also raise problems of privacy and other sociological issues.

If we consider again the new usage scenarios mentioned above, then these tasks can now be supported as computers with less desk-bound interfaces are emerging, as discussed above. Computer usage in non-office environments in turn raise further requirements for human-computer interaction. The same task, e.g. notetaking, or information access, can require different interaction techniques depending on the environment. In many environments users can not use their hands to operate their mobile devices, e.g. when driving a car or operating another machine. In these cases, audio-based interaction would be appropriate, whereas in other scenarios, e.g. in noisy environments, audio would be inappropriate. Another requirement can be *heads up*, e.g. in a meeting mobile device operation should not require the user to shift his attention away from communication partners. These examples show that mobility has far-reaching effects on application development (in these examples in particular on user interfaces).

1.3 Multimedia - Multimodal Usage and Orthogonal Support

Multimodal usage: in daily life, humans utilize many different media and modalities[1] for communication based on the experience that some media and modalities are more effective than others in certain contexts. Obviously, human-computer interaction can improve considerably, if different media are integrated for information presentation, and if different modalities can be employed for interaction. With the advent of multimedia on the desktop, applications such as hypermedia information services, point-to-point audio/video conferencing, and, in some research labs, media spaces were developed. Despite this trend, we still observe poor media-integration is user interface design. First of all, we observe media separation (*media modality*, cf. [10]) in applications and user interfaces: Media such as video commonly appear as encapsulated chunks of coarse granularity. Applications and user interfaces fail to sufficiently abstract from differences in media handling at operating system and networking level, where different storage and transport requirements lead to media separation. Secondly, media-integration is hampered by attitudes users and designers have to different media. Video e.g. is associated with TV and thus considered inherently non-interactive and even suspicious with respect to the conveyed information.

Orthogonal support: media-integration has to take place at various levels. At the media level, more abstraction from underlying representation differences is required to enable tighter linkage of media to multimedia objects. An important aspect is the granularity of information stored in databases or presented in user interfaces. For some media, e.g. text, we find very fine granularity (here, characters) which allows to link different pieces of information very effectively. It also provides the user with more support for searching and browsing. Other media typically have very coarse granularity, e.g. video. Currently, frame numbers are the only means for establishing intravideo granularity, which of course is not very helpful for defining links to other media, and for support search capabilities. Instead, content-based referencing and retrieval needs to be supported.

Media-integration at software engineering level first of all requires explicit support for different media and modalities. Different media have to be treated as building blocks of equal rights for application development. Whereas in traditional user interface design media and especially modalities have been implied, media-integrated user interface development has to support a choice of media as explicit design decision. Further, media-integration requires some sort of common grip for media handling and manipulation, based on commonalities among media. Finally, the ultimate form of media-integration would be based on media understanding. Media understanding would be the basis for automated conversion among media, or for advanced support of human-human interaction in CSCW (e.g., coordination of meetings based on their content).

This orthogonal support has further facets such as *media data integration* (augmenting conventional software by support for multimedia data handling) and *workplace-integration* (support for the coupling of the conventional software with new, telecooperation-type applications like audio/video conferencing; thereby, the various activities of a user must be mediated by a comprehensive "access point" to the system as either human-to-human or human-machine interaction in a consistent, software-integrated way).

---

1. We use the term *modality* in the sense of 'way of interaction'. The terms *media* and *multimedia* are prefered when primarily concerned with the representation of information, whereas *modality* and *multimodality* are used when concerned with the dynamics of interaction.

282

1.4 Cooperation: Prescription vs. Description

Just as the availability of small and mobile devices, the availability of efficient distributed systems leads to new ways of computer usage. Traditionally, computers function as tools for support of single-user tasks. On the basis of distributed systems they can assist humans in a wider scope of their work, which does not consist of isolated tasks but spans a network of human interaction. Computers can now support tasks that involve many users, leading to the new discipline of computer supported cooperative work (CSCW).

Descriptive cooperation: currently, CSCW is mainly used to label applications in which humans are tightly coupled and interact rather synchronously in often unpredictable and less controlled ways. Such applications, commonly called groupware, comprise multimedia conferencing, media spaces, and shared applications. Within this new class of applications, computers are increasingly perceived as medium rather than as tool. Coordination of cooperation in these groupware applications is usually up to the participating humans, and generally based on their social behavior.

Prescriptive cooperation: besides in groupware we find support for cooperative work in application integration systems. These have first been investigated in the domains of office automation and computer-integrated manufacturing, and now receive much interest under the label *workflows* which refers to long-living activities within large organizations. In workflow applications, human activities are rather loosely coupled, interaction is mainly asynchronous, and coordination is well-defined and controlled by the system. Individual workflow participants are usually only partly aware of the coordination, much like individuals in organizations usually only have partial understanding of how the organization is run.

Human cooperation generally requires the establishment and maintenance of a shared context. Commonly, this shared context is based on exploitation of shared information repositories, yet we find access rights and transaction management as implemented in present databases hampering cooperative usage severely [21]. Access rights are bound to users, whereas they should be bound to roles abstracting from individuals. As a partial relief, so-called roles can model the function a user has in a specific task and thus determine the actions she or he can perform on a shared information repository. A user can than play more than one role, associated e.g., with different levels of rights.

With respect to user interface design and management knowledge of cooperation semantics, i.e. role-task bindings, enrolment rules, etc., is elementary. The user interface to an information repository has to fully reflect the role of its user, which will not only be manifest in the set of actions provided in the interface, but also in different views of the data.

The following arguments illustrate again the mutual influence of the five major challenges described in this chapter, i.e. that cooperation support is closely related to

- Distribution: cooperating teams must be supported, working together usually at different locations and either at the same time or at different points in time.

- Mobility: Software is integrated into complex distributed applications. Since a large physical space (distributed system) is covered, *mobile software objects* (both data *and* functions) must be handed over from one computer or one user to another.

Since a large spectrum of usage is covered by the computer and software, the above mentioned "access point" (e.g., portable computer) becomes ubiquitous and thus has to follow *mobile physical objects* (users, goods) as these travel around.

- Multimedia: since the scope of usage ranges from (traditionally keyboard-mouse-monitor driven) human-machine interaction to (traditionally voice-image driven) human-to-human interaction, and since mobile physical objects (particularly. users) tend to carry along their (tiny, portable!) 'terminal' device, a broad range and combinations of user interface technologies (modalities) have to be supported, not just the ability to handle multimedia data.

1.5 Usability - Liberation and Internationalization

It is in the context of support for the aforementioned four challenges that finally a very old challenge may be met: the demand for highly flexible applications that can adapt to the individual users to a large degree.

Liberation: Traditionally, computer applications come with one-fits-all user interfaces; advanced cooperative applications have quite often copied the same error and were developed with a single cooperation strategy in mind. Such lack of liberation limits use to rather homogeneous groups of users who speak the same language (literally and metaphorically), and excludes people with special needs. Now, we experience an application pull for support of inhomogeneous user groups (global markets, travelling people, home computing) as well as a technology push (availability of world-wide networks, mobile computing). On an experimental base, adaptive user interfaces and systems *do* exist very well, even based on sophisticated user models. But just as observed in former subsections for other challenges, liberation can not be well supported by a single 'glorified' approach or user model. Rather, it is important to provide the functionality and integration techniques for building suitable liberation support.

Internationalization, more particular than liberation, means culture-based adaptation of applications and user interfaces to increase usability for the individual. Required adaptation can range from large scale (e.g., language and writing system) to details (e.g., date/time/address formats). Besides issues of information representation, different work habits and problem solving techniques have to be taken into account. Similar to cultural adaptation, increasingly widespread use of computers and liberation demands of people with special needs requires user interface adaptation, here according to skills and abilities. Again, adaptation can require very general design decisions (e.g., choice of modality to compensate for disabilities) as well as minor adaptations (e.g., speed of interaction).

1.6 Integrating Software Technology: Items

The above discussion should have shown that the five major challenges, distribution, mobility, multimedia, cooperation, and usability, are very much interconnected and that they are, at least partly, orthogonal to any modularization of a software technology view.

Therefore we propose a *framework* for the development of *media-integrated cooperative software*. Fig. 1 shows a three-tiered view onto such a framework which is currently developed in our group, called Items[15]. Items is based on earlier projects

284

investigating distributed application development [16] and cooperative multimedia in the CAL domain [17]. Items is partly discussed in this paper.

As fig. 1 depicts, the five major challenges are reflected in three key domains of the Items framework: ubiquity, modality, and synergy. These three domains should *not* be considered as separate layers of a layered architecture, but as equally treated sets of so-called aspects, cf. below.

Using Items, software engineers start by developing an object-oriented design for the software under development. Over time, they can add an arbitrary number of so-called *aspects* to the objects designed (in our terms, this adding of aspects augments objects to *items*). Every aspect treats a very specific facet of the system under development; the semantics of an aspect are known to the system i.e. software development tools, so that a high degree of development support can be offered to the software engineers. The aspects are logically grouped into three different sets as indicated in fig. 1.

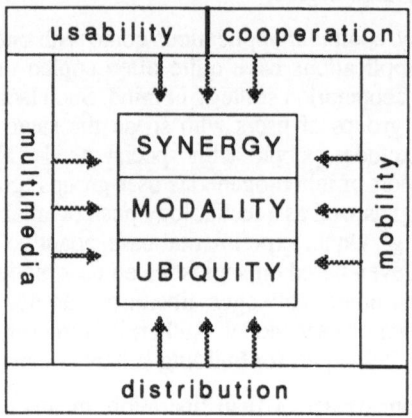

Fig. 1. Framework for cooperative media-integrated software: three sets of aspects

The *synergy* domain integration relates items in the context of long-living cooperative activities. The whole spectrum from rather prescriptive (workflow-like, multiuser) aspects to rather descriptive ('CSCW'-like, rule / constraint based, rather liberal) cooperations is covered here. The *synergy* domain is closely related to the cooperation challenge, but on one hand it is also largely influenced by all the other challenges and on the other hand further domains (modality, in particular) are also reflecting cooperation needs.

The *modality* domain accounts for the 'multimodal' and 'multimedia' aspects which can be perceived at the interaction interface of applications to their users. The other challenges (in particular cooperation, usability, and mobility) have largely influenced the design of the modality domain.

In the *ubiquity* domain, distribution and mobility are combined into a sophistication level which allows users to access applications at almost any time and location. Scalable use of multimedia and a high degree of adaptation are supported here. The aspects of the ubiquity domain include, e.g., customized briefcase support, basic for disconnected operations, and heuristics support for mobile objects in distributed systems.

It has to be retained that the three domains mentioned represent software support facilities in the first place. Services and runtime systems are only provided for generic functionality, the focus lies on development support for complex customized applications.

In the remaining two chapters, the synergy and modality domain will be described in more detail, the ubiquity domain will be left out due to its limited importance in the context of multimedia.

2 Modality: Design and Management of Multimodal Interaction

User interface development involves a number of distinct design decisions that differ in their dependencies. This is particularly true for the development of UIs for cooperative media-integrated applications, as additional challenges are imposed by aspects such as distribution, mobility, cooperation, media-integration. Yet, in existing approaches, UI design decisions remain poorly structured and lack integration with other software engineering aspects, as will be pointed out below. Then, we introduce a new approach for structured UI development based on a set of aspects, denoted as MMI aspects, which constitute the modality domain in Items.

2.1 Software Technology for User Interface Development

We have pointed out a number of aspects that ought to be considered explicitly in user interface development to ensure usability. Subsequently, we will discuss how these challenges relate to existing user interface development and management tools and methods. We will discuss the toolkit approach to user interface development, and user interface management systems (UIMS). Then, we will summarize the shortcomings in these approaches.

Toolkit-based UI Development. The currently predominating approach to user interface development is the use of toolkits. Toolkits provide user interface developers with sets of building blocks for particular interaction styles and aspects. In particular, many toolkits have been introduced for graphical user interfaces. These toolkits are strictly bound to the desktop metaphor and to direct manipulation as interaction paradigm. Further, they are platform-bound, thus hampering user interface development for heterogeneous environments. Only few so-called portable GUI toolkits abstract from platforms, e.g. XVT, Open Interface, and Galaxy. Here, platform-independence is achieved by limiting support to the least common denominator of underlying lower-level toolkits, sacrificing platform-specific strength. More recently, multimedia toolkits are becoming available, e.g. Xmedia. Also, several GUI toolkits are being extended with audio/video capabilities, cf. [25]. Further, the cooperation aspect is supported by toolkits such as GroupKit [22]. Yet, the toolkit approach has several well-known deficiencies:

- Toolkits come with complex APIs which the developer has to master on top of a programming language. Even if the complexity of a number of APIs is mastered, integration of different toolkits remains very difficult and often impossible.

- Toolkits hardly support abstraction from user interface details, so interface construction becomes very time-consuming. To address this concern, interface builders have been introduced, which allow interface design in a direct manipulative way. Yet, the only design decision supported by interface builders is instantiation of presentation objects, neglecting the important aspect of interaction dynamics.

- Focus in toolkits is on presentation, rather than on more important semantic design issues such as dialogue structure.

- Toolkits do not provide design assistance: interface designers easily make poor widget choices, yielding interfaces of low usability.

- Integration of toolkit objects with semantic objects is weak; interface objects do not know the semantics of the concepts they present and control.

The listed drawbacks of the toolkit approach are particularly limiting with respect to the UI development challenges listed in table 1. Toolkits are platform-bound and thus pose problems in a heterogeneous environment. They impose metaphors, modalities (usually mouse/keyboard-gesture and graphics display), media, dialogue structure, and even programming styles (e.g., GUI toolkits imply event-based programming). With user interface toolkits, important design decisions are not supported explicitly, and thus get hidden in application code. This results in user interfaces difficult to port and extend, and difficult to adapt to, e.g., user preferences. Further, the complexity of integrating different toolkits renders them inappropriate for integrating different media, and for integrating interaction techniques for multimodal interfaces.

User Interface Management Systems. Over the last decade, many user interface management systems (UIMS) have been proposed. UIMS aim at generating user interfaces based on application models and style rules. With this approach, a user interface designer is relieved from presentation details and can concentrate on design of interaction semantics. There are a number of existing approaches which have demonstrated the feasibility of automating user interface design tasks. E.g., with ITS [29] a user interface designer specifies *dialogue content* in addition to an application's *data definition*. ITS then generates dialogue boxes using a reusable *dialogue style* rule set. In ACE [7] the interface developer describes dialogue in terms of *selectors*, which are semantic-based controls as opposed to presentation-oriented widgets. Selectors particularly aim at tight integration with application semantics. UIDE [26] goes beyond other UIMS approaches by using an application model not only at design time but also at run time for dialogue management, e.g. for automatic help generation. Automation of presentation tasks such as window and menu layout commonly yields limited user interface designs. HUMANOID [27] addresses this concern and provides *templates* as abstract presentation building blocks. At run time the user interface management system selects specific widgets as subtypes of templates based on the application data to be displayed.

Only few UIMS have investigated user interface generation beyond single-user applications. CHIRON-1 [28] is a distributed UIMS which strictly separates interface code, underlying toolkits, and application code. RENDEZVOUS [6] is a language based approach for building multi-user multi-media user interfaces. Its abstraction-link-view paradigm supports coordination of multiple views based on constraints.

UIMS so far have focused on graphical user interfaces. Even for this rather limited class of user interfaces better models need to be developed to enable production quality user interface generation. User interface generation so far employed style and layout rules. In order to extend UIMS capabilities to generate multimodal and internationalized interfaces, a broad understanding of different media, modalities, usage scenarios, and cultural issues needs to be developed and formulated in rules. So far, support for multimodality is only found in first attempts at structuring the MMI design space [19], and modelling user preferences [5].

Open Issue: Integration of Tools and Methods. In present user interface development we observe to major deficiencies: lack of integration of different interaction techniques and interaction aspects, and lack of methodological support for good design practice.

User interface tools have made progress in producing widget sets and construction environments for designers for interfaces consisting of standard menus, windows, boxes and buttons. Increasingly, construction sets also become available for other interaction techniques, e.g. device-dependent toolkits for audio and video. All these tools are narrow in the scope of user interfaces they cover. For the construction of more sophisticated dialogues including multiple users utilizing multiple modalities (or media, from a system's point of view), the major challenge is the integration of lower-level toolkits.

Besides integration, methodological support is required to ensure good design practice. Within the HCI community a variety of methods have been proposed for task analysis and dialogue modelling, however, they have not gained much acceptance. As with tools, we find that methods commonly only address rather small parts of the design problem. In order to improve user interface development substantially, a framework is required which brings together different tools and different methods (at present, integration of methods and tools is only found in style guides). As user interface design and management is highly dependent on so many systems aspects, as pointed out by us, such a framework should be tightly integrating user interface development in software engineering.

2.2 MMI Aspects: A Structured Approach to Development of Multimodal Interaction

User interface design involves decisions with various dependencies, e.g., depending on application models, user models, user preferences, human factors, device technology, metaphors, etc. As has been shown, this is particularly the case in the context of telecooperative applications. Distinct design issues ought to be supported by distinct tools and methods. Yet, in existing approaches user interface design decisions remain poorly supported. In the Items framework, we integrate a new structured approach to development of multimodal interfaces based on MMI aspects.

In a first step, a software engineer must identify those objects and operations of the application core which shall be visible to the user. This step is driven by the task structure of an application, i.e. its decomposition into tasks. The resulting description of the application interface must fully abstract from interaction metaphors (e.g., object-oriented descriptions do not impose a direct manipulation metaphor, neither do procedural descriptions imply command-response style). Following this first step, a number of MMI aspects has to be considered (cf. fig. 2). It should be retained that not all aspects necessarily need to be specified. Specification of aspects are not required steps to make an object complete. Further, there is no strict order in which to specify different aspects, though there are dependencies. The purpose of MMI aspects is to structure distinct design decisions, and to model them explicitly so they can be maintained.

Interaction Semantics. For specification of interaction semantics mere type information of those application objects and operations that interface to the user is not sufficient. E.g., if interaction requires to enter a date that lies in the future, type information does not suffice for validity checking. Thus, additional semantic information is required:

- pre- and postconditions, constraints and defaults that apply to data entry (selection of values) or operation invocation (selection of actions)

- selection semantics (discrete/continuous sets; selection of 1 or many or intervals)

- argument semantics (required, optional, default)

This additional information augments application objects and operations with interaction context and extends them to abstract interaction objects and actions. These are absolutely independent from implementation issues, e.g. whether the interaction style is direct manipulation or command/response. A textual as well as a visual specification language for interaction semantics are currently prototyped within Items.

Roles. The role a user plays in a dialogue may depend on his expertise (*novice - expert*), his rights (*read/write - read/only*) or his part in a cooperative task. For support of different roles, abstract interaction objects and actions need to be extended for description of role-specific interaction semantics. Further, for cooperating roles there is a need to express the effects which role activities have on other roles, e.g., the rate at which interaction participants are updated on actions of their partners. In Items, a generic language for group interaction in CSCW [23] is currently integrated with a deliberately more complex role concept as presented as part of the 'cooperation' set of aspects in chapter 3.

Structure. A typical interactive application will exhibit a multitude of objects and operations at the user interface. Thus, structure is an important design issue, driven by human factors considerations. Structure is required to decrease cognitive load of a UI, thus to increase user performance. As a consequence, dialogue structure is dependent on the user model (an expert user may perform better with a less structured dialogue than a novice). A major constraint is the available modality: e.g., a voice-only interface will, because of the transient nature of its media, require different structure than a graphics interface. Structuring introduces composite interaction objects, either representing aggregations or choices.

Navigation. Dialogue control defines the context of user interaction at any time. It partly depends on interaction semantics and partly on human factors. To some extent, the dialogue control can be derived from pre- and postconditions of user actions, which determine that at any time only valid actions can be performed by the user. In addition, dialogue control is responsible for navigating the user through the dialogue in a way that increases user performance. A dialogue control decision would be, e.g., whether the thread of dialogue in a hierarchical menu should on completion of a task return to the parent menu or to the root menu. With more complex structures, e.g. hypertext-style interfaces as increasingly found in multimedia applications, good navigation design becomes crucial for usability. In Items, we use PreScripts [20], a typing approach for hypertext traversal, to design and manage this aspect.

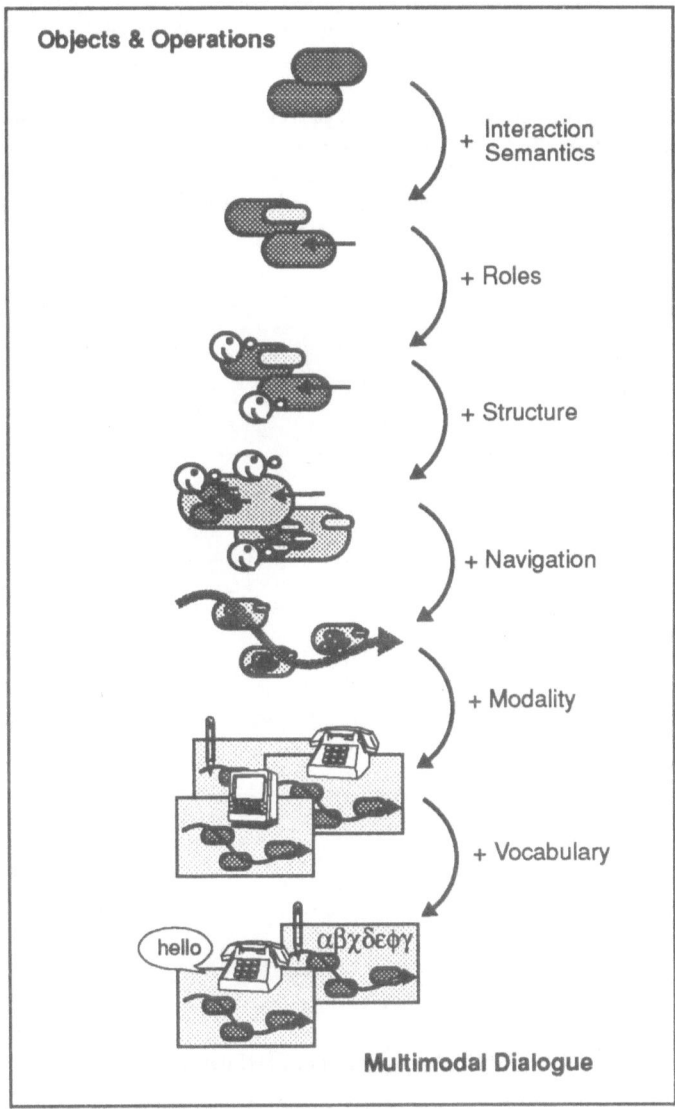

Fig. 2. From objects to MMI items by adding aspects

Modality. With the advent of new interaction techniques and new usage scenarios (support of out-of-office tasks) dialogue modality is becoming a central design issue. Different modalities exhibit different characteristics: e.g., sound is good for gaining

290

attention, graphics have their strength is conveying spatial data, text is appropriate for formulae. In a multimodal design space, issues are not only which modalities to choose, but also how to combine modalities to increase bandwidth, to provide alternatives, to support concurrence, or to achieve redundancy. Combination of modalities occurs at lexical level (multimodal symbols, involving synchronization of input events), syntactic level (combination of symbols expressed in different modalities to commands), and semantic level (interpretaion of commands depending on their modality).

Vocabulary. The choice of the symbol set, or vocabulary, to be used in human-computer interaction depends mainly on the media employed. Of course, for a certain medium, the choice depends on the user model, mainly his/her culture (language, writing system, culture-related icons and sounds, ...), and skills (e.g., a large vocabulary imposes high cognitive load but eases expression of concepts).

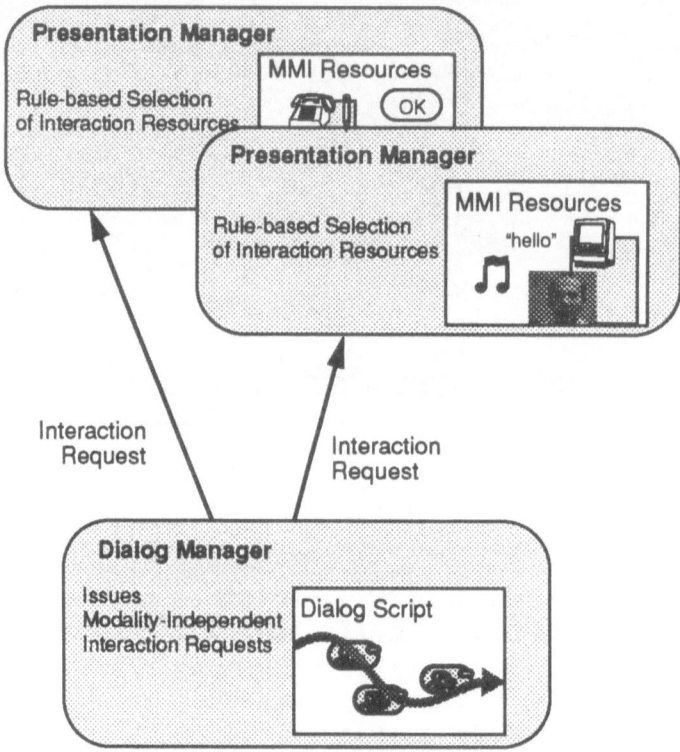

Fig. 3. Management of MMI items

Figure 3 sketches out exploitation of the aspects-based approach in a run time scenario. Dialogue managers control different threads of interaction. For each user involved, a presentation manger enrols with a dialogue manager to receive interaction requests. These can range from vague (few aspects specified, e.g. "display New York") to very specific ("show MPEG video of New York with jitter < 10 ms, latency < 20 ms, synchronized with Sinatra's *New York, New York*").

2.3 Items Context

For the ongoing implementation of Items, we use an open architecture for cooperative tools which is based on a Linda tuplespace for communication and on the EXL language, which is purpose-build for prototyping cooperative interactive applications [11]. Figure 4 depicts a UIMS implemented on this architecture. Applications and user interfaces, which are executed by the EXL interpreter, are effectively separated by a tuplespace. This yields a number of advantages such as support for multi-processing (cf. [13] for a more detailed discussion). Further, a PreScript engine controls interaction of user interfaces and applications by monitoring the tuplespace and issuing control tuples. A role resolution tool is responsible for matching application-specific roles against user roles represented by EXL processes. Further tools, e.g. a logging process, can easily be integrated without effecting the existing ones.

While figure 4 depicts only a management scenario, the same architecture is also exploited at design time. A number of specialized tools cooperate via tuplespace. E.g., graphical editors, interface builders, and conventional programming languages are employed to generate distinct design artifacts which are cooperated on via tuplespace.

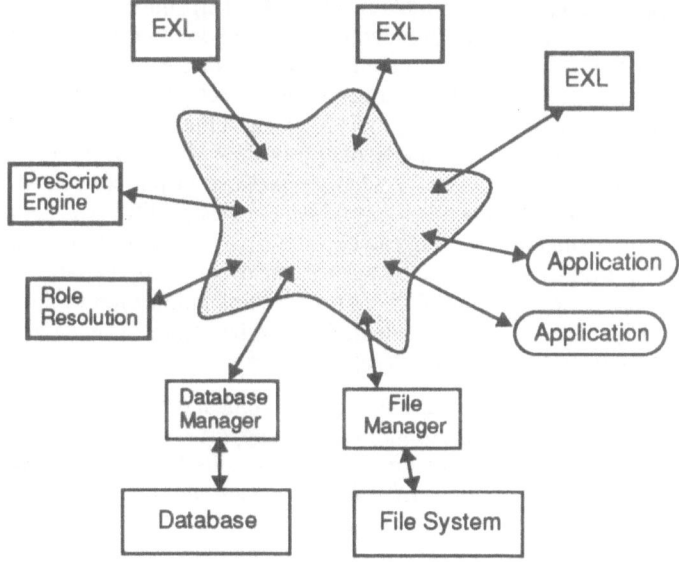

Fig. 4. A tuplespace-based UIMS

3 Synergy: Workplace and Enterprise Integration

3.1 Motivation for Synergy

Looking at the state of the art in software support for cooperative work, we find two different approaches, related to two different *kinds* of cooperation:

In *workflow-type cooperations*, interrelated automated or manual activities are loosely coupled via few well defined, predictable, and usually asynchronous interactions. The nature and description of the encompassing cooperation(s) is often invisible to the individual participants (rather, users expect support for the coordination of their individual action items, e.g., in the form of to-do lists or priority lists - a simple form of workplace-integration). The loose coupling and invisible cooperation structure makes implicit, user-driven coordination between cooperating partners hardly possible. An explicit and firm coordination must therefore be imposed by the system [30]. *Prescriptive* approaches to coordination definition dominate, prescribing an interaction algorithm, the interaction activities and subactivities, and their sequence.

In *CSCW-type cooperations*, cooperating human parties are tightly coupled, usually interacting in a rather implicit and personal, synchronous, but less controlled and less predictable way. Users often do not want more than a framework of loose guidelines. The purpose of cooperation support in the CSCW context is to offer a set of interaction mechanisms (i.e., subactivities) together with coordination rules and invariants that have to be met by all interactions within the cooperation [22]. Cooperation here is usually based on a *descriptive* coordination definition.

Both cooperation types usually are based on different (multimedia) interaction techniques and tools. Typical tools for CSCW-type cooperations are, e.g., AV-conferencing tools and application sharing technologies (e.g., [1, 12]) supporting tight coupling and personal interactions with only little 'conferencing style' coordination. Asynchronous interactions for workflow-type cooperations on the other hand are generally based on mail services (e.g., [14]), media servers and (mono-media) coordination tools (e.g., [8, 30]). Although specialized modeling tools for each of the cooperation types are widely available (e.g., [23, 24]), there is a lack of approaches which cover and integrate them. Such a uniform approach is exactly what we propose in the context of the 'synergy aspects' of Items. This approach has several advantages: CSCW-type cooperations like conferencing or application sharing can become a part of a workflow-type cooperation and vice versa; instead of a choice between two extremes, any variation in a spectrum can be realized; a smooth migration from one cooperation type to another becomes possible; finally, better workplace-integration can be achieved, integrating traditional computer use and telecommunications applications.

The Items cooperation approach is based on a graphical definition of cooperations and comprises design-level as well as runtime-level support. The model is centered around the notions of tailorable *cooperation description units (CDUs)*, *coordination*, and a *role resolution*. The latter relates *task roles*, *organizational roles* and real life *cooperation participants*, as described in section 3.4.

3.2 Cooperation Description Units

In a top-down modeling approach a cooperation is decomposed into subactivities. The 'leaf' elements of the hierarchy are so-called role actions. Role actions are beyond the modeling scope of the cooperation: they may represent other items (cf. section 2), may not be subject of the actual cooperation (legacy software), or may be modeled elsewhere (reusability support).

A CDU may have several input and output *parameter groups*, used to trigger a CDU and to return its results. Within an input or output group, each typed data unit is of one out of four basic parameter categories: control flow, data flow, role flow, or resource flow (cf. below). An input triggers a CDU as soon as all required parameters of the input group are valid. Multiple input groups provide for potential parallelism, both inside a CDU and with respect to workflows. Usually, multiple input parameter groups represent multiple 'workpieces' which can be processed to a certain degree independent from one another. Thus, a CDU can 'start working' as soon as one of its 'workpieces' is ready. Multiple output parameter groups in turn can be used to model alternative potential results or different output states.

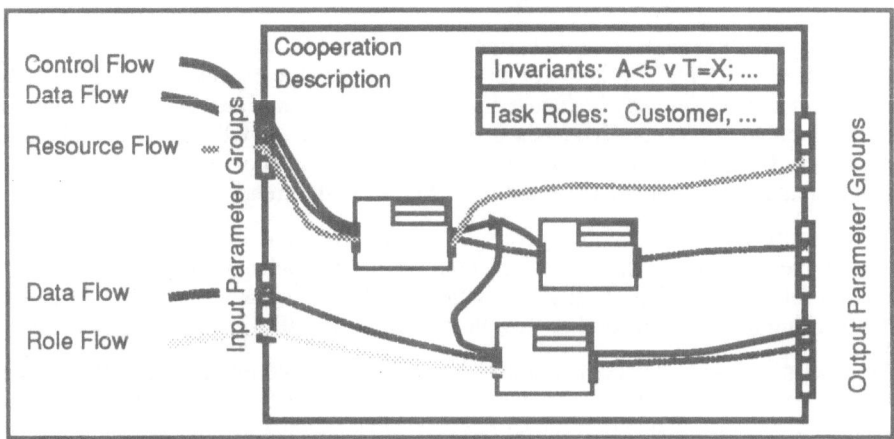

Fig. 5. Sample Cooperation Description Unit (CDU) with subactivities and coordination

3.3 Coordination

After the decomposition of a task a coordination may be imposed on the resulting set of subactivities. The principle coordination element in our model are *rules*. A CDU definition includes a set of rules which provides guidelines for the execution of its subactivities. Rules may define trigger or termination conditions for a subactivity, or invariants for subactivities of a CDU. Thus, coordination rules define the behavior of the cooperation. Typically, three different kinds of rules are defined:

- **anticipative rules** defining coordination which is known apriori, i.e., describing the 'usual' behavior of the coordination;

- **reactive rules** defining reaction on (un)expected exceptions at runtime, and

- **organizational rules** defining constraints imposed by the embedding organization. Thus, organizational rules taylor cooperations for the different organizations in which they are executed.

As rule-based specification of behavior constitutes is a somewhat low level of abstraction, *links* between subactivities are introduced as shortcuts for trigger and termination rules. They also provide the glue for defining prescriptive cooperations. Corresponding to the four basic parameter categories for input and output data units, four different types of links are available for connecting input and output groups, e.g., a control flow link between subactivities A and B describes the rule "B is triggered when A is terminated".

The separation of parameters and connecting links into four principle categories bears the opportunity of modeling cooperations according to their underlying metaphor and nature, and according to the "thinking" of the software engineer. E.g., control flow links are suited for procedure-based modeling similar to [2], and data flow links may be used for form-based modeling (cf. [8]) or to provide compatibility with many existing workflow systems like Lotus Notes. The combination of data flow and control flow links provides for a new style of modeling with more explicit semantics, integrating procedure-based modeling (often used in early stages) and data oriented modeling (typical for more detailed description).

Invariants finally denote conditions that must remain true during the execution of all subactivities of a CDU. Violation of an invariant during the execution of a subactivity results in an event that may be handled inside or outside the CDU. Invariants augment the declarative power of CDU based modeling. Based on CDUs, rules, links and invariants, the above-mentioned two cooperation types (and combinations thereof) can now be realized by applying the semantics of CDU in different ways:

For prescriptive modeling, a cooperation tasks is decomposed into a set of *required* subactivities, and the subactivities are connected with links (providing an ordering relation for the execution of all subactivities). Links and subactivities together define an algorithm (control flow or data flow based) which specifies *explicit* coordination.

For descriptive modeling, cooperation tasks are decomposed into a set of subactivities which are modeled with respect to the way in which they *may* help to meet the cooperation goal. I.e., the cooperation is decomposed into a selection of (redundant) subactivities which seem to help to meet the cooperation goal. The subactivities are complemented with a set of invariants (general cooperation rules which must always hold) and an overall cooperation goal, both defined in a declarative way as rules. The lack of links leads to a high degree of freedom in the ordering of subactivities by the cooperation participants..

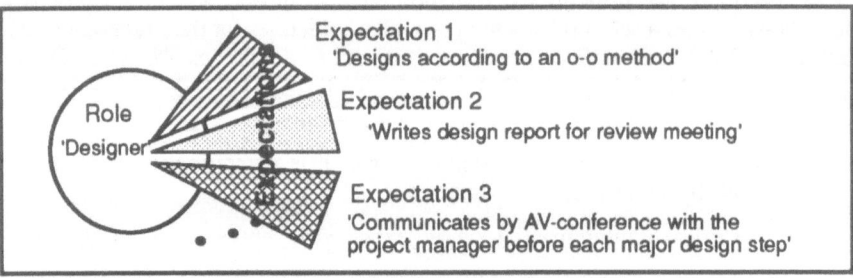

Fig. 6. Task roles are a collection of expectations

3.4 Role Resolution

Until now, the cooperation modeling is based on 'activities' and 'rules'. The concept of *roles* finally introduce a means for the separation of the actual cooperation participants ("performers") from the cooperation itself. The role concept is used to match capabilities of concrete participants to requirements defined in cooperation descriptions. A three-tiered model is used here, consisting of the following elements:

- *Task Roles:* in the hierarchical decomposition of CDUs into subactivities, the leaf nodes must eventually be role actions, as mentioned above. Task roles are used for defining task specific requirement sets. Task roles can be considered as collections of expectations a specific cooperation descriptions has towards the capabilities of a particular cooperation participant (cf. fig. 6). By specifying such task roles, the software engineer (cooperation designer) models tasks by decomposition of activities and groups basic activities to cooperation specific actors.

- *Organizational roles*, representing capabilities or positions inside organizations of potential cooperation participants, or mapping these capabilities to other representations. Organizational roles themselves may be interrelated in various ways, according to the specific interrelationships relevant to a given organization (like command hierarchies, knows relations, etc.).

- Surrogates of *real life cooperation participants* in the systems (e.g., a user interface for a particular person or a memory or network address of a process)

A sophisticated role resolution procedure is launched at initialization time of a cooperation, mapping task roles via organizational roles to the real life cooperation participants (cf. fig. 7).

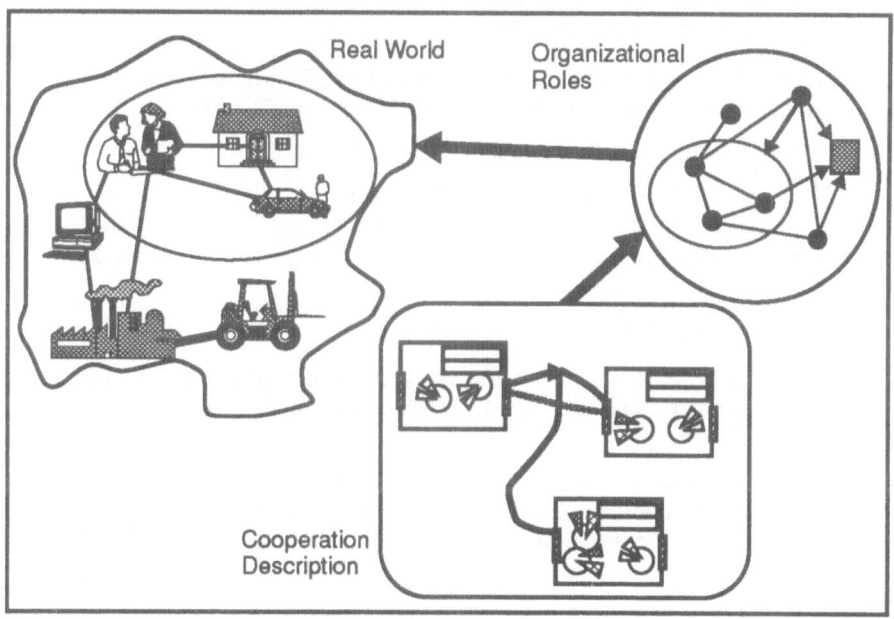

Fig. 7. Role resolution procedure

4 Conclusion

We presented a discussion of challenges posed on development of cooperative media-integrated applications. We pointed out the strong mutual influence of different software technology aspects, which are commonly approached separately. Thus, we argue that development of cooperative media-integrated software can only be effective within a software engineering framework integrating different tools and techniques. We presented such a framework, Items, as currently developed by our group. Within

Items, we define three key domains: ubiquity, modality and synergy. Within each domain, development support is founded on the notion of so-called aspects modeling distinct design and management concerns. A more detailed discussion of aspects was presented for the modality and synergy domains. Implementation of Items is currently carried out on a tuplespace architecture, which stresses integration of very inhomogeneous tools for largely autonomous support of the three key domains.

References

1. Altenhofen, M., et al..: The BERKOM Multimedia Collaboration Service. In: Proc. of ACM Multimedia '93, Anaheim, CA, June 1993.

2. Blakowski, G.: Development and Runtime Support for Distributed Multimedia Applications. Shaker, Aachen, 1993. Dissertation, in German.

3. Buhr, R., Casselman, R.: Architectures With Pictures. In: Proc. of OOPSLA'92 Vancouver, BC, Oct, 1992, pp. 466-483.

4. Gellersen, H.-W.: Graphical Design Support for DCE Applications, In *Proc. of International DCE Workshop*, Karlsruhe, Oct. 1993, pp. 267-281.

5. Glinert, E., Blattner, M.: Programming the Multimodal Interface. In Proc. of ACM Multimedia '93, Anaheim, CA, June 1993, pp. 189-197.

6. Hill, R.: The Abstraction-Link-View Paradigm: Using Constraints to Connect User Interfaces to Applications. In: Proc. of CHI '92, pp. 335-342 (May 1992).

7. Johnson J.: Selectors: Going Beyond User-Interface Widgets. In *Proc. of CHI '92*. May 1992, pp. 273-279.

8. Karbe, B., Ramsperger, N., Weiss, P.: Support of Cooperative Work by Electronic Circulation Folders, COIS90 - Conf. on Office Information Systems, Cambridge, MA, Apr. 1990.

9. Lauesen, S., Harning, M.B., Bøving, H.F.: Dialogue Independence Based on a Structured UIMS Interface. In: Grechenig, T., Tscheligi, M. (eds.): Human Computer Interaction, Vienna Conference, VCHCI '93, Vienna, Austria, Sept. 1993. Springer 1993 (Lecture Notes in Computer Science, vol. 733, pp. 279-290).

10. Laurel, B., Oren, B., Don, A.: Issues in Multimedia Interface Design: Media Integration and Interface Agents. In: Proc. of CHI '90, pp. 133-139 (April 1990).

11. Leidig, T.: Development of Cooperative Graphical-interactive Applications. University of Kaiserslautern, Germany. Dissertation, in German (Mar. 1994).

12. Macedonia, M., Brutzman, D.: MBONE, the Multicast BackbONE. Technical Report, Naval Postgraduate School, January, 1994, available at file://taurus.cs.nps.navy.mil/pub/mbmg/mbone.hottopic.ps

13. Masui, T.: User Interface Programming with Cooperative Processes. In: Myers, B.A. (ed.): Languages for Developing User Interfaces. Boston London: Jones and Bartlett 1992, pp. 261-277.

14. Moeller, E., Scheller, A., Schürmann, G: The BERKOM Multimedia-Mail Teleservice. In: PIK 16, No. 3, 1993 (in german).

15. Mühlhäuser, M. and Frick, O. Towards a Modeling Framework for Cooperative Multimedia OLDAs. Objects in Large Distributed Applications (OLDA-II) Workshop, OOPSLA '92, Vancouver, October 1992.

16. Mühlhäuser, M., Gerteis, W., and Heuser, L. DOCASE: A Methodic Approach to Distributed Object-Oriented Programming. *CACM 36, 9* (Sept. 1993), pp. 127-138.

17. Mühlhäuser, M. and Schaper, J. Project NESTOR: New Approaches to Cooperative Multimedia Authoring/Learning. In *Tomek, I.: Computer Assisted Learning,* Springer Berlin, 1992, pp. 453-465.

18. Nielsen, J.: Noncommand User Interfaces. Communications of the ACM 36 (4), 82-99 (April 1993).

19. Nigay, L. and Coutaz, J. A Design Space for Multimodal Systems: Concurrent Processing and Data Fusion. In *Proc. of INTERCHI '93*. April 1993, pp. 172-178.

20. Richartz, M. and Mühlhäuser, M. PreScripts: A Typing Approach to the Construction and Traversal of Hypertext. In Proc. of ED-MEDIA '93, Orlando, June 1993.

21. Rodden, T., Mariani, J.A., Blair, G.: Supporting Cooperative Applications. Computer Supported Cooperative Work (CSCW) 1, 41-67 (1992).

22. Roseman, M., Greenberg, S.: GroupKit: A Groupware Toolkit for Building Real-Time Conference Applications. In Proc. CSCW '92.

23. Rüdebusch, T. CSCW–Generic Support for Teamwork in Distributed Systems. DUV (Gabler, Vieweg, Westdeutscher Verlag), Wiesbaden, 1993. Dissertation, in German.

24. Schäl, T., Zeller, B.: Supporting Cooperative Processes with Workflow Management Technology. Tutorial on ECSCW '93, Milano, Italy, Sept. 1993

25. Schnorf, P.: Integrating Video into an Application Framework. In: Proc. of ACM Multimedia '93, Anaheim, CA, pp. 411-417, 478 (1993).

26. Sukaviriya, P., Foley, J.D. and Griffith, T. A Second Generation User Interface Design Environment: The Model and The Runtime Architecture. In *Proc. of INTERCHI '93*. April 1993, pp. 375-382.

27. Szekely, P., Luo, P., Neches, R.: Facilitating the Exploration of Interface Design. In: Proc. of CHI '92, Monterey, CA, pp. 507-515 (1992).

28. Taylor, R., Johnson, G.: Separation of Concerns in the Chiron-1 User Interface Development and Management System. In: Proc. of INTERCHI '93, Amsterdam, pp. 367-374 (April 1993).

29. Wiecha, C., Bennett, W., Boies, S., Gould, J. and Greene, S.: ITS: A Tool For Rapidly Developing Interactive Applications. *ACM Trans. on IS 8, 3* (July 1990), pp. 204-236.

30. Winograd, T. et.al: The Action Workflow Approach To Workflow Management Technology. In Proc. CSCW '92, Toronto, Oct. 1992

CSCW
and
Information Services

Principles of a Public Multimedia Information Service

M.J. Hoogeveen & F.C.I. van den Eijnden

Department of Telematics Services, PTT Research
P.O. Box 15000, 9700 CD Groningen, The Netherlands
E-mail: M.J.Hoogeveen@research.ptt.nl

Abstract. A next generation of public information services will include multimedia information services, and will have distributed characteristics. In this contribution light is shed on the principles of a Public Multimedia Information Service (PMIS) from the perspectives of end-users, information providers, service providers, network providers, and financial parties. A PMIS can form the basis of a Virtual Market (VM), the electronic market place which may become the most important economic exchange mechanism of the next century. A PMIS can be set up with current technology, but first organisational (e.g. standardisation) and economic (e.g. communication costs) bottlenecks need to be resolved.

1 Introduction

The next generation of public information services will encompass multimedia information services in a Virtual Market (VM) environment. Public information services have distributed characteristics by nature. The main objective of distributed multimedia systems is, according to Davcev et al. [5], to integrate multiple databases, to provide efficient multimedia information retrieval and transparent services to the end user. The main objective of public services in this context is to offer transparent broadband communication between the access and service points.

A growing interest can be seen in multimedia telecommunication and distributed multimedia systems for education [6, 12], multimedia teleconferencing [4] computer supported co-operative work based on broadband [10, 15], electronic publishing [3], medical imaging [20], Virtual Reality [16], video on demand [19], financial services [1] and for many other areas of application. Such multimedia systems may once be accessible by an integrated Public Multimedia Information Service (PMIS), i.e. a multimedia information service which is accessible through public networks.

Current public information systems, which are often based on Videotex, although still expanding, never reached the market penetration in most European countries that was initially predicted [14]. Some of the reasons for this are their limited functionality, user friendliness and media richness compared to the demands of consumers and business users as is reflected in state-of-the-art consumer electronics and computer technology. Reinforced by dropping hardware costs and transmission costs in a liberalising telecommunications market, a next generation of more processing-intensive multimedia information retrieval technology will solve these problems and will gradually be introduced in the next decades.

The technical feasibility and commercial viability of a Public Multimedia Information Service, which provides a VM environment, is addressed previously [8]. Laboratory experiments have made clear that a PMIS is technically feasible, although problems related to large-scale introduction need yet to be solved.

This paper deals with the issue of describing a PMIS from the perspectives of the VM actors involved, namely the end-user, the information provider, the service provider, the network provider, and involved financial parties. For each viewpoint advantages and realisation bottlenecks are given. In the conclusion the main advantages and bottlenecks are shortly discussed and a preview is given.

This paper is written in the context of the PTT Research PROMISE project, which is directed at defining multimedia information management services in support of marketing and sales applications. PROMISE elaborates on previous multimedia service projects, experiences with Videotex, and EURESCOM IMS1 (Integrated Multimedia Service at 1 Mbit/s) results.

2 A PMIS from different viewpoints

2.1 Introduction

A PMIS can be characterised by its types of users, the types of applications or services it provides, the types of information it delivers, and the types of functions that are included. Below we will discuss these characteristics to elucidate what a PMIS is.

Types of actors. The *End-users* can be seen as the customers of an information provider. There will be both professional and non-professional users.

The *Information Providers* (IP) of a PMIS are those companies or persons who invested in a certain application, a certain information service. An information service consists of the provided information and the programmed functions to handle this information.

An example of an IP is Time Warner involved in a video-on-demand market pilot in Orlando, Florida.

Service Providers (SP) consist of the parties who offer the PMIS service to their customers. They maintain the information servers, the connections to the information servers and may be involved in the production of an application or specific information service.

Network Providers (NP) play second fiddle in the PMIS concert. Their role is to provide the network connections between the involved entities and to offer - simply said - bandwidth.

Financial Parties (FP), like credit card organisations or banks, need to open their financial infrastructures for the PMIS service in order to support real-time financial transactions during a PMIS session.

Types of applications and business. In the history of Videotex most applications fell in the categories banking and insurance, retailing and distribution, electronic publishing and travel agencies. [14]. In a multimedia successor new applications can be added which require video and/or audio, like video on demand (see also the introduction).

In principle there is no limitation to the number and types of applications that may be offered by a PMIS. There will naturally be a kind of self-selection due to the commercial viability of an application. Typical categories of multimedia applications of interest are, in addition to the categories given above, marketing and sales, education, entertainment, medical care and videoconferencing.

Types of information. Depending on factors like costs of transmission and production of information and the value added of video and audio information applications may include multiple information types. Multimedia information may consist of information types like text, video, graphics, speech, music and structured data. Different types of information raise different kinds of requirements to the network, regarding acceptable delays, needed capacity, burstiness, etc. It is also very important that standard file formats and documents formats are supported. Interesting evolving document standards, although not yet accepted by the market, are the HyTime ISO 10744 [13] extension on SGML, and HyperODA. Important current information coding standards are JPEG for stills, Px64 (CCITT H.261) for videophony, and MPEG1 (ISO 11172) for video and audio data streams of various quality.

Types of functions. All functions that are considered to be necessary in the non-public variant of applications need to be supported in similar PMIS applications. It is important that the complete life cycle of information, including creation, editing, management and distribution, is supported. Extra functionality is related to on-line, eventually real-time communication with others, e.g. for CSCW or financial transactions using smartcard technology. New functionality is related to the distributed management of

multimedia databases, multimedia communications, video and audio encoding and decoding, and multimedia user interfaces including speech recognition and production, and optical and intelligent character recognition. If the information is non-sequential, or if associative searching is needed hypermedia features, encompassing hyperlinking, graphical browsing and path definitions for backtracking through hypermedia documents may also be supported.

2.2 Viewpoints regarding the functionality of a PMIS

The baseline for the PMIS functionality is the widely accepted, state-of-the-art functionality, which is offered by environments like Apple OS, MS Windows on Intel-PC's and OS/2. A main consideration is that the introduction of a PMIS would benefit from the presence of a large installed base, which leads to the MS Windows environment in the office or the TV at home. More advanced environments like the object oriented NeXT Step environment are problematic from the perspective of the magnitude of the installed-base.

Important basic requirements are user friendliness, transparency, media richness, and parallel multiple user sessions.

In the following sections the PMIS is described from the different viewpoints of successively the end-users, the information providers, the service providers, the network providers, the financial parties.

2.3 End-user: Access to multimedia applications

From the point of view of an end-user the multimedia service consists of a terminal, a layered user-interface and a number of specific applications of interest to him or her. He knows that he is not alone, that he can perform transactions and eventually communicate real-time with others. For the end-user it is an access point to a common information market. The fact that it offers multimedia information is only important as a derivative of the application he wants to use.

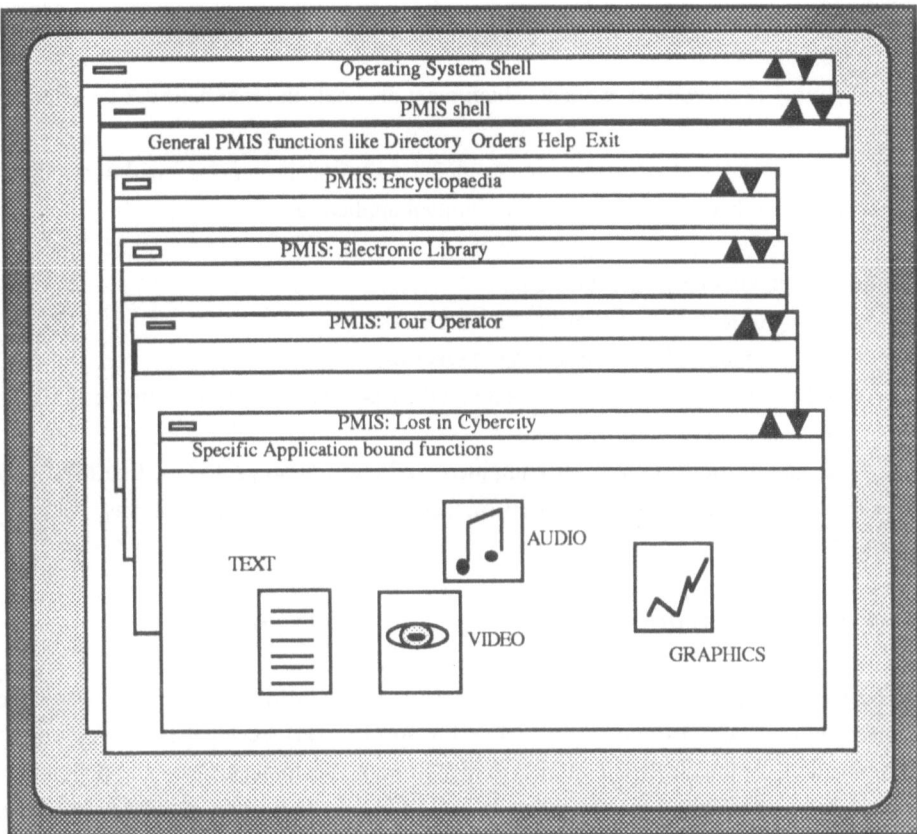

Fig. 1. View of what the end-user will see on his screen: the operating system shell, the PMIS shell or environment and the specific applications he activated.

On his screen the end-user encounters in a multi-session windowing environment three layers:

- the local operating system shell, e.g. DOS and MS Windows for a PC or RTOS for CD-I, is used with its related functions;
- the PMIS shell, which is activated from the operating system shell, and which contains general PMIS functions for accounting and billing, accessing the PMIS service directories, getting general help, copying information to a personal directory or printing certain information, controlling the remote connection, changing the set-up (for example the language), and quitting the PMIS shell;
- the specific applications or information services which are activated by selecting one from a PMIS shell.

The main advantages for the end users are:

306

- quick and unhampered access to services of information providers from the desktop;
- getting new types of services which meet demands not met before, like a personal news magazine;
- getting access to world-wide, or at least European, services without social or language barriers. (In case of multilingual applications).

Introduction bottlenecks are related to:
- pricing of terminal equipment and bandwidth;
- business value added of information services;
- end-user acceptance, which depend on the usability of the PMIS (applications) and resistances to change;
- standardisation of end-user equipment and end-to-end protocols, like MHEG for exchange of multimedia and hypermedia objects between (sub) systems.

2.4 Information provider: offering on-line services

From the viewpoint of an information provider (IP) a PMIS is a generic service which offers him the opportunity to introduce his specific service, in the form of a PMIS application, on the electronic market to many remote customers. Once an application is produced and installed the service sells itself and asks only little maintenance in most cases, except when the ageing of information goes at a very high speed like in a news application. The news may be updated every 15 minutes, or even continuously! Slower is the ageing of an electronic handbook for car repairs, which may be updated once a month. Real low is the update need for an electronic encyclopedia, this may be done once a year.

The IP has the possibility to update his own application on-line, he also may farm out this to a subcontractor or the service provider. The IP has, depending on the application, the possibility to review the usage of his applications, gets orders from client users and payment from financial parties.

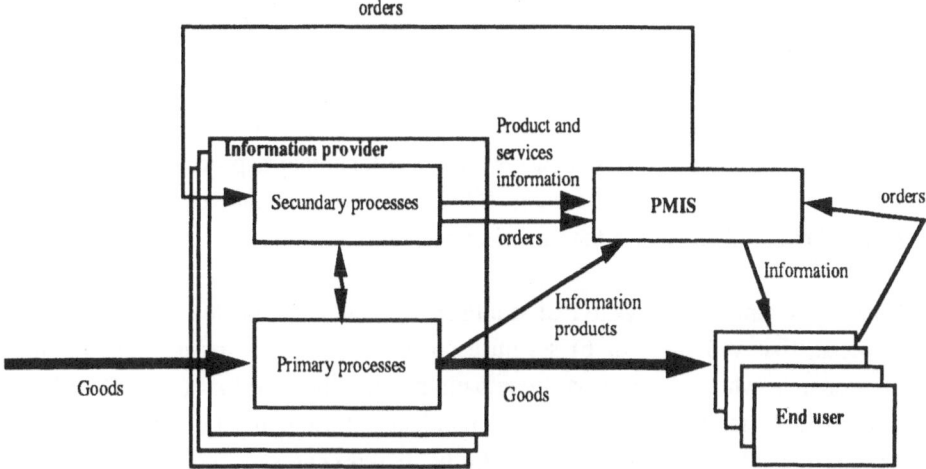

Fig. 2. For information providers a PMIS is an electronic platform to extend their business: to get their information better to their customers and to generate more revenues.

For an IP the PMIS is primarily a platform to extend their business. They can use it for marketing purposes as a vehicle for information about their products and services. They also can use it as a distribution channel for their information products, like an electronic encyclopaedia, and information services, like providing tourist information. Of course they can place orders themselves as well and use the PMIS as an end user.

The advantages for IPs are that they:
- get immediate and precise information about customer behaviour;
- get immediate access to their market
- reduce transport delays for information products and information services;
- (depending on the number of PMIS access points) extend their market penetration

Introduction bottlenecks are related to:
- the initial costs for setting up an information service;
- the difficulty to predict the actual benefits;
- lack of experience with multimedia publishing;
- copyright protection of information provided;
- high costs of bandwidth;
- standardisation of an open authoring environment for handling multi-format multi-protocol information;
- definition and standardisation of a comprehensive end-to-end MM service protocol.

2.5 Service provider: keeping the service in the air

Probably, most of the complexity of the PMIS is revealed to and handled by the service provider. The service provider is the one who needs to keep the PMIS in the air and shields-off the other parties or users from the technical aspects (complexity). The service provider needs to guarantee 100% availability of the service, to implement copyright control and check for authorisation.

There are mainly two ways to realise a PMIS: a) gradually update existing information services, like Videotex, or b) set up a complete, new and for its tasks optimized environment which is downward compatible with older services (and offers for that purpose Videotex emulation). This is a political and economical decision for involved organisations. We will not elaborate it further in this context.

The SP is responsible for one or more service environments, support of the end-user environments, and may offer a production environment as a payed facility for IPs. In the production environment the information services are created. Therefore content data need to be created, gathered, edited and prepared digitally. Also the information services need to be authored, tested and transposed to the service environment. For the production an application development toolkit needs to be composed.

There may be many distributed service environments, which are managed by one or more service providers. Typical functions in these distributed environments (see Fig. 3) are application installation and maintenance, accounting and billing (see also section 3.7), service supervision and control, service and network access control, and queuing and rerouting of user requests. The PMIS service must present itself as a whole to the user, although many service environments may exist (in different countries) which may make use of many information servers (per country). The development of operating systems that support distributed multimedia systems would be very useful [11].

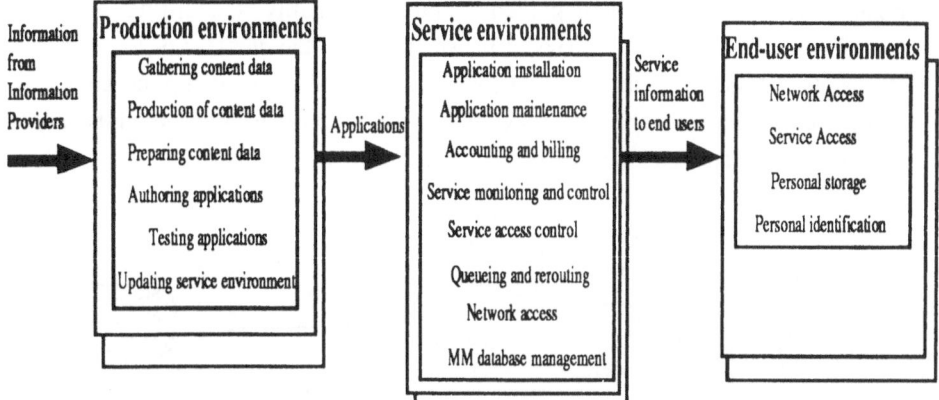

Fig. 3. Overview of service related functions in the production, service and end user environments.

In the many end user environments, user functions like service access, personal information storage and personal identification can be located. Dependent on the type of use, more functionality can be located in the end user environment. Examples of such functionality are printing, electronic payment, and editing of information. Serious problems that need to be solved for the service are clock synchronisation, out-of-sequence data packets, packets-to-packets jitter, and lost data packets [17].

The main advantages for the service provider are:
- it generates revenues and profits, if the service can be set up cost effective;
- it will generate extra revenues for the shareholders, probably network providers, some large information providers, existing service providers like Videotex and Minitel, and perhaps financial parties.

Introduction bottlenecks:
- compared to normal telephony up to 30 times higher demands related to throughput, access times of storage media and processing power in the service environments; this requires large investments and distributed solutions;
- lack of experience with multimedia service provision, e.g. multi-user aspects in relation to real-time use of an application.

2.6 Network provider: offering bandwidth

Network providers view a PMIS just as a specific VANS (Value Added Network Service). It consists of variable bandwidth connections between access points for users, hosts, and the service management centres. Probably accounting and billing functionality of the network provider is used to assess the duration of PMIS sessions. Payments of End-users will be partly based on the fixed connection price and the price of network usage. (The price for the complete service will also depend on the prices of information and application usage).

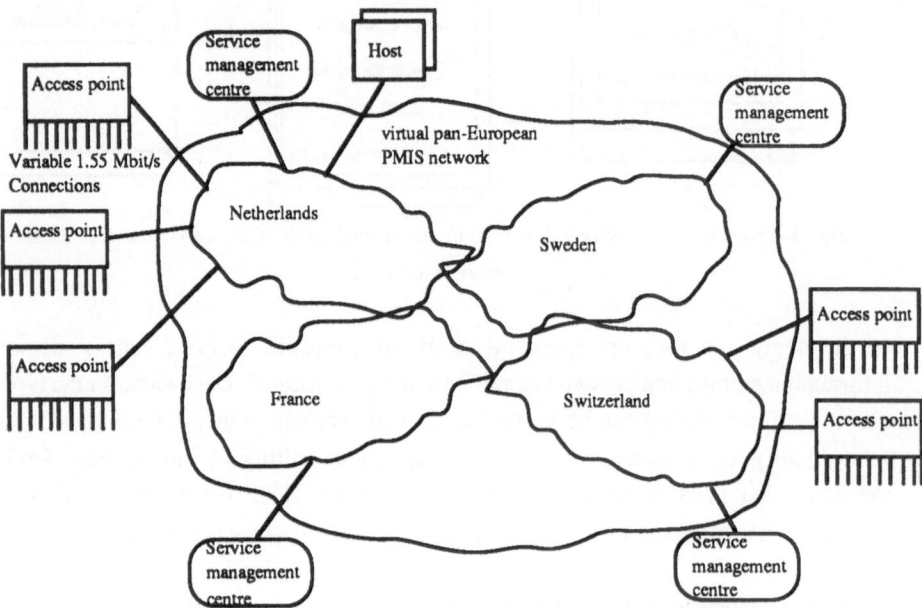

Fig. 4. An example of the composition of a virtual pan-European PMIS network.

It is the task of the network providers to offer the necessary bandwidth for PMIS sessions. They need to 'create' a virtual PMIS network (1.544 Mbit/s is enough for real-time MPEG1 data stream with video and audio), consisting of many national networks which are interconnected. They need to offer variable bandwidth connections to the users and service nodes in the virtual PMIS network. This requires that investments need to be made to offer at least 1.544 Mbit/s to the home. Possibilities for this are advanced copper systems like ADSL (Asymmetric Digital Subscriber Line) or HDSL (High-bitrate Digital Subscriber Line) [8], and PONs (Passive Optical Networks) [18]. ADSL and HDSL can be used in combination with basic rate ISDN (2B + D) on the same twisted pair. Currently, ISDN-30 meets the MPEG1 bandwidth requirement, although it does not meet the efficiency requirement regarding variability of bandwidth (variable bit rate). The price of ISDN-30 connections is also about 10 times the pricing of basic rate ISDN. An interesting alternative is formed by ATM in combination with PDH, for which standards are developed.

A growth path towards higher video quality, requiring 4-10 Mbit/s for MPEG2, should be anticipated. Moreover, if multiple video application sessions may run in parallel manifolds of 1.544 Mbit/s bandwidth are required. This means that ATM-based Broadband ISDN comes into the picture if no stronger compression (e.g. fractal compression) is used. Very encouraging are the results with ATM based multimedia services [2]. An alternative is formed by the possibility of using CATV networks, although huge investments in introducing switching technology need to be made.

Advantages for the network provider are:
• more network traffic;
• more connections are 'sold'

Realisation bottlenecks:
• at least 1.544 Mbit/s bandwidth to the home is needed;
• high bandwidth (at least 1.544 Mbit/s) switching functionality is needed;
• standardisation of reliable, switched broadband services for unhampered international multimedia data tranmission.

2.7 Financial parties: Real-time transactions

The financial part of the PMIS functionality is maybe not the most technically complex, but nevertheless one of the most important issues. Financial parties, like banks and credit card organisations, need to be connected to the PMIS in order to allow for real-time financial transactions when services or information are provided to an end user. (Financial parties can also act as an information provider, offering their financial services, like GIROTEL in the Netherlands, directly to end users).

312

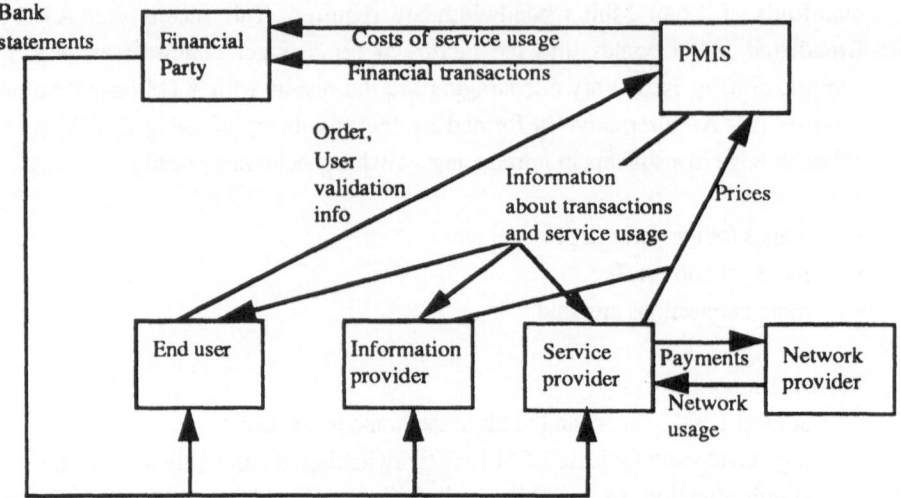

Fig. 5. A scenario for data flows concerning financial transactions

In the figure above a scenario for the data flows between the involved entities is given. The information provider and service provider are feeding the PMIS with price information about products, business services, and the costs of information service usage. Hence, when an end user places an order the transaction costs can be calculated. Also the dynamic costs of service usage can be calculated. All these costs calculations will be sent to a bank, which will carry out the necessary financial transactions and send bank statements to the involved parties. Meanwhile the PMIS has provided the end user and concerned information provider with information about the transaction directly. The service provider obtains information about service usage continuously. In this scenario payment for network usage is settled between the network and service provider, unrelated to the PMIS. In this case, the service provider will pass on these expenses to the end user.

Another scenario in which the accounting and billing functions of network providers are used is not just hypothetical.

Advantages for the financial parties are:
- they can improve their service to their customers (this is a competitive advantage);
- transaction processing is automated to a higher degree, which may reduce further the amount of manual data-entry by bank employees;
- more use is made of special financial services (e.g. credit card transactions).

Realisation bottleneck:
- standardisatin of financial interfaces and protocols.

3 Conclusion

An overview is given of a PMIS, which may support a variety of applications, multimedia information, and potentially a tremendous variety of user specific tasks.

The main potential advantages for the involved types of actors are made clear. The technical bottlenecks, although often complex, do not seem invincable. The most important technical challenge is to offer MM elements for a reasonable price (e.g. ADSL is yet very expensive). Sometimes low cost hybrid solutions can be found, which use the current communication infrastructure. The major bottlenecks are related to organisational and financial issues: Can we agree on MM protocols and international standards? How to set up a profitable information service? Which applications offer enough value added to be appealing to enough numbers of end users? How to be sure that a PMIS would give Return On Investment for a service provider?

Experiences with Videotex in many countries are, from the point of view of the Videotex service providers, not so rosy to justify large investments in multimedia upgrades. On the other hand, upgrading in the direction of Photo-Videotex can be noticed. If Information Providers discover attractive business opportunities for multimedia services, e.g. tele-sales or tele-marketing, renewal in the direction of multimedia will be accelerated.

One of the major bottlenecks is formed by the costs of equipment and communication. These costs (expressed in bits/s) are dropping considerably, especially in the liberalising communication markets. The main costs stem from the access network, because access network sharing is in most cases limited to the members of a household.

We presume that in the next century in most western countries the necessary investments in the access network are made to form an electronic data highway. Then PMISs on such an electronic data highway will be the backbone of the VM, and will boost new types of economical activities.

Abbreviations

ATM   Asynchronous Transfer Mode
CATV   CAble TeleVision
CSCW   Computer Supported Co-operative Work
FP   Financial Party
HyTime   Hypermedia and Time Based structuring language
IP   Information Provider
ISDN   Integrated Services Digital Network
ISO   International Standardisation Organisation

314

IT	Information Technology
MPEG	Moving Pictures information coding Experts Group
MS	Multimedia System
NP	Network Provider
ODA	Open (Office) Document Architecture
PMIS	Public Multimedia Information Service
RTOS	Real-Time Operating System (for CD-I)
SGML	Standard Generalized Markup Language
SP	Service Provider
VM	Virtual Market

References

1. Arbuthnot, C.P., Khalil, H.: RACE project DIVIDEND - an application for the finance sector. BT Technol J 11(1), 12-18 (1993).
2. Armbrüster, H., Wimmer, K.: Broadband Multimedia Applications Using ATM Networks: High-Performance Computing, High-Capacity Storage, and High-Speed Communication. IEEE Journal on Selected Areas in Communications 10(9), 1382-1396 (1992).
3. Consulting Trust.: New Opportunities for Publishers in the Information Services Market. (Report EUR 14925 EN). Commission of the European Communities DG XIII (1993).
4. Crowfort, J., Kirsten, P.T., Timm, D.: Multimedia teleconferencing over international PSDNs. Computer communications 14 (7), p 433-437 (1991).
5. Davcev, D., Cakmakov, D., Cabukovski, V.: A Distributred Multimedia System. In: Spaniol, O., Danthine, A. (eds.). High Speed Networking, III (IFIP). Amsterdam, The Netherlands: Elsevier Science Publishers BV (North-Holland) 1991, pp. 241-254.
6. Gullickson-Morfitt, M., Southworth, J.H., Young, D.B., Moore, D.L., Uvarov, A.: Development of Intergrated Multimedia Telecommunication Utilization for Project Management: The International Network for Education in Science and Technology Project (NEST). In: Proc. Pacific Telecommunications Council Fourteenth Annual Conference PTC'92. Honolulu, HI, USA: Pacific Telecommunications Council 1992, pp. 462-471.
7. Hoogeveen, M.J.: Multimedia. Infrastructuur voor tekst, beeld en geluid. [Multimedia. Infrastructure for text, video and audio (in Dutch)]. Rijswijk, Netherlands: Lansa Publishing 1993.

8. Hoogeveen, M. J., Andersson, J.: Specification of a Public Pan-European Public Multimedia Information Service. In: Proceedings of the AAIM conference on Multimedia in Education & Industry, Savannah, GA, p 97-101 (1993).

9. Hoogeveen, M.J., Van der Meer, K.: Full Integration of Information Retrieval and Database Management in Support of Multimedia Police Work. Journal of Information Science, in print (1994).

10. Kindt, A., Reible, V., Vöge, K.H.: Broadband Based Cooperative Work. In: Bullinger, H.J. (ed.). Human Aspects in Computing: Design and Use of Interactive Systems and Information Management. Amsterdam, The Netherlands: Elsevier Science Publishers 1991.

11. Leslie, I.M., Mc Auley, D., Mullender, S.J. : Pegasus - Operating Support for Distributed Multimedia Systems. (Pegasus paper 92-2). University of Cambridge Computer Laboratory/University of Twente Faculty Computer Science 1992.

12. Mühlhäuser, M.: Computer Based Learning with Distributed Multimedia Systems. In: Bullinger, H. J. (ed.). Human Aspects in Computing: Design and Use of Interactive Systems and Information Management. Amsterdam, Netherlands: Elsevier Science Publishers 1991.

13. Newcomb, S.R., Kipp, N.A., Newcomb, V.T.: The HyTime Hypermedia/Time-based Document Structuring Language. Communications of the ACM 34(11), 67-83 (1991).

14. Online.: Proceedings of Videotex'84 International. London: Online Publications 1984.

15. Pehrson, B., Gunningberg, P., Pink, S.: Distributed Multimedia Applications on Gigabit Networks. IEEE Network Magazine, 26-35 (1992).

16. Ramanathan, S., Venkat Rangan, P., Vin, H.M.: Integrating Virtual Reality, Tele-conferencing, and Entertainment into Multimedia Home Computers. IEEE Transactions on Consumer Electronics 38(2), 70-76 (1992).

17. Richard, W.D., Costa, P.: The Washington University Broadband Terminal, IEEE Journal on Selected Areas in Communications 11(2), 276-282 (1993).

18. Van Vaalen, M.J.M.: ATM PONs for PSTN and ISDN access. RACE Open Workshop on Broadband Access. Nijmegen, Netherlands, June 7-8, 1993.

19. Venkat Rangan, P., Vin, H.M., Ramanathan, S.: Designing an On-Demand Multimedia Service. IEEE Communications Magazine, 56-64 (1992).

20. Vöge, K.H.: BERKOM-Anwendungsprojekte. Entwurf und Erfahrungen. Nachrichtentech., Elektron. 42(2), p. 49-53 (1992).

Supporting Cooperative Software Development through a Multimedia Environment

Adérito Marcos

Fraunhofer Institute for Computer Graphics
Wilhelminenstr. 7, 64283 Darmstadt, Germany
marcos@igd.fhg.de

Abstract. Systems to support Cooperative Software Development (CSD) have as main goal to enable several users connected over a network to work together in order to develop software. They have to solve problems such as: coherence maintenance of the software project through the distributed system by managing possible conflicts between local versions of each group member and promote the necessary mechanisms for the inter-group awareness and integrity.

The objective of the current paper is to introduce a distributed and multimedia solution to support CSD. We describe here our own CSD prototype - it enables a group of developers (2 to 4), possibly located at remote places and connected over network, to develop software together. A cooperative multimedia editing environment is available for the whole Development Cycle, enclosing mechanisms of computer-conferencing (text, audio and video communications).

1 Introduction

The evolution and improvement of both network and workstation technology made possible the realisation of several distributed environments to support group work. This comprehends the accessibility to more cheaper and powerful resources on video-conferencing, data-transfer and multimedia capabilities which are becoming common place and used as bottom platforms to cooperative solutions.

We deal here with the problems posed by Cooperative Software Development - a specific case of CSCW (Computer-Supported Cooperative Work), which encompasses the questions of supporting the activities of a group of people that cooperates in order to produce a piece of software. We mean as Software Development those tasks relating directly with code programming and software research implementations not expressively using CASE (Computer-Aided Software Engineering) technology.

The work in development and maintenance of software is typically alternating between tasks involving many persons and individual assignments [10]. This development work is performed following a Software Development Cycle (SDC) which includes activities like conceptualisation, design and specification, editing, integration of software components, debug, test, review, and others.

As a first step, the group has to conceptualise and decide guidelines and strategies to be used during the development process, and also divide implementation tasks and responsibilities among themselves. After this phase each developer will concentrate in his own tasks, and starts properly the development process.

It has been verified that almost all the implementation work tends to be done asynchronously and more or less independently, where each developer only carries out the task(s) assigned to him. However, points exist during the development when two or more developers want to collaborate by completing together a specific goal (sharing or not software object(s)), or simply exchange opinions about details on the software project [12].

Global meetings occur when the group needs to (re)consider together the software project state (e.g. test up results or redefine strategies). Then, all the changes achieved in the system by each developer appear to fit in an unique version, turning the system to the same global state. However, and due to the distributed characteristics of the development process, changes performed by one developer can conflict (*merging conflicts*) with the changes made by the other users in the system. This represents the main difficulty of CSD processes, i.e., support of consistency. A solution must be taken from negotiations and organisational protocol strategies [14]. We can easily devise how important (if not crucial) is allow efficient direct inter-user communications features in order to facilitate negotiations and promote the group work.

Accordingly, we have adopted a strategy following two guidelines: first, prevent *merging conflicts* from arising by avoiding absolute forms of parallel work; and second, support a strong awareness within the group by allowing mechanisms for a easy inter-group communications. In fact, when several developers want to edit in the same software object (but not in the same point), the object is divided among the candidates in strict reserved areas (not overlapping), for their own exclusive use. This permits a broad way of parallel work, in the sense that no different logical versions are created, but the same software component is being simultaneously changed. When contentious situations appear, referring to areas or even a whole object access, they can be solved by direct human (user-user) negotiations or asking the intervention of the group's moderator.

An important characteristic of any computer user-oriented system is the interface model it supports. This is particularly true when considering specific systems requesting information expressiveness or graphical visualisation (presentation) of the involved data. However, in recent years and due to the increased evolution on multimedia technology, system designers are adopting more or less complex interface models in almost all areas.

In the case of CSCW systems and specially the CSD ones, the use of multimedia can improve the process in two global ways: to effectively support the necessary group communication links; and to enhance the expressiveness of the related information in the development cycle (see [18]).

We describe here the decisions and solutions adopted in our approach - a computer-supported cooperative work architecture for software development. It includes a complete software development cycle (C, C++ programming dependent) and is implemented over a multimedia environment (see [17]) It enables a group of developers (2 to 4), possibly located at remote places and connected over network (LAN or WAN (Internet and ISDN)), to conceptualise, decide strategy, edit and integrate software components, comment on, debug, compile, test, perform code inspection and review, and generate reports.

The system provides group awareness by allowing the traditional paradigms of cooperative editing: personalised multiple cursors, WYSIWIS (What You See Is What I See), social roles, developers' identification, tele-pointing, multi-user interface, multi-user communication. The media available for communication are text, audio and video. The media available for editing in the several phases of the development cycle are text and graphics. The developers can exchange ideas about pieces of information in the editing phase by commenting on (doing public comments) in text, graphics and audio.

In this paper we firstly expose the global architecture and algorithm adopted. Next, we explain in detail the development cycle and finally we draw our future work directions and conclusions.

2 The CSD system strategy

We mean as architecture the way the cooperative system is organised in order to enable the cooperative work. This organisation concerns about the distribution of the physical processes and files over the different machines where the users are located, as well as the way the communication is enabled. In context of CSD, the architecture concept also includes the organisation strategies of the software project.

On the other hand, the algorithm to support the CSD process encircles the strategies to control the information flow through the distributed system, concerning the issues to maintain global coherency.

2.1 System architecture

CSD systems require special attention due to software consistency support. Indeed, CSD architectures should take in consideration where and how the software project data can be physically organised according to its parts already stated as consistent and stable (commonly used as source for the current and subsequent development), and also those components being changed (potentially inconsistent).

Usually, stable software components are stored as belonging to the current global project version, and must be independently preserved from inconsistent changes. Consequently, the centralised architecture seems to be the adequate solution.

On the other hand, most of the times changes being generated by each developer are temporal (or volatile), in the sense they are not yet integrated in the global version. Therefore, for efficiency reasons, developers' workspaces should maintain, more or less independently, these temporal changes in local copies.

In conclusion and following the above guidelines, we have adopted a hybrid architecture able to support a centralised control of global versions and also local structures of developers' workspaces.

An external process (see the *Global Server* in Fig. 1) synchronises all the developers' actions and is also responsible for the global software project management.

All the connections between the *Global Server* and the developers' processes and between the developers' processes themselves are made using Ethernet-LAN functions (TCP/IP) or ISDN-WAN [19].

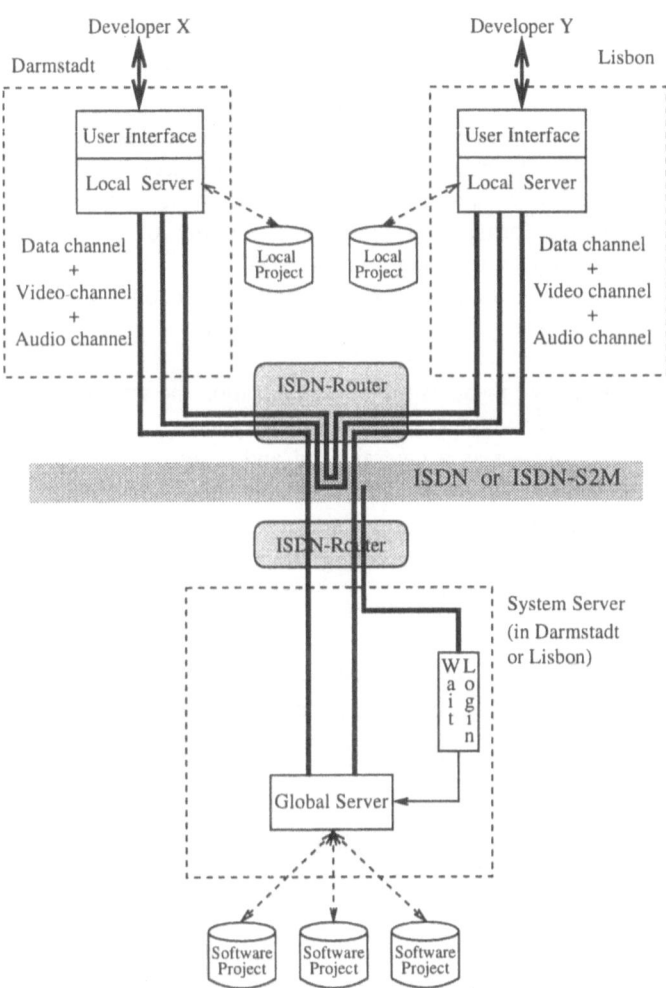

Fig. 1. An overview of the main architecture (using ISDN-WAN)

Each user starts a process on his own workplace which establishes a communication link with the *Global Server* (which is started automatically if it does not exist). After this connection is established, the *Global Server* sends all the information concerning about the current software project (if it does exist) necessary for the new developer process to register itself has one more developer in the editing session. Each developer process, supports several structures needed to sustain locally a version of the software project. Also updated copies of the editing state of the other developers are kept, which permits to pursue a strong awareness within the group.

The *Local Server* functionalities avoid the overload of the network by handling the traffic between developer process and *Global Server*.

The architecture also allows each process on the developer workplace to connect to another workplace via a text, audio and video channels. This allows inter-user communication without the *Global Server* control and consequently promotes the integrity and effectiveness of the group task.

The video communication uses the JPEG codec standard (see [8]) for the video frames, and VideoPix hardware or IndigoVideo on Sun or SGI workstations respectively. For audio, we provide crossplatform usability, by using a common intermediate exchange format and realising a number of on-line bi-directional converters supporting different code formats (see [21]).

Finally, the text communication follows an improved version similar to UNIX/Talk feature.

Project organisation. We mean as project organisation the way its involved entities are conceptually located and the kind of relation they have.

We define *software project* as a central head and a set of *components*. The head includes the *makefile* and the data referring to the project design and conceptualisation. The *components* are pieces of text or graphics, with or without logical or hierarchical relations, consisting of parts of a whole, i.e., the project structure. These *components* can be:

• *Units*: the traditional C program elements (modules, headers and libraries). They are in practice the *software* components of the project environment.

• *Reports*: text or graphics files manually or automatically generated, including considerations about the development task.

• *Documents*: refers to any documentation file about the software project.

• *History*: text file automatically generated, which holds a logical narrative of the developers' actions along the development process.

The *software project* environment comprehends also entities such as compilers, debuggers, or any tool assisting the development process.

In fact, our considerations about consistency are strictly related with *units* (precisely with modules) and their management. They represent the "physical" *software project* being produced.

Each *unit* has one creator and one or more developers. During the development process, successive versions for each *unit* are stated stable (or consistent) and integrated in the global *software project* version located in the *Global Server*.

In order to avoid interference between individual developments, the system supports for each developer workspace, local versions of the *units* being changed. Each changed *unit* becomes "visible" to the whole system, only when is integrated (if no conflicts exist) in the global version. The management of the different project versions is performed by the *Global Server* process. It keeps a set of tables controlling the state of each machine/developer.

2.2 The cooperative algorithm

It is easy to devise that different architectures adapt better to different algorithms. For example, centralised architectures adapt better to Client-Server algorithms and replicated architectures to Order algorithms.

We have adopted a hybrid solution, incorporating concepts from Client-Server (see [3]) and also Order algorithms (see [9]) and adapted to the system architecture. On one hand, there is a *Global Server* process to perform the management and on the other hand, by means of the *Local Server*, the user process gets more "intelligent"

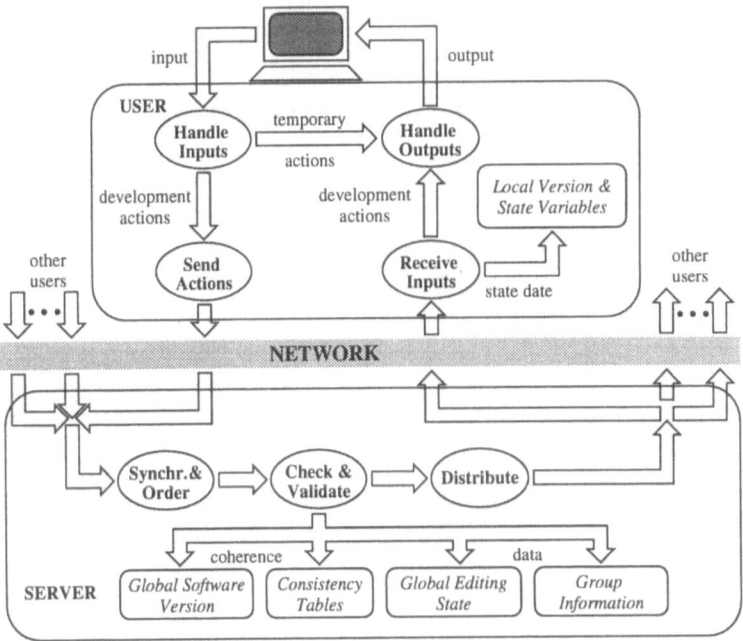

Fig. 2. A global overview of the cooperative algorithm

helping in the synchronisation problems.

As the development actions are performed by each of the developers, they are transmitted to the *Global Server* which re-transmits them to all the developers (including the one who originated it). There is no direct communication for development actions between the users in the system. The *Global Server* receives and dispatches the users' requests using a FIFO rule. Therefore, this guarantees mutual exclusion and serialisation of the users actions. There exists no parallelism in the answer time [19]. The *Global Server* has locally a set of consistency tables containing the current development state of the whole software project. Access

322

conflicts, updating requirements, or general coherency violations, are checked using the consistency tables.

By receiving the actions from the *Global Server* each user process executes them either by changing the development state or by outputting a result (see Fig. 2). The user actions are only definitively executed after receiving the *Global Server* answer (agreement). During the development process, the local versions are being successively updated by receiving, through the *Global Server*, the changes (stated consistent) from the other developers. Actions such as local debug or test, even passing through the *Global Server*, are always executed using the contents of the local workspace. Global test or debug demands, for purposes of coherence, the integration of all the local changes in a same global version.

The *Global Server* process is the only one with real access to the global version of the Software Project being developed and each one of the user processes has only a copy of the Software Project (local version). Precisely the maintenance of the consistency of these copies and also of the global version, is the main goal of the algorithm.

3 The cooperative software development cycle

The development of software is necessarily a set of cyclical tasks, following a common goal, i.e., the production of a "satisfactory" package of software. These set of tasks, commonly named as the Development Cycle, represent in practice the system interface to the users. The Multimedia mechanisms/metaphors play here a

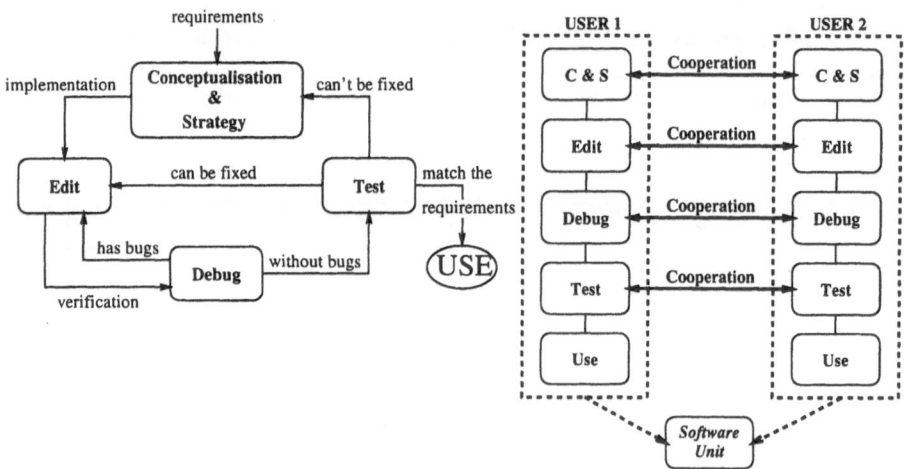

Fig. 3. The *traditional* software development cycle performed by an individual developer(left), and the *cooperation role* in the cycle (right)

decisive role by enhancing the expressiveness and a best manipulation of the involved information, and consequently improve the editing environment of the Development Cycle. The media used in our system during the Development Cycle are text, graphics (raster and 2D) and audio. For the inter-group communications there are three media channels: text, audio and video.

The software development performed by individual or small groups of developers usually follows more or less the traditional "four-steps" cycle strategy (conceptualisation, code editing (programming), debugging and testing). Moreover, we have verified this strategy adapts quite well to cooperative environments, where certainly, we need to take into account the specific requirements of the transition from individual to group work.

Accordingly, we have defined a Cooperative Software Development Cycle (CSDC) as having four inter-connected phases:

- *Conceptualisation and Strategy* - the cycle's first step, where the group decides together the strategies for the project development. It represents a convergence of the whole group.

- *Editing* - in this phase each developer performs his task as decided in the conceptualisation step, and can be done alone or together. It encloses the environment of creating and changing project *components*.

- *Debugging* - it is the common compiling and syntax error fixing task, and can be done with the other developers' help.

- *Testing* - after producing an executable program the developer should test the results, with or without the group collaboration.

Tasks as review or inspections, are not properly independent development steps, and consequently are included as a part of the editing environment.

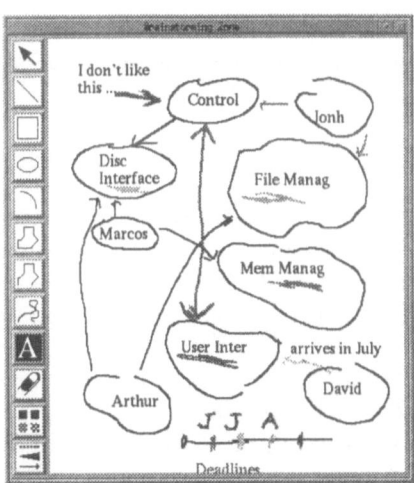 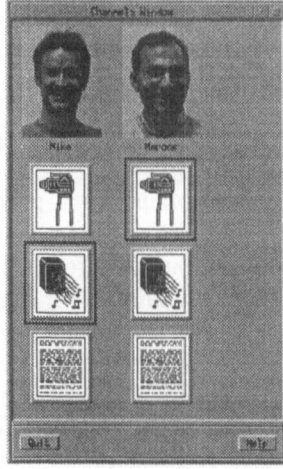

Fig. 4. An example of a common drawing area (raster graphics) used for brainstorming (left) and a window used to establish the communication channels among users in the group (right)

Social roles. As the CSD work is a task performed by a group of people, consequently it must include some kind of inter-coordination in order to promote the work performance. One response to the problem is the definition of social roles. The social roles we have adopted are Moderator - chairs the session, Developer - one of the participants in the team that actively contributes on the development process, Reviewer/Inspector - does not participate directly on the development work., but contributes to the CSD process by commenting on the software project. This can be done informally or executing a well defined Review/Inspection task..

The social role of each of the participants in the meeting is defined during the login time or in the *Conceptualisation and Strategy* phase.

Developers can also assume another role in the system, i.e., as *expert*. The *expert* is any active developer in the system, who has some understanding on specific areas of the project. The developers can ask him opinions about conceptual things or send him an error report while looking for help. An *expert* affects a special importance in the *debugging* phase, where difficult syntax errors can be more easily solved with colleagues' help.

3.1 Conceptualisation and strategy

We define *Conceptualisation and Strategy* as the first project step where the group' members decide together things as: conceptual guidelines, global resolution strategies and tasks distribution. From here, the development responsibilities are divided amongst the team members and each one should promote the work in his specific part. This phase implies always a convergence of the whole group and consequently comes to be extremely important be supported through efficient tools for inter-group communication and group awareness.

We provide *Conceptualisation and Strategy* in our system by a set of brainstorming tools that includes:

• *brainstorming zone* - is a shared drawing area where all the users can sketch simultaneously. Each one sees instantaneously the inputs of the others;

• communication channels (video, audio and text);

The *brainstorming zone* plays here the role as a traditional shared "white board" often used in face-to-face meetings, which holds informal schemes generated during the discussion. Therefore, each group' member can add (draw) new details while looking for attention to a specific idea. This information can be stored as an report and recovered subsequently.

In the *brainstorming zone* (see Fig. 4) all the editing actions of each user occur with his personalised cursor, which allows the individual recognition.

The conferencing process of this phase is coordinated by using the established group' members *social roles*.

3.2 Editing

As we referred before, the editing phase encloses the environment to manipulate project *components*. A *component* is a piece of text or graphics that can be edited by one or more developers. Two specific cooperative editors (text and graphics) support the *components* editing. They include strongly the WYSIWIS and multiple cursors paradigms. The system also presents a global environment where the user can edit at same time several *components* and organise them (see Fig. 6 (top-left window)).

The manipulation of *units* as software objects, represents the main goal of the editing phase, and must be considered under the global consistency strategy adopted.

Indeed, only two editing modes are permitted:

- *turn taking* - only one user can edit at a given time, i.e., the *unit* is locked.

- *split & combine* - allows simultaneous user editing. Even so, each user has a reserved area for his own strict use and cannot interfere in the other users' parts. Anyway, he is completely aware of the other actions

The *turn taking* mode concerns about the exclusive use of *units*. In fact, this mode encircles the possibility of the other users waiting indefinitely for the lock to be released. In such case, direct user-user communications can be used to find out an agreement, or as a last resource, ask for the Moderator intervention who has

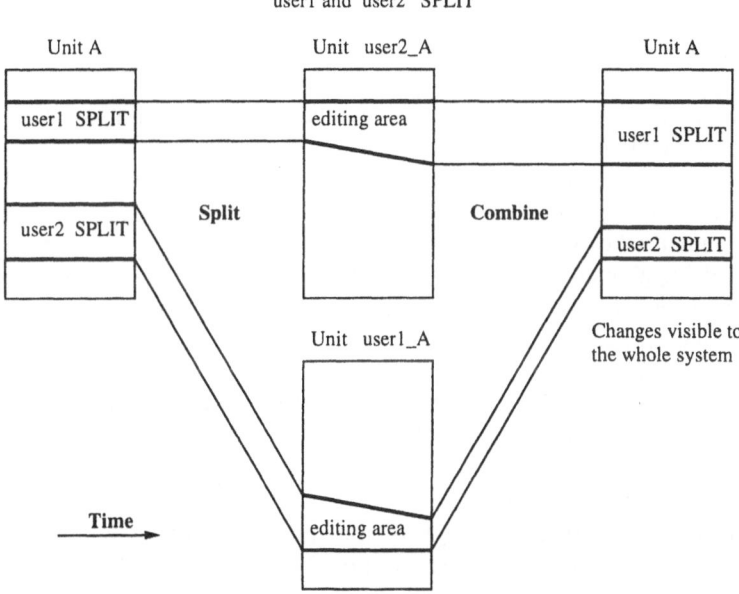

Fig. 5. Creation of two alternative *units* and their merge

authority to break the lock and free the *unit*.

The *Split & combine* mode demands a merge mechanism in order to integrate the various changes. However, as no absolute parallel development exists and also no physical "collisions" are generated, consequently the merge function is reduced simply to a copy of the changed areas to the original *unit* (see Fig. 5). Human intervention can always be used to repair difficult merge cases, usually coming from logical dependencies between changed parts from different users.

When a Developer leaves a whole *unit* or simply a reserved area, the related changes are sent to the *Global Server*, integrated in the global software version and finally distributed to all the other developers local versions in the system.

Code review/inspection. Code Review is the inspection and analysis of source code *units* by developers who are knowledgeable in the application domain and programming environment. Code reviewers analyse individually the *unit* to be inspected, looking for coding errors, portability problems, violations of coding standards, etc. Thus, review is mainly based on commenting on the software source code. These comments are fragments of information referring to a certain piece of text in the code, and express considerations about this related text area.

Our system supports public comments and private annotations. They can contain textual, graphical and voice information. Their function is based on the traditional hypermedia paradigm - they can be accessed by following a link when clicking on the area. The comments are immediately distributed after their creation to all users. They are then common knowledge to the group and can be further edited by anyone [18]. Annotations are appropriate to privately generated ideas, which may subsequently be communicated to he group.

3.3 Debugging

We define debug as compiling and syntax bugs fixing. Thus, in most of the cases, it is a closed individual task.

The cooperation can appear in all the situations where a developer needs to ask for someone else's opinion about details such as errors or software characteristics. Our environment takes that into account by permitting developers to send errors or the whole debugging environment such as windows or *units* to an e*xpert*. The *expert* can be any of the other users. Therefore, a sub-group or all the group can follow out and help in the debugging process of a member.

The cooperation occurs also in the manipulation of a specific debugger tool (the current prototype version supports only the UNIX debugger dbx). Several developers can perform inputs and receive outputs in a shared interface, following the paradigm of WYSIWIS. This aims to maintain a "on line" discussion over the related local or global version being debugged.

The input/output control strategy of the running debugger is similar to the one approved in the testing phase (see section 3.4). The only difference resides on the related executable file.

3.4 Testing

Testing is essentially the assessment of the current results achieved on the *software project*.

This process can be made locally or globally. In the first case, consists in a private test where the developer uses his local project version in way to evaluate his own changes.

The global test happens when the group decides to integrate all the local versions and observe the whole aspect of the project. Then, one of the machines is adopted to hold the running process, which is usually the one of the developer who requested the global test.

Testing globally involves a shared interface and the control of the several input/outputs coming from the group. The principle of WYSIWIS must be followed, permitting as much as possible the awareness within the group. The input flow can be controlled by two modes:

- *token-ring*: only one developer (who has the token) can perform input.

- *free-for-all*: all the group ' members can enter inputs.

The *token-ring* mode, refers to the classical token strategy, i.e., only one developer has the turn to perform input. The turn can be given or lost to another user.

When testing with *free-for-all* mode, all the developers can perform inputs, and the *Global Server* takes the responsibility to solve possible conflicts. In fact, a strategy of global stamps is used, i.e., each developer process has locally a total sequence order, referring to the inputs accepted by the *Global Server*. This sequence is the same in the whole system, and reflects the inputs serialisation performed by the *Global Server*. When the *Global Server* process accepts an input, it firstly informs all the developers (including the owner) which was the accepted input and who is the owner, and only after dispatches the related input request. Inputs arising out of the global sequence are discarded. This scheme permits to sustain coherently the sequence of input/outputs through the system.

4 Future work

Even though the prototype offers a complete Software Development Cycle, we still have a number of research directions underway.

We are already doing the first steps in what we call our priority goal - a generic multimedia cooperative environment able to integrate non-cooperative applications. It comprehends a complete computer-conferencing top level structure which allows people to share their own tools and environments to enforce a best continuity of the cooperative framework.

Another important point we want to pursue is the support of remote software packages demonstrations and consulting. It has to combine: forms of logical representation of editing actions, multimedia, hyper-organisation of objects and transfer mechanisms over network, to enhance an interactive generation of presentation sessions.

Also we have under consideration the use of ATM and "mobile" technology for communication proposes.

Finally, we want to improve the cooperation mechanisms and integrity of the system, doing it gradually able to be used as a general platform to support Software Engineering in its several tasks.

6 Conclusion

In the last years, more and powerful cooperative systems have been developed following the evolution on technology and performance of both network and workstations platforms.

One of the group' activities being supported cooperatively is Software Development. The software development process is usually not pursued by only one person. Most of the times it involves the work of software designers, programmers, engineers, end-

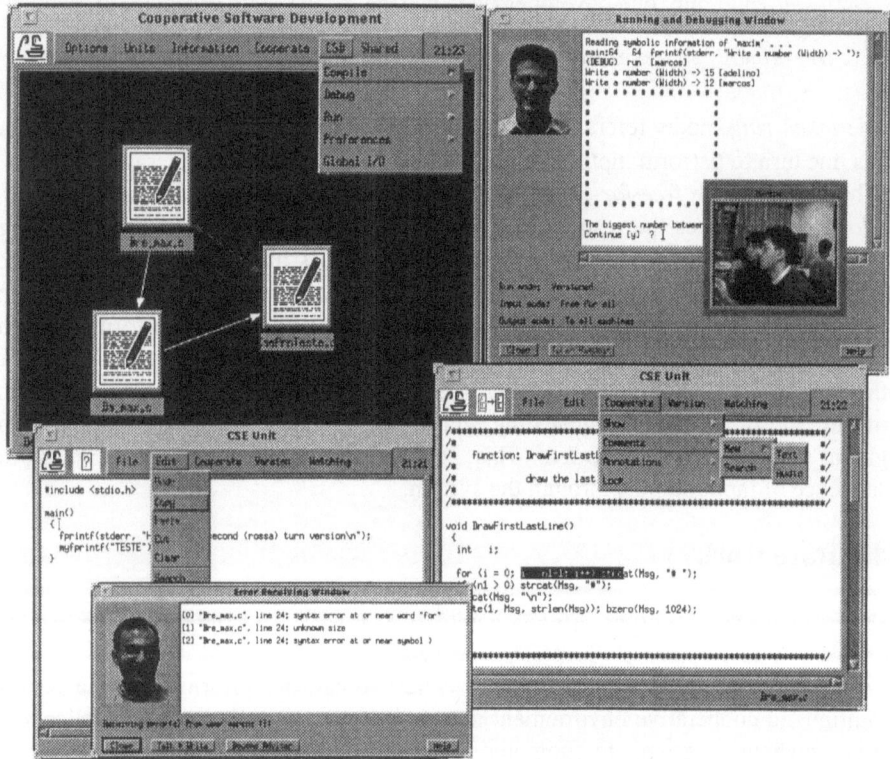

Fig. 6. An overview of the CSD system. The *units* organisation environment (top left), with two open *unit* editors (bottom right and left), *expert* window (bottom left), the *debug* window (top right), and also video channel window (top right)

users, reviewers, etc., not located in the same geographic place, i.e., expertise is not located in just one place. Therefore, the development of software products can be dependent on the cooperation of many people.

In this paper we have introduced a global distributed multimedia environment to support CSD. An architecture and algorithm were explained, and also the Development Cycle. These have enclosed issues such as: the way the software project is organised through the distributed system, or which kind of strategy was used to perform the software development process in its several steps.

Acknowledgements. We thank Prof. José L. Encarnacao for the opportunities given, Dr. Ch. Hornung and Adelino Santos for the useful suggestions and discussions and finally the student José Rossa for the help in the implementation. This work is partially funded by a CIENCIA scholarship (BD/2663/93-IA).

References

1. Adams E., Honda M., and Miller T.: "Object management in a case environment", in Proc. of 11th ICSE, IEEE (1989).

2. Dunn R., "Software Quality: Concepts and Plans", Prentice Hall, 1990.

3. Greenberg S., Roseman M., Webster D. "Human and Technical Factors of Distributed Group Drawing Tools", in Proc. of the Workshop on Real Time Group Drawing and Writing Tools, CSCW'92 (1992).

4. Harrison W., Ossher H., and Sweeney P., "Coordinating concurrent development", in Proc. of CSCW'90, ACM (1990).

5. Hornung Ch., Jäger M., Santos A., Tritsch B., "Cooperative Hypermedia: an Enabling Paradigm for Cooperative Work", The Visual Computer: an International Journal of Computer Graphics, (in press).

6. Ishii H., Kobayashi M. "Integration of Inter-personal Space and Shared Workspace: ClearBoard Design and Experiments", in Proc.of CSCW'92, Toronto (1992).

7. Johnson P., Tjahjono D., "Improving Software Quality through Computer Supported Collaborative Review", in Proc. of ECSCW'93, Milano, Sept. 1993.

8. "JPEG Technical Specification", Joined Photographic Expert Group ISO/IEC, JTC1/SC2/WG8, CCITT SGVIII, Aug. 1989.

9. Lamport L., "Time, Clocks, and the Ordering of Events in a Distributed System", Communications of the ACM, July. (78).

10. Magnusson B., Asklund U., Minör S.,"Fine-Grained Version Control for Cooperative Software Development", Tech. Report No.LU-CS-Tr:93-112, Dept. of Computer Science, Lund University, 1993 Sweden.

11. Marcos A., "Cooperative Editing of Static Images and 2D-Graphics in CoMEdiA", Tech. Report FIGD - 92i014, Aug. 1992.

12. Marcos A., Hornung Ch., "Using Multimedia to Support Cooperative Software Development", in Proc. of VI Portuguese Conference on Computer Graphics, Braga Feb. 1993, Portugal.

13. Marcos A., "A Distributed Environment to support Cooperative Software Development", in Proc. of 5th IFIP HPN'94 (Conference on High Performance Networking), Grenoble, June 1994.

14. Narayanaswamy K., Goldman N.,"*Lazy* Consistency: A Basis for Cooperative Software Development", in Proc. of CSCW 92, Toronto, 1992.

15. Neuwirth C., Kaufer D., Chandhok R., Morris J., "Issues in the Design of Computer Support for Co-authoring and Commenting", in Proc. of CSCW'90.

16. Ricart G., Agrawala A., "An Optimal Algorithm for Mutual Exclusion in Computer Networks", Communications of the ACM, Jan. (81).

17. Santos A., "A Cooperative Architecture for Hypermedia Editing - CoMEdiA", in Computer Graphics Forum, Vol.2, N.5, Dec.92.

18. Santos A., Tritsch B., "Using Multimedia to support Cooperative Editing", in Proc. of EUROGRAPHICS'93, September 1993, Barcelona.

19. Santos A., Marcos A., "An Algorithm and Architecture to support Cooperative Multimedia Editing", in Proc. of 4th Workshop on Future Trends of Distributed Computing Systems, September 1993, Lisbon.

20. Santos A., Marcos A., "CoMEdiA: A Tool to support Multimedia Editing", in Proc. of V Portuguese Conference on Computer Graphics, Aveiro, Feb 1993.

21. Tritsch B., Hornung Ch., "Cooperative Multimedia on Heterogeneous Platforms", in Proc. of Dagstuhl Workshop on Multimedia System Architectures and Applications, Dagstuhl, 1992.